ALSO BY JAMES RESTON

Prelude to Victory (1942)

The Artillery of the Press (1967)

Sketches in the

S A N D

Sketches in the
S A N D

JAMES RESTON

NEW YORK · *Alfred A. Knopf*

1 9 6 7

THIS IS A BORZOI BOOK
PUBLISHED BY ALFRED A. KNOPF, INC.

PUBLISHED SEPTEMBER 18, 1967
SECOND PRINTING, NOVEMBER 1967
THIRD PRINTING, DECEMBER 1967

Copyright 1941, 1943, 1948, 1952, 1954,
© 1955, 1956, 1957, 1958, 1959, 1960, 1961,
1962, 1963, 1964, 1965, 1966, 1967
by The New York Times Company.

All rights reserved under International
and Pan-American Copyright Conventions. Distributed by
Random House, Inc. Published simultaneously
in Toronto, Canada, by Random House of Canada Limited.

Library of Congress Catalog Card Number: 67-18613

MANUFACTURED IN THE UNITED STATES OF AMERICA

For My Gal Sal

"A puzzled man making notes...

drawing sketches in the sand,

which the sea will wash away."

WALTER LIPPMANN

The New Republic, AUGUST 7, 1915

CONTENTS

INTRODUCTION

THE ARGUMENT AGAINST PICKLING A LOT OF OLD NEWSPAPER LEFT-
overs in a book is almost as powerful as the argument for throwing everything out of the attic, but not quite. A newspaper
column, like a fish, should be consumed when fresh; otherwise
it is not only undigestible but unspeakable. Mark Twain called
such collections "mortuary volumes." E. B. White, an opponent
of all pea-cockery, was even more severe. "Old newspaper
stories," he observed (when putting out a collection of his personal remainders), "have an odor all their own; they are extremely hard to run down, and after you find them, you wish
you hadn't. It is a bad moment. . . . Even the perfect newspaper
story dies like a snake with the setting of the sun . . ."

Still, old opinions have some value, even if they merely expose
the impermanence of old fevers. Nothing cuts a man down to
proper size quicker than prowling through the graveyard of old
clippings for a few signs of life. One recalls the mood of the day
when they were written: how sure one was that the facts were
right, the criticisms fair, the analogies apt, the conclusions
sound; and now, in another time and mood, how they mock and
rebuke the pretensions of the past.

I have tried to deal with this by following Sir Arthur Quiller
Couch's advice to all writers: "Murder your darlings." Well, this
I have done, perhaps not as ruthlessly as I should. I have killed
the worst offenders and dismembered quite a few others. Here
and there I have eliminated references to forgotten or meaning-
less events, and run together a couple of pieces on the same
subject, or added a paragraph for clarity. Where I have deleted

more than just a sentence or a phrase, I have indicated this by points of ellipsis.

My excuse for publishing what remains, leaving aside vanity and greed, is that I want to say a good word for my craft.

In another generation, at the rate things are now going, concentrated power in a crowded world, while inevitable, will take a lot of watching: the more people, the more congestion; the more congestion, the more government control; the more government power, the more danger of corruption and war—and the more need for a vigilant and skeptical press. Therefore, I think newspapering is important, to say nothing of being fun. It not only involves a man in the struggles of his time, thus keeping him from going to sleep, but gives him the opportunity, unmatched by the university or the law, to write on the big issues when people are paying attention, which usually means when they are startled out of their normal preoccupations by some thunderclap in the news. Besides, any craft that gets a man out of the house into different experiences every day and brings him home with something worth talking about, even if late to dinner, is worth defending.

This is not, however, a simple task. After over thirty years in this business, I get the impression that most newspaper readers have only the dimmest idea about what a newspaper column really is. There seems to be popular support for the notion that a good column is one that supports the reader's convictions and a bad column one that does the opposite, but the reason and purpose of the thing are not well understood.

Maybe this is because the American newspaper column was created, not by popular demand, but by economic necessity. The more the country got involved in the affairs of the world, the more costly it became to pay the carfare and the expense accounts, particularly the latter, of reporters in Washington and overseas. By sharing the costs of a syndicated writer, hundreds of papers could expand their coverage at little expense. Publishers welcomed it: they could buy opinion and even philosophy by the yard at a weekly fee less than the cost of copy boy or a janitor, and meanwhile avoid the awkward business of having to produce and defend ideas of their own. Reporters, of course, loved it: if they could get a column, they could escape at last from the clutches of the enemy copyreaders. Of course, they might write rubbish, but it was their own rubbish, and after a hard day's work and a good night's sleep, they could field the morning paper on the first bounce and glory in their own unmolested prose.

As for the public, they seem to be irritated by columnists a good deal of the time, and no wonder. For here we are every day or so, blowing through our hats about a whole variety of complicated subjects that normally baffle and humble even the most intelligent members of the human race. How could you be so almighty smart? they ask us. Who hired you to save the Republic? Why should we take your judgments when government has more information about almost everything than you have?

The main answer to this, I suppose, is that a democratic society is expected to operate by the consent of the governed. The final judgment lies with the people, who make up their minds by watching and listening to their officials, following the arguments of the political opposition, listening to the news on the radio and television, and reading the reports and comments in the newspapers and the magazines. Reporters and commentators merely try to make this process a little easier for the citizen. The voter cannot read every document or hear every argument going on in the capital, any more than he can deliver his own mail, and democratic governments cannot be left to pass judgment on their own acts any more than a baseball player can be allowed to call his own balls and strikes.

The newspaper column is merely one of the instruments in this process, and it differs widely from one writer to another. Some think of it as an instrument of ideology, and comment on the news from the left or the right. A few regard it as a means of supporting one political party and opposing the other. Probably the most popular are the backstairs columnists who undertake to expose whatever hanky-panky they know or believe is going on behind the scenes. The column thus has great flexibility. It can be merely a signed personal opinion. It can serve as a filter to catch some of the official trash. It can be an analysis of a man or a policy. Or it can be a beanball aimed at some particularly stupid or corrupt knucklehead.

Each writer follows his own bent. I have tried merely to pass on some informative footnote to the news of the day, as if in a letter to a thoughtful friend. Most of the time this is not a personal opinion, but merely some bit of background gathered from the experts on the particular subject of immediate interest. A good deal of the time I have been writing about the problems of change. This has seemed to me the central issue of the age. My generation came to maturity in the economic depression of the early thirties, and since then has lived through a series of wars, rebellions, and revolutions of the old empires, the new nations, the races, the scientists, and the economists. This transformation of the United States from an isolated, laissez-faire country to the most powerful and deeply involved nation in the world has challenged most of our assumptions and attitudes and forced all our institutions from the government to the church, the university, and even the family to adapt to a wholly new set of facts and responsibilities.

I have not, I hope, approached this reporting of trends in a dogmatic spirit. Walter Lippmann described the newspaper commentator in 1915 as "a puzzled man making notes . . . drawing sketches in the sand, which the sea will wash away." That's me. The elevator operator in the *Times* building in Washington used to ask every night as I went home: "Any news tonight or is it the same thing worded different?" I'm afraid there were all too many nights when it was hard to pretend there was anything new, yet we must print on time, and alas, the Scotch cannot help preaching and raising hell.

This may explain a curious paradox and even contradiction in this book. The shorter daily columns are full of grumbles that we are not changing fast enough to keep up with the times; the longer pieces on the deeper trends are more optimistic about our progress and ultimate success. Yet both the lag and the progress are part of the story of this convulsive period, and the theory, at least, is that by harping on the lags, we may speed the progress.

Officials, of course, regard this constant carping as a bore, and no wonder. The difference between opinion and policy is very great. It is obviously easier to say what has not been done or even what should be done than it is to devise acceptable policies to do it. No generation of American officials ever had to face such a torrent of intractable new problems—from the closing of the banks to the falling of the old empires and the uprising of new peers and nations. Yet despite the irritation of officials with those of us who think our job is to watch and criticize whatever government of whatever party is in power in Washington, most of them put the right of criticism, even when they think it is unfair, ahead of their personal grievances.

The newspapers, on the whole, do the same thing. No doubt they too are annoyed from time to time with the presumptuous conclusions of their employees, but they give us more freedom to write as we please, perhaps, than any other press in the world.

I am grateful to *The New York Times* and the other institutions that sponsored these pieces in the first place, and to the interns in my office over the years—Jonathan Yardley, Christopher Willoughby, Steven Roberts, Craig Whitney, and Iver Peterson—who have rescued these few remainders out of the files of the *Times*.

Finally, I am especially indebted to my wife, Sally Fulton Reston, who not only had to endure the production of these pieces in the first place, pretending the next morning to like them, but what was even harder, to read them all over again and help with the selection.

Fiery Run, Virginia
September 5, 1966

1

PERSPECTIVE

"We should behave toward our country as women behave toward the men they love. A loving wife will do
anything for her husband except to stop criticizing and
trying to improve him. That is the right attitude for a
citizen. We should cast the same affectionate but sharp
glance at our country. We should love it, but also insist
on telling it all its faults."

J. B. PRIESTLEY

FEBRUARY 22, 1955

The Limitations of Power[1]

WE NEED TO DEVELOP A PHILOSOPHY ABOUT OUR COUNTRY'S
place in the world today, a way of looking at the endless scare
headlines. Otherwise, I fear, the constant press of events will
drive us into a state of indifference, which is a menace to democratic government, or into a condition of constant anxiety, which
destroys both a tolerant public opinion and private tranquility.

I have no doubt whatsoever about the outcome of the cold
war. No handful of men in the world are smart enough to run
this vast Communist empire. The thing is against human nature,
and its inner contradictions will bring it down if we are strong,
vigilant, and patient.

But this is a marathon, and we're running it like a hundred-
yard dash. It might be useful, therefore, to suggest a way of
looking at this struggle. Our need, I repeat, is for a workable
philosophy about contemporary history, and I will try to contribute one or two ideas toward this end.

First of all, I suppose it is necessary to say that we have to
have a foreign policy. We can no longer safely avoid the entangling alliances General Washington warned us against. There is
no return to the old unencumbered, unentangled days.

If anybody is looking for "normalcy," let him look around the
world at his leisure. This is it—what we have now. Today, in
1955, it is Quemoy and Matsu. Tomorrow it will be South Vietnam. Yesterday it was Europe. Now it is Asia and tomorrow it
may be Africa or Latin America. It is obvious, I think, that the
only power in the world equal to the power that threatens our
civilization is the power of the United States. . . .

Second, I suppose we should remember that foreign relations
are foreign. They concern our contacts with other independent

[1] Taken from the Gideon D. Seymour Memorial Lecture. Published by
the University of Minnesota Press.

nation-states, most of whom are as proud and cantankerous as we are. We cannot legislate beyond our own frontiers. We cannot buy the consent of others. We cannot change the French constitution. We cannot make India stop lecturing the world from its pinnacle of neutrality, much as we did in the nineteenth century. In short, we have power in this field, but we are not omnipotent. We cannot play God.

A third fundamental follows from this: Nations, like individuals, have to limit their objectives, or take the consequences. Napoleon and Hitler refused to limit their objectives, and were destroyed. The Japanese did the same thing when they set themselves the objective of destroying the power of the United States at Pearl Harbor.

This business of limiting one's objectives, however, is difficult for Americans to learn . . . We are accustomed to doing the impossible in America. It is a part of our national psychology. It is a glorious tradition which cleared the American frontier of trees and built a fantastic society. But in foreign policy it can be awkward. People and nations are more stubborn than trees. They cannot be moved so easily. Consequently, it is not a bad idea in foreign affairs to keep your commitments in line with your power, and to avoid demanding things you are not willing to pay for.

Fourth, the main objective of our foreign policy is very simple: It is to defend the security of the American people. It is not to remake the world or protect the status quo or to win wars. It is to guard the safety of our people, to encourage an environment in which they can enjoy the blessings of liberty and to prevent the outbreak of an atomic war.

Finally, these foreign-policy questions are difficult, not because the Democrats are disloyal or the Republicans stupid, but because Asia is in revolt, Soviet and Chinese power have vastly increased, British and French power have greatly declined, new techniques of war—from atom bombs to subversion—have been devised, and all this has become part of our responsibility before we have had time to adjust our habits of mind or our institutions to our new role in the world.

This, at least, is the way I look at it—I think we have to begin with the assumption that nations, like people, want contradictory things; that each has to limit its objectives and do without the things it is not willing to pay for; and that this is an endless process of conciliation and adjustment, like life itself, in which nobody is ever likely to get exactly what he wants.

Under these circumstances, it is not a good idea to expect too much. The great antagonists of the world—the United States and the USSR—have contradictory views of the end of life itself and, unfortunately, they are not only the two most powerful nations in the world today but they are also the least experienced of the major states in the conduct of foreign policy.

In these terms, rather than in the terms of the perfectionists, I think we are doing pretty well. The United States has learned the lesson of the major British failures of the early part of the century. Very often, it seems, our "muddling through" has merely replaced *their* "muddling through," but there is this important difference: They did not deter the big war when they had primary responsibility and, so far, we have.

The British did not raise enough strength in the critical periods of the century—from 1908 to 1914 and from 1933 to 1939 —to keep the Germans from thinking that they could win without being severely punished. They would not raise their defense budgets to meet their commitments. They would not break up the family and conscript their sons until it was too late. Nor were they able to put together an effective coalition of nations to deter the potential aggressors.

The United States has learned these lessons. It reversed its League of Nations decision of 1920. It has conscripted its men ever since the war. It has maintained enough offensive power to restrain the Russians. It has stationed its young men all over the world. And it has committed itself to oppose aggression from the north cape of Norway right through the heart of Europe to Trieste; thence across Turkey to Pakistan, Southeast Asia, Formosa and the Pescadores, Korea, Japan, and deep into the South Pacific.

When I think back to my early days as a foreign correspondent, when the British and the French were saying, in the thirties, that all would be well if only the United States would make clear that it would oppose aggression, I am amazed at our progress and appalled at the complaints we now hear about America in London and Paris.

A generation ago men were saying the American Constitution divided power so evenly that no important treaty with another country would ever again pass the Senate. Ten years ago it was said that the power of the Presidency would always be paralyzed at the time of crisis. All this was said about our selfishness and the rigidity of our political institutions.

The American capacity for unity, however, has proved to be greater than the predictions. The Republican party, which was supposed to go isolationist as soon as it came into power, has not only sustained the defense treaties made by the Democrats but has extended our commitments to Pakistan, to most of Southeast Asia, and to Korea, Formosa, and the Pescadores.

Three years ago, in 1952, Western Europe had an alliance with the Democratic party; today it has an alliance with America. And the astonishing thing is that the main foreign-policy opposition in the Republican party today comes from those who want us to do not less, but more.

In the meanwhile, the American people, despite their frustrations about it all, have poured out their substance to their allies, to the neutrals, and, on occasion, even to those who have sworn to destroy everything that gives meaning to our society. All this is so remarkable and is so widely overlooked that I sometimes think the world has lost its sense of wonder. There has been nothing like it in the history of sovereign nations.

Moreover, we have not only organized our power but we have used it effectively and with restraint. It is popular now to dismiss Korea as a disappointment, if not a failure. But in the long story of the twentieth century I think it will look very good alongside the names of Abyssinia and Spain and the occupation of the Rhineland.

Ever since late in June 1950, when the American planes went into action against the first Soviet open aggression at the 38th parallel, the men in the Kremlin have had to reckon with the very real possibility that any open aggression against the free world might be struck by the power of the United States. This, then, is the central fact, it seems to me, of the postwar era: The New World has been equal to the latest challenge to Western civilization.

It does not, however, follow from this that the battle is over. Much of our national frustration today springs from the illusion that foreign policy has a beginning and an end, like a football game. We are willing to sacrifice, but we want it to end almost right away. It is significant, I think, that we talk about the Soviet Union as a "headache," and keep on looking for a pill that will make it go away. We have been so fine-favored by the Lord and have been so successful that we expect to win every time we enter the arena. Foreign relations are like human relations. They are endless. The solution of one problem usually leads to another. We tackle pestilence in Asia, improve the sanitation, and find at the end that we are prolonging the lives of more people than we can feed. Administrations come and go, but the Russians are still around. It is all very strange. One sometimes wonders if everything said in political campaigns is absolutely true.

So, while I sincerely believe that America has just passed through one of the great decades of its history, this is a perplexing, shifting, perpetual business which demands new methods, new men, and new ideas all the time.

The first objective of the cold war was to keep the 175 Red Army divisions from marching at a time when there were only about ten Allied divisions between the Elbe River and the North Sea. It was equally important to prevent the economic disintegration of Western Europe, to build and organize the military forces of the free world into an effective coalition, and to stop the Communist resort to armed force in Korea.

These things were done, and they were remarkable achievements. But Korea deranged our whole cold-war effort. It turned our minds almost wholly to the problems of military power. In the belief that Korea was the first act in a world war, Washington concentrated on questions of force, played up military aid to the allies, and played down economic aid to other countries, though the Marshall Plan and the Point Four program were extraordinary accomplishments.

This is what almost always happens in Washington. Like all

institutions, government clings to the familiar, often long after it admits conditions have changed. Almost everybody in the government talks about adjusting to the more subtle and perplexing tasks of the cold war—of getting its economic and information programs back in balance with the military—but the budget and the thinking in official circles still reflect an official preoccupation with questions of military power.

This, of course, is a matter of opinion, but I believe we are now out of balance and a little out of date. The United States has won the first phase of the cold war and doesn't know it, and has moved into the second phase, and isn't ready for it.

We have to move along now, it seems to me, not on one but on many fronts. We have to have a "new look" military establishment in the event of a catastrophic test of strength, but we also have to have an "old look," for the police problems we face in the jungles of Asia are in some ways more similar to the tasks of the French and Indian Wars than to anything else.

The deterrent power of the strategic air force and its family of atomic weapons and guided missiles has to be kept up to date, of course. This is our shield. In the present uncivilized state of the nations, it is the foundation on which everything else rests. But we dare not allow this obvious need to prepare for the big war— which may never come if we maintain the shield—to dominate our budgets and our energies to the point where it will keep us from waging the war that is here right now. . . .

I don't know what percentage of our atomic-energy budget and our scientific brains is going into the development of atomic and thermonuclear weapons and what percentage is going into the development of atomic energy for peaceful purposes. We are not told, and probably should not be told, such things. But I suspect that a disproportionate amount is going into big weapons.

We are power-minded, and that is all right. But a capacity to destroy all life in a twenty-mile-wide belt from Chicago to Milwaukee with a single H-bomb ought to be enough to deter the Russians. Meanwhile, a great deal more of our energies in this field might be applied more usefully to the peacetime projects. In the long run, the atomic-electric-power race may prove to be more decisive than the atomic-bomb race.

The lag in our information program illustrates the same problem. It is almost impossible for any speech writer in Washington today to write a speech without saying something obvious about "the war of ideas," but I haven't run into anybody with a new idea in this field since the President produced his "atoms for peace" plan.

Everybody agrees that we are in an ideological war, but the ideology of this great country is being distorted at home and misunderstood all over the world. We won our independence with a flurry of the finest pamphlets ever written in the English language, and we have devoted more time and money and energy to the arts of persuasion than all the countries of the world combined. Yet our information program is pedestrian and ineffective, and even our allies are left in monumental ignorance of what kind of people we are and what we are trying to do.

One reason for this is that we have concentrated almost entirely on ways of saying things or on psychological tricks, rather than on what to say. Almost every debate on the United States Information Service is dominated by discussion about transmitters on land and transmitters on sea, and how clever we are at floating balloons back of the Iron Curtain.

Meanwhile, platoons of thoughtless Senators and Congressmen and retired generals, who forget that their voices carry beyond the county line, send up clouds of banalities which frequently blur and muffle the true and generous voices of America.

We can never speak with a single voice and never should, but somebody, sometime, should try to remind the politicians that what they say is part of the Voice of America, too. We cannot measure the effectiveness of our information program in megacycles. A poor distribution system is better than a good distribution system if we say the wrong thing, for a powerful system merely multiplies our mistakes and carries them farther across the world. . . .

Let me summarize: It is not surprising that we have concentrated on questions of power in the last decade. It was necessary; we have to save our lives before we can decide what to do with them. But I believe we have done that part of the job and know how to keep on doing it, and we must now concentrate a little more on this fifty-year war the President talks about.

There is no escape into the unentangled world of George Washington's dreams. It vanished with the guided missile, the intercontinental-supersonic bomber, the atomic bomb, and an enemy who is sworn to the destruction of everything that gives meaning and purpose to our lives.

The old Biblical injunction applies here: We must, it seems to me, be willing to cast away our lives in order to save them, but if we are willing to cast them away, we shall probably save them. Meanwhile, I hope we can be a little more hopeful and a little less flighty. A man can't stay breathless for fifty years. People keep wanting to jump from one extreme to the other. We need balance, but Congressmen either go fishing or go crazy.

The future, we may be sure, will produce as many surprises as the past, and require as much industry and imagination. The world is changing fast. Our own country's population has doubled in the last fifty years. We are in more than an arms race. We are in a race with the pace of our own history, and the pace is so swift that our habits of mind and our institutions are lagging behind.

If we limit our objectives, however, and judge our progress by something short of perfection, there is no need, it seems to me, for despair. The need is for a patient, well-informed people, both attentive and unafraid, who know what this great country stands for and are willing to die for it if necessary. . . .

JUNE 20, 1960

Purpose and Leadership

IF IT IS TRUE THAT AMERICA NEEDS AND LACKS A SENSE OF purpose, the history of the nation suggests a remedy. For if George Washington had waited for the doubters to develop a sense of purpose in the eighteenth century, he'd still be crossing

the Delaware. In fact, most of the great political crises of the
American past have been resolved, not by the zeal and purpose
of the people, but usually by the willpower or obstinacy of their
leaders.

No doubt the massive thirst of a long-tormented majority
brought back 3.2 beer, but the plain fact is that in most other
emergencies, a resolute minority has usually prevailed over an
easygoing or wobbly majority whose primary purpose was to be
left alone. John Adams estimated that one third of the population was against the American Revolution, one third for it, and
one third indifferent. And this is the way it has usually been.

Some farsighted character like Thomas Jefferson or Teddy
Roosevelt was always buying Louisiana or the Panama Canal
when nobody was looking, and writers have always been grumbling, mainly to each other, about the feebleness of the national
will. The main difference between today's lamentations and those
of the past is that the language is milder and the pay better.
Thomas Paine, roaring about America's mulish indifference in
1775, makes today's orators sound complacent. And even Ralph
Waldo Emerson, who was really a pretty cheery fellow, could
wail in 1847: "Alas for America, the air is loaded with poppy,
with imbecility, with dispersion and sloth. Eager, solicitous, hungry, rabid, busy-bodied America: catch thy breath and correct
thyself."

Thus, criticism of the American people for lack of purpose is
not new. What is new is that leaders now seem to think they
must follow the nation instead of leading it. What is new is that
a hostile coalition of nations now has the military power to destroy the Republic. The margin of error granted to us in past
wars and crises has vanished. What could be won before with
partial effort, late starts, feeble alliances, and mediocre administration can no longer be won in a contest with the Communists.

It is not that they are so efficient but that they are so purposeful. They are all working on the main target and we are not. Life,
tyranny, and the pursuit of capitalists is the Russian way of life.
They have obliterated the difference between war and peace.
They are always at war, all of them, women as well as men,
teachers, philosophers, scientists, engineers, lady discus throw-
ers, airmen, and three or four million foot soldiers. None of this

need trouble us very much except for *their* national purpose, which is simply to replace our system of individual freedom with their system of state control wherever they can, including regions vital to our security such as Germany, Japan, and even Cuba.

I must say they have been very frank about it. They have given us timely if not fair warning. They are directing all the energies of all their people to that goal. They are not arguing about the conflict between private interests and the national interest. They have simply eliminated private interest. They have put everybody to work on "burying" capitalism, and, since our national purpose, among other things, is to avoid being buried, this creates an awkward and even nasty situation.

How then, shall we approach the problem? I was brought up on the Church of Scotland's shorter catechism, the first question of which is: "What is the chief end of man?" Accordingly, I am all for self-direction and self-criticism. Nevertheless, I have my doubts about the imminence of any self-induced renaissance or epoch of austerity.

When I consider attacking the problem through the people, I think of Harry Ashmore's old story about the man who acquired a reputation for training mules with honeyed words and kindness. Hearing about this remarkable achievement, the Society for the Prevention of Cruelty to Animals dispatched a lady emissary to present the mule trainer with a medal. Upon arrival, she asked for a demonstration. The trainer obligingly trotted out a young mule, reached for a long two-by-four, and clouted the beast over the head. As the mule struggled back to his feet the good lady exclaimed in horror, "Good heavens, man, I thought you trained these animals with kindness."

"I do, ma'am," he replied, "but first I got to git the critters' attention."

I don't know how just anybody gets the attention of 180 million people these days. They are engaged in the pursuit of happiness, which, incidentally, the Declaration of Independence spells with a capital "H," and to be frank about it, I suspect that public debates on the national purpose give them a pain.

It will not, I think, be wise to underestimate America's current resistance to exhortations from the preachers, professors, columnists, and editorial writers of the nation. For unless I miss my guess, the Americano, circa 1960, is in no mood to rush off on his own initiative to "emancipate the human race," or to set any new records as the greatest benefactor of all time, or engage in any of the other crusades mapped out for him in Cambridge, Mass.

He may do many of these things because he is honest enough to know that he doesn't know all the facts of this dangerous and complicated era, but he is not likely to set out to do them because of his own "reflection and reason" or the arguments of talkers or writers he seldom sees. Accordingly, we must, I think, start with the national leadership, partly because this is the engine that has pulled us out of the mud before, and partly because this is an election year, when we will be picking a President, probably for most of the 1960's.

The President of the United States is the one man who can get the attention of the American people. If he says the nation is in trouble they will listen to him. If he addresses himself to their doubts and questions, they will hear him out. If he presents programs and legislation to do what he thinks is necessary for the safety of the Republic and explains and keeps explaining why these are essential, he may very well prevail.

All the magazine articles on the national purpose, all the reports by all the foundations on all our manifold weaknesses, all the speeches by Adlai Stevenson, Jack Kennedy, Lyndon Johnson, and Stuart Symington on the wickedness of the Republicans, all the exhortations to return to the faith of our fathers—all are nothing compared to serious programs eloquently expressed and strongly pushed by a determined President of the United States.

"His is the only national voice in affairs," wrote Woodrow Wilson. "Let him once win the admiration and confidence of the country and no other single force can withstand him, no combination of forces will easily overpower him. His position takes the imagination of the country. . . . His is the vital place of action in the system. . . ."

Of course, he has to act. He cannot ask for half measures and run away. But once he expresses the national need, once he decides to try to remove rather than to perpetuate the illusions of the past, then his specific remedies will affect the spirit and direction of the nation.

I remember when the Marshall Plan for Europe was devised in Washington. It was perfectly obvious that the sickness of the European economy was creating a crisis of great magnitude, and the bare bones of a four-year plan, costing perhaps as much as $20 billion, were worked out and approved by President Truman. I printed a long story about it one Sunday in *The New York Times*, and by ten o'clock that morning, the late Senator Arthur H. Vandenberg of Michigan, then chairman of the Foreign Relations Committee, called me at home and said: "You must be out of your senses. No Administration would dare to come to the Senate with a proposal like that."

Yet once the lead was taken and the need documented, Senator Vandenberg ended up as a key supporter of what almost everybody now agrees was the most farsighted piece of legislation since the war.

I do not underestimate the task. I agree with much that has been said about the slackness of our society, but I find the present mood understandable, perhaps inevitable, under the circumstances, and not without hope.

At the end of the last war, the American people made a genuine effort to clear the wreckage and understand the new situation. They went through the biggest geography and history lesson in their history, always with the false optimism that they were dealing with a temporary situation that would eventually go away. Instead of going away, the problems became larger and more complex: After Europe, it was the Middle East; after the Middle East, the Far East; after the Far East, Africa; after Africa, outer space, and after outer space a lot of inner tensions over U-2, me too, inflation, deflation, rising cost of living, balance of payments, nuclear testing, sputniks, luniks, and a lot of other things that everybody seemed to be differing about.

There was no panic about any of this. The people merely turned from what they did not understand to what they did understand. They turned inward from the world to the community and the family. In the fifteen years of the atomic age, they increased the population of the nation by more than 40,000,000, which is not the action of a frightened people, and which is interesting when you think that the entire population of the country at the start of the Civil War one hundred years ago was only 31,000,000.

A distinction has to be made, I think, betwen the façade of America and the other more genuine America. There is, of course, this big obvious clattering America of Hollywood and Madison Avenue and Washington, but there is also the other quieter America, which has either kept its religious faith or at least held on to the morality derived from religious tradition.

I do not wish to glorify the multitude. Much can be said about the dubious effects on the American character of very early marriage, easy credit, cheap booze, cheaper TV, lower education standards, and job security even for sloppy work. Nevertheless, there is more concern for the outside world, more interest in its problems, more generosity, and more resourcefulness in this society than in any free society I know anything about.

If it is true, as I believe, that this generation of Americans is doing less than it could, it is also true that it has done everything it was asked to do. It may be more concerned about its private interests than about the public interest, but if a man is offered a choice between a Cadillac and a swift kick in the pants, we should not be surprised if he doesn't bend over.

What has it been asked to do that it has not done?

It was asked to restore the broken economy of Europe, and it helped bring that continent within a decade to the highest level of prosperity in history.

It was asked to accept high taxation and military conscription to police the world, and it has done so from the north cape of Norway to Japan and Korea.

It was asked to keep a standing army of a quarter of a million men in Western Europe, and it has done so for fifteen years with scarcely a murmur of protest from a single American politician.

It was asked to abandon its tradition of isolation, and it took on more responsibilities involving more risks—in Korea and elsewhere—than the British ever did at the height of their imperial power.

These are not the acts of a slack and decadent people. There is nothing in the record of free peoples to compare with it. This is not a static society. The problem is merely that the pace of history has outrun the pace of change. Ideas and policies have lagged behind events so that by the time policies were formulated, debated, and put in force, the situation they were intended to remedy had changed. Thus, in a torrent of change, in a revolution of science, a social revolution at home and an unprecedented political revolution in Asia, Africa, and Latin America, it is scarcely surprising that there is a crisis of understanding in the nation.

This is all the more true because there has been a serious weakening of the ties between the men of ideas and the men of politics in this country during the past decade. "Our slow world," wrote Woodrow Wilson in 1890, "spends its time catching up with the ideas of its best minds. It would seem that in almost every generation men are born who embody the projected consciousness of their time and people.

"Their thought runs forward apace into the regions whither the race is advancing, but where it will not for many a weary day arrive . . . the new thoughts of one age are the commonplaces of the next. . . .

"The men who act stand nearer to the mass than the men who write; and it is in their hands that new thought gets its translation into the crude language of deeds. . . . "

It cannot be said that the men of ideas of the country have not performed in these last few years their traditional tasks. They have observed the convulsions of our time and let their minds run ahead to the logical consequences for the nation. I cannot remember a time when there has been more purposeful thought on contemporary problems in the universities and foundations than now. Their reports and conclusions would fill a good-sized library, but the alliance between them and the White House has been feeble, and somehow it must be restored.

What, then, can be done? We can, at least, look at the world as it is instead of the world as we would like it to be. . . .

Since the last war, 1.2 billion people have changed their form of government in the world, and 800 million of these have achieved independence for the first time. These new nations are determined to be industrialized, ready or not. Hunger and pestilence are not new in the world, but the 2 billion hungry people are less willing to tolerate hunger and pestilence now that they know something can be done about it.

How these new governments develop, in freedom or by the quicker way of state control, may very well determine, not only the climate of freedom in the world, but the balance of power as well. Thus the primary problem of foreign affairs may very well be, not the East-West problem we hear so much about, but what Sir Oliver Franks calls the North-South problem: whether the nations of the south, in Africa, Asia, and Latin America, develop along the lines of the free industrialized nations of the north, or the state-controlled methods of the two large Communist northern states of the Soviet Union and China.

We have tended to make several assumptions about this: first, that most nations wanted to develop like the United States, that knowledge cannot develop except in a climate of freedom, and that the Western powers could deal with the underdeveloped nations without interfering much with present concepts of sovereignty or commercial practice.

All these assumptions are now under challenge. The Soviet Union has shown that spectacular scientific progress can be made in a closed society. Cuba, to take only one example close at hand, has not only indicated contempt for the American system of free enterprise but is now organizing its whole society under state control.

The problem is not that the Soviet Union produces better engineers than the United States—though it certainly produces more—but that it can direct its engineers into these new countries or anywhere else that helps promote the purpose of the state. . . .

My conclusions about all this mysterious sociology and economics are unoriginal, vague, and even modest. All I know about the "rate of growth" is what happened to three boys of my own in the last twenty-three years, and even that is a little confusing . . .

First conclusion: An honest debate on the issue might not be a bad idea. Maybe we cannot do everything everywhere. Maybe after 125 years of isolation and a generation of internationalism, somebody should call out once more to America: "Catch thy breath and correct thyself." But anyway, a revival of honest plain talk in the country wouldn't do any harm.

Second, in the face of the clear facts, anything less than the highest possible standard of education for the children of America is obviously a disgrace. We cannot punch kids out like cookies and drop them into slots, and wouldn't if we could, but we ought to be able to spend more money on their education than we do on all that sexy advertising.

Third, offhand, I would guess we were kidding ourselves in thinking we could do this job with the kind of people now working on it overseas or that we could do it without far more cooperation and coordination among the allies.

If the main war is the battle in the underdeveloped areas, why not offer talented young men of draft age the option of using their brains in a civilian service in Indochina rather than sentencing them to Army KP in Hoboken? It is not fair or accurate to say that the voluntary system cannot compete with the directed system in recruiting men for service in the underdeveloped areas, for no really imaginative effort has been made to attract the volunteers.

Thus, wherever you look it is hard to escape the conclusion that our response is unequal to the threat. We are in what Professor Walt Whitman Rostow of the Massachusetts Institute of Technology calls one of those "neurotic fixations of history." These are periods when nations are confronted by radically new situations but hang on to old policies that are increasingly divorced from reality.

This is what George III of England did when confronted by what he called the "rebellion" of the American colonies; what Edward VIII did when he hung on to Wally Simpson; what Stanley Baldwin did when he refused to rearm Britain in the face of Hitler's challenge; and what the United States did when it clung to isolation after the rise of Nazi Germany.

Isolation is now gone, but the hangover of the old habits of the days of isolation remains: in our assumptions that we can meet the Soviet challenge with the same school system, the same political patronage system, the same diplomatic sytem, the same attitudes toward politics and the public service, and the same old chestnut about private interests inevitably serving the public interest.

It is not so much that we have lost our way forward but that we have lost our way home. This is the country of freedom, youth, experimentation, and innovation; of pioneers and missionaries and adventurers.

If you ask whether we can meet the Soviet challenge by concentrating on our private interests instead of on the public interest, by losing a great many of our best young brains in poor schools before they ever get to the college level, by not using our intelligent women when the Russians are using theirs, by not making a genuine effort to get our best brains into the most effective jobs to serve the nation, why I'm bound to say that the answer is "no."

I believe, however, that there is still a lot of spunk and spirit in this country that can be brought by free methods into the service of the nation, provided Presidential power is used to clarify where the nation stands.

The first national purpose is to know who we are and what we stand for, and it would be an impertinence to try to improve on the second paragraph of the Declaration of Independence as a guide to the problem.

"We hold these truths to be self-evident," it says in the first sentence. It thereupon lists, as if they were the indisputable facts of last Sunday's American League batting averages, a whole catalogue of wonderful things that are not only not "self-evident" in 1960, but are actually in violent dispute among men all over the world, including quite a few in our own country.

"All men are created equal," it says, and of course this is just the trouble, for you can get an argument on that one anywhere in the Province of Georgia, USSR, or the State of Georgia, U.S.A.

In the minds of the Founding Fathers, the moral idea came before the political, and the latter was merely an expression of the former. This, too, was apparently the idea Matthew Arnold had in mind when he came to this country before the turn of the century and discussed our national purpose in New York. He made two points:

"We must hold fast to the austere but true doctrine," he said, "as to what really governs politics, overrides with an inexorable fatality the combinations of so-called politicians, and saves or destroys states.

"Having in mind things true, things elevated, things just, things pure, things amiable, things of good report: having these in mind, studying and loving these, is what saves states."

However, the old gentleman, when writing these exuberant sentences, had no illusion about their being put into force by the majority. These moral concepts would prevail, he said, only as they were upheld by "the remnant" of leaders and thinkers who loved wisdom, for the majority, he insisted, was full of "prosperities, idolatries, oppression, luxury, pleasures and careless women . . . that shall come to nought and pass away."

"The remnant" in America of those who love wisdom and have the ability is very large. It has greatly increased as the population of the nation has increased, but it needs to be brought to bear on the great purpose of the nation more than it is today, and this is obviously one task of Presidential leadership. Meanwhile there is no cause to despair over the evidence of disorder and menace, for in all the golden ages of history, disorder and hazard have existed alongside Vitality and Creativeness.

"Surely our age shares many characteristics with the earlier golden times," Caryl P. Haskins, president of the Carnegie Institution of Washington, has written. "There is the wide feeling of insecurity, the deep-lying anxiety, the sense of confusion, not unlike the earlier times in general character . . .

"But there is likewise the same intense concern with new ideas and new concepts, the same eagerness for widened vistas of understanding . . ."

What Mr. Haskins did not say was that these golden ages were also periods of great leaders who knew how to bring ideas and politics together, and this seems to me to be the heart of our present problem.

The Ideal of Unity

INTERNATIONAL CRISES HAVE THEIR ADVANTAGES. THEY FRIGHTEN the weak but stir and inspire the strong. In sound societies they purify and clarify, elevating what is primary above what is secondary.

This is what happened at the beginning of this country when the idea of independence in a few powerful minds gradually overcame conflicting ideas of personal and commercial interest as the pressure mounted. This is what happened again in the Civil War when the preservation of the Union took priority over everything else in Lincoln's mind, even over the issue of slavery. This is what tends to happen in every critical moment in the history of a nation: In due course a single idea gains command and points the way not to a solution of the crisis—for there are no total solutions these days—but to a tolerable existence.

If there is such an idea today in the free world it is the idea of unity, not of a grand design of political union, but of a kind of practical, well-organized partnership based on necessity, on mutual interest, and on wider concepts of loyalty and patriotism.

This is the thing the Russians fear the most and what, ironically, they are gradually bringing about. First the Wall, then the Bomb, then the new threats to Finland and the West—are clarifying the path upward into greater unity rather than terrifying the free nations into disunity. Every Communist act that defies the spirit of the civilized world, like the explosion of the Bomb or the building of the Wall, makes it more possible for the leaders of the Free Nations to draw closer together, to overcome the narrow disintegrating forces in their societies, to add to their national loyalties wider philosophic loyalties, to think in continents large and strong enough to match the power of their adversaries.

The question now is not what the Russians are going to do, but what the West is going to do in response. What the Russians are doing is clear enough: they are consolidating an empire by force of arms, and doing everything they can to block the voluntary consolidation of the Old World of free Europe with the New World of America.

The Wall and the Bomb are not alone symbols of Communist strength but also of Communist weakness. Having failed to convince the East Germans, the Soviet Union had to wall them in. Having failed to negotiate an uninspected test ban with the free nations, they tried to terrorize them—and failed again.

Over the short run of a few more years, the tactical advantage may well lie with Moscow, and it is a formidable advantage. In rocketry, though not in nuclear power, the Communists are ahead and may well remain so. The underdeveloped world, still in the agony of transition, remains vulnerable to the sorcery, the subversion, and the techniques of Communist organization and conspiracy. But these advantages may very well pass away.

This is why Khrushchev is in such a hurry. Having awakened the free industrial nations to their responsibilities in the field of weaponry, and having shown his contempt for the independence of the new nations, he has to be quick. He is, in Walt W. Rostow's vivid phrase, "the scavenger of the transition," and as the Twenty-second Communist Party Congress shows, there is "trouble in paradise."

The Russians are still fighting with the Chinese Communists over the underlying dilemma of the need for centralized power in the Communist system and the increasing demands in the Soviet empire and even in the Soviet Union itself for the decentralization of power. For the increasing cries for a better life, the Soviet leadership has only more promises of "jam tomorrow." Meanwhile, Western Europe, which was supposed to collapse, is booming and uniting; and even the United States is entering into closer economic consultation with the Common Market.

The pace of events in the East is faster than in the West, and nobody can say that the West will accelerate the pace of interdependence fast enough to create an effective combined strategy for economic, political, and military cold war, but the direction of salvation is clear enough. In order to see it clearly, all that is necessary is to observe what the Russians are trying to break down. They are trying to break the Western Alliance. They are trying to destroy Germany's participation in the Common Market. They are trying to dismember the force that makes it unprofitable to seek Soviet aims by force of arms.

Whatever else it does, the Bomb at least has provided a flash of light on the way to go. It is, or so it seems to me, in the direction of unity at home and within the free world, toward a commonwealth of free nations, free as in the British Commonwealth to stay in or get out, but with a central strategic command that can mobilize the still-immense energies of those who really believe in liberty.

2

THE PROBLEMS
OF CHANGE

"The jangle you hear is not so much national anthems out of tune as clocks out of time. The primeval tom-tom still beats while the atom bomb ticks. Russia is straddling the centuries, in victory more than ever pounding backward to Peter the Great and racing at the same time to overtake Henry Ford and Henry Kaiser before she has caught up with Thomas Jefferson. The clocks of Europe are turning back and the clocks of Asia are turning forward. And there are places where time stands still because the night does not lift and there is no tomorrow."

Anne O'Hare McCormick

The Fertile Human Animal

THE BIG NEWS IN THE WORLD TODAY IS NOT WHAT THE POLITICIANS
and statesmen are saying but what the people are doing.

Almost everywhere the activities of Governments are running
behind the activities of the people. This week the population of
the United States reached 185,000,000. It has gone up over
3,000,000 since President Kennedy was elected—it has almost
doubled in the forty-four years since he was born.

For years now the headlines have centered on the political
squabbles of the nations, but all the time there has been this
fantastic human growth, which is likely to be far more important
in the end than the political fencing of the day. Despite all the
talk of the rising authority of government, it is the energy of the
family, the creativity of the scientist and the engineer, and the
willful purpose of millions of individuals in all the continents
that are shaping the modern world.

Even the Communist system, that symbol of authority, cannot
control it effectively. They have to build a wall in East Germany
to keep the people from running away. They revolutionize their
agriculture in Communist China, but the population rises by
16,000,000 a year and they are crippled by famine.

In the underdeveloped nations the Governments are also feeling pressure from below. The word has got around: hunger is not
inevitable but intolerable; machines can relieve endless labor,
and medicine can prolong life. Life expectancy in India before
the last war was thirty-two years; since then it has gone up to
forty-seven.

Even in the United States the human animal keeps moving
and changing things beyond the calculations of the great men in
Washington. The American Negro moves out of the agrarian
South into the large cities of the North. White workers from the
North follow jobs into the rising industrial regions of the South.

Newcomers move westward into California at the rate of 1,500 a day and create a new empire which nobody planned or quite knows how to control. . . . New suburban developments with their long, low, colorful one-story ranch houses are spreading out from the cities, but the housing shortage continues despite all the efforts of private and public enterprise.

Airports are obsolescent almost before they are completed. The biggest road-building program in the history of the country cannot keep pace with the size and prosperity of the population or the wider, faster, longer cars produced each year in Michigan. Everywhere in the West, municipal officials are overwhelmed by the problems of financing new facilities for a population that is moving westward again, marrying earlier and having more children.

The big story in Denver this week was that the City Council voted seven to two for a city income tax designed to meet the vast new expenditures for slum clearance, new streets, sewers, schools, viaducts, and bridges to keep pace with the city's growth. On the day the Russians announced that they had developed an accurate long-range intercontinental ballistic missile, and the House of Representatives finally passed the Civil Rights Bill in Washington, the main headline in the Denver *Post* was: "Suburbs Fight Income Tax."

In Aspen, Colorado, last night, the town forum debated not the great issues of world politics but: "What are we doing with our leisure?"

Around the periphery and to the west of the Great Lakes the question is not about the development of the Middle East, but what the ocean-going traffic through the St. Lawrence Seaway is doing to the Middle West.

The story in Western Europe is not quite the same, but meanwhile, not only a common market but a common political life is now beginning to emerge in Europe. A mass-production industry has replaced the batch-production system of prewar Europe. Labor is moving freely from one country to another, Commerce is not following the flag but the flag is following commerce, and creating in the process one of the most productive areas and attractive markets in the world. . . .

What is happening, therefore, is clear enough:

It is not only the races that are being integrated but the regions and the nations, and even the continents. On the surface the waters are ruffled and confused, but deep and powerful tides are running underneath toward the interdependence of the free nations. . . .

LOS ANGELES, CALIFORNIA

OCTOBER 19, 1958

The Changing West

THE ANNOUNCEMENT FROM THE CENSUS BUREAU IN WASHINGTON was brief and mathematical. On Thursday of this week, it said, the population of the nation passed 175,000,000.

An aircraft approaching Los Angeles from San Francisco says the same thing, only better. Here below in the morning mist is the dramatic symbol of the dry statistics: a vast community of restless Americans, drawn from the whole Republic, stretching from the Pacific deep into the surrounding hills as far as a man can see. Across the Baldwin Hills and the Santa Monica Mountains the great machine glides, over the Hollywood Hills and deep into the San Fernando Valley, descending and veering now across hundreds of thousands of new homes, perched on the dramatic slopes of a community more startling than the vaguely imagined Eldorado of the ancient legend.

From a small, moving window in the sky the story of America seems quite clear. It is the old, majestic story of an energetic people constantly moving, constantly changing, forever tearing down the old and building up the new. It is only when the scene is reduced to political terms on the ground that it loses its grandeur.

The politicians of California are engaged now in a squalid struggle over the political control of the commonwealth. They are not talking of the glory and the grandeur. They are fighting like petulant children over petty things: Knowland condemning Brown, his opponent for the Governorship, over some vague and ancient connection with some crooks; Knight nursing his wrath against Knowland for elbowing him out of the Governorship; Nixon hopping about the state exposing the inaccuracies of Harry Truman (as if anybody cared); and the President using up his precious store of energy crying for unity.

California is an illustration today of the persistent fact that everything in America changes faster than its politicians. Its population is increasing by more than 1,000 every day; actually at the rate of half a million a year.

In 1950 it was 10,586,000; in 1955, 12,961,000; in 1960, on the Census Bureau's projection, it will be 15,273,000, and by 1970 it will have passed New York as the most populous state of the Union and its most powerful political entity, with a population of 20,296,000.[1]

A visitor venturing up and down the tidy streets and approaching the low, rectangular California suburban houses is soon made aware of a few simple facts. The young women who come to the doors are not concerned with the squabbles of the politicians. They are preoccupied with children, schools, mortgages, and prices at the neighborhood supermarket.

The old folks are more interested and better informed. They know about war and the accidents of life and are therefore more interested in Quemoy and Matsu. They are acquainted with illness and are therefore sympathetic to the President. They are concerned with taxes and Social Security. They remember the depression of the Thirties and lean accordingly to the Democrats.

What the Bureau of the Census said this week, however, is the main thing. In 1952, when President Eisenhower ran for the first

[1] Actually, in September 1966 the Census Bureau reported that California's population as of July 1, 1966, was 18,918,000, and that California had become the most populous state sometime in 1964.

time, the population of the nation was 155,384,000. Now it is almost 20,000,000 beyond that, an increase equal to nearly half the people of Britain or France.

Even in the westward thrust of the gold-rush days there was nothing in California to compare with this astounding revolution. The people are moving from the older Democratic cities of the East into the Republican areas of the West. They are moving from New England with its equalitarian traditions to the conservative, segregated South. The Negro from the old Confederacy is trekking northward to Los Angeles, San Francisco, Chicago, Detroit, Philadelphia, and New York and taking his politics with him.

These are the things that are slowly but surely changing the political patterns of the Union, more than what the politicians proclaim or the President says or the Supreme Court decrees. . . .

PITTSBURGH, PENNSYLVANIA

APRIL 2, 1963

The Darker Valleys

THE PROSPERITY OF AMERICA IS ASTOUNDING BUT UNEVEN. THE new industries of the space age are centering on the sunny crescent from Los Angeles down through Texas to Florida and creating new problems for the old centers of the American industrial revolution of the past. No doubt this will change again in the future, but the dark and stagnant valleys still remain.

Pittsburgh these days illustrates the point. The promise of spring was on the hills here today. The willows stand out soft and green on the grim and wrinkled river slopes, like daffodils scattered on a slag heap. The spectacular roller-coaster highways hum with traffic above the Golden Triangle, and the sky is stained with copper-colored iron-oxide smoke from the great steel mills along the Ohio.

Yet Pittsburgh is not exactly in a hopeful springlike mood. It is a crippled giant, immensely powerful but chained by unemployment, potentially a vast unified industrial empire stretching up the river valleys, but actually a politically divided complex of almost 200 different municipal authorities. All the political, economic, and social problems of urbanized and industrialized America are dramatized here: the conflict of men and machines, the conflict of city and suburban governments, the waste of idle men and machines, the paradox of too few skilled workers and too many unskilled workers in the increasingly automatic factories.

Not since the Korean War in 1951 has there been anything approaching full employment in the four counties of Allegheny, Beaver, Washington, and Westmoreland that make up the Pittsburgh labor area. It was down to 2 per cent then. Now it is well above the national unemployment average, with 10.7 per cent out of work, and over 20 per cent of the steelworkers either unemployed or underemployed.

In Allegheny County alone, there are now 92,675 persons living on relief benefits, 66 per cent of them within the city limits of Pittsburgh. And in the four counties, the unemployment total is 97,800.

The expectation of the Fifties that the demand for steel would rise with the gross national product has not been realized. The best peacetime year in the steel business was 1955, with a total production of 117,000,000 tons. This dropped to 85,000,000 in the slump of 1958, and has leveled off in the last few years at around 98,000,000 to 99,000,000.

Oddly, there is not a great deal of grumbling here about the competition of new substitutes for steel or the competition of overseas producers of steel. Nor is there any talk of strike in the air, though the steelworkers union could give notice to terminate their open-ended contract any time after May 1.

The economy has simply not created the demand for more steel than can be produced on a part-time work schedule, and neither the steel managers nor the union leaders are very confident that it will under present private and government policies.

The reaction here to this part-time working life is rather strange. Unemployment is slowly poisoning the community, but like animals that can adjust to deadly poisons or men who can learn to breathe at altitudes they could not at first endure, the steelworkers and their union leaders seem to have adjusted to a diet of part work and part relief.

The French coal miners seem to be the only humans on earth who can impress De Gaulle, and the British unemployed, with only half our percentage out of work, storm the House of Commons in protest. But the steelworkers here don't go crazy: they go fishing.

The political implications of all this are difficult to analyze. This is Democratic territory, but, even at the steelworkers headquarters in the Commonwealth Building, there is evidence of disenchantment with the Administration in Washington. Significantly, the union leaders, a year after President Kennedy's row with Roger Blough of the U.S. Steel, are not condemning Blough but saying it was wrong to put pressure on him to hold prices down when little effort was made to hold down prices in other fields.

There is quite a bit of muttering in the unions too against President Kennedy's budget. The criticism here is that the President says unemployment is the nation's major economic problem, but puts $5 billion into space, which produces few jobs, rather than putting at least part of this into urban transportation and housing that would create jobs.

Washington seems far more optimistic about its manpower-retraining schemes and the human relations committee of the steel industry than Pittsburgh. The unemployed do not want to leave these stark but elemental river valleys. They do not see satisfactory jobs at the end of the retraining period. Their seniority piles up even when they are on the loose and on the dole; and while they grumble they keep hoping that somehow somebody will "get this country moving again" and transform these river banks once more into a productive inferno.

Thirty years after the start of the New Deal, the record of the welfare state around Pittsburgh seems oddly paradoxical. It has helped the steelworkers get better houses, many of them owned by the workers. It has produced service jobs for their wives but not steady jobs for the men. So they paint their houses or do other jobs around the basement when they are out of work, and bet on relief and their union pensions. This clearly has not satisfied them, but it has muffled them. It is not a crisis, but a tragedy.

BIRMINGHAM, ALABAMA
SEPTEMBER 20, 1963

The Changing South

THE STRIKING THING ABOUT BIRMINGHAM TO AN OUTSIDER IS that it seems so advanced industrially and so retarded politically. It has seized the scientific revolution and rejected the social revolution of our time. Accordingly, it is engaged in a remarkable and hazardous experiment: it is trying to back full speed into the future.

The visible and audible symbols of the city dramatize this paradox. It lies in a long valley surrounded by lovely flowering hills. On a peak above the forest of smoking chimneys stands a vast stainless-steel statue of Vulcan, like some hideous modernistic monster out of the German Ruhr. Yet down below in the city the symbols are not of the fires of the future but of the fires of the past. The Confederate flag is painted on the cars and helmets of Governor George Wallace's state troopers, now very much in evidence here, and the biggest clock in town booms out across the city from the tower of the Protective Life Insurance Company a few bars of "Dixie" before it strikes each hour.

Look to the industrial future, says the gleaming Vulcan.

"Look away, look away, look away, Dixie Land," chimes the clock.

That Birmingham should have become the symbol of Southern defiance adds to the paradox, for it did not come out of the tradition of the old agrarian, slave-holding, plantation South. It was not even incorporated until December 1871, in the decade after the War Between the States; it was populated from the North more than almost any Southern city, and its commercial and industrial ties now run to New York and Pittsburgh rather than to Atlanta or New Orleans.

Like most industrial cities it does have a tradition of putting private interests above public interests and it does have a history of violence. It was for many years an overgrown mining camp, populated by rough men from all sections of the country. Convict labor from the state prisons worked in the mines until the early 1920's, and National Guardsmen first went on strike patrol during the coal miners' walkout here in 1894.

Thus Birmingham is not like any other city in the country. Industrially it is ahead of much of the North; politically it is behind most of the urban South. It pays its Negroes better and in some ways treats them worse than most Southern towns, partly because it suffers from some of the worst aspects of both industrialization and segregation.

No generalization about Birmingham is safe, but its history does help suggest one possible explanation about the present attitude of many of its most influential leaders. This is not a city dominated by inherited wealth. More than in most Southern cities, Birminghan's commercial and industrial leaders are self-made men, with the self-made man's feeling that others can be just as successful too if they will only work.

Many white leaders here created their own fortunes, others are managers under pressure from Northern headquarters to produce the maximum at the minimum cost. As human beings, they are probably no better or worse than business leaders in other cities, but there is something in the history and atmosphere of this place, some relationship between the idea of the supremacy of the dollar and the supremacy of the white man, that has made them feel they could hold out longer against social change.

It isn't that they wanted more than other white leaders in Atlanta and elsewhere, but merely that in this particular city they thought they could get away with demanding more. The result is that the leaders of Birmingham are trapped for the time being in the struggle. For the more they have delayed making concessions to Negro equality, the more the Federal Government has dramatized their dilemma, and the more the Negroes have demanded, and the more business the city has lost.

The death of the four Negro children in this week's bombing of a Negro church has merely brought all this to a head. It has shocked the community, but there is little evidence that it has changed the convictions of the white leaders about what they regard as the proper (separate) relations between the races. They merely seem a little more convinced now that the continued uproar here is not good business, and Birmingham wants good business, even if it has to obey the Federal law to get it.

FIERY RUN, VIRGINIA

NOVEMBER 22, 1959

Old Echoes, New Sounds

THE OLD CURRIER AND IVES AMERICA OF THE THANKSGIVING DAY prints has not wholly vanished. The towns and suburbs are creeping in on the Blue Ridge from Washington, and the youngsters are leaving the land for the cities along the Potomac and the Rappahannock in the valley, but there is still a lot of plain living and high thinking in the American countryside.

The world is well acquainted with the America of Washington, D.C., Hollywood, and Madison Avenue and a little dismayed by what it sees, but there is still another America, far larger than the world imagines, where the family, the church, and the community are still the foundation of a generous and simple life. By other men's standards the farmers on these stony, red-clay hillsides have few material blessings, but they will be in John Marshall's parish church at Leeds tomorrow giving thanks just the same. They have their farm problems. They have their social problems with the Negro and the public schools, but the church is still the center of their social lives, and this is an aspect of America that is too often overlooked.

The cities of America are full of self-questioning. The pulpits ring with the old incessant questions: Where are we going? What is the purpose of our society? Economists such as John Kenneth Galbraith at Harvard decry the direction of our "affluent society"; Max Ways and Henry Luce cry out from their opulent tower in Manhattan for some new relationship between politics and philosophy, means and ends. And now this week Secretary of State Christian Herter has joined the reflective chorus.

"We have, of late," he said on Monday in New York, "been too much absorbed, I feel, in the mere enjoyment of a prosperous life behind our defensive curtain of nuclear power.

"We must realize instead that the fateful competition with Communism has placed a first claim on the energy of and interest of us all. That means subordinating our private interests to the paramount public interest. It also means using our economy less for the things which do not really matter and more for the things which do—for the uses which would train and inform our minds, promote the health of our society and keep our country free."

Few people up here in the hills would argue with this reflection of Christian Herter's New England conscience, or know what to do in a practical way to cooperate. The will to cooperate in anything "to keep our country free" is as strong in America as it ever was, but in this kind of complicated world rhetoric is no substitute for policy.

The people cannot do more than they are asked to do in the war Mr. Herter is talking about. They are being told these days that the main problem now is not to do more for defense, but to get the other industrial nations to do more. They are being deluged with speeches about balancing the budget, and this, like calling on others to take their fair share of the burden, is an important objective, but it is not exactly a rallying cry equal to the challenge.

The dominant sound in American ears today is the endless babble of commercial advertising, interlarded with Elvis Presley and the singing commercials. Night and day this incessant tribal beat goes on and the hawkers "train and inform our minds" in you know what. So long as this is the dominant voice of America, the quiet, courteous, and sensible words of the Secretary of State will be overwhelmed. Is this inevitable? Is there no way for the *highest* common denominator to be heard above the din?

Washington might have done something about this while the country was ashamed of the TV scandals. The President can still do a lot by personal persuasion with the leaders of the mass-communications industry. He could do a lot, too, with a 30,000-mile tour of America, probably more than in a good will tour of the world.

For it is not true that the American character has been debased. It responds to what it hears. It will respond again to the old echoes still heard among the hills. But somebody has to strike the note, clearly and steadily, and appeal to what is best instead of what is worst.

DECEMBER 25, 1960

Washington's Pioneers

THE BREATH OF HISTORY LIES ON THE COOL WASHINGTON AIR this Christmas. One hundred years ago South Carolina passed its "solemn Act of Secession." On Christmas Day, 1860, the Richmond *Examiner* called on the citizens of Maryland to join with Virginians in seizing the Capitol.

Then, as now, the Capitol Building was being extended, and Captain Montgomery Meigs of the Army Engineers, presiding over the clutter of Corinthian columns and marble blocks strewn over Capitol Hill, was known as "Meigs among the ruins of Carthage."

Then, as now, one Administration was giving way to another amid solemn warnings of decadence and decay. Yet the Christmas spirit went on. Gautier, the fashionable French caterer, was taking orders for Christmas cakes, Margaret Leech tells us. Madame Delarue announced a shipment of full-dress bonnets and Jouvin's gloves from Paris, and some businessmen in Washington were taking their usual wide view of history. "Readers," said one advertisement, "the Union is in danger but by buying your holiday presents at Lammond's you may save it."

Then, as now, the British were condemning our "intellectual barbarism." Lord Lyons, the British Minister, complained that Washington was a dreadful place for young men: it had no clubs and no good restaurants, no permanent theater or opera, but plenty of saloons, lots of gambling, and—interesting word—a "suitable" complement of brothels.

Anthony Trollope was no more impressed. Most of the Federal capital, he wrote, was "wild, trackless, unbridged, uninhabited, and desolate . . . tucking your trousers up to your knees, you will wade through the bogs, you will lose yourself among rude hillocks, you will be out of the reach of humanity. . . . If you are a sportsman, you will desire to shoot snipe within sight of the President's house."

Yet there were other men with other dreams, and whatever was wrong with them, they were never "out of reach of humanity." Sam Clemens, son of the middle border, was piloting a steamboat between St. Louis and New Orleans. Sam Grant, an ex-Army captain, was running a leather business in Galena, Illinois, and Walt Whitman was working for the Government (until they fired him) and writing poetry.

> "Have the elder races halted?
> Do they droop and end their lesson,
> Wearied, over there beyond the seas?

We take up the task eternal,
And the burden, and the lesson
Pioneers! O pioneers!"

Well, it is a different Washington now, but the spirit of hope is not dead, and because it survives there is some genuine happiness in the world today. If the bruise in our souls has not vanished one hundred years after the secession of South Carolina, we are at least united enough to keep the free world breathing and dreaming. In fact, there is a kind of pause in the active wickedness of international politics today not merely because of Christmas but because America has paused to say so long to one generation of leaders and install a new generation in its place. And what is this new generation saying?

It is lisping something very much like the lines of Whitman. It doesn't have the words yet, but it has the melody. It is optimistic and generous, restless and self-critical. We are ranging widely once more, forever pilgrims in our native land. And yet, the theme of our national policy, like the theme of Christmas, is concerned with responsibility for those in distress; in short, with the common destiny of mankind. What that forlorn and tragic figure, President Buchanan, said about the United States one hundred years ago is true today of the whole world. "Our Union," he said, "rests on public opinion and cannot be cemented by the blood of its citizens shed in civil war. If it cannot live in the affections of the people it must one day perish."

Washington still doesn't have that good restaurant, or that permanent theater or opera, but for all its transient population, it has a sense of history, and it has more tradition than it understands. It has survived a lot and will survive a lot more. This always seems more apparent at the end of each year, and it is particularly apparent in relation to that melancholy Christmas of one hundred years ago.

The Faith of Berlin

BERLIN HAS A SPECIAL SYMBOLIC MEANING IN CHANGING EUrope this Christmas. The Wall of misunderstanding that divides the human family is tangible here, but Berlin has something else. It has that quality of spirit so closely associated with the idea of Christmas: a gift for seeing beyond the walls that divide men, a confidence in things unseen, even a childlike belief in the elements of goodness and magic.

When Winston Churchill came to Europe soon after the end of the last war, he said: "We must turn our eyes away from the horrors of the past toward the future. If Europe is to be saved from infinite misery, and, indeed, from final doom there must be an act of faith in the European family and an act of oblivion against all the follies and crimes of the past."

All the great things that have happened in Europe since that time have been acts of faith. The Marshall Plan was an act of faith by the New World in the Old. The reconciliation of Germany and France was an act of faith by De Gaulle and Adenauer. The Common Market was an act of faith in the essential unity of the Western European nations. And Berlin is the most dramatic act of faith of all.

There is nothing logical about it as it stands. The Soviets have 1,200 tanks within fifty kilometers of the Brandenburg Gate. They have even brought up some new amphibious tanks which have been seen crossing the Elbe River. There are some ninety divisions of Soviet troops, according to Chancellor Adenauer, between the Soviet border and the Iron Curtain. And here is this hideous Wall cutting Berlin in two, dividing family from family, one generation from another, and otherwise distorting the whole human and commercial life of the community.

The Berliners are not a particularly religious people. They did not, like the people of Adenauer's Cologne, grow up in the shadow of a cathedral. Even in their present troubles, there has been no dramatic rise in churchgoing. But history and geography have taught the Berliners to be patient. Maybe this is what keeps them going. Adenauer told this visitor the other day: "One day we will be reunited. The Europeans know how to wait. They have a long history."

The logical, legal, factual approach to the German problem today, therefore, is the thing men like Mayor Willy Brandt of Berlin fear the most. One hears far less talk of the "economic viability" of Berlin here than in Washington. Brandt talks about spirit and confidence and patience and faith in the future.

Brandt and Adenauer do not talk about big plans. They are not trying to work things out legally and economically in accordance with some large design, and for good reason. This is of course what Hitler did: he bet everything on a grand design which if everything had worked out precisely as he planned would no doubt have established the Reich as he promised "for 1,000 years." The trouble was he made no allowance for chance and the peculiarities and capriciousness of the human spirit.

The Berliners are now reversing the process. They are putting everything on an act of faith. Maybe this thing won't work, but they are going on with it and are more confident in their future than all the logical and reasonable men farther west.

One wonders here whether Berlin would be divided by the Wall if we farther west had had a little more faith ourselves. We talked a lot, earlier this year, about the "logical facts of history," about the "division of Europe, Germany, and Berlin." We saw Berlin as an island, when, in fact, until the Wall, it was a bridge from East to West, not only for the refugees but, more important, for hundreds of thousands of East Germans who crossed back and forth every week.

This assumption of a sharp division may have been a great mistake. The Wall was in our minds before it was in Berlin. We had divided the city in our thoughts, one part free, one part Communist, and it was only after Khrushchev saw this and found us talking almost exclusively about "rights of access to West Berlin" that he ordered the Wall put up.

So here it is for the present, but it will come down. It is too unnatural, provocative, and dangerous to last. The Berliner is sure of it. He does not know when the miracle will happen. He does not know how it will happen. But he knows, even though he can't quite tell you why.

LONDON, ENGLAND
AUGUST 11–14, 1963

The Decline in Ideology

THIS IS THE NINETEENTH YEAR AFTER THE SECOND WORLD WAR, and to an American who first came to this old city to work nineteen years after the First World War, the contrast is spectacular.

Now, as in 1937, a whole generation has grown to manhood since the armistice. Britain is engaged in a savage debate about the politics, morals, economics, and education of the nation, most of it reflecting a deep sense of insecurity, suspicion, and resentment about Britain's changed position in the world. Yet in the perspective of this past convulsive quarter of a century, the outlook for the present postwar generation is infinitely better than the prospects of the nineteen-year-olds in 1937.

The great difference now is that the postwar generation can plan its life with reasonable assurance that it will have a life to plan. Britain was so concerned with saving its life in 1937 that it had no time to think about what to do with life. Then the nation was talking about whether its Cabinet ministers were asleep; now it is talking about whom they are sleeping with.

It is an instructive difference. Literally nobody seems worried about the prospect of a major war. Britain is frustrated and spiritually lonely now, but it is not alone. The forces of peace in the world have balanced the forces of war, and it is precisely because there was not this combination of will and power in the free world in 1937 that Hitler was by then in the Rhineland, the Japanese were deep in China, Mussolini was in Abyssinia, and France was moving on Madrid.

Accordingly, one now finds Prime Minister Macmillan musing in the Cabinet room at Admiralty House as if the cold war in Europe were about over, and worrying instead about Moscow's growing navy and the threat of China east of Suez. He has just ordered a new aircraft carrier at immense cost, not to cruise around the Atlantic but because he expects the battleground in the war with Communism to shift from the possibility of nuclear war in Europe to conventional wars and revolts in Asia. Similarly, the British Foreign Secretary, Lord Home, while slightly more skeptical than Macmillan, seems convinced that the Soviet Union is giving priority to its national interests over international Communist interests.

Maybe this reviving hope about the Soviets is as misguided as Chamberlain's wishful thinking about the Nazis, but two events have apparently convinced the leading British politicians and civil servants that we are now entering a historic new and hopeful phase in our relations with Moscow. These are the bitter ideological conflict between the USSR and Communist China, and the American willingness to risk a major war with the Soviet Union last winter over Cuba.

Particularly those leaders of Europe who lived through the drift and indecision that led to the two world wars of this century are inclined to identify President Kennedy's confrontation of the Soviet Union in the Caribbean last year as one of the decisive acts of the age. It is their view that such a direct challenge to Germany in 1914 or at any time in 1937–9 would have prevented both world wars, and therefore they cannot understand how it is that America itself has underrated Kennedy's retreat-or-fight challenge to Khrushchev last year.

This view is shared, incidentally, by the British Labor party leaders, Harold Wilson and George Brown, and like Macmillan and Home they seem willing to base policy on the assumption that the ideological differences between Moscow and Peking are irreconcilable.

The mood of Britain in the summer of 1963, then, is full of

paradox. It is more optimistic than America about the conflict with Communism, but pessimistic about itself. The air is full of clashes between the parties and between the allies, between the classes and between the sexes, but the big thing that permits these lesser controversies to preoccupy the nation is that the elemental fear of major war has receded. This is the great change between 1937 with Joseph P. Kennedy in Grosvenor Square and 1963 with his son in the White House.

"The new Europe," wrote Arthur Koestler in *Encounter* the other day, "is not Huxley's brave new world or Orwell's 1984. . . . Ideologies are on the wane, poverty is on the way out. The new structure which is taking shape is the society of managers, technocrats, official planning, chromium, motels and motorways."

It is a good comment. To an American, the mood of Western Europe today seems a little like the mood of the United States in the Twenties. Economically, it is prosperous; one sees far less poverty even In the Scottish Highlands than in the American South. Politically, it seems increasingly isolationist. Morally, it is even wilder than we were in the Jazz Age. Spiritually, it is adrift from its past.

This is, admittedly, a poor time to judge. Europe is in a kind of intermission between the great acts of history. The old political leaders are too stubborn to leave the stage and the new generation is too weak to take over. Job security and military security are better now than at any time since the war and, ironically, prosperity and not religion seems to be the opium of the people.

Accordingly, Europe is relaxing and enjoying the pause. It is developing its own life behind the American nuclear shield just as we, with even more indifference, developed our continent behind the shield of the British navy in the nineteenth century. For the time being, the private purposes of life are taking precedence over the larger public purposes, and this naturally makes one wonder whether the new postwar generation will be different.

So far as a visitor can judge, the young people who have grown up since the war are not dominated either by the "angry young men" of Britain, or by the weirdies and beardies who want to ban the bomb in Trafalgar Square. The charge against this emerging generation is not that they believe in wrong things but that they don't believe in anything.

They are what Koestler calls "The Silent Generation." They seem, he observes, "to have no aspirations except getting on in their professions, marrying early, and going on holidays in the family car. Thus, this super-historical age has produced a generation which seems to live outside history . . ."

Aldan Crawley, British Member of Parliament, and his wife, the writer Virginia Cowles, recently made a tour of the universities of France, Italy, and Germany. They came back "depressed" by the lack of ardor for European political union or any other large public design.

"The dynamic had gone out of Europe," Crawley wrote in the *Sunday Times*. "The vision which Sir Winston Churchill resuscitated in 1945 of the world's most talented peoples joining together to rekindle the flame of Western civilization, in alliance with, but not dependent upon the United States—in opposition to Communism but also in the hope of being a catalyst which would bring understanding with the Communist world—is dying."

Sleeping may be a better word. President de Gaulle, by his rejection of Britain in the Common Market, has interrupted, though he has not stopped, the movement toward European union. His was the only eloquent voice in Europe and when he said "no," he broke the momentum toward unity but did not kill the idea.

Politically, there is very little progress toward union, but defense, learning, and commerce are all becoming more international and interdependent, and the soldiers, teachers, scientists, and businessmen are all forcing acceptance of "foreign" ideas. Also, it is difficult to sleep for long in a country with as soft an economy and as lively a tradition of political criticism as Britain. Nothing escapes the witty disloyalties of the demolition crew in Fleet Street, not Macmillan or Wilson, not Oxford or Cambridge, not the Blimps in Pall Mall or in the unions, not what Malcolm Muggeridge calls "this empire on which the sun never rises."

Thus, in due course, a growing and changing Europe will

probably be forced by a growing and changing world to develop new public purposes and policies. Western Europe is now taking America for granted and enjoying the materialism they used to criticize in us. But European reliance on U.S. power will create economic and political problems just as U.S. reliance on European power created desperate problems in the Thirties. For the time being, they are copying, not the best in America, but some of the worst, and as we discovered to our sorrow, a combination of isolation and materialism has its limitations.

JUNE 6, 1965

Unlimited Ends and Limited Means

AN IMPORTANT CHANGE HAS COME INTO AMERICAN LIFE. IT IS NOT that the old optimism has vanished, but that serious doubts have arisen about applying the optimistic assumptions of America to the rest of the world.

This is the root of the anxiety in the country today about many of the Administration's policies and much of its evangelical rhetoric: not that the people differ with the objectives of peace abroad and equality at home, but that they have begun to doubt, almost for the first time since the last war, that the Administration is willing or able to provide the means to achieve the exalted aims it proclaims.

About the objectives of blocking Communist expansion in Southeast Asia and producing full employment, equal opportunity, and decent housing for the poor in America there is little controversy, but about the means and even the will of the nation to achieve these noble ends there is a great deal.

All the debate on the crisis in Vietnam comes back to the fundamental question of ends and means. Some think the means being applied there of bombardment are too severe, others think they are not severe enough; but both those who want more bombing and more Marines and those who want less agree that the ends and means of our policy seem to be out of balance.

Somehow they have to be brought into line. The mathematics of both bombardment and guerrilla warfare are fairly clear. Bombing at the present level and defense against the Vietcong at the present level are not adequate to the objectives of stopping the flow of Communist guerrillas from the North or defeating them in the South. Therefore, either the ends or the means have to be changed.

The danger at the moment is that neither will be, and this is the greatest danger of all. For it takes ten or twenty to one to defend against guerrilla attack, and there is no evidence that the South Vietnamese army, even with our bombing and defensive aid at limited points so far, can make substantial progress toward ending the Communist advance.

Either this dilemma will be faced, or we will be trapped into a piecemeal involvement in a ground war without adequate forces on terrain highly favorable to the enemy. When a sizable South Vietnamese unit got into a losing battle with the Vietcong the other day, it naturally called on the American forces to come to their aid on the ground. In this particular case, an air attack on the Communists eased the pressure, but it is virtually certain that similar calls will go out in the future, and what will the President do then?

He has said the defense of South Vietnam is "vital" to the United States, which is quite a statement. With every speech he increases the commitment of the United States to prevent the defeat of the South Vietnamese army. Accordingly, he cannot very well let them be cut up, but he does not have the forces on the ground to prevent it—especially since the Communists in the North have an army of over 400,000 that has not yet been committed to the battle.

Somehow, the American people seem to understand this contradiction between what they want and what they are willing to pay for, and this helps explain the anxiety in the country about the way things are going in Southeast Asia.

In fact, the same conflict between ends and means is also present on the race question at home. Again, the President has recently been saying on the commencement circuit that the inequality of the American Negro is intolerable, that the Negroes must be taken out of the slums and given jobs and housing that will make their new legal rights a reality. How this is to be done, however, without a massive public-works and public-housing policy is not clear. Again the objectives are expressed in eloquent words, but not carried out in public policy.

The President has defined the Negro's problem: thirty-five years ago, Negro unemployment in America was about the same as white; now it is twice as large. Since 1947, the number of white families living in poverty has decreased 27 per cent, while the number of poor nonwhite families living in poverty decreased by only 3 per cent; and now 73 per cent of the American Negroes are living in cities, most of them in slums.

Yet on this question, as on Vietnam, the disparity between ends and means is startling and disturbing. For the means proposed to achieve the solution of the problem are clearly inadequate, and this is what creates the uneasiness over what is said in Washington and what is done.

Therefore, if there has been a decline in American optimism it is not only because we do not know how to solve our problems, but because we do not yet know how to discuss them. The politicians insist on pretending that everything is soluble—that we can achieve almost unlimited ends with limited means—and, while the people would like to believe it, they increasingly have their doubts.

Power, Violence, and Purpose

POWER AND VIOLENCE ARE NOW DOMINATING THE HEADLINES. MORE and more bombing in Vietnam. Riots and the National Guard in the streets of Chicago. Most of the airlines and most of the newspapers in New York paralyzed by strikes. And beyond this, the majority of the American people looking on in wonder, troubled but helpless. Is it as bad as it seems? What happened to all the talk of a few months ago about peace abroad and a Great Society at home? Are the problems of the cities and the races, the contending nations and philosophies, beyond rational control?

Sometimes it seems they are, but the larger picture is probably not so dark as the headlines suggest. Power is being used in the world but it is also being restrained and its limitations are being exposed. The bomber is not prevailing in Vietnam. "Black Power" is not prevailing in America. They are not dramatizing the problems but demonstrating that they cannot solve the problems. The rule of physics tends eventually to prevail in politics; force produces counterforce, and in the end is likely to create balance.

We are going through a difficult experiment with power at the moment both in Vietnam and at home. Power is being used both places, paradoxically, to prove that power will not prevail. It is invoking fear, again paradoxically, to encourage reason, and power will probably continue to be used both at home and in Vietnam until reasonable remedies to those problems begin to be discussed.

Both sides, fortunately, are afraid. In fact, the only thing we have to cheer is fear itself. And this is true in the wars at home as well as in the war abroad. Everybody is using power but is afraid of it. Everybody is threatening to use more of it, but is holding back. So there is still a chance that a balance of power will eventually be established and lead to common sense.

Unfortunately, there is very little evidence in Washington that the Johnson Administration has an adequate sense of priorities in dealing with all this violence at home and abroad. It has a policy for dealing with each problem—whether it is hands-off on the newspaper strike or limited intervention in the airplane strike, or more legislation in the racial war, or more bombing in the Vietnam war—but no sense of relationship between all these difficult questions.

This is odd, too. For the President has been converted by Secretary of Defense McNamara to the managerial techniques of "cost accounting." He loves to talk these days about how McNamara showed the Pentagon how big-business methods in Detroit applied to big Government problems in Washington.

Under the McNamara plan everything should be put to the test of "cost and benefit." Each purchase of planes or missiles, each decision about new weapons systems must demonstrate that the benefits equal the costs. Yet there is very little evidence that the McNamara system has been applied to the Johnson Administration's program as a whole. The cost of the Vietnam policy, for example, is well over a billion dollars a month, and over one hundred lives a week—to say nothing of the wounded, and the diseased, and the corrupted. The cost to the South Vietnamese is hard to calculate or even to imagine.

What is the cost of a "victory" that would humiliate China? What the cost of a prolonged war that would block progress with the Soviet Union in the control of nuclear weapons? No doubt we can eventually prevail on the battlefield, if the Chinese stay out, but what benefits will match the hostility of the 700,000,000 Chinese people in the future? And what would a cost-benefit test tell us about spending enough money in Vietnam and on the moon to wipe out most of the slums and illiteracy in the American cities?

The Johnson Administration does not give the impression of having a sense of relationship on all these things. It wants everything: peace in Vietnam on our terms; the abolition of inequality and poverty; a Great Society—but it could, the way things are going, end up first in peace, first on the moon, and last in the big American city slums.

It is this lack of skill and scope, of proclaiming great goals and raising vast hopes, which is adding to the doubts of the American people today. The demoralization of disappointed hopes is now fairly evident in the violence of the slums.

"A demoralized people," Walter Lippmann wrote during the depression, "is one in which the individual has become isolated and is the prey of his own suspicion. He trusts nobody and nothing, not even himself. He believes nothing, except the worst of everybody and everything. He sees only confusion in himself and conspiracies in other men. That is panic. That is disintegration. That is what counts when in some sudden emergency of their lives men find themselves unsupported by clear convictions that transcend their immediate and personal desires."

There is no such clear conviction in the country today. The use of power and violence dramatizes the point. But the violence may, hopefully, have positive results. It may, both in Vietnam and in the American cities, demonstrate its own impotence and thus finally bring the nation back to a redefinition of purpose and priority, which all the changes of the past have confused.

MAY 8, 1966

"Too Damn Big and Rich"

MOST OF AMERICA'S TROUBLE IN THE ALLIED WORLD TODAY IS simply that it is so rich and powerful. No nation ever had such power to dominate or so little desire or will to dominate, as the United States, but it dominates anyway—inevitably, indirectly, and almost absent-mindedly.

The recent outcries among our best friends in Canada against our economic influence in that country are the best illustration of the point, though Europe is worried about the same problem. Through investment in Canada, Americans control 60 per cent of the Canadian petroleum industry, 52 per cent of mining and smelting, 35 per cent of paper and pulp, almost all of the Canadian rubber and auto industries.

Corporate decisions made in the United States about investment, production, and markets affect incentives, initiatives, employment, and the standard of living in Canada. Most of the time these American decisions help the Canadians. What we do south of the border means more employment, more opportunity, and a higher standard of living for Canadians. But the decisions are made in the United States, and this is just the problem. For Canadians, it is a rich neighbor–poor neighbor relationship— convenient, pleasant, but unequal and therefore irritating even when the rich folk are nice about it.

The Canadian Minister of Finance, Mitchell Sharp, issued a "manifesto" the other day calling for the reversal of trends toward what he called U.S. "domination" of the Canadian economy. His predecessor in that office, Walter L. Gordon, went even further toward a kind of declaration of independence from U.S. economic control.

This may not be serious economically, but is deadly serious psychologically. "We like you," Beland H. Honderich, editor of the Toronto *Star*, told his American newspaper associates last year, "but we are worried about you. American cultural, economic and political influences so pervade our way of life that we have begun to wonder if our relatively small nation can retain its independence in face of the strong pressures generated by our giant neighbor to the south."

The problem is not that the Canadians really seriously question American motives. They used to fear that we sat around plotting to annex them. Now they fear that we don't think much about them at all but just do what comes naturally—work, produce, invest, and distribute wherever we can make a profit—and in the process help them, corrupt them, and dominate them without really realizing what we are doing.

The elements of irony, paradox, and even tragedy in all this are interesting. The U.S. does not intentionally use its power to dominate other friendly nations, but it does so anyway. It opposes the spirit of domination but it dominates. It yearns to create the spirit of independence in other nations, but with foreign aid and business arrangements, unintentionally makes them dependent.

In the last few days the businessmen of the United States have illustrated a remarkable concern about social justice and good relations among nations. Henry Ford made a speech the other day in which he sounded like a volunteer in Lyndon Johnson's war against poverty. A few days later Douglas Dillon took some of the most powerful leaders of American big business to Paris—the heads of U.S. Steel, General Electric, Corning Glass, etc.—to discuss with French business leaders what could be done about the decline in Franco-American relations. But the problem of American commercial interests and American power on the one hand and American foreign policy on the other still remains and it is still unresolved.

Maybe this is what Lord Acton meant by the problem of power—of power corrupting, but he didn't really foresee the American experience. For there is honestly no will to corrupt here in the United States either in the Government or consciously in business, no desire to dominate or humiliate Canada or Western Europe. It is mainly, as Ambassador Charles E. Bohlen said in one of his undiplomatic moments—"We are simply too damn big and rich."

Report from the
University of Alabama

IT IS NOW ALMOST FOUR YEARS SINCE GOVERNOR GEORGE Wallace stood in the door of Foster Auditorium and defied the Federal Government to bring Negroes into the University of Alabama. Things are quite different here now.

There are now 298 Negroes at the university. They have made their way into everything except the fraternities and Bear Bryant's football team, and the students have just put on a two-day convocation in this same Foster Auditorium which was as free and outspoken as anything ever presented at Berkeley or Cambridge.

The Student Government Association's program for the convocation carried articles by the Chairman of the Joint Chiefs of Staff in Washington, General Earle G. Wheeler; by Roy Wilkins of NAACP; Stokely Carmichael, the prophet of Black Power, and even Bettina Aptheker, the Communist student leader at the University of California.

When Secretary of State Rusk arrived in Tuscaloosa, he was greeted by the anti-Vietnam picketers, four of whom insisted on being arrested in order to test the law forbidding outsiders from demonstrating on university property. And when he finished his speech before over 4,000 Alabamans, he was presented with a petition from the students of the Negro college at Tuskegee, charging that Negroes were bearing a disproportionate share of the fighting in Vietnam.

This is quite a change. There was a kind of lust of enmity on the race question here just a few years ago, but the focus of attention in this conference was on a dignified Negro, Dr. Stephen J. Wright, president of the United Negro College Fund and former president of Fisk University, who discussed the Negro revolution in the South and was treated by the vast audience with the utmost courtesy and even enthusiasm.

He was quiet, plain, witty, and even blunt, as if he were talking in his own house to a misguided white friend. He told them he had stopped for the night on the way down from New York at an "uppity" hotel in Birmingham, Alabama, and everybody treated him so casually, he said, that he was almost disappointed. This was progress, he conceded, but nobody should be deceived.

He had come to Tuscaloosa not to discuss the Negro "revolt," for "revolt" meant merely a protest which might or might not be successful. He had come, he explained, to discuss the Negro "revolution," and "revolution" was the right word because, he said, "the fundamental objective of all the civil rights activity we have witnessed during the last several years has been to overthrow the social, economic and political system of the White Establishment."

Dr. Wright expressed with disarming courtesy what had been achieved in the last few years, but insisted that the battle was just beginning for Negro equality in housing, in the administration of justice and public services, in employment and educational opportunities. He almost gave his audience a timetable for the troubles ahead in Cleveland, Pittsburgh, Chicago, Los Angeles, Newark, and New York, followed, as he explained, by more trouble in Baltimore, Birmingham, and Memphis, and he predicted the Negro leadership would become "increasingly radical" in the "next decade of revolution," unless the problem of Negro jobs, housing, and education were tackled much more aggressively and effectively than now.

The audience in Foster Auditorium, which had come in out of the lovely flowering Southern spring, obviously was not representative of general opinion in Alabama, and certainly not representative of the Wallace government in Montgomery (George is still damning "the moron professors"), but it gave Dr. Wright more applause than any other speaker except the Secretary of

State, and Dr. Wright's only embarrassment came, not from whites, but from a Negro student from Tuskegee who condemned him for "smiling" when he talked to the white people in the audience.

The students in this vast hall were even bolder than Dr. Wright. They marched to the microphones and told Secretary Rusk that they thought he was "sincere" but hopelessly wrong about Vietnam. One Negro student startled the audience by asking why a country that discriminated against Negroes should ask him to fight against the poor nonwhites of Asia who have been "cut up" by the white man for centuries.

The audience obviously did not like that, and it was visibly embarrassed by the hostility of the questions and speeches addressed to Secretary Rusk, but Rusk, who was born in Cherokee County, Georgia, was more impressed by the free and even pugnacious spirit of the meeting than by anything else.

None of this made the newspaper headlines outside of Alabama. University officials were so apprehensive about what might happen when the picketers arrived that they had the police out patrolling the campus and watching for the Klan, but there was little news, because "nothing happened."

Nothing, that is, but the triumph of dissent; nothing but the emergence of a few young white and Negro leaders in Alabama who are determined to challenge the comfortable falsehoods of the past; nothing but the willingness of the university president in Tuscaloosa to take the social and political risks of the meeting; nothing, in short, but the demonstration that Alabama is beginning to have a university where ideas, no matter how defiant of the established order, can be discussed. And this could be "news" of some importance.

3

⁂

PORTRAITS

Arthur Vandenberg[1]

THE GREAT THING ABOUT THE LATE SENATOR ARTHUR VANDEN-
berg was that he was a pretty good symbol of America in the
Thirties and Forties. In the Thirties, like the United States, he
was isolationist, boastful, inexperienced in the field of foreign
affairs, idealistic, contradictory, fiercely suspicious and combative, sharply critical of things he knew little about, dogmatic,
and often hypocritical.

In the Forties, also like America, he was internationalistic, he
was energetic, enterprising, sometimes naive and erratic, and
very often wistful about the simple past and resentful of the
responsibilities of the present.

Accordingly, his private papers are not merely one more book
about the great revolution of American foreign policy. They are
an intimate record of the conversion of a man and a nation
during one of the most critical periods of world history. They are
a most revealing account of the way in which foreign policy is
made in a government of divided powers. They are the story of a
complex and fascinating human being, who played a critical role
in the development of American leadership in the world, and
fortunately, they are written by the man himself and not, like
most of the postwar reports of the mighty, the work of a competent ghost. . . .

Senator Vandenberg's great contribution was that he did not
believe in an "inevitable war" between the East and the West.
And he did not believe in an "inevitable war" between the internationalists and the isolationists at home. Once he came to the
belief that America could not be isolated, or even, as he called it,
"insulated" from the wars of Europe and Asia, he set himself the

[1] A review of *The Private Papers of Senator Vandenberg*, ed. Arthur H.
Vandenberg, Jr., and Joe Alex Morris (Boston; 1952). Published in *The
New York Times Book Review*.

task of trying to find ways and means of bringing the Congress and the State Department and the internationalists and the isolationists together on a common policy.

It is impossible to read these diaries without coming to the conclusion that he was essentially a great mediator. He was not an originator of ideas. But once a Marshall Plan, or a North Atlantic Treaty, or a Greek-Turkish aid program was put before him, he had a genius for seeing precisely how and when it could be qualified and presented so as to win the consent of the Senate. His capacity to anticipate opposition on the Hill, to find the area of agreement between the State Department and the Senate, and finally, to find language which would express that agreement in acceptable terms was extraordinary.

Great emphasis has been placed upon Senator Vandenberg's courage in abandoning the isolationist policy in public and thus making it easier for others to follow his lead. An equally important contribution, as this book makes clear, however, was his realization that men in public life do not like to change their minds in public and his conclusion which flowed from this realization, namely, that techniques must be found to remove objections to legislation on Capitol Hill before, and not after, prominent legislators had taken a public position.

These papers are full of stories about how Senator Vandenberg developed these techniques: how he worked with Cordell Hull during the war to establish regular contact between State Department officials and members of the Senate Foreign Relations Committee; how he induced the State Department to change its approach on the Greek-Turkish aid bill; how he worked with former Under Secretary of State Robert Lovett and General George C. Marshall for weeks on the preliminaries to the North Atlantic Treaty and induced the Senate to approve the Vandenberg Resolution—which was the forerunner of this treaty —before many members of that august body really knew what was happening.

It must be said, however, that this is an uneven book, as, indeed, Senator Vandenberg, like most human beings, was an uneven performer. He did not participate at all in many great foreign-policy decisions of the last decade, and therefore there are great gaps in his knowledge, or at least in the record published in this volume. Also, he let weeks and often months go by without writing in his diary, and then wrote from memory, or did not catch up at all. This was particularly true when he was in the midst of a political battle in Washington, or when he was mortally ill in 1949 and 1950.

Consequently, the record is not only incomplete but it is not wholly accurate on one or two important points. The impression given by the editors, and by the diary itself, is that Senator Vandenberg patiently modified his former isolationist philosophy between 1941, when the United States was attacked at Pearl Harbor, and January 10, 1945, when he carefully planned and produced his extraordinary proposal: that the United States should abandon its policy of no entangling alliances and enter into a long-term alliance with Britain, France, and the Soviet Union to block any revival of German aggression.

It is true that the Senator modified his position shortly after Pearl Harbor. He talked a great deal about the necessity for American participation in maintaining the peace in 1942, 1943, and particularly in 1944, when he came under the influence of John Foster Dulles. He said in many private conversations in those days that the invention of the pilotless aircraft, used so effectively against Britain, had shaken all his beliefs about America's "ocean barriers."

What startled the Senate and the nation, however, was the specific nature of the proposals made by the Senator in his speech of January 10, 1945. Many former isolationists, including the Senator from Michigan, had talked about the necessity of American participation in postwar arrangements to keep the peace, and many others, also including Mr. Vandenberg, had complained in public about the Soviet Union's aggressive tendencies in Eastern Europe.

But nobody in Washington—not even the most prominent of the internationalists—had dared to suggest, as Mr. Vandenberg did in that speech, that the thing to do was offer the Soviet Union an alliance against the revival of German or Japanese aggression, and thus take away from the USSR the excuse that she was grabbing territory in Europe and Asia in order to protect herself against the possibility of future German or Japanese attacks.

What is interesting about this is that only a few days before the January 1945 speech was delivered it did not contain any such proposal at all. The speech originally was a protest against Russia's policies in Eastern Europe, and particularly in Poland. This speech was, as Mr. Vandenberg wrote in his diary six months later, shown to several reporters in Washington. One of them told him it was a good speech but that it offered nothing concrete or positive, that it was merely one more complaint against Soviet policy and would do nothing but aggravate the frustrations of the people about Soviet policy.

Asked for a suggestion about what could be proposed, the reporter then outlined the proposed treaty which would take the debate on the postwar settlement out of the realm of generalities and into the realm of the concrete by offering an American alliance. Senator Vandenberg decided at the last minute to adopt the proposal, and the response to it was, as he later said, "so sensational that it bowled me over."

It has often been said that Senator Vandenberg gave America a decisive lead away from isolation, and this is undoubtedly true, but it is equally true that America, by its reaction to his speech, also produced the final evidence that changed him. Nothing that he had done in public life until that speech brought him such a response. Men and women from all over the nation poured out their hearts in long and eloquent letters to him. They came from a type of citizen that had seldom written to him before. The press, from left to right, hailed his positive stand. And perhaps more than anything else, this response convinced him that he had struck a theme that was close to the heart of large numbers of the American people.

The popular Vanderberg story is the story of the courageous convert, who, having seen the need for change after Pearl Harbor, patiently planned his great conversion speech and thereafter led his party into another era. It is a good story and it is largely true, but it is not as good or as human a story as the real Vandenberg story. For the real story is far more exciting.

Senator Vandenberg was beset by doubts about American foreign policy until his death. He felt in his bones that America had to cooperate with other nations and share their risks. He was sure that a "bad world for others can't be a good world for us," and after the January 1945 speech had crystallized him in the new role of the Republican convert, he kept this idea uppermost in his mind and used his remarkable powers of mediation, persuasion, and definition to help unify America on an internationalist policy.

Always, however, when a new program came up, or the British or the Russians did something he didn't like, or United States policy suffered a reverse, as in China, the weight of his responsibilities and the endlessness of his country's problems revived his old fears and hesitations. . . .

Nor did he ever really take an entirely nonpartisan view of foreign policy, despite all his tireless efforts in its behalf. He complained bitterly in public that he was never consulted about Far Eastern policy, yet the truth is that he did not want to be consulted about it.

He once explained this apparent paradox to this reporter in these terms: "I cannot be effective as a mediator if I forget the realities of politics. My party has a fundamental problem. It is still divided between those who do not want to assume world responsibilities and those who do. The Republican party has this dilemma: if it does not cooperate in the world, it will be blamed for destroying the peace, as in 1920. If it cooperates too much with the Democratic Administration, it will be charged with having no policy of its own. Therefore, as I see it, we must cooperate in the theatre where we could lose everything, which is Europe, and oppose the Administration in the Far East, where there is no solution that I can think of anyway."

It is precisely because he never forgot the realities of politics and could honestly voice his dissents and his doubts until the end that he was so effective. The true believer, the convinced convert has no doubts and can pursue his role with equanimity, but Senator Vandenberg's role was never that simple. He persevered in spite of his doubts toward goals which he often saw very vaguely or not at all. This was both his ordeal and his triumph and it was really a greater achievement than these fascinating documents make out.

Robert Frost

EVERY TIME ROBERT FROST COMES TO TOWN THE WASHINGTON Monument stands up a little straighter. The old gentleman was here this week just when everybody was down in the dumps about the Russians, but he was full of bounce and confidence.

The beauty of life, said he, looking out on the golden maples on R Street, lies in struggle and change and taking tough decisions. When he heard people complaining about the Russians and the sputnik, and the endless standoff with Moscow, he said he had trouble suppressing a mocking frivolity.

"We ought to enjoy a standoff," he remarked. "Let it stand and deepen in meaning. Let's not be hasty about showdowns. Let's be patient and confident in our country."

At 83, Mr. Frost is still full of poetry and plans, still wandering about the world talking to kids about what it means to be an American, still taking long walks through the Northern woods, and still urging everybody to talk up and be sassy. He is against everything and everybody that want people to rely on somebody else. He is against the United Nations. He is against the welfare state. He is against conformity and easy slogans, and Madison Avenue, and he hasn't seen a president he liked since Grover Cleveland.

"I keep reading about old Grover, and after sixty years I have to admit there were one or two things that could be said against him, but I concede it reluctantly. As Mencken said, Cleveland got on in politics, not by knuckling to politicians but scorning and defying them. He didn't go around spouting McGuffey Reader slogans or wanting to be liked."

The United Nations, disturbed by Mr. Frost's opposition, suggested to him recently that he might like to write a poem celebrating the ideal of the interdependence of the nations. Sweden had given the UN a huge chunk of solid iron and somebody thought that this should be built into the UN building as a symbol of nature's strength and unity.

Frost was not interested. Iron, he said, could be used to strengthen the UN building or it could be used for weapons of war. That was the way with nature, he said; always confronting mankind with decisions. So he rejected the invitation with a couplet:

> Nature within her inmost self divides
> To trouble men with having to take sides.

His pet project at the moment is to band together all men and women who want to stamp out "togetherness." The glory of America, he says, has been its pioneers, who celebrated "separateness" and who were not always seeking protection. "There is," he remarks, "no protection without direction."

Mr. Frost is still a physical phenomenon. There is a comfortable, shaggy look about him but great physical and mental power. He has a pair of shoulders like a Notre Dame tackle, a shock of disobedient white hair, and a vast solidity, like a great natural object.

His idea, one gathers, is that America should act in the face of the Communist challenge as a great man would act. It should not be dismayed. It should not be boastful. It should be calm and watchful and industrious. It should avoid pretension and sham. It should say clearly and calmly what it means and do what it says it will do.

"The question for every man and every nation," he says, "is to be clear about where the first answerability lies. Are we as individuals to be answerable first only to others or to ourselves and some ideal beyond ourselves? Is the United States to be answerable first to the United Nations or to its own concept of what is right?" Once we get this straight, he believes, the United States will be less entranced and preoccupied with the Soviet world, more self-reliant, more prepared psychologically for the endless struggle of existence.

Transition and change do not bother him. He is pleased with Dean Inge's reminder that when Adam and Eve were kicked out of the Garden of Eden Adam was heard to remark, no doubt by a reporter of the *Times*, "We sure are living in a period of transition."

"All life," he says, "is cellular. We live by the breaking down of cells and the building up of new cells. Change is constant and unavoidable. That is the way it is with human beings and with nations, so why deplore it?"

To Mr. Frost most of the political pronouncements of the day are just "corn-meal mush," put out by politicians who think their "first answerability" is to what will get them re-elected instead of what is right and true.

But he isn't worried. "I stand here at the window and try to figure out whether American men or women swing their arms more freely. There cannot be much to fear in a country where there are so many right faces going by. I keep asking myself where they all come from, and I keep thinking that maybe God was just making them up new around the next corner."

MARCH 2, 1956

Richard Milhous Nixon

THE MAN IN THE NEWS TODAY (WHO WISHES HE WERE NOT QUITE so much in the news) is Richard Milhous Nixon, the 43-year-old Vice President of the United States.

He is the lightning rod of the Republican party. All the flashes of Democratic anger and frustration descend on him. Harry S. Truman, Adlai E. Stevenson, Governor Harriman of New York, and Senator Estes Kefauver of Tennessee may differ on a thousand things. But in their personal antipathy to Mr. Nixon they are united. Why is this?

Part of the explanation is in the role he has played since he became Vice President. He has taken on, at the request of the President, who does not like party politics, the role of principal party spokesman. For the last three years he has been the prosecutor of the Democratic party. He has, in short, been the point of the Republican spear.

Part of the explanation, too, is personal. Like Thomas E. Dewey of New York, his personal appearance, his dress, his platform manner are all impeccable but seem contrived. If President Eisenhower is the football-coach image in American life, Mr. Nixon is the Hollywood image, as well groomed and smooth as an actor, but as serious and determined as Billy Graham.

At the same time he has what the Democrats call "an instinct for the jugular." In his campaigning, he conveys an impression of righteous sincerity, but he concentrates on the inflammatory issues and constantly manages to imply that the Democrats were not only wrong but that they were wrong for sinister reasons.

In the 1954 campaign, he asserted in Las Vegas, Nevada, that Adlai E. Stevenson "has not changed since he testified for Alger Hiss." Mr. Stevenson had given an affidavit in regard to Mr. Hiss at the request of the court. In mentioning Secretary of State John Foster Dulles, Mr. Nixon said on March 15 of the same year: "Isn't it wonderful that we finally have a Secretary of State who isn't taken in by the Communists, who stands up to them?"

He is not controversial mainly because he has raised the Communist issue and blamed the loss of China on Democratic "softness on Communists"—many Republicans have done that —but because he has implied dishonorable motives while claiming virtuous motives for himself and his party.

These things, however, have had political consequences, which is why Mr. Nixon is in the news today. Some influential members of his own party have said that he is now such a controversial figure that he would hurt the party in a campaign with an ailing President. Others, with powerful support in the party organization, applaud the very tactics the Democrats and others condemn and think he is precisely the kind of spear the GOP needs in a war with the Democrats.

Thus, he is at a critical point in a remarkable career. He has fought his way up the hard way and is now at the $32,000 question. He came from a poor Quaker family, was graduated second in his class at Whittier College in 1934, won a scholarship to the Duke University Law School, and worked his way the rest of the way through there. He left there with honors in 1937.

He was married in 1940 to Pat Ryan, a pretty Whittier schoolteacher whom he met while playing a district attorney in a local theater group. He came to Washington a month after Pearl Harbor to work as a lawyer in the Office of Price Administration. After six months he joined the Navy and ended up as an operations officer in the South Pacific Combat Air Transport Command.

No man in American politics with the exception of President Eisenhower has gone so far during the last ten years. He represented the old Twelfth California district (eastern part of Los Angeles County, including Whittier and San Marino) from 1947–50, ran successfully for the Senate in 1950 and remained there until the 1952 Presidential race. President Eisenhower listed his name with four others as possible Vice Presidential material. A committee of Eisenhower political advisers picked Mr. Nixon.

It was while he was in the House that he was assigned to the Un-American Activities Committee and played an important, perhaps even the decisive role, in pursuing the investigation that led to the exposure and conviction of Alger Hiss. In this he was greatly assisted by the late Bert Andrews, former chief Washington correspondent of the New York *Herald Tribune*.

As Vice President he may have infuriated the Democrats and alienated many independents, but he won the respect of the President and the Cabinet. Even his political enemies concede that he conducted himself during the critical part of the President's illness with restraint and mature responsibility. His political advisers urged him to seek a commitment from the President on a second Vice Presidential nomination before the President made up his mind—a maneuver that many observers here think would have succeeded—but he refused to do so. "Let's leave that to the President," he said. And that's where the decision lies now.

Eugene Black

GENE BLACK, THE GREATEST NATURAL WIZARD TO COME OUT OF Georgia since Ty Cobb, is thinking of retiring soon. He is head of the World Bank and one of that remarkable breed of international civil servants who have done so much for the reconstruction of the old world and the development of the new nations since the last war.

When the history of this first postwar era comes to be written, it's a good bet that the political figures in the cold war will seem less important than they do now, and that a few creative pragmatists in the international community will loom much larger.

Among these are the late Dag Hammarskjold, Secretary General of the UN; Jean Monnet of France, whose quiet and persistent wisdom guided the unification of Europe; Per Jacobsson of Sweden, head of the International Monetary Fund; Sir Oliver Franks of Britain, who helped persuade the United States to launch the Marshall Plan; and Gene Black, whose political genius, charm, and cool competence have guided the World Bank through a remarkable period.

Gene Black—out of the University of Georgia at 18, Phi Beta Kappa, "the seasickest ensign in the U.S. Navy" in the first World War, investment banker in Atlanta for the New York investment firm of Forbes & Co., vice president of the Chase National Bank in 1937, student of Shakespeare and connoisseur of the four B's (baseball, bridge, bourbon, and Balzac), came to the World Bank first as executive director for the United States and then as president in 1949.

His story since then illustrates the flexibility of the American mind and the development of these new international institutions as instruments of peace.

First, he concluded that it was important to develop what the

London *Observer* has called "an international social conscience
—a feeling that extreme differences of wealth and poverty were
as intolerable among nations as, during the last hundred years,
they had come to be regarded among individuals within the same
nation."

Second, he concluded that the development of the new nations
of Africa and Asia meant nothing less than "exporting the industrial revolution, with all its political and social implications."

Third, as Black himself said, "the most necessary requisite for
development may be reform . . . and since resources will at best
be limited, careful planning is necessary . . ."

Thus the orthodox conservative American banker out of Atlanta via the Chase National became a kind of international
social reformer and managed to do it not with grants but with
sound self-liquidating loans. In the process he has not only won
the confidence of the lenders of the world but of the borrowers as
well, and gradually, as a result of this confidence, he has been
forced into the role of mediator between governments in international disputes such as those between Britain and Egypt over
the Suez Canal, and India and Pakistan over the waters of the
Indus River.

The weakness of greatness, however, is that it tends to be
irreplaceable. Replacing such a man will, because of the financial
power of the United States, start with President Kennedy, but it
is an international responsibility which cannot be met in accordance with the normal process of American politics. . . .

Meanwhile Gene Black has bought himself a house on Brooklyn Heights, from where he can watch the skyline of downtown
Manhattan and carry on his duties as chairman of the finance
committee of the Ford Foundation and read Shakespeare.

He won't leave until he is satisfied with the transition, but
when he goes it will be a sad day in the capital. For this breed of
international civil servants—the Monnets, the Hammarskjolds,
the Frankses, and the Blacks—were not only great servants of
the world but they were among the most articulate and charming
men of their time.

Felix Frankfurter

Dr. George A. Kelser, Jr., of Washington said yesterday that Justice Felix Frankfurter had suffered "an acute cerebrovascular insufficiency," and was "resting" in the hospital, but this could not possibly be true.

Judge Frankfurter never had an "insufficiency" of anything in his life. His problem is not "insufficiency" but oversufficiency. He has more surpluses than the Department of Agriculture. His difficulty is not a shortage of anything, except maybe size, but too much blood and energy, too many ideas, interests, and opinions racing too fast through too small an area.

What clearly destroys the doctor's medical bulletin is his reference to the Justice "fainting" and then "resting." He has made strong men faint all his life, but he has never done the thing himself, and as for "resting," this is obviously ridiculous. He has never rested, night or day, and he's not likely to start at 79.

The explanation of what happened to the Judge is really very simple: he blew a gasket. He has been doing it all his life, and the reason is clear enough. Every man has some weakness, and Mr. Frankfurter has a weakness for olives and newspapers. He is incontinent about both.

He is not a secret drinker but a secret reader. He has a little second-floor study in his Victorian house in Georgetown, and when his lovely wife, Marian, and his faithful friend, Matilda, are not looking, he sneaks in there and reads newspapers from all over the world. What is worse, he thinks newspapers should be logical or at least sensible—an obviously preposterous idea— and over the years this has had certain medical effects on him, which Dr. Kelser did not mention. The Judge has taken an overdose of printer's ink into his bloodstream. His memory is overdeveloped, and when he reads some particularly outrageous bit of nonsense the ink momentarily clots the blood.

Thus, as Dr. Kelser explained, there can be "a temporary narrowing of blood vessels in the brain, rupture of a brain artery, or blockage of a brain artery by a clot. The Justice is believed to have suffered a spasm, a sudden narrowing of a brain artery, which relaxed before any real harm was done."

Precisely. But it was not an "insufficiency" of blood that did it, but an oversufficiency of ink and nonsense. This city is an intellectual midden of illogical rubbish, and anybody who has ever watched the Judge read a newspaper about events in Washington knows that he gets an average of at least one spasm on every page.

Dr. Kelser was no doubt right about one thing. He said that Judge Frankfurter's condition cleared up "spontaneously." This is precisely the word that describes most things about the Judge. He is a "spontaneous" character given to "spontaneous combustion." This explains why he has an oversufficiency of both friends and enemies.

The other night Robert Frost was here for a big, splashy eighty-eighth birthday party and the Judge was there till one in the morning singing the old poet's praises and listening to Frost's remarks. "All there is to life," said Frost, "is getting a meaning into a lot of material. . . . You've got to be sweeping and you've got to be pointed. You've got to come out somewhere, just as plain as a wisecrack or a joke."

Frankfurter was so enthusiastic in his applause that he probably overdid himself right there, and no wonder, for this is precisely what F. F. has been doing all his life—getting a meaning into a lot of material, reducing diversity to identity, coming out somewhere, plain as a wisecrack, to the delight of many and the despair of many more.

Maybe the doctors are right that age has something to do with the Judge's physical problem, though not because it has narrowed the arteries but because it has widened the mind and deepened the memory. The Judge, bless him, can't help thinking that the Constitution is important and that people are important. His enthusiasms are boundless. If he is a little tired, it is because he has paid attention to so many things and inspired so many youngsters here and in Cambridge over so long a time.

There is now some talk here of replacing him on the Supreme Court of the United States, but this is as silly as the doctor's bulletin. They may eventually put somebody in his place, but they won't replace him.

OCTOBER 21, 1964

Herbert C. Hoover

HERBERT HOOVER'S LIFE, WHICH CAME TO AN END TODAY, GIVES US some perspective on our own age. He was born in 1874 of a family that came to Iowa from Canada by prairie schooner. His great-grandmother, Rebecca, was still alive when he went east of the Mississippi River for the first time at 23. She was born in 1801 during the Administration of Mr. Jefferson. Thus these two members of a single family lived through almost the entire course of the American Union.

The population of the country in the year of Mr. Hoover's birth was 44,040,000. Since he left the White House in 1933, it has increased by over 67,000,000, and it stood at 192,985,643 on the day of his death.

Federal Government expenditures in the year of Mr. Hoover's birth totaled $302,634,000. In the last year of his Presidency, with the economic depression already on and Hitler just coming to power, the Federal expenditures were $4,659,203,000. The present Federal budget is $97,900,000,000.

About the only thing that sounds familiar about those "good old days" ninety years ago was the public outcry against the state of public and private morals. In Hoover's Quaker household in West Branch, Iowa, thee was religious or else! His great-grandmother, Rebecca, was opposed to the screening of windows against insects as somehow an interference with the Lord's will. But his mother, Huldah, seems to have taken part in street demonstrations against Demon Rum.

Mr. Hoover was born during the Grant Administration, when many politicians seem to have regarded honesty as an eccentricity. Sensational frauds were uncovered in the War and Treasury Departments in 1874. Grant's private secretary, O. E. Babcock, was implicated in the famous "whisky ring" which defrauded the Government of millions of dollars in taxes on distilled whisky.

That same year the Secretary of the Treasury, W. A. Richardson, hastily resigned to avoid a vote of censure by the Congress; Secretary of War William Belknap later was caught selling Indian post-traderships and got out to avoid impeachment, and Secretary of the Navy George M. Robeson accumulated a fortune of several hundreds of thousands through kickbacks on business contracts. It was quite a time.

Mark Twain even wrote a novel in 1874 entitled *The Gilded Age*, parts of which read like the campaign speeches of Barry Goldwater today. "Every individual you encounter in the city of Washington," wrote Twain, "represents political influence. . . . Mere merit, fitness and capability are useless baggage to you without influence. . . ."

The "memorable dates" of those first few years of Mr. Hoover's life were marked by events reminiscent of many of the conflicts of the present time. William M. ("Boss") Tweed of New York City was convicted of 204 charges of fraud in 1874, for example, and there was a Negro demonstration in 1874 in Vicksburg which ended with the death of seventy Negroes.

There was also much discussion over both public and private morals. The nationally known preacher Henry Ward Beecher, pastor of the Plymouth Church, Brooklyn, was sued in 1874 for $100,000 by one Theodore Tilton, who accused the holy man of committing adultery with Tilton's wife. Edward Eggleston, worried about the easy life, wrote a major novel called *The Circuit Rider*, extolling the glories of hardship; and in Ohio, a militant band of women formed the Woman's Christian Temperance

Union in Cleveland, and took to the streets to stamp out booze.

Even overseas the news was not entirely different in 1874. The British had another important election in which Disraeli succeeded Gladstone as Prime Minister. The Chinese had trouble with foreigners in Formosa, this time the Japanese. The Russians began to bother their neighbors by introducing compulsory universal military service for the first time. There was a revolution in Cuba, and trouble with the French over the Monroe Doctrine in Mexico.

None of this public violence and personal ambition seems to have corrupted the simple life of Herbert Clark Hoover off there in Cedar County, Iowa. His father died when he was 6 and his mother when he was 8. It is true that he drifted away from some of the externals of his Quaker faith later on. The matriarch Rebecca chastised him for fishing on Sundays, which probably explains why he got such a kick out of sneaking away from the White House to the Rapidan River later in life. At college, he took up ballroom dancing to please the girl who afterward became his wife. It is even said that he came to enjoy the movies, the theater, good cigars, and even playing cards later in life, without noticeable degeneration of his character.

In short, he not only overcame the political morals of his youth but helped transform them. He had the last laugh. He convinced most of his critics in the end and outlived the rest of them. And few politicians manage to do that.

Edward R. Murrow

EDWARD R. MURROW LIVED LONG ENOUGH BEFORE HE DIED THIS week to achieve the two great objectives of a reporter: He endured, survived, and reported the great story of his generation, and in the process he won the respect, admiration, and affection of his profession.

The Second World War produced a great cast of characters, most of whom have been properly celebrated. Roosevelt, Churchill and Stalin are gone. Chiang Kai-shek is now living in the shadow of continental China, which he once commanded, and only De Gaulle of France retains power among that remarkable generation of political leaders formed in the struggle of the two world wars.

The great generals of that time too, like MacArthur and Rommel, have died or, like Eisenhower and Montgomery, have retired; but in addition to these there was in that war a vast company of important but minor characters who played critical roles.

History would not have been the same without them. They were the unknown scientists like Merle Tuve, who invented the proximity fuse and helped win the air war, and Chiefs of Staff like Bedell Smith, and the Foreign Service officers like Chip Bohlen and Peter Loxley of Britain, and on the side, the Boswells of the story, like Ed Murrow of the Columbia Broadcasting System.

It was odd of Ed to die this week at 57—usually his timing was much better. He was born at the right time in North Carolina—therefore he was around to understand the agony of the American South. He went West to the state of Washington as a student and therefore understood the American empire beyond the Rockies; and he came East and stumbled into radio just at the moment when it became the most powerful instrument of communication within and between the continents.

He was part of a remarkable company of reporters from the West: Eric Sevareid, Ed Morgan, Bill Costello, whom Murrow recruited at CBS; Hedley Donovan and Phil Potter, out of Minnesota; Elmer Davis, Ernie Pyle, Tom Stokes, Bill Shirer, Raymond Clapper, Wallace Carroll, Webb Miller, Quentin Reynolds, Wally Deuel, the Mowrers, and many others, including his dearest friend, Raymond Swing, who played such an important part in telling the story of the Old World's agony to America.

But Murrow was the one who was in London at that remarkable period of the Battle of Britain, when all the violence and sensitivities of human life converged, and being both sensitive and courageous himself, he gave the facts and conveyed the feeling and spirit of that time like nobody else.

It is really surprising that he lived to be 57. He was on the rooftops during the bombings of London, and in the bombers over the Ruhr, and on the convoys across the Atlantic from the beginning to the end of the battle. Janet Murrow, his lovely and faithful wife, and Casey, his son, never really knew where he was most of the time, but somehow he survived.

In the process, he became a symbol to his colleagues and a prominent public figure in his country, and there was something else about him that increased his influence. He had style. He was handsome. He dressed with that calculated conservative casualness that marked John Kennedy. He was not a distinguished writer, but he talked in symbols and he did so with a voice of doom.

It is no wonder that the British, who know something about the glory and tragedy of life, knighted him when they knew he was dying of cancer at the end. Their main hope in the darkest days of the German bombardment of London was that the New World would somehow understand and come to the rescue of the Old, and if anybody made the New World understand, it was Murrow.

He hated the commercial rat race of the television networks, and fought their emphasis on what he regarded as the frivolities rather than the great issues of life, and talked constantly of escaping back into the small college atmosphere from which he came. He never made it, and probably wouldn't have liked it if he had.

Those who knew him best admired him most. He was a reporter of the old school and a performer of the new. In radio and television, there is no written permanent record. Only the memory of the listener remains. And the memory of Ed Murrow will remain for a long time among people who remember the terrible and wonderful days of the Battle of Britain.

JULY 15, 1965

Adlai E. Stevenson

AMERICA CELEBRATES SUCCESS, BUT OCCASIONALLY IT PAUSES TO REgret the men who didn't quite make it—the also-rans, the good men who arrived near the top at the wrong time, the rejected and the disappointed.

Adlai Ewing Stevenson of Illinois, who collapsed and died on July 14 on a street in London, was such a man. He was the man of thought in an age of action. He was in tune with the revolutionary spirit of the age, but not with the more moderate spirit of his own country, and no one knew this better than he.

He was sad at the end, not because he was rejected for the Presidency by his fellow countrymen, but because he felt his ideas were rejected by the leaders of his own party—President Kennedy and President Johnson.

He never expected to be President. I spent two hours with him alone at the Roger Smith Hotel in Washington immediately after President Truman called him to the White House at the end of January 1952, and asked him to seek the Democratic party's Presidential nomination with Mr. Truman's support.

Later he accepted the nomination on the ground that Senator

Robert A. Taft of Ohio might be nominated by the Republicans, and that Senator Taft was "an isolationist," but that night, he was sure that General Eisenhower and not Senator Taft would be the Republican nominee, and he was sure not only that General Eisenhower would win, but that maybe the General should win.

Was it not time, he asked, for the Republicans to come to power after twenty years of Democratic rule? Was it not true that the absence of power, as well as the exercise of power, tended to corrupt? Would not General Eisenhower finally lead his party away from its isolationist tradition, and was this not good for the country?

Later he changed, but this objective quality of mind in Mr. Stevenson was precisely why he was so respected by the intellectual and diplomatic communities, and why at the same time he was so unpopular with the most political elements of his own party.

His disappointments came later. He wanted to be Secretary of State more than he expected to be President, but both Mr. Kennedy and Mr. Johnson passed him over for the job, and while they listened politely and often reluctantly to his advice, they did not follow it—or at least, he died believing that they were more interested in power and politics and did not agree with him about Vietnam, or the Dominican Republic, or the importance of the spirit of the United Nations.

He talked many times about resigning, from the Bay of Pigs to the bombardment of North Vietnam, but at the same time, he loved the stir and prominence of public life, he hated "scenes," and could not quite bring himself to the point of getting out.

Even so, when he died in a London street today, he left a good legacy. He brought a certain chivalry to American politics. He elevated the political dialogue in America and he contributed much to the style and the policies later adopted by Presidents Kennedy and Johnson. His insistence, for example, on proposing a nuclear test-ban treaty in the Presidential campaign of 1956 was widely criticized at the time, even by his own campaign managers, but he was around long enough to see the treaty signed.

A man has to have a strong sense of self-importance in order to feel up to the staggering tasks of the American Presidency, and Stevenson was not a self-important man. He used to say that flattery was all right "if you don't inhale it." He had a way of looking at himself from a distance, as if somehow he were another person who merely happened to have stumbled into Presidential politics.

One day he was riding in a car on Michigan Boulevard in Chicago with a friend. When they stopped at a traffic light, a man in another car recognized him and said, "Hi, Adlai." When they drove on, Stevenson's friend said: "Did you know him?" And Stevenson replied: "No, he wasn't talking to me, he was talking to Adlai."

He was deeply hurt by the collapse of his marriage. "When women ask me," he once said, "how I could hold the country together when I couldn't even hold my family together, I don't know what to say to them."

"There are two ways of being a politician," Paul Valéry once wrote. "The first is to bring to politics all one's ideas, energies and even possessions; to enrich it with one's own riches, and yet in the midst of it, to maintain one's own intellectual and inner preoccupations, so that the management of public affairs may be ennobled by them.

"The second is the exact opposite: it consists in taking from politics all one's ideas, along with power and many other resources. This is living off politics instead of giving it life." Stevenson met the first test perhaps as well as any Presidential candidate of this century.

He was not bitter about not being President or Secretary of State. He was too full of self-doubt and even self-mockery for that. It was not his ambition but his pride that was affronted by what he thought was the rejection of his advice to rely more on United States moral than military power.

For example, he wanted President Johnson to reassure the United Nations that the United States wanted to end the legal dispute over financing the United Nations, but the President rejected his advice only a few days ago and exhorted the United Nations merely to follow American policy.

The tragedy of Adlai Stevenson, however, is not that the

United States has lost a representative at the United Nations, but that the Western world has lost another of its few eloquent men.

Language is power, and in the last few years the West has lost most of the men who could define its purposes—Churchill and Gaitskell in Britain, Kennedy in the United States, Hammarskjold at the United Nations, Nehru in India, not to mention those spokesmen of the Western literary world, Frost, Faulkner, and T. S. Eliot.

Maybe Mr. Stevenson's critics were right—he may have been primarily a writer and a public speaker, rather than a political leader. But as Churchill proved, speaking and writing are important in politics, and the only one now left with the gift of articulation in the West is De Gaulle, who is using his eloquence, not on behalf of Western civilization, but on behalf of the French alone.

Even after he was nominated for the Presidency at the Democratic convention in Chicago in 1952, his doubts and his eloquence were apparent: "I would not seek your nomination for the Presidency," he said, "because the burdens of the office stagger the imagination. Its potential for good or evil now and in the years of our lives, smothers exultation and converts vanity to prayer.

"I have asked the Merciful Father—the Father of us all—to let this cup pass from me. But from such dread responsibilities one does not shrink in fear, in self-interest, or in false humility.

"So, if this cup may not pass from me, except I drink it, Thy Will be done."

Yet at that same convention, he startled the delegates by his power of expression in his welcome to Chicago: "Here on the prairies of the Middle West," he said, "we can see a long way in all directions. We look to east, to west, to north and south. Our commerce, our ideas, come and go in all directions. Here there are no barriers, no defenses to ideas and aspirations. We want no shackles on the mind or the spirit, no rigid pattern of thought, no iron conformity. We want only the faith and conviction that triumph in free and fair contests."

When he was defeated he summed up the spirit that endeared

him to the people he admired the most in these words: "Looking back, I am content. Win or lose I have told you the truth, as I see it. I have said what I meant and meant what I said. I have not done as well as I should like to have done, but I have done my best, frankly and forthrightly; no man can do more and you are entitled to no less."

And, despite defeat and disappointment, he had the saving grace of humor. After General Eisenhower had obviously defeated him on election night of 1952, he went on television and turned to President Lincoln, as always, for the expression of his feelings: "Someone asked me, as I came in, down on the street, how I felt," he said. "And I was reminded of a story that a fellow townsman of ours used to tell—Abraham Lincoln.

"They asked him how he felt once after an unsuccessful election. He said he felt like a little boy who had stubbed his toe in the dark. He said that he was too old to cry, but it hurt too much to laugh."

He did not do so well in the campaign of 1956, when he was renominated, for by that time he had been persuaded that his idealistic and objective approach to Presidential politics was not effective, and he relied on a more traditional and partisan approach.

Yet, on the whole, he tried to impose his own principles and conscience on American politics—whether as Presidential nominee or as United Nations delegate, knowing most of the time that it probably wouldn't work. In this sense, it must be said of him that he had the courage to fail.

Maybe it is too much to say that Stevenson joins that remarkable company of also-rans who were better than the men who defeated them—Webster, Clay, Bryan, Hughes, Stimson, Al Smith, and John W. Davis—but he was a shining figure, and he lived long enough to know that he had the respect and the admiration, perhaps not of the masses or his leaders, but of people he personally admired the most.

Aleksei M. Kosygin

TALKING TO PREMIER ALEKSEI M. KOSYGIN OF THE SOVIET UNION is a little like pitching batting practice to the New York Yankees. You throw a question, then duck.

Soviet officials do not converse with foreigners: they compete. There is no searching for understanding in conversation as we understand it in the West, no effort at accommodation of the mind, not even the slightest hint or suggestion that the Soviet Union has ever done anything that was in any way wrong or even unwise, imprudent, or intolerable. Their idea of give and take in a talk is simple; you give, they take.

The manner of speech here differs, of course, from official to official. Khrushchev was volatile, earthy, vivid, and emotional. Kosygin is as unemotional as the multiplication table. He insults you quietly.

Kosygin is undoubtedly as angry and frustrated as he sounds about Vietnam and Germany, but he refuses to start at the beginning of the story. He begins not with the Communist actions in these places but with America's reactions. He assumes that it was perfectly proper to divide Germany and put her and all the rest of Western Europe under the threat of Soviet rockets. He assumes it was not only all right but even noble to help the Communists in Vietnam launch a guerrilla war to achieve political control of that country. These acts he regards as past and beyond dispute. They are settled. This is not, in his view, using force in Vietnam or the threat of force in Germany: it is "liberation" and "self-defense" and it is immutable.

That the Germans may not want to be divided and helpless and that the non-Communist South Vietnamese may not want to be taken over seems to surprise him, and that America should help them militarily seems to him an intolerable and wicked affront.

It is easy to understand his irritation—after all, we are getting in his way—but it is difficult to comprehend his self-righteousness. If the Communists use force in Vietnam it is a crusade: if America uses force it is "aggression." If the Soviet Union threatens Germany it is natural and permissible, but if America defends Germany it is an outrage, and a threat to world peace. And if you suggest to him that all this is a monstrous distortion of the fact he merely looks surprised.

I mentioned to Kosygin on the way out of his office in the Kremlin that a great opportunity had been missed when Kennedy tried to reach an understanding with Khrushchev at Vienna in 1961 and was bullied and threatened with war over Germany in reply. It was this violent intimidation, I said, that led to the buildup of U.S. arms in Germany. And later in 1961 in Vietnam.

Kosygin puzzled over the word "bullied"; then when he understood it he smiled and condemned not the bullying but the buildup. "Politicians should use reason, not force," he said. "When you have time," he added at the door, "you may want to give some thought to what I have said."

His meaning was perfectly plain and his manner a little like that of a confident headmaster who knows about wickedness but never indulges in it himself. He was clearly right, he seemed to be saying, and any sensible person who thought about it would realize it was true. And this is precisely the problem. For as Michael Stewart, the British Foreign Minister, discovered here last week, negotiating with the Russians is a mysterious business. He said at the end that he did not recognize the Germans as they were described here, but still thought he had reason to believe that maybe the Russians would not reject any and every effort to bring Germany safely into the nuclear defense of the Atlantic.

He had scarcely reached London, however, before Tass put out a statement saying he was absolutely wrong: the Soviet Union, Tass insisted, would indeed reject any and every attempt to let the Gemans into an Atlantic nuclear community.

There is still, therefore, a problem about how to deal with these diplomatic problems. We are not only not solving them with the Russians, but haven't even found an effective way to talk about solving them. There is not only no agreement but no spirit of agreement.

"Only a few years ago," wrote Paul Valéry in 1933, "we still thought that in the world of the mind there were definite values, that a certain way of thinking, a certain general freedom of thought, a will to intellectual sincerity, intellectual precision had somehow gained, once and for all, the confidence of all humanity." Even then, Valéry had his doubts about the mind of Europe, and the mind of Russia is even more of a puzzle.

MARCH 20, 1966

Charles de Gaulle

PART OF PRESIDENT DE GAULLE'S GREAT INFLUENCE IS THAT HE throws such an elegant monkey wrench. If it weren't for the consequences, it would be almost a pleasure to be kicked out of France in such style. Since the death of Churchill, Nehru, and Kennedy, De Gaulle is the last man in the world politics who knows how and when to speak, and he seems to be the only leader in the free world today who really knows what he wants.

It is too bad that he wants such contradictory things: glory without power, strength without unity, equality without size, "a nation of heroes and saints" in a world of atomic bombs and scoundrels. Nevertheless, it is important to try to understand his grievances and yearnings.

Even when his manners are poor, which is quite often, it is easy to share his regrets and dreams. Like so many of our own restless young people in the universities, he resents this big clattering homogenized world. He longs, as we all do, for the romantic life where poetry does not come out of an IBM computer. His memoirs are full of the old noble words—honor, dignity, sacrifice, independence, courage, and grandeur—and he resents the fact that Europe, the center of the political and cultural world for a thousand years, the common home of Dante and Goethe, should be dominated in the west by the United States and in the east by the Soviet Union.

What could be more natural? Such a Europe would, he fears, become a kind of tourist's museum "without a soul, without backbone, and without roots," and his aim is to create a league of independent European states strong enough to look after themselves, to persuade both the United States and Russia to loosen their ties, and to serve as a powerful balancing third force between the Goliaths.

It is here that romance and reality come into conflict and French logic seems rather odd. How do you make a league of independent states strong enough to balance and banish America and Russia? His aim is clear enough. He is not alone in resenting the overwhelming power of the United States Government in Washington. This is shared by most of the governments and peoples of free Europe, and even by many of the American people. But there are really only two ways to deal with this vast disparity of power.

One is to break up the United States, which would be awkward, and the other is to build up Europe into a unified political and military force, which could then negotiate an equal partnership with the United States.

President de Gaulle cannot arrange the first and is not interested in the second. He is unalterably opposed to the principle of integration of either political or military power, either with the United States or with his allies in Europe. He wants to go back to the Europe of separate but equal states, which of course was precisely the divided system that led to the two German wars and resulted in the intervention of Washington and Moscow in Europe in the first place.

There is one other awkward fact. The other allies in Europe are not interested in De Gaulle's proposals. They do not want to exchange American influence and power, which irritates but protects them, for French influence and power, which also irritates but does not protect them. This does not seem to the Germans, for example, to be a very good bargain, and the British don't like it either, for they suspect that under De Gaulle's plan, Germany and not France would eventually emerge as the most powerful nation in Western Europe.

It is difficult, therefore, not to sympathize with De Gaulle's aim of a Europe that would be free of both American and Soviet political, and eventually military predominance, but even more difficult to see how this aim can be achieved by keeping the European states separate and independent.

De Gaulle is undoubtedly right that an Atlantic alliance would always be dominated by the United States, and that the domination will always be resented by the Europeans, but only a unified Western Europe can create the balance he wants, and this he is determined to oppose. Thus he is caught in a contradiction which separates the United States, divides Europe, and isolates France with a policy and a Constitution that are not likely to endure after De Gaulle is gone.

President Johnson has responded to all this very cautiously and prudently. De Gaulle has struck him with a NATO crisis in the middle of the Vietnam crisis, which is a little like Johnson threatening to break up NATO in the middle of De Gaulle's Algerian crisis, but Johnson has put France ahead of De Gaulle and acted on the assumption that France and the alliance will prevail long after De Gaulle and Johnson are gone.

No doubt President de Gaulle will have his way. He has the power to kick America out of France and to weaken the alliance, but not to put anything effective in its place. Even so, President Johnson will confirm his commitment under NATO to defend France, and may even go to Paris to make this point clear. Then it will be up to De Gaulle to take personal and historic responsibility for weakening the alliance which was the foundation of his own remarkable career at home.

Dean G. Acheson

THE MOST VIVID PERSONALITY IN WASHINGTON TODAY OUTSIDE OF the Big Man himself is Dean G. Acheson, the former Secretary of State, who is now almost 73, going on 50. He is the most active, interesting, and pugnacious character in town—a poet among the mechanics, a believer among the skeptics, and almost the last of our contemporaries who believes that history and power have a future.

Dean Acheson is a symbol of the irony of the present age. He was vilified by the liberals when he broke with Franklin Roosevelt and resigned from the Treasury on monetary policy in the early days of the New Deal. He was the arch villain of the conservatives when he opposed General MacArthur's Caesarism during the Korean War. He was condemned when he suggested that the practical line of effective American power lay outside continental Asia where air and naval power could operate effectively in blue sky and blue water. But who, after Vietnam, is to testify now that he was wrong?

He did more to help America reconstruct Europe and create the North Atlantic alliance than anybody else. He will deny it, but the Marshall Plan was more the Acheson Plan than anything else. He is the most loyal of all the loyal associates of President Truman, but the fact is, and President Truman would be the first to concede the point, that behind the remarkable Truman foreign-policy record was Acheson.

Many of Mr. Acheson's contemporaries will disagree, not about his achievements but about his tactics. He is not a mild man, but he is a man. He says what he thinks, which is a bold and rather old-fashioned thing to do in Washington these days. He does not suffer fools gladly, which is rather awkward in a capital where fools are not in short supply.

This has not helped him. He was never quite able to see

behind the slow and even stupid Congressman the sensitive and intelligent citizens the Congressman undoubtedly represented, and he has often been ungenerous to all the other men who were struggling to understand the mysteries and dilemmas of our foreign affairs—Dean Rusk, who became Secretary of State on his recommendation; Bill Fulbright; Adlai Stevenson; McGeorge Bundy; and Walter Lippmann—whose views he often condemned with eloquent contempt.

Yet even the men who have suffered under his scornful shafts have to deal with his ideas. He believes we are in trouble in Europe not because we have failed but because we have succeeded in restoring Europe and containing the Soviet Union beyond our dreams. He believes in power and feels that the decisive question in the world lies not in Africa or Asia or Latin America but in the Atlantic.

"Unique among commentators on American foreign policy," he wrote in the current issue of *Foreign Affairs*, "I do not believe that the difficulties which the alliance confronts today are the result of American ignorance, ineptitude or mistakes. Not that our Governments since the war have not made mistakes, and serious ones; but our problems do not stem from them. Rather they are the result of our own successful policies and the relaxing effect of prosperity. To this must be added a measure of bad luck in the appearance on the scene at a critical moment of General de Gaulle's atavistic mysticism and its effect on the most promising development in Europe since the Middle Ages."

Dean Acheson may be right or he may be wrong, but the main point is that he is almost the last of the free spirits in Washington who says bluntly what he thinks and says it with clarity, ardor, and style. At 73, he is beyond ambition. If the President asks his advice, as he does quite often, Mr. Acheson is pleased and honored, but if the President rejects his advice, which he does quite often, he goes back to his law practice, his cabinet-making, his dahlias, and his writing without resentment or remorse. He makes furniture at his farm in Sandy Spring, Maryland, because, as he says, a table is not like a foreign policy: "You don't have to wait twenty-five years to see how it comes out."

He writes—and he writes better than any man in public life in

America today—not about his problems but only about his pleasant memories. In short, he has come to terms with life. He has reconciled his professional and his private life, as few do. He may be savage in his criticism, but there is no bolder mind in Washington today, no more thoughtful friend, no better talker or writer, and no more eloquent critic in a city that has forgotten the function of eloquence, criticism, and style.

APRIL 22, 1966

Robert McNamara

SECRETARY OF DEFENSE MCNAMARA IS A PUZZLE. HE IS PROBABLY the most energetic, efficient, and dominant Secretary of Defense since Forrestal, but he is energetic, efficient, and dominant in a very special way.

To accuse him of "shocking mismanagement" of the war in Vietnam, as Congressman Ford of Michigan has done, is silly, and he has dealt with this charge to the satisfaction of most people here, but that was never really the question about McNamara. The question is not about his management of the war but about his judgment.

He has been very efficient in establishing civilian control of the Pentagon, in reorganizing the armed services for limited as well as nuclear warfare, in ending the perennial feuds between the Defense and State Departments, in winning the confidence of both President Kennedy and President Johnson, and in winning his arguments against those who were against the Bay of Pigs adventure, who thought it was unwise to land 25,000 marines in the Dominican Republic, and who oppose the successive commitment of U.S. power in Vietnam.

This issue about the Secretary of Defense is not over his inefficiency but his decisive efficiency in putting over dubious policies. Nobody in Washington is a more persuasive advocate. He marshals his figures down to the last decimal point. He is tidy, he is confident, and he has the sincerity of an Old Testament prophet, but something is missing: some element of personal doubt, some respect for human weakness, some knowledge of history.

McNamara is an intriguing question, for the private McNamara is quite different from the public McNamara. He is not a computer but a philosopher. He is probably more interested in disarmament than any other Secretary of Defense in the world today. In his private life he is a searching, sensitive, modest man, longing not for power and prominence, but for serenity and even obscurity, but in his public life he is machine-tooled—every hair and argument in place.

His testimony before the Foreign Relations Committee this week illustrates the paradox. "The governing principle of our military assistance programs," he said, "has been and is that the vital interests of this country in the defense of the free world are dependent upon the strength of the entire free world and not merely upon the strength of the United States." He went on to argue that the United States cannot do everything everywhere and that success in the world struggle depends on "staunch friends well armed, ready to do their part of the job." All of which is true, except that McNamara himself knows better than anybody else that our "staunch friends" are not "ready to do their part of the job."

He assumed that our staunch friends would prevail in Cuba in 1961, and that our staunch friends would pull together for freedom in Vietnam in 1963–5, but it didn't work out that way. He went to the meeting of the North Atlantic Council last year and told the Atlantic allies that they must consider what was to be done about the aggressive tendencies of China. But they listened politely and did nothing.

Yet McNamara persists. He is supposed to be a pragmatist, but he is an incorrigible idealist. He has read more about the religious, regional, and ethnic differences in Vietnam than any other member of the Cabinet, yet he told the Senate Foreign Relations Committee: "I strongly resent the implication that the war in Vietnam is in any sense a civil war."

Nothing could be more misleading than that McNamara is guilty of "shocking mismanagement" in Vietnam. He is a good manager if nothing else. He is the new mathematics allied to the old church, the computer and the missionary, and nobody quite knows what to do about this combination.

He appeals to everybody. The President is attracted to both his facts and his idealism. The Congress resents his assurance but doesn't know what to do about it. The Joint Chiefs hate his challenge to their tradition but dare not oppose him publicly. The press is troubled about him, especially when he loses his temper, but they are not worried about his efficiency. They are worried about his power and his judgment.

PORTLAND, OREGON
OCTOBER 25, 1966

Robert Kennedy

ROBERT KENNEDY IS RISING AND CHANGING FASTER THAN ANY OTHER political figure in the nation today. He is turning the legend he inherited from his brother into a powerful political movement, and he is coming out of the 1966 elections a winner, regardless of what happens to the Democratic or Republican party.

Even his famous brother at age 40, though only three years from the Presidency, never created the stir or drew the crowds outside his own state Bobby has been getting in the present tour through the West. The Labor Temple here in Portland was so jammed last night that even the Senator's aides and the crowd of reporters following him by jet across the country couldn't get into the hall.

The Seattle *Post-Intelligencer* gave him three whole columns on the front page this morning ("Bobby! Demos Beam as Students Scream"), and the *Oregonian* here in Portland led the paper with a headline ("Youths Mob Bob Kennedy") that overwhelmed the news out of the Manila conference.

This is no longer the stunned young man who walked through the political crowds in a trance two years ago and sounded uncertain and squeaky in his political talks. He is turning into an accomplished public speaker, and he is not only wooing the young jumpers and squealers, but putting a lot of influential Democratic candidates in his debt.

His platform manner is a faithful copy of his brother's. In these last few weeks the reporters following him feel he has improved substantially.

He starts each political talk with the same kind of self-mocking wit, quiet, brief, and conversational. He says he is glad to see such a big crowd, but as Churchill remarked, the crowd would have been twice as large for a hanging. Noting the youngsters, he jokes about wanting the voting age lowered to fifteen. Observing that the President, the Vice President, and Congress are all out of Washington, he says he has just had a wire from his brother Teddy: "Everybody's gone: Have just seized control." Much of this is carefully contrived, but he is quick and deft at turning aside hostile questions with a gibe or a wisecrack, and he seems increasingly bold and self-confident.

He didn't hesitate to tell the students in Washington and Oregon that he didn't like the present student-deferment system under Selective Service. Nor did he hesitate to make clear that he opposed the hawkish Vietnam policy of the Democratic candidate for the Senate in Oregon, Representative Robert B. Duncan, though he came here primarily to support the Democratic candidates for the House and Senate.

This, however, is not so much a trip to expound Kennedy's policies as it is to exploit Kennedy's personality, gain publicity, and win influential supporters in the Democratic ranks. He remains ambiguous about Vietnam, but the main impression he leaves is that he is for peace, for composing differences with the Soviet and the Chinese, for escalating the war on poverty rather than the war in Vietnam, and always, while saying an occasional good word for President Johnson, he talks about his brother and takes up a position a little to the left of Mr. Johnson's policies both at home and abroad.

1966, then, is obviously a training ground for a Kennedy Presidential bid in the future, but here the parallel with his brother breaks down. In the off-year elections of 1958, when John F. Kennedy began his campaign for the White House, the Republicans were in charge of the Government, and the field was clear for all Democrats, with Adlai Stevenson hesitating to run and Lyndon Johnson carrying the burden of liberal Northern opposition.

Robert Kennedy is not so fortunate. Actually he has more executive experience at 40 as Attorney General and first assistant to President Kennedy than J.F.K. ever had until he reached the White House. But Bobby has Johnson in his way, which is quite a barrier; and he will be 46 in 1972 and could easily be a grandfather by that time, which might make a difference to the students whose votes he is trying to get.

Nevertheless, his progress is significant. He is growing in experience and in poise. He is benefiting from the popularity of his brother and the personal unpopularity among many young people of President Johnson, and this is enough to keep alive the Kennedy mystique.

Averell Harriman

THE MOST DURABLE PUBLIC OFFICIAL IN WASHINGTON TODAY IS W. Averell Harriman, diplomat, croquet champion of the universe, and dean of Yale's "old boy network," who came here temporarily in 1934 and just got back this week from a world peace mission in time to celebrate his 75th birthday.

Somehow the right honorable gentleman manages to bridge the generations and the factions in this restless political city. Bobby Kennedy gave him birthday party the other night. Hubert Humphrey was a principal speaker, and the prophecy of the evening apparently was that Harriman would probably outlast both Kennedy and Humphrey. In any event, he lasted till three in the morning and was at his desk in the State Department at nine.

There must be something unusually tough about these Yale men. The Harvards of the New Frontier have all but vanished, and the Yales are not only multiplying but taking over some of the toughest jobs.

At last count they were running the Poverty Porgram (Sargent Shriver), the Treasury (Secretary Henry Fowler), the Federal Reserve Board (William McChesney Martin), the Army (Secretary Stanley Resor), and the Foreign Aid program (William S. Gaud). Then, of course there are the two new Under Secretaries of State from the Yale Law School, Nicholas deB. Katzenbach and Eugene Rostow; William P. Bundy, Assistant Secretary of State for Far Eastern Affairs, not to mention the four Yale Law School men on the Supreme Court of the United States (Fortas, White, Stewart, and Douglas, who taught there).

As for Harriman, his assignment is merely to see if he cannot help find and negotiate a settlement of the war in Vietnam. He is the elder member of President Johnson's diplomatic fire brigade, which includes Dean G. Acheson and Ellsworth Bunker, both of course from Yale, and John J. McCloy and Eugene Black, a couple of deprived citizens from Amherst and the University of Georgia.

There is a certain logic to Mr. Harriman's new assignment. He has been doing unlikely things all his life. He was a rich New York banker, almost "a malefactor of great wealth," so he joined Franklin Roosevelt's crusade against the bankers. He knew next to nothing about Russia or diplomacy, so he made himself an expert on both. He couldn't make a public speech, so he went into politics and became Governor of New York. Everybody said he was finished when Lyndon Johnson became President, but he didn't retire to write that book and probably never will.

Mr. Harriman's formula for survival seems to be that he doesn't get lost in details or devoured in personal feuds. He has the memory of a computer and a good diagnostic mind, but his process is intuitive rather than intellectual, and his gift of expression, while not wholly defective, is not effective either. Nevertheless, he has been uncannily right on the great questions of foreign policy in the last generation and somehow manages to feel rather than think his way through the thickets of controversy.

He came back from his post as Ambassador to the Soviet Union in 1945 and shocked observers at the UN San Francisco conference by announcing that the objectives of the United States and the USSR were "irreconcilable." But once Moscow had atomic weapons he concluded that in some fields these objectives had to be reconciled.

Accordingly, he contributed greatly to the negotiation of the test-ban treaty with the Soviets during the Kennedy Administration, and more than many of his associates in the State Department, he is convinced now not only that the way to peace in Vietnam lies through Moscow but that he may just be the man to make that journey.

If necessary, he will walk it. At 75, he could shinny up the Washington Monument. Like Dean Acheson, he has kept himself young by sitting up late talking politics and diplomacy with young people. Otherwise he is a temperate man, who has managed to serve the Government for over thirty years without falling into the deadly Washington habit of thinking he is what he merely represents.

This is perhaps why he has served longer in higher and more diverse posts than any other American official of his time. He didn't let pride and vanity get in his way. Having been Governor of a great state, Secretary of Commerce, Ambassador to Moscow and the Court of St. James's, he didn't hesitate to take less prestigious jobs as time went on. It's too bad about that book, but it's a wonderful human story anyway.

4

POLITICS

"Politics was at first the art of preventing people from minding their own business, A later age added the art of forcing people to decide what they did not understand. . . ."

"All politics are founded on the indifference of the majority of those involved. . . ."

Paul Valéry

The Independent Spirit

THE AMERICAN VOTER IS AN AMUSING FELLOW. HE WILL NOT BE roped or measured. What he does one year he may very well repudiate the next. How the Negro or the Catholic votes in one city is no sure guide to how he will vote in another, and this is the genius of the system.

It is the despair of those who want the parties to represent tidy principles and ancient conflicts, but it has its points. It is as varied and flexible, as vital and changeable as life itself. It adapts to the different conditions of a vast continental country, and it changes with time and place.

One by one the so-called rules of politics are broken by an increasingly sophisticated and independent electorate. They would not put a Catholic in the White House, it was said, so they elected Kennedy. They would not elect a Southerner, so they gave Lyndon Johnson the biggest victory in the history of the Presidency.

Most of the assumptions about New York politics were rejected this week: the Democrats could win with anybody, the Republicans couldn't win even if they were united. Goldwater had chased all the Negroes into the Democratic camp for good. Some fool even wrote about New York as "the city that quit."[1] It was all very traditional and all very wrong.

The Republicans won in New York with the help of the Negroes. Same in Philadelphia and Louisville. But in Cleveland a liberal Negro running for Mayor as an independent almost defeated the Democratic incumbent, and polled far more votes than the Republican candidate.

Putting calipers on all these voters is not easy, and finding national voting patterns is almost impossible. The Democratic

[1] Reston of the *Times*.

candidate for Mayor in New York lost despite the help of the President, the Vice President, and Bobby Kennedy; but in Virginia the conservative Democrats won the governorship with the help of the Byrd machine and the Negro and labor-union leaders.

Appeals to religious voting did not produce the desired results. In New York Abraham Beame, a Jew, ran well behind his party's normal vote in the areas occupied by Jews, though public appeals were made in these areas to put a Jewish Mayor in City Hall for the first time. Lindsay, a Protestant, won with powerful support in the Jewish and Catholic precincts.

Appeals to prejudice did no better. In New Jersey the Republican candidate for Governor, Wayne Dumont Jr., tried to beat Governor Hughes by arguing that the Governor should have fired a state university teacher who had said he would welcome a Vietcong victory in Vietnam. Hughes won in a landslide.

All this tells us something about the American political system. Where there is so much variety and independence, even a massive defeat such as the Republicans suffered in the Presidential election of 1964 can be overcome.

Herbert Croly of *The New Republic* once said that the two American political parties were indestructible because they were low-grade organisms without a brain or a heart, and therefore they could be cut in pieces and the bleeding fragments would somehow wiggle on and survive.

Actually there are not two great central parties but a hundred different parties, two in each state, run by different men and often by different principles for different objectives.

It is not a disciplined system. It does not follow the same tendencies in off-year elections as in Presidential elections. What is a savage issue in one area can be a bore in another, and this prevents the country as a whole from dividing into two unreconcilable groups.

This is probably the most encouraging thing about the system. It avoids precisely the kind of sharp ideological commitment the extreme conservatives want to encourage. Both parties are appealing to the widest possible electorate, even if they have to repudiate their own party label occasionally in order to make that appeal.

When one party rejects this approach, as Goldwater did in 1964, it gets in trouble. When the Democratic leaders of New York think they can count on party regularity and racial and religious affiliation to put over a mediocre candidate, they too get in trouble, and so it goes.

If anything, with the increase in mass higher education, and the dissemination of information by television, the tendency toward independent voting is increasing. The professional politicians do not like it, but that may merely prove that it is a good trend.

JANUARY 31, 1954

The Decline of Eloquence

WHEN LORD BRYCE WROTE HIS MEMORABLE STUDY OF *The American Commonwealth* near the end of the last century, he was so impressed by the eloquence of American politicians that he devoted an entire chapter to this subject. The gentle peer, one of the most perceptive and sympathetic critics of our society, should have been in the Senate this week for the so-called great debate on the Bricker Amendment. He would have been appalled by the gush of platitudes and full of wonder at the decline of this most natural of American talents.

Lord Bryce did not think the substance or literary form of our political speeches was better than Britain's in the Nineties, but he observed: "There is more fluency, more readiness, more self-possession. Being usually quicker and nimbler in mind than an Englishman, and feeling less embarrassed on his legs, an American is apt to see his point more clearly and to get at it by a more direct path.

"He is less frequently confused and clumsy, less prosy also, because his sympathy with the audience tells him when they begin to tire, and makes him sensible of the necessity of catching and holding their attention."

There is scarcely a word in this passage which could accurately be applied to this week's debate in the Senate. . . .

Nothing is more revealing than to read the debate in the House of Representatives in the 1830's on Greece's fight with Turkey for independence and the Greek-Turkish debate in the Congress in 1947. The first is dignified and eloquent, the argument marching from principle through illustration to conclusion; the second is a dreary garble of debating points, full of irrelevancies and bad history. . . .

JANUARY 21, 1966

NO CAPITAL EVER TALKED SO MUCH ABOUT "GREAT DEBATES" OR HAD so few of them. The Senate has not been performing its constitutional function of "advise and consent" on the critical issues of foreign affairs during the bombing pause in the Vietnam war, for example. The Senate has been tugging and hauling on the President in a series of disjointed and unconnected statements, speeches, and television remarks, most of them made outside the Senate chamber.

The opposition party did not launch a debate on the President's State of the Union message. It put on a television show featuring Senator Dirksen and Representative Ford in a recitation which differed wildly from most of the things they have said about the war in the past.

Secretary of Defense McNamara went before the Senate Armed Services Committee today and when he and the Senators emerged from the privacy of the committee chamber the scene was about as orderly as the end of a professional football game. Senator Richard Russell of Georgia told the crowding reporters that the general tone of McNamara's private remarks was that time was running out on the peace offensive. "Never even mentioned it," the Secretary said later.

No doubt the discussion inside the committee room was better, but ever since the start of the peace offensive the public statements have been a babble of disconnected shouts. One day a general comes back from Vietnam and calls for a resumption of the bombing in North Vietnam. The next a Senator offers his opinion that escalating the war now would be "sheer madness."

Yet there was no reason why the two houses of Congress could not have taken a week for a serious discussion of the President's State of the Union message. It was at least a clear picture of a perplexed man. It defined the dilemmas if not their solutions.

In any other democratic country the parliament would have regarded such a message at such a time by the head of the government as an invitation to a debate. The leader of the opposition in both houses would have replied at length, defined the areas of agreement and disagreement. Experts on both sides of the aisle would have talked on the aspects of the message they know best. And at the end of the debate, the leaders of the majority party would have tried to answer the questions raised.

Such a procedure not only clarifies the feeling of a democratic Congress, but is often useful to the Government executives who finally have to make the decisions. But no such orderly clarifying procedure has been following here.

It may be objected that a public debate in the midst of the peace offensive would dramatize the divisions in the country on Vietnam—they are being dramatized anyway—but there is no reason why the Government, if it fears this result, cannot debate the issue in private. This was done during the last war, and while there were the inevitable leaks, these did little damage.

The present situation is remarkable in a number of other ways. President Woodrow Wilson died believing that the power of the Senate was so great in the field of foreign affairs that it could virtually paralyze the President, but today the President alone can decide whether to renew the bombing or extend the pause, to raise or lower the level of violence on the allied side, to bomb Hanoi and mine the harbor of Haiphong or leave them alone, to attack the Soviet ships carrying supplies to North Vietnamese or ignore them, without even listening to the Senate.

There has been no real debate on the China question, which lies behind the whole war. It is not even clear whether the North Vietnamese and the Vietcong have increased the number of attacks on our positions since the start of the peace offensive, for the Pentagon has testified that the attacks have increased and the President has said they have decreased.

If the purpose of all this is to confuse the enemy, it must be a success—for the so-called debate is certainly confusing everybody else. The American people are entitled at such a time to a candid and searching discussion of the issues in the Congress assembled, but this is precisely the one thing they have not had.

MARCH 7, 1954

The President and McCarthy

THE WHITE HOUSE IS PLAYING A WAITING GAME WITH JOSEPH R. McCarthy. Men around the President have a theory that the American people will get bored with the Wisconsin Senator or that he will discredit himself or come to an abrupt political end.

They may be right—anything can happen when honor is challenged almost every day—but McCarthyism is not likely to go away, regardless of what happens to McCarthy. So long as the nation lives in fear of atomic war, unadjusted to the new and terrible responsibilities of world leadership, there will be McCarthys of one kind or another exploiting the fears and frustrations of the people.

It is not an entirely new thing in our history. One of the factors in the tyranny of the Salem witch trials was a widespread fear that the world was coming to an end at the close of the century. Accordingly, with the community facing the possibility of imminent death, it was felt that all men must accept the common faith; the right of dissent could not be tolerated, the heretic must be put to the rack. We do not go quite so far today, but fear is again the root of the problem—greater fear than ever in our independent history—and again the dissenter is under attack.

Senator McCarthy did not create this situation; he merely exploited it, increasing the fear in the process, but he has been permitted to exploit it so successfully that he has established a technique which is likely to go on regardless of his presence.

In this sense Senator McCarthy has already won a considerable victory. He has demonstrated, in this atmosphere of fear, that violence and deceit can be made to pay in American political life. He has silenced many honorable men in Congress and elsewhere, seized at least part of the machinery of his party, and tilted successfully with the President himself. Already one hears young men on Capitol Hill talking about him as if notoriety and fame were synonymous. The new ones come here to the House of Representatives full of the idealism of America. At first they are industrious, constructive, and usually moderate.

Then they note that, except for the well-established Senators or Representatives, it is the violent and outrageous men on the extremes who attract the attention of the press gallery. This was a problem long before McCarthy ever arrived in Washington, but with every victory he has scored the tendency toward extremism has increased.

Confronted by the Senator's rough tactics in the Zwicker case the President said this week that the "conscience of America will clearly discern" how to be both vigilant and fair in dealing with the menace of Communist subversion. He added that the Congress reflected that conscience and "we can be certain" that its members will act to defend the American sense of justice and fair play.

In view of the history and habits of the Congress, particularly since the rise of Senator McCarthy, this Presidential statement created something of a surprise in Washington. On this question of dealing with McCarthy there is very little evidence that the Congressmen are being faithful to their own consciences, let alone to the conscience of the nation. Not only the young ones, dazzled by his success, but the old-timers avoid his wrath.

Senators by the dozen will fume outrageously about McCarthy in the privacy of comfortable dining rooms, but they will do nothing about making any fundamental changes in the rules to curb his powers. The Democrats will occasionally make acid remarks about McCarthyism, but when it comes to defending General Zwicker they aren't present for the fight.

Finally, even after the President's remarks about "effective steps" being taken on Capitol Hill to establish codes of fair procedures in the investigating committees, the Republican leadership turned the question back to the committee chairmen, including Senator McCarthy. The job of minimizing the atmosphere of fear and getting somebody to reflect the "conscience of America," therefore, is not likely to be done by the Congress.

Senators and Representatives are not so accustomed to thinking about "the conscience of America" as they are about the special interests of their own districts and States. The President, however, is elected not by part of the nation but by the whole nation, and the responsibility inevitably bounces back to the White House.

"[The President] cannot escape being the leader of his party," said Woodrow Wilson, "except by incapacity and lack of personal force, because he is at once the choice of the party and of the nation. . . .

"His is the only *national* voice in affairs. Let him once win the admiration and confidence of the country, and no other single force can withstand him, no combination of forces will easily overpower him. His position takes the imagination of the country. He is the representative of no constituency, but of the whole people. . . .

"He may be both the leader of his party and the leader of the nation, or he may be one or the other. If he leads the nation, his party can hardly resist him. . . ."

Funny People, The Americans

THE AMERICAN VOTERS ARE FUNNY PEOPLE: THEY DON'T LISTEN. Once every four years they are courted and coaxed by Presidents and would-be Presidents, by Democrats and Republicans, by commentators, reformers, socialists, teetotalers, vegetarians, and prohibitionists, but they don't listen.

They have more radios and television sets, more loudspeakers and hearing aids than all the rest of the people in the world, but they don't listen. They talk more politics, they start more arguments, they attend more rallies, they watch more political forums, they tune in on more "press conferences" than all the other peoples in all the other elections in Christendom, but they don't listen.

The American voters are funny people: they don't read. They buy more newspapers and subscribe to more magazines than the British, the French, the Germans, and the Italians, but they don't read them. They line their shelves with them, they start fires with them, they make hats for their children with them, they pack dishes in them, but they don't read.

For their special benefit, the presses turn out scores of political books, pamphlets, charts, cartoons, histories, and biographies, but they don't read them.

Armies of correspondents interview politicians and taxi drivers, housewives and bartenders, farmers and trade-union leaders, political-science professors and editors, mayors, sheriffs, county clerks, and policemen—all for the special benefit of the voters—but they don't read.

Serious novelists take time out from their life's work, Harvard historians and economists are excused from classes, distinguished magazine writers and college professors get a leave of absence—all to write speeches designed to persuade the American voters—but they don't read what is written.

They are told that the future of the Republic depends on the re-election of Everett McKinley Dirksen of Pekin, Illinois, as United States Senator; they pay no attention. Billboards are purchased in the working-class district of Portland, Oregon, to convince the laborers that a vote for Wayne Morse is a vote for slavery; they won't look at them.

Brochures are printed by the ton and circulated in Cos Cob, Connecticut, to prove that the President and Senator Prescott Bush of Connecticut are "tools of Wall Street . . . instruments of big business . . . hard-hearted men who love General Motors and hate Joe Smith"; nobody sees them.

The American voters are funny people: they don't vote. They present themselves to the world as the most successful republic in history—a model of democracy, the most responsible and best-educated people on earth—but they don't go to the polls. They are critical of the British, the French, the Italians, the Belgians, the Dutch, the Indians, the Japanese, the Germans—all of whom have a higher percentage on Election Day than we have—but they don't vote.

The farmers swear by the Republican party but go fishing on Election Day. The industrial workers complain to their long-suffering wives about the Republican Administration but forget to register. The white-collar slaves proclaim their superiority, condemn their fate, and whine about inflation and discrimination, but they don't vote.

They complain. They criticize. They condemn. They philosophize. But when the contention ends, when the people they like and the people they don't like have had their say and the great day comes around, they don't vote.

The American voters are funny people: they don't care. They are told that the Russians have slipped into the Middle East for the first time in 200 years, that the Chinese Communists are quietly building a vast empire in the Pacific, and that the British and French empires are breaking up before their very eyes, but they don't care.

They are told that the Secretary of State has outraged every major-league statesman in the world and is now working on the bush-leaguers; they pay no attention. The President is portrayed to them as a man with nothing but a smile and a prayer; they won't believe it. The Democratic nominee is condemned as an egghead with nothing but brains; they're not interested.

The English tell them their Constitution is unworkable; the French criticize their logic and their cooking; the Communists foretell their inevitable destruction; the Socialists predict their economic collapse; the moralists wail about their children; and they don't give a damn.

They don't listen. They don't read. They don't care. But that's all right. They don't need to; never did need to. They get along. And think of the nonsense they miss every four years.

FEBRUARY 3, 1957

"Charlie's Jessie Ann"

THE CHIEF CHARM OF WOMEN IN OFFICIAL WASHINGTON—ASIDE, of course, from their reckless beauty—is that they are essentially more honest than their menfolk.

The men who come down here into lofty executive jobs invariably lose their individuality to the organization. The demands of the big Government machine, the pressures for conformity with the official "line," and the dictates of ambition squeeze all the spunk and personal distinction out of most of them.

But their women are different. Except in rare instances they are not surrounded by droves of bureaucratic drones and press agents. They are not protected and puffed up by official aides and are therefore not so likely to confuse themselves with power.

They stay in their homes during most of the day. They remember more vividly who they really are. They have "the humbling job" of raising the children, who are not impressed by all the trappings of official life, and therefore they remain more human, more direct, and more honest.

Once in a while, however, some courageous female rebel gets thoroughly fed up with all the sham and hypocrisy of the big Government hive and shakes creation with some lovely backfence commentary. This is what the wife of Secretary of Defense Wilson did this week and it is the nicest thing that has happened in this town since Bess Truman told Harry to watch his language.

Not since the invention and official recognition of "togetherness" has anybody on the Eisenhower "team" dared to whisper a word of criticism of the President of the United States. Mrs. Harold Talbott did say that it was "a dirty, low-down, sneaking group" that was trying to "get" her husband, the former Secretary of the Air Force, but even she subsided into wifely silence once the President decided that Mr. Talbott should go away.

Mrs. Wilson, however, said for publication—and she wasn't kidding—that the President was unfair in criticizing her husband's remarks about the draft-dodging in the National Guard: she implied that she thought her husband had done as good a job as Mr. Dulles, whom the President praised in the same news conference, and that she wished that Mr. Wilson would quit. "I've stood back and listened to criticism until I'm tired of it," she said. "I've been very, very careful not to make any criticism of any kind. But you reach a point sometimes—and this was it."

Whereupon Charlie issued an official communiqué saying he was "very proud" of his wife, told a committee of the Congress that he wouldn't be around to be badgered any more next week, and took his Jessie Ann off to Florida for a vacation.

This is a reminder of a very important point in life—namely, that a man's first and last line of defense, even if he is the Secretary of Defense, is his wife. And it is a reminder of some other things.

Among these is the fact that these famous officials, who are supposed to do no wrong in a world where it is almost impossible to be right, are men who have wives with feelings, even as you and I. The pity is that they don't speak up more often, for while the pleasures of official life are many, the ordeals are at least as great.

Save for the butterflies, who love the parties and the ridiculous social pretenses of this expense-account town, the Government officials' wives are not as a rule at ease in the big official limousines, the endless receiving lines, and the big crystal-chandelier dining rooms.

They come to these things, most of them, late in life from simpler backgrounds. They worry about their children growing up in what seems to many of them an unreal and bogus atmosphere. They are properly impressed by the majesty and tradition of this beautiful community, but they see their husbands working too hard and gradually being more impressed than they should by the endless flattery that goes with power.

Men such as Dulles and Nixon and Stassen get inured to criticism, for they dish it out, they love the struggle, and they get the satisfactions of pride and position. But what of their wives?

This is one of the endless perils of official life in Washington. The men learn to say a lot of things without disclosing anything. Indeed, saying nothing at great length eventually becomes a rather pleasant official game. But their women are accustomed before they come here to saying what they think and it is only later that they discover that outgoing spontaneity is a menace to themselves and their husbands.

"I've been very, very careful," said Mrs. Wilson. "But you reach a point sometimes—and this was it."

Nixon's Political Coup

VICE PRESIDENT RICHARD M. NIXON HAS DEVISED, OR STUMBLED into, the perfect way to launch a campaign for the American Presidency.

Instead of throwing his hat into the ring, he is throwing Nikita S. Khrushchev. He is running on an anti-Communist ticket, courtesy of the Soviet Government. Instead of sharpening his political techniques at $100-a-plate Republican dinners at home, he is training in Siberia and the Urals.

This is largely due to the capriciousness of American politics. Traditionally, a Vice President's political ambitions are frustrated by the purely ceremonial responsibilities of his office. In this case, however, a ceremonial assignment has suddenly cast Mr. Nixon into the politically favorable role of defending the principles of the West inside the Soviet Union at a moment of international tension and national political decision.

His manner of campaigning here is very similar, indeed it is almost identical, to his procedures at home. He started in Novosibirsk this morning climbing over a new hydroelectric dam project, shaking hands with workers, chucking youngsters under the chin, and arguing agreeably with anyone in the crowd who wished to challenge his pitch. He ended up here tonight in Sverdlovsk shouting agreeable nothings to a crowd of two to three thousand around the steps of the City Hall. Here he also toured the largest heavy engineering factory in the Soviet Union.

All this was standard campaign practice. What was new was the location, and this makes all the difference.

Mr. Nixon did not necessarily plan it this way. He came here to open the American National Exhibition in Moscow and he has stuck to his international assignment. But in the process, either innocently or otherwise, he had engineered a domestic political coup.

What he did was to provide something new. He made available to the American press the first nonstop American jet flight in history from the United States to Moscow. The trip assured him an audience of more than fifty United States reporters. They tagged along here not primarily to see him but to see the Soviet Union, and they brought with them all the engines of American mass publicity.

He then proceeded accidentally to get in a public row with the Soviet Premier, before a color television camera. He opened the fair with a slam-bang speech proclaiming the benefits of Western democracy over Communism. He followed this with a weekend of hobnobbing with Mr. Khrushchev at the United States Embassy and the Premier's dacha along the banks of the Moskva River.

As if this was not enough, he was able to please the women voters at home by having Mrs. Nixon and Mme. Khrushchev present during the six-hour conference with the Soviet Premier, thus producing perhaps the first mixed-foursome meeting in diplomatic history.

Whereupon he flew off with three planeloads of assorted commissars, reporters, photographers, and advisers to Leningrad and the grim but exciting "closed" industrial cities of Siberia and the Urals.

In the long history of international diplomacy, to say nothing of United States Presidential politics, there has never been anything like it. Mr. Nixon flies thousands of miles in a few hours in Soviet jet planes and comes down in cities that have seldom seen an American, let alone an American Vice President.

His arrival at each city here is a politician's dream. Beautiful children dressed in colorful costumes greet him with bouquets. Stolid commissars in funereal clothes welcome him like a potentate. They ply him with vodka and caviar and take him to the ballet in vast opera houses with ready-made audiences measured in the thousands.

If he were launching his campaign at home he would have to

agonize over an announcement speech, paying attention to every comma, every active verb, and every powerful regional bloc in the nation. But here he does not even have to prepare a speech. All he has to do is say "peace and friendship" in bad Russian and everyone applauds as if he had suddenly ended the "cold war." Not only are the reporters and photographers present to take it all down, but they can actually get it back to the voters at home free of censorship.

In all, Mr. Nixon has produced the first innovation in American politics since the women's vote. Is Mr. Nixon pleased? He has not been so happy since the resignation of Harold Stassen!

He went out to the Uralmash factory tonight like St. George looking for a dragon. This is a fabulous, roaring engine of a factory, which almost seems to have been designed for manufacturing iron curtains. Far from avoiding words with quarrelsome Communist workers, who had obviously been told to ply him with embarrassing questions, he welcomed them. Meanwhile, just to top it all off, the rest of the world remained quiet so that his adventures in the Urals and in Moscow and in Siberia could dominate the front pages.

He did, however, encounter one problem. His only competitor for the Republican Presidential nomination, Governor Rockefeller of New York, was about to get into the limelight at next week's Governors' Conference in Puerto Rico. But Mr. Nixon dealt with that, too. He simply agreed to go to Poland next week. That visit will undoubtedly produce more news and more headlines than anything Mr. Rockefeller can do in Puerto Rico.

COON RAPIDS, IOWA

SEPTEMBER 24, 1959

Khrushchev's Odyssey

WHEN PREMIER KHRUSHCHEV ARRIVED AT THE GARST FARM HERE
today, everything was wired for sound but the hogs. The Associated Press had taken over one barn, United Press International
another.

The upper pasture sported a new high steel television tower,
and there were more photographers in the trees than birds. Tall
TV booms for high-angle cameras stuck up above a forest of
new telephone poles, and while all this produced more corn—
journalistic corn, that is—than normally grows in the whole state
of Iowa, it also illustrated a problem.

This is that Mr. Khrushchev cannot see America for all the
cops and photographers. There are so many newsmen reporting
his trip that they change the course of events. They are not the
obscure witnesses of history, but the principal characters in the
drama, whose very ubiquity is such that most of the time Mr.
Khrushchev is addressing them, or addressing others with them
in mind.

The newsmen are not covering this visit; they are smothering
it, and each other at the same time. Rarely in the history of
journalism have so many resourceful scribblers kept each other
from following closely such a major event. Rarely have they
written so much about a person they could not hear and often
could not see. There were so many newsmen here today that they
changed everything at the Garst farm but the smell.

All this, mind you, gives Mr. Khrushchev no pain. He is less
interested in seeing America than in having the world see him in
America, and for this purpose the reporters, photographers,
technicians, and all their gear are not only useful but indispensable. Millions of feet of film have been taken on this astonishing

odyssey. If it were all put together it would produce a remarkably accurate but devastating record of the "new diplomacy."

It will be interesting to see what comes out in Asia and Africa when the Soviet propagandists get through cutting the film record to size and shape. You can bet your last ruble that it will show Mr. Khrushchev getting an enthusiastic welcome. Whoever said pictures do not lie is the biggest liar of all, for this film can be made to show anything. The silent crowds can be eliminated and the applauding crowds can be retained; Mr. Khrushchev's good jokes can be kept and his bad jokes cut; the simple people of this little Willa Cather town can be forgotten, and the Hollywood girls in their black lace tights can be immortalized along with the can-can.

In a worldwide propaganda battle, this is not frivolous nonsense. It is deadly serious, for while it was inevitable that Moscow would be given much raw material for propaganda in the neutral countries, it was not inevitable that clumsy administration should make things worse.

Washington did not minimize but actually doubled the damage. For this is, to put it mildly, the worst-run political trip since Estes Kefauver ran for the Vice Presidency. Mr. Khrushchev was President Eisenhower's guest, but the President's press secretary, James C. Hagerty, who knows how to avoid public-relations disasters, bowed out after the party left Washington.

This left the show to the State Department, but Andrew J. Berding, who is in charge of public affairs, avoided it, too. Thus the job fell by default partly to Henry Cabot Lodge, Mr. Khrushchev's official host, and partly to minor officials of the State Department's Press Division.

The result has been turmoil with nobody anticipating obvious problems, with planes not arriving on time, with Western European correspondents denied any chance to get close to the Soviet visitor, with local officials playing politics on the side, and the Soviet delegation laughing contemptuously at America's reputation for efficiency. . . .

What Kind of a President
Do You Want?

PRESIDENT EISENHOWER'S REMARKS YESTERDAY ABOUT THE LUNCH-counter controversy in the South tell a lot about the concept of the Presidency. More important, they provide a specific incident by which the nation can help decide the major political question of the day—namely, what qualities are needed in President Eisenhower's successor.

The President put a sharp limitation on what he regarded as his right to intervene to help the Negroes achieve equal status at the lunch counters in the South. He dealt with the legalities of the problem but not the moralities. He supported the Negro's right of peaceful demonstration for equal rights. He deplored any use of violence on either side. He implied that the Negro had a constitutional right to eat alongside whites in public places oper-ating under "public charter," but not in privately owned estab-lishments. In sum, he gave his "understanding" of what was legal but not what he thought was right, and this raises some interest-ing questions for the future:

Is the President's obligation fulfilled when he meets the legal duty to "take care that the laws" are "faithfully executed," or is there also a moral obligation to speak out for the equality of all the people?

Which of the two historic conceptions of the Presidency do we need: a Presidency "active and reformist" or a Presidency pro-tective of the established order?

What are the requirements of the Sixties: for an assertive "reformist" President like Jackson, Wilson, and the two Roose-velts, or for the weaker Presidents of 1809–29 and 1865–85, or for something in between?

President Eisenhower has usually acted to protect the established order, as an honest conservative usually does, but he has not always refrained from taking the lead against powerful opposition. He led the debate against inflation, and swung the sickle in that "dread field" of foreign aid. But he has shied away from the moralities of the civil-rights debate.

He landed the troops in Little Rock to meet what he regarded as the legal obligation, to enforce the Supreme Court's public-school-integration decision, but he has not said yet that he thinks the court's decision was right. Why? He said yesterday that he did not want to make any judgment about the lunch-counter demonstrations "because I'm not in a position to." Why isn't he? "I know about these [lunch-counter demonstrations] as they come briefly to my attention," he added. Why briefly?

The reasons for these attitudes are not hard to find. President Eisenhower believes with great sincerity that the "active, reformist" concept of the Presidency has gone too far. As he told the reporters yesterday morning: "I am one of those who believe there is too much interference [by the Federal Government] in our private affairs. . . . I would like to diminish rather than increase it."

For this reason, he would leave the question of eating in private establishments in the South to the local authorities; he would leave the allocation of the nation's resources primarily to private choice, rather than increase the flow of funds into education, hospitals, and defense. He would leave the development of Latin America primarily to private venture capital (which takes one look at Castro and flees) and avoid any direction of television, no matter what commercial television does to debase the national taste.

He believes in the noble theory which Jefferson proclaimed (and didn't always follow)—but will it work in the Sixties? Will the local communities really make peace at the lunch counters, or vote the funds to provide the education necessary in this kind of world? Will private capital voluntarily develop the underdeveloped countries in freedom, or give us educational television?

There are a lot of people here who honestly think the answer to these questions is "no." They understand the conservative limitation of Presidential power in a period of consolidation. But they think the President, one hundred years after Appomattox, ought to be willing to say at least a word for the Negro trying to eat a hamburger next to a white man in Atlanta, and they insist that the next President, whoever he is, will need to use all his powers to meet the problems of the Sixties.

MARCH 25, 1960

THE "OTHER AMERICA" WAS BACK IN THE NEWS TODAY: NOT "THE affluent society" we hear so much about, but the indigent society that once dominated the front pages.

In a country with the unbelievable annual personal income of $393 billion (as of February), there are still 32,200,000 people living on less than $50 a week for a family of four. Included in these 32,200,000 are one fifth of the nation's children, and 8,000,000 over 65.

This raises again the insistent questions of the Presidential campaign: What are the role and scope of the Federal Government in maintaining the public welfare? How should the resources of the nation be used? Should the President grapple with the problem, or pass by on the other side?

President Eisenhower chose this week to pass by on the other side. The Congress was dealing with the problem of health insurance for the aged. The President opposed the legislation under discussion. His Secretary of Health, Education, and Welfare proposed that the Administration immediately offer its own substitute bill to deal with the problem, but the President opposed that too.

About the facts there is no dispute. As the President himself has often emphasized, the inflation of the last generation has been particularly hard on the old people. The 8,000,000 over 65 in the low-income bracket cannot afford decent housing, proper nutrition, or adequate medical care.

Taking all aged individuals—16,000,000 of them now and 20,000,000 fifteen years from now—almost 60 per cent have less than $1,000 a year in money income. In 1959 two out of five of them had less than $200 for emergencies.

The main question here is not the specific bills introduced by Representative Forand of Rhode Island or Senator Kennedy of Massachusetts. Both involve the compulsory principle—supported by all the Democratic candidates—of increasing the Social Security tax of people still paying that tax for the benefit of all old people who are now its noncontributing beneficiaries.

There are good arguments against this. One, for example, is that the proposed bills would subsidize the rich when they are old as well as the poor. Beyond this is the root question of paternalism and where the welfare state is to stop.

Life in youth-tide can care for itself. The welfare state does not have to relieve the young men in the Air Force from doing kitchen duty, as it just has. But people in affliction and adversity, standing on the summit of lean and slippered old age, are something else. Many of them have nothing to count but their years. Many more are in that witless stage of life and cannot even enjoy their memories. If they are not a charge on the richest state ever devised by man, then they are a least a charge on the national conscience. Vermont Royster wrote a lovely editorial about them this morning in the *Wall Street Journal*, which is not an organ of rebellion. He is against the Forand and Kennedy bills. He hates the welfare state but he has a sense of pity.

So does the President. As a human being he has retained as much humanity and compassion as anyone in the capital. Also, he has this problem of caring for the aged in his own wife's family. But this merely brings us back to the main point: What kind of President do you want? It is not the President's humanity that is at issue but his concept of the Presidency. It is not Eisenhower who is the issue but the man to succeed him, and the concept of government to follow after him.

This whole question of how we allocate and spend the nation's resources has unfortunately drifted into black-and-white issues of whether we want tail fins with freedom or security with Government control. But before we get to the question of directing the nation's resources, there is the question of directing the President's resources.

Obviously, the voluntary way is better, but if justice to the old people is not freely given, even then, before direction, comes the obligation of persuasion. The answer to the old people may be that the Government can't afford it, and shouldn't try to do more, but the point has to be explained. For if the old folk can't eat, at least they can vote. And so can the people who have to care for them.

APRIL 17, 1962

Conflicts of Interest

THE SENATE OF THE UNITED STATES IS WORRYING ALONG EASY-LIKE these days about conflicts of interest in Washington. Not the Senators' conflicts of interest, mind you, but other people's. (A conflict of interest is the sort of thing that could arise if an Internal Revenue agent audited his own income-tax return.)

Anyway, it's a problem. When the Government spends over $90 billion a year, there is always the chance that some miserable sinner might try to nip off a little on the side, and the laws to discourage such nipping are antiquated, silly, or worse.

As the Association of the Bar of the City of New York pointed out in a careful study of the problem starting seven years ago, the main conflict-of-interest statutes are directed at a world that has ceased to exist. They were directed broadly at that pork-barrel class of petty political appointees who looked on a Government job as a means of legalized graft. They were dealing with an age when there was a clear separation between private business and Government business, and in a narrower sense, they aimed at eliminating hanky-panky in the fields of Government claims and Government contracts.

Accordingly, these laws on the books do not deal with an America whose Government is deeply involved in the industrial and commercial life of the nation; whose Government employees come largely from a vast civil service, a temporary, revolving group of political appointees, and an increasingly diverse army of men and women who work part-time for the Government, part-time for industry, part-time for universities—and very often for all three at the same time.

Nor do the present laws take into account the widespread development of stock-buying, and institutional security through company insurance, retirement, and other welfare plans. As a matter of fact, the laws not only permit some officials to hold stock at considerable gain, but deny the same right to other Cabinet officers.

The system, in short, is unequal and even dangerous. It penalizes some officials and not others. It denies to the Government many essential and competent citizens who don't like the idea of losing pensions and retirement funds in order to work eighteen hours a day at less pay under the skeptical eye of a hostile Congress and a cheeky press.

Finally, the system does something else that is little realized. By forcing some men to sell all their stocks and jeopardize their positions in their former companies, it is almost an incitement to these men to use their Government positions to favor other companies that might give them cushy jobs as a reward when they get out. . . .

The biggest uncovered conflict of interest in the capital today lies with the Federal legislators, who can hold all the stocks they like and benefit through their law firms even when those firms continue to represent companies that benefit from Federal legislation.

Who will investigate the investigators? It is true that their problem is different in many ways, but they are not interested in tightening up their own conflict-of-interest regulations, and they are not even very enthusiastic about modernizing the laws that deal with officials of the Executive.

The Senators cannot say they were not warned. Even before the Sermon on the Mount was warning about not serving two masters and not leading us into temptation, Plato, a republican from Athens, was forbidding his philosopher kings to have any personal economic interests whatever. . . .

NOVEMBER 9, 1962

Richard Nixon's Farewell

THERE WAS AN ELEMENT OF TRAGEDY IN RICHARD NIXON'S SOUR reaction to his defeat for the Governorship of California. Two years ago he was within 100,000 votes of the American Presidency and today, unelected and unmourned, he is an unemployed lawyer in Los Angeles. No wonder he slammed the door as he went out.

The British do it better. They find a "safe seat" in Parliament for the defeated leader of a party, and, being sensitive to human frailty, pass him along in later years to the dignity of the House of Lords. Our politics are more savage. The gap between victory and defeat is almost too wide. The winner gets more than he can handle and the loser more than he can bear. We put them in the White House before they are ready and retire them before they are ripe.

It was this system that produced Nixon in the beginning and destroyed him in the end. He came to power too early and retired too soon. He mastered the techniques of politics before he mastered the principles, and ironically it was this preoccupation with techniques that both brought him forward and cast him down.

Dick Nixon got into national politics by using his bad qualities rather than his good qualities—of which he has many—against

Jerry Voorhees and Helen Gahagan Douglas, and he reached almost to the pinnacle of our national life at least partly by accident. For he came along at a time when the Republicans happened to be looking for a Vice Presidential candidate who could symbolize "youth," the growth of the West, and anti-Communism. This was what the system required in 1952 as a running mate for Eisenhower—this and Nixon's political skill to back up Ike's lack of political experience. So he was nominated and elected, and then another ironical thing happened.

Like most Americans who reach the top councils of their Government, he grew up with the job and used his good qualities in the performance of it, but the job itself dragged him back into the political arena. To Eisenhower, who didn't like political rallies until he retired, Nixon was the Vice President in charge of the party. He was the point of the Republican spear, always tilting with the opposition in the exaggerated rhetoric of the political wars, and inevitably this pugnacious and aggressive role perpetuated his reputation as the symbol of everything that is harsh and devious in American political life.

Maybe this had something to do with his defeat in 1962. Maybe it was merely his appearance. Yet there was something else: the American people will put an aggressive district-attorney type into almost any office. But the Presidency, they seem to feel, requires that power be tempered by wisdom and even by mercy, and these were certainly not his most obvious qualities. See, also, Tom Dewey.

What was most obvious about Nixon, particularly to the press, those recorders of the obvious, was his preoccupation with the machinery of politics. Everything seemed to be contrived, even the appearance of naturalness. He attacked planning but planned everything. He seemed bold and elaborately objective in public, but in private seemed less composed, even uneasy and disturbingly introspective.

This was the root of his trouble with the reporters; not that they were refusing to report what he said but that they were insisting on reporting all the rest of the picture—not only the words but the techniques, not only the public posture but the private posture, not only the lines of the play but the elaborate stage directions.

Always here in Washington there was this terrible feeling among reporters that seemed to come out only in flashes in private or under pressure in public—that there was a vast difference between appearance and reality and that it was important, maybe even important to the nation, to try to define which was which.

Even in his farewell address, he insisted on taking responsibility for "any mistakes" in the campaign, and then blamed his "magnificent" staff for blowing the election. Similarly, he said he "respected" the reporters while accusing them of betraying their responsibility.

No public figure of our time has ever studied the reporters so much or understood them so little. He thought the reporter should merely be a transmission belt for what he said, not of why he said it. Like the cigarette man, he insisted that "It's what's up front that counts," while the reporter, constantly haunted by the feeling that he might deceive the reader merely by reporting the carefully rehearsed lines in the play, insisted on recording what was going on backstage.

Nixon always resented this. He never seemed to understand the difference between news and truth. To him what he said was "news" and should be left there. Maybe he was right. It could be that the "real Nixon" was the one onstage, but that is beyond journalism now and will have to be left to the historians and the psychological novelists.

The Art of Quitting and Firing

THE ART OF QUITTING AND FIRING HAS ALMOST VANISHED IN WASH-
ington. Officials are never "fired" these days, they are merely
"called to fields of higher dedication." They never quit on principle: they slip away silently, blaming "family considerations."

Baseball is the last of the professions where losers are booted
out publicly. When the Washington Senators lost ten out of
eleven games recently, which is only slightly worse than their
average, Mickey Vernon, the manager, was canned on twelve
hours' notice. But even he issued a communiqué of unsurpassed
sweetness. "I just feel disappointed," he said. "But I think I've
been treated very well."

How John McGraw would have hooted at that! He would
have kicked in the clubhouse door. He would have declared that
even an act of Congress couldn't get the Senators out of the
American League cellar. And, so saying, he would have shoved
over the Washington Monument and left town in a blaze of
profanity.

This, however, is the age of evasion. We haven't had a good
slam-bang exit since General MacArthur. Even Sherman Adams,
who was supposed to be the curmudgeon's curmudgeon, took his
rug and flew softly away, and Allen Dulles, as a reward for
Cuba, was all but canonized at the end.

Under President Kennedy the system is remarkably smooth.
He is a master of the delayed shift. Chester Bowles is the best
illustration of the technique. If the man doesn't measure up as
Under Secretary of State, or somebody at the White House
thinks he doesn't measure up, he is not called in and asked to go
away, but is shifted to the White House and given a fancy title as
adviser to the President on Africa, Asia, Latin America, and
underdeveloped points east. There, then, he sits in lonely splen-

dor, like a deviationist in Siberia, until he is sufficiently softened up to want out, at which time he is smuggled off to India without a fuss.

Sometimes the direct-transfer or consolation-prize technique is used. For example, if Admiral George W. Anderson is being stubborn, awkward, or too talkative, or all three, as Chief of Naval Operations, he is given the option of retirement or opulent banishment to a new post which, the President explains, "requires a good deal of skill and a good deal of dedication." All men who get this treatment are "dedicated."

From the Administration's point of view the system has certain advantages. Mainly it muffles the struggling on the back stairs and keeps a lot of awkward questions from being debated in public. What is harder to explain is why the victims go so quietly. Here the expert is former Secretary of State Dean G. Acheson, who after long personal study and experience has a taste for stylish resignations and deft decapitations.

Mr. Acheson believes that officials stay on partly because of the boredom of private life, partly because "making a fuss" has gone out of style, partly because "saving face" has become increasingly important in the Western world, and partly because officials, like other people, like to eat.

One result of all this is that a good deal of informed and dissenting opinion within this Administration is not getting out. Equally important, the dissenters are hesitating more and more to push their views up to the top in private.

Every President has this problem sooner or later. As time goes on and problems and frustrations build up, officials hesitate to add their own doubts to the President's worries. Meanwhile, Presidents hesitate to provoke dissent, important as it is. This problem increases in direct proportion to the respect and affection inspired by a President in the members of his staff. The more they admire him and sympathize with his burdens, the more they hesitate to question or challenge him. And this is a real problem for President Kennedy, for he has both the respect and admiration of his staff.

Accordingly, the decline of the volcanic resignation is a loss. This is not to say that tame and deserving bureaucrats, like condemned convicts, do not deserve a good dinner before they go, but an apoplectic dissenter on his way out had a certain therapeutic and educational value.

Anyway, the polite habits of the Government establishment do not have to be transferred to baseball. The opposite might even be preferable. For the old rule of professional baseball was that losers were either benched, traded, or sent back to the minors whence they came. McGraw didn't transfer hitless infielders to the outfield, or tanglefoot outfielders to the infield. He didn't ask whether they were nice guys, either. He just sent them back to Topeka.

NOVEMBER 17, 1963

The Moral Indifference
of Congress

THE CONGRESS OF THE UNITED STATES HAS SELDOM APPEARED more futile, divided, confused, and morally indifferent than it does these days. It is not its legislative record alone that is so spotty—after eleven months there is still no indication that it will deal effectively with the problems of unemployment, education, or civil rights—but its attitude toward public criticism is even worse.

When Representative Wayne Hays, Democrat of Ohio, was criticized for taking Ernest Petinaud, the headwaiter in the House restaurant, on an official junket to Paris at Government expense, he dismissed the whole thing with unoriginal contempt as "a tempest in a teapot."

When the House and Senate got into a row over the right of

House members to send out free mail, Representative Tom Steed, Democrat of Oklahoma, threatened to disclose the name of a Senator who, he said, had two call girls on his payroll unless the Senate yielded to the House on the junk-mail issue. "I was only trying to defend the rule of comity," Representative Steed said today. "If the Senate is going to defy that rule and interfere with the House's standards, I have every right to discuss their standards."

These are not minor or eccentric members of the Congress but prominent and influential men. Even Representative John W. Byrnes, Republican of Wisconsin, the ranking GOP member of the Ways and Means Committee, didn't see anything wrong in doing a favor for a Wisconsin insurance corporation and then buying $2,300 worth of stock in the company, now worth about $25,000. Representative Byrnes is being promoted in Wisconsin as a favorite-son candidate for the Presidency of the United States.

These attitudes are in some ways more important than the recent disclosures of influence peddling in the Baker and Korth cases, for it is this easy "anything goes" approach that makes the influence peddling possible.

The point is not that the conduct of Senators and Congressmen is worse than it used to be. In many ways it is better than in the old days when men were sent to Washington by and for powerful vested interests. But Congressmen now seem much more casual about what anyone thinks about their conduct.

The more the Government has got into the economy of the nation with its vast defense and space contracts, its large financial grants for research and development, and its huge contracts with foreign governments, the more Congressmen have found themselves in a morally ambiguous position.

Many of them retain connections with law firms that benefit from the private and public beneficiaries of Government funds. Many of them are constantly voting on questions that affect their private interests. And almost all of them are under financial pressure from the high cost of campaigning, the high cost of living, and the high rate of taxation.

Unfortunately, the prospect for the future is even darker than the condition of today. Senator Joseph Clark, Democrat of Pennsylvania, is one of the most unpopular members of the Senate today simply because he has sought to break up the conservative Establishment of that body.

The outlook for Congressional reorganization is not good. President Kennedy's legislative program is paralyzed by the Tory coalition and by Southern chairmen of his own party who hold ten of the fourteen major chairmanships in the Senate. . . .

The main thing is that the Congress feels that nothing can be done either about conflicts of interest or Congressional reform. Representative government itself is increasingly the object of ridicule in the capital, but the men who have the power to improve it are either indifferent or helpless.

JANUARY 17, 1964

The Press and the Congress and the Nation

THE PRESS HAS GIVEN THE IMPRESSION IN THE LAST YEAR THAT THE Congress of the United States is in a bad way, which is true, and that very little can be done about it, which is not true.

The newspapers themselves can do something about the Congress—not much but something—if they will look at the primary elections and tell the truth about the many duds and incompetents who represent their states and districts on Capitol Hill. In many cases, if they tell the truth, they will support the incumbents for re-election, for the majority of men and women in the House and Senate are able and industrious public servants, but as the editors know, there is a minority of numbskulls in the

Congress whom no self-respecting editor would trust to cover the local City Hall.

The time to do something about these characters is now upon us. The filing deadline for the primary elections is coming up, and Ohio and Oklahoma are indicating what can be done about getting new figures into the race by talking up the names of John Glenn, the astronaut, and Bud Wilkinson, the talented football coach and administrator at the University of Oklahoma.

Replenishing the tired blood of the Congress, however, takes forethought and leadership. Most newspapers pay little attention to the primary elections. They wait until the general election in November, which often means that they are merely left with a choice between two mediocre candidates, and then, more often than not, they go sled-length for the second-rater of their own political persuasion.

It would be difficult to overestimate the damage done to the quality of Congress by the amiable good-fellowship of newspaper editors and owners. Usually they know their Senators and Congressmen very well, and often go on backing them long after age or sickness has impaired their usefulness. Lacking any lead from the papers, the voters do the same. They get accustomed to their representatives. The world changes, but they vote them back into office anyway and pass up innumerable good potential replacements in the process.

The sad case of Senator Clair Engle of California illustrates one aspect of the problem. He has suffered a severe stroke and has not recovered his normal capacity of speech. He was a good Senator and a friendly, popular man, but he is clearly not able to do his job now.

Similarly, the voters of Arizona, having an affection for Carl Hayden, who was elected to the Congress when Arizona first became a state, re-elected him again in 1962 when he was 84, and now, at 86, he is second in line for the Presidency after Speaker John McCormack, who is first in line at 72.

The Congress of the United States, like the editors, often puts personal considerations ahead of public duty. This is what it has done for years in failing to provide adequately for the death or incapacity of the President, and this is what it is doing now in the case of Speaker McCormack. Few members think he is competent to be President, but few are prepared to do anything about it, lest they hurt his feelings.

Most cases, fortunately, are less difficult. The editors in every community usually know men in their states and districts who would make better Senators or Representatives than the men who will soon be seeking re-election, but they seldom make any effort to urge them to get into the primaries.

It is not, admittedly, an easy job. New candidates need money even to make a trial run in the primaries. They have to expect a hard and sometimes ugly fight. They are trying to unseat an officeholder who is usually better known and enjoys the extra advantage of an organization and free mailing privileges. So, many competent men hold back unless they are pushed forward by the papers. . . .

What the Congress needs is not reorganization—though that would help—so much as it needs to be reinvigorated by men who have the brains and energy to keep up with the present torrent of work and change on Capitol Hill. This will not be achieved by editorials on "The Constitutional Crisis in Washington," real as it is. The editors will not help change the Congress until they change themselves.

MAY 10, 1964

Touring Dixie with LBJ

TOURING THE SOUTH WITH PRESIDENT JOHNSON IS A LITTLE LIKE going back to the old evangelical Chautauqua Circuit. He is Andy Jackson in a jetliner vaulting the Appalachian Range in a half an hour, and loving and exhorting the South at every stop. The exhausted Washington press corps chases after him in amazement, noting down all the flattery and exaggeration, but this combination of his Southern origins, his present power, and his political skill may very well prove the most significant part of his Administration.

He turned out more than half a million people in the streets of Atlanta this week. In Rocky Mount, N.C., and Gainesville, Ga., his audiences were larger than the total population of the two towns, and his message was perfectly clear. His speech, his manner and address, his stories, his reminiscences of the past, his emphasis on family and friendship, his fantastic personal recollections of local and state politicians, were all so genuinely Southern that nobody could possibly challenge him.

But his point was unmistakable. "Justice," he said, referring to the motto of the State of Georgia—Wisdom, Justice and Moderation—"means justice among the races. . . . I will never feel that I have done justice to my high office until every section of this country is linked in a single purpose, a joint devotion to bring an end to injustice, to bring an end to poverty and to bring an end to the threat of conflict among nations."

The South would probably hesitate to take this from anybody else, but even the most segregationist Southerner cannot wholly disown President Johnson.

When his daughter Lynda was born twenty years ago, the first man he called up to announce the news was Representative Carl Vinson of Georgia, who was on the platform with the President here this week. When Lynda was introduced to the Georgia legislators at Friday's breakfast, she said simply that she felt at home in Georgia and referred to Georgia's Senator Russell, who is leading the fight against her father's civil-rights bill and was conspicuously absent at the breakfast, as "my beloved friend, who helped raise me."

Even the members of the Georgia Legislature, who hate Johnson's civil-rights bill and who applaud Senator Russell's decision not to attend the Johnson breakfast, knew that this just happened to be true.

They may disagree with the President, but he is one of them. When he talks about civil rights he quotes not Northerners but Southerners like Atticus Haygood, the president of Emory College, who said in 1880: "We in the South have no Divine call to stand eternal guard by the grave of dead issues."

When the President talks about poverty, he says: "Over my bed in the White House in Washington I keep a little picture of the tiny, three-room home where I was born, the son of a tenant farmer who worked on the 'halves,' and his cotton crop was about eight bales a year. It reminds me every day where I came from. But, more important, it reminds me of the people I serve."

He knows the history of the South and he tells them exactly what role Georgians played in the writing of the Constitution and how many went to the last three wars and how many died. He knows they still respect Franklin D. Roosevelt, and he has Franklin D. Roosevelt, Jr., on the platform with him. He knows most of them oppose his program of equal rights, yet he says, using the Biblical idiom of the South:

"In God's praise and under God's guidance, let all of us resolve this morning to help heal the last fading scars of old battles. . . . Heed not those who would come waving the tattered and discredited banners of the past, who seek to stir old hostilities and kindle old hatreds, who preach battle between neighbors and bitterness between states. That is the way back toward the anguish from which we all came."

The South has never lacked for spokesmen who have urged it to look to the future. It has produced probably more good newspaper editors in the last generation than any other section of the country. It has listened attentively but skeptically over the generations to Walter Prescott Webb telling it what oil, modern insecticides, the new fertilizers, water power, milo maize, and air-conditioning were going to do for the South in the last half of the twentieth century. It has heard the faith and the wondrously disarming stories of Henry Grady about the glorious future of the South, but all this was less important.

Now it is the President of the United States who speaks not only for but to the South, and the difference is important. It is a long time since the South has had a voice in the White House that it really listened to, and this may prove a most important fact of our time.

Goldwater's Attraction

SENATOR BARRY GOLDWATER HAS NOT ONLY WON A SPECTACULAR victory. He has also shifted the whole American political battleground to the conservative right.

President Johnson, it can be said on good authority, will not follow him in emphasizing the widening ideological differences between the parties. He does not want to inflame or envenom the almost theological issues between Republicans and Democrats that have been dramatized here. He will undoubtedly move now to the right to capture the nonattached, nonideological voters in the decisive center.

Mr. Goldwater's militant foreign policy, although highly troublesome to our relations overseas, does not worry the White House as a domestic political issue. His total-victory, religious war against the Communists is regarded by influential Democrats as both bad policy and bad politics. But Mr. Goldwater's overtures to the South, his moral appeal to middle-class ethics, his nostalgic and obviously sincere longing for simple answers to complicated problems, his fervent protests against the devilish obscurities of an urbanized, computerized secular society are a formidable argument that do worry the people around the President.

The political implications of Mr. Goldwater's nomination are just beginning to be discussed here and in Washington. Despite all the Republican appeals to unity, it has clearly split the party and it has had its effects on the Democrats as well.

With the campaign moving a little right and south of center, Attorney General Robert F. Kennedy, who is unpopular in the South, will now probably be dropped as a Democratic Vice Presidential prospect; and Secretary of Defense Robert S. McNamara, who is popular with many Republicans, and Senator Hubert H. Humphrey of Minnesota, who has some of the militancy of the Goldwaterites, are now reported to be the main contenders as Mr. Johnson's running mate.

A wholly new alignment of political forces in America is now forming, however, so new in fact that all the assumptions of the past about the parties are unreliable.

The story of San Francisco is much more complicated and interesting than the battle between the single-minded, industrious Goldwater pros and the tardy sophisticated, disorganized liberals. It is also more complex than the fight on television over "extremists," civil rights, and who controls "the Bomb."

There are deep historical and psychological tides running here. It would probably be a profound mistake to regard all this as a Goldwater triumph of personality, or as a cunning takeover by well-financed and well-organized conspiratorial forces winning over the disorganized noblesse-oblige liberals. Mr. Goldwater may attract all the ultras, and the antis—the forces that are anti-Negro, antilabor, antiforeigner, anti-intellectual—but he also attracts something else that is precisely the opposite of these vicious and negative forces.

Mr. Goldwater touches the deep feeling of regret in American life: regret over the loss of religious faith; regret over the loss of simplicity and fidelity; regret over the loss of the frontier spirit of pugnacious individuality; regret, in short, over the loss of America's innocent and idealistic youth.

It is easy to scoff at all this, and to demonstrate that the effects of Mr. Goldwater's policies on the Negro revolution and the Communist problem are reckless, but in this complicated and baffling era it is not surprising that many people put the family before the community, the community before the state, the state before the nation, and the nation before the world.

All this has been fairly obvious in San Francisco, not perhaps on the clamorous floor of the Cow Palace, or on the television screen, but in the private conversations on the fringe, and even in the savage outcry against the newspaper columnists and the television commentators on the floor.

There is a bitter paradox in the Republican party between its respectability and its frustrations. It knows instinctively that the most vicious elements in our national life, from the Birchers and Ku Kluxers to the protectionists and the isolationists, are supporting Mr. Goldwater, but it is so frustrated and so genuinely opposed to the trend of modern life that it seems to be willing to use any means to oppose what it believes to be the wicked ends of a planned, international, interdependent, coexistence policy.

All this has come out here, even occasionally on the convention floor. The delegates are so involved in the game of politics that they do not listen, but the speeches are full of laments for our innocent past, of longings for the character of a more austere age, of disillusion with the consequences of success and prosperity.

Somehow, along the way, all these frustrations have been transferred into political terms, and the true Republican believer —not the extremists in the party but many of the most moderate and respectable Republicans—have come to identify the Democrats with everything from the decline of individual responsibility to unemployment, racial tension, international confusion, and juvenile delinquency.

The liberals, in this present Republican mood, have become responsible for the destruction of authority and tradition. The threats and seductions of the radical innovators have produced, as they see it, moral confusion. The license of liberal doctrine has created a conflict in their minds between faith and reason, and produced a kind of intellectual and moral bankruptcy for which the Democrats, as they see it, are responsible.

This is what explains at least part of the revivalist atmosphere of the convention here on July 14 and 15. The Goldwater-controlled convention would concede nothing, not even to those who were trying to compromise with them. The Democrats, the liberal Republicans, the sophisticated and "decadent" East, the wicked, debased internationalist Eastern press—all were the enemies, not only of victory for the "right" here in San Francisco, and in Cuba, and in Vietnam, but also the enemies of the true objectives of the American dream.

No doubt there was an element of expediency and revenge in

this atmosphere in the Cow Palace. Many delegates merely felt that Barry would help them in their own district to win in November. Many more were getting even for the liberal victories in the conventions from 1940 to 1960. Quite a few were still resentful about the Eisenhower triumph over Robert A. Taft in the convention of 1952, and wanted to score over Henry Cabot Lodge and Christian A. Herter, who led the Eisenhower campaign in that convention.

But back of all this is the deep feeling that is seldom reported: That the nation, in many Republican minds, has drifted into attitudes and policies that debase and weaken the American character, and threaten the security of the nation. This thesis—right or wrong—is the "sleeper" in this election, and Mr. Goldwater is its symbol. It is surprising, therefore, that the Goldwater did not support on the convention floor the efforts to condemn the Birch Society and the other extremists, for Mr. Goldwater does not agree with them. Besides, they would vote for him even if he repudiated them.

Also, it is surprising that he opposed the moderate civil-rights compromise put forward by Governor George Romney of Michigan, who made the most moving appeal of the whole convention. For Mr. Goldwater's main hope in this election, as at least some observers here see it, lies, not in winning the South or the vote of the extremists on the far right, but in convincing the uncommitted and the troubled voters in the middle that there is something basically wrong with the trend of our national life.

Mr. Goldwater's dilemma now is quite clear. On the one hand, he is arguing for the New Morality, but on the other he is supporting a racial policy that seems to many deeply immoral and attracts the most negative forces in the nation. On one side, he is arguing for allied unity, but on the other he is proclaiming policies that will clearly split the Western Alliance.

The convention has insisted after protracted debate on defending the right of dissent by the John Birch Society, but it has violently booed the right of dissent by the American press. It has argued for a more militant policy toward the Communists one minute and called for a cut in expenditures and taxes in the next. It has asked for the cooperation of the liberals in the election campaign, but has refused even to grant them a few vague compromises in the platform that would ease their obvious embarrassment.

Accordingly, Mr. Goldwater is facing the most militant and ideological election campaign of the century with a divided party, and although he can undoubtedly force President Johnson to the right, he has to win in the center, where Mr. Johnson feels more comfortable than anyplace else.

AUGUST 6, 1965

The Quiet Revolution

PRESIDENT JOHNSON IS BEGINNING TO MAKE FRANKLIN ROOSEVELT'S early legislative record look like an abject failure. He's getting everything through the Congress but the abolition of the Republican party, and he hasn't tried that yet.

It is a political miracle. It has even surpassed his own expectations, which were not modest, and while he's still a long way from achieving a Great Society, he is at least making progress toward a more equal and compassionate society.

In a single evening this week, the Senate passed the most liberal voting-rights bill in the history of the Republic, and sustained the Supreme Court's ruling that the state legislatures must be reapportioned to give equal voting rights to the steeply rising urban and suburban population of the nation.

In this first session of the 89th Congress, the Federal legislature has also passed the medical-care bill under Social Security, a housing bill with an experimental system of Federal rent subsidies for the poor, education and poverty bills that bypass the ancient conflict over Federal aid to religious institutions, a constitutional amendment to deal at long last with the danger of

Presidential disability, a bill for the relief of the depressed areas of Appalachia—all this and a lot more and a tax cut too.

Mr. Johnson is giving us a revolution in the binding of a hymn book. He has broken the consolidating spirit of the Eisenhower era. He has sounded more conservative but acted more radical than his mentor, Roosevelt, and he has presided over more legislative innovations on the home front than any other President in any other single session of the Congress in this century.

This is not, of course, due entirely to Lyndon Baines Johnson's particular brand of political magic, though that hasn't hurt. The New Deal's day has finally come. The radical ideas of the early Thirties are now winning instead of losing. There seems to be a new sense of social responsibility in the country—a growing feeling that racial discrimination, bad education, inadequate medical care, and degrading poverty are intolerable in a fabulously wealthy nation.

Other factors have helped. The Democratic landslide in the Presidential election of 1964 gave the President's party large majorities in the House and Senate; the new members in the 89th Congress have been overwhelmingly for the President's program; the old conservative coalition of the Southern Democrats and Midwestern Republicans has been broken, and the Republican leadership has not only gone along with but sometimes has led the fight for equal civil rights.

This is a development of worldwide significance. It is not so long ago that students of Government in other lands were perplexed about the erratic nature of the American economy, the verbal violence of American politics, and what they regarded as the rigidity of the American Constitution.

They were not sure that the United States could maintain economic growth and stability, that it would apply the new techniques of tax and monetary policy, that it could provide continuity of purpose from one political party to the other, or that a Federal Government of proud and numerous states with an attic full of hobgoblins about the welfare state and the planned economy could achieve social progress over an entire continent and bring its military power to the defense of freedom in other parts of the world.

Well, it begins to look as if the people will take the welfare state and the planned economy if you just don't mention the names, mainly because, wicked or not, they seem to work. The gross national product rose by $9.2 billion in the second quarter of 1965—from a 1964 level of $622 billion to an annual rate of $658 billion.

Something, in short, seems to have happened to the old popular assumptions that the American economy wouldn't work if the Government tinkered with it; that the White House and the Congress couldn't get along unless both were reorganized; that Federal money couldn't be channeled to the private and parochial schools without the immediate retaliation of a vengeful God.

So maybe there's some zip in the old system yet. In his State of the Union message, President Johnson said the time had come to give more attention to the home front. He promised to try to keep the economy growing, to extend the prosperity to more people, and to try to improve the quality of life for all. And even his critics here concede he has kept his promise.

NOVEMBER 7, 1965

The Decisive Political Center

THE HISTORY OF AMERICAN POLITICS SINCE THE WAR OF 1939–45 seems to support three propositions: (1)—The political spirit of the majority of the American people varies from moderate to progressive; (2)—either major party that takes its stand on this middle ground with an attractive world-minded candidate can win the Presidency; and (3)—there is plenty of room for vigorous and constructive party warfare on this center battlefield between the Tweedledum Republicans a little right of center and the Tweedledee Democrats a little left of center.

These propositions may not be true in some areas of the country—for example, in some predominantly Democratic states of the South and some predominantly Republican states of the Middle West, where the spirit of the people is more conservative. But in national terms, it is difficult to argue from the record that either party can win the Presidency or even an effective national opposition if it defies these propositions.

Dwight D. Eisenhower accepted all three propositions and won for the Republicans in 1952 and 1956. Lyndon Johnson accepted them in 1964 and won by the largest margin in the history of the Presidency. Barry Goldwater defied them and not only lost but weakened his party's capacity—in the Congress and the state capitals—to serve as an effective opposition party. Even in so Democratic a city as New York, John Lindsay saved the Republican party by repudiating it, and won the mayoral election by appealing above party to all moderates and progressives, while the Democrats lost by appealing on narrow partisan grounds.

Individuals may ignore and even resent the success of these moderate-to-progressive candidates of both parties, but political parties cannot. For the function of a political party in this country is not to preside over a philosophical debate, but to control and direct the struggle for power, and no party can do this successfully unless it appeals to many diverse economic, regional, religious, and racial groups all over the continental United States.

Ideological conservatives like Goldwater and Buckley in New York are quite right in asserting that acceptance of the policies of the American "center" means acceptance of a strong trend toward "the welfare state" and "the planned economy." They are right too—though their opponents usually will not admit it—in charging that American politics are moving to the left and adopting many of the aspects of a "Socialist society."

Where they are wrong, or so it seems to me, is in basing the political action of a large national party on narrow ideological grounds and on what people say or pretend instead of on what people really do. Almost everybody says he is against "the welfare state" and "the planned economy," but most of them vote for both without thinking much about either.

Almost everybody in this country is for "the common welfare," and the most successful "planners" in the United States are the Republican big businessmen who plan every automobile or other commercial product to attract popular support. People are not as rigid as political doctrines. They often denounce in theory the things they support in practice, and the successful politicians of the last generation have been those who have appealed to the people's interests and not to the people's pretenses.

The record simply does not support the notion that moving the Republican party from the center to the conservative right strengthens the Republican opposition and helps restore a balance in American political life. It does the opposite. It gives the people a clear "choice" all right, but a choice they are not prepared to accept. It does not balance or weaken the left but strengthens the left. It increases the noise and it envenoms the political argument, but it actually reduces the power of the Republican opposition.

Eisenhower and the British Conservatives have demonstrated that the best way to gain national power in a Western democracy is not by moving to the right and exaggerating the differences with the party on the left, but by commanding the center, accepting the best of the liberal policies, and arguing that the moderates can administer them more efficiently. Eisenhower accepted all the domestic and foreign policy forms which the Democrats introduced and his own party opposed in the Thirties and Forties, and thus managed to be the only Republican President in the last thirty-three years. Goldwater gave the impression that he was against these reforms and was overwhelmingly defeated.

This is still the main political lesson of the postwar era. The decisive battleground of American politics lies in the center and cannot be captured from either of the extremes, and any party that defies this principle does not improve its chances of national power or even effective opposition, but precisely the opposite.

The Tragedy of the Republicans

THE TREND OF REPUBLICAN PRESIDENTIAL POLITICS IS NOW FAIRLY clear. It has narrowed down to Governor George Romney of Michigan or former Vice President Richard M. Nixon against Lyndon Johnson in 1968. Nobody quite knows why it has come down to this, and the party is not very happy with the choice, but this is the way things are going.

The logic of politics is hard to fathom. The strongest Republican candidate against President Johnson would be one who is experienced in foreign affairs, but the only two Republican Governors who have any claim to special knowledge in this field—Rockefeller of New York and Scranton of Pennsylvania—have just taken themselves out of the race. This leaves the choice between Nixon, who has some experience in foreign affairs, and Romney, who hasn't, and the chances are that the GOP will take Romney, who is not well known, rather than Nixon, who is too well known.

The lesson of recent history for the Republicans seems simple enough. In the thirty-six years between 1932 and 1968, they have won only with Eisenhower, a national hero and political amateur and outsider who expanded all the welfare-state and internationalist policies his party had fought against in the previous generation. All the Republican political insiders, from Dewey on the left to Goldwater on the far right, were defeated, and the further right they went, the more spectacular their defeats.

If the purpose of a political party is to control and direct the struggle for Presidential power, the logic of this is that the GOP should be looking for one of two things: either an attractive new "outsider" who might have a chance of beating Johnson in 1968; or if this seems unlikely, as it does, a young man with some determination to deal with the growing problems and masses of the cities, who can be prepared for the future political battles of the Seventies.

At the present time, the Republicans are doing neither. They are not looking for new personalities in their ranks who might provide a hopeful alternative to President Johnson in 1968, and they are not looking for young men who could provide an effective opposition and still be young enough to run for the Presidency in 1972.

The Republicans are not without leaders. They have no national hero like Eisenhower. They talk vaguely about General Lauris Norstad, Eisenhower's successor in the NATO command, an attractive and highly intelligent officer, and about General Westmoreland, the American commander in Vietnam. But Norstad has not been well, and Westmoreland, unlike Ike, is not yet the hero of a victorious American army. Nevertheless, the Republicans still have some able "outsiders," and this is just the problem: they are "outside." They are either not interested, or not considered, or working for Johnson, and this complicates the Republican political future.

The two most powerful and impressive members of the Johnson Cabinet today are both Republicans: Robert McNamara, the Secretary of Defense, and John W. Gardner, the Secretary of Health, Education, and Welfare, who are two of the most attractive and intelligent men to come into the top of Government since the New Deal. The Republicans somehow overlooked them during the Eisenhower Administration, and it is probably ridiculous for the Republicans to think about them in Presidential terms now.

Still, there are others, most of them, for some odd reason, Yale men. Kingman Brewster, the president of Yale University, William McChesney Martin, Jr., the chairman of the Federal Reserve Board, McGeorge Bundy, former foreign affairs assistant to both Presidents Kennedy and Johnson and now president of the Ford Foundation, Associate Justice Potter Stewart of the

Supreme Court of the United States, and Mayor John Lindsay of New York—all of them Republicans and all of them unconsidered.

This is, of course, a crazy parlor game rather than a political reality, yet who is to say that Romney or Nixon would be a better President than any of these men, or than Robert Anderson, former Secretary of the Treasury, whose politics are ambiguous, or Douglas Dillon, who served at both State and Treasury, or the former Attorneys General under Eisenhower, Herbert Brownell and William Rogers.

If Ronald Reagan of California is suddenly put on the list of Republican Presidential possibilities, why not Brewster of Yale, who may, though we will probably never find out, be another Woodrow Wilson? Mr. Reagan is an actor, which is really in his favor, for all politicians are actors. But if Goldwater, the authentic conservative article, could not make it, why a Hollywood type playing the role of Goldwater?

The point is that the Republican party, overwhelmed by defeat during the last generation, is not really analyzing its problem or mobilizing its resources. It is divided and frustrated. It is playing the professional game, which the Democrats invented. It is up against Johnson, the most accomplished political pro of the century, representing an urban, working-class, union-oriented party with a yen for reform and spending; and trying to beat him with its own political professionals, representing a rural, middle-class, old-stock, business-oriented, status-quo tradition.

In this kind of conflict, Democratic political pros against Republican political pros, Johnson against Romney or Nixon, the outlook is fairly certain. It is the Green Bay Packers against Harvard, and the irony of it is that the Republicans have the men to make a race of it, but do not mobilize their strength.

5

EDUCATION

Advice to a College Freshman[1]

PART OF THE DISCIPLINE OF UNIVERSITY LIFE IS TO LISTEN PATIENTLY
to middle-aged bores, and you might as well start now.

I was here as a freshman in the latter part of the Middle
Ages.[2] This was away back in the days when women wore skirts.
The president of the university then was David Kinley. He was a
Scot with a strong conviction that all men and some women
shared the burden of original sin—especially college undergraduates. He assumed that the students of that day were willful, and
potentially wicked, children—particularly when gathered together as males and females—so he believed they had to be
policed like prospective criminals. This task he assigned to the
Dean of Men, Mr. Thomas Arkle Clark, who looked like Mr.
Chips and acted like J. Edgar Hoover. Dean Clark was assisted
by the Dean of Women, Miss Leonard, who warned the girls that
wearing red might arouse the passions of the men.

I should say in passing that I myself married a recklessly
beautiful girl whom I first saw here on Wright Street wearing a
scarlet coat. I will spare you the happy story of my life, but in
any event, we got a new president at the end of my sophomore
year, who ran the place on the totally opposite theory that all
undergraduates were mature ladies and gentlemen, who needed
very little supervision or discipline. I have often wondered since
then who was right, but the contrast between Presidents Kinley
and Chase was so striking that it illustrates really the only point I
want to make to you about university life.

This is that the approach to a new experience or problem is
fundamental. What assumptions you bring here with you at the
beginning may be more important than what you take away at

[1] From a talk given to the 3,000 members of the freshman class at the
University of Illinois.
[2] Class of 1932.

the end, for your approach to the beginning often determines the end. What I want to talk about, therefore, as frankly as I can, is how to approach university life at a time of great upheaval and convulsion in the world.

When Gilbert Keith Chesterton, one of the great Victorians, wrote his autobiography at the end of a long and useful life, he set himself the task of defining in a single sentence the most important lesson he had learned. And he concluded that the critical thing was whether one took things for granted or took them with gratitude. This, I think, is a good place to begin, and it has a special reference to the Class of 1969.

This country is at war. My generation may have staggered into it, but yours is fighting it. I have just come from the battle of Chu Lai up near the 17th parallel in South Vietnam. Americans, who by the accident of birth happen to be a little older than you are, fought and won that critical opening test of strength with the Vietcong. Other Americans of your own age, most of them probably a little poorer than your parents, are now registering not for classes but for uniforms. I don't want to make too much of the point, for all wars are unequal, but the fact that you are here and they are there is not the sort of thing that should be taken for granted, but should be regarded, perhaps, with a little gratitude.

I leave aside the people of Vietnam, who have a life expectancy of thirty-eight years, and have been at war for over twenty years. The theory of our public policy on the draft is that you will do more for the development and security of your country by studying here than fighting there. I think it is a good, if often an unfair, policy, but it does place upon you an obligation to do your best and at some time to repay the nation for the opportunities provided for you in this place.

A respect for fact is another useful companion at the beginning of your journey. You are not obliged to be grateful for the present tumult of the world, but you have to live in it. You may have any opinion you like about Lyndon Johnson, but he's the only President we have. He is a fact—and some fact! You may not like the war in Vietnam, but it is also a fact. You may not like the size of this university—it is certainly not a small monastery—but you have to deal with the world as it is and not with the world of your desires and dreams.

It may be a significant fact that you entered the university in the week when one fifth of the human race on the Indian subcontinent started bombing one another, and China, which contains one fourth of the human family, gave India a seventy-two-hour ultimatum to abandon her military bases in the disputed areas of the Himalayas. We all have our thoughts about this madness. China is undoubtedly a nuisance, but even though we do not recognize China, it will not accommodate us by going away.

I have to tell you bluntly that the outlook for the rest of the Sixties is not entirely rosy. My generation has had to deal with its share of moral monsters and staggering and blundering governments, but there is an important difference. Our problems were primarily in Europe and in Russia, which to some extent has come under the influence of a civilization we know something about. But your generation will be dealing with Asia, which comes from a much different culture and has a majestic disregard and even contempt for many of the fundamental things we proclaim in the Declaration of Independence to be "self-evident."

Our assumptions are not self-evident to the turbulent peoples who live between the Yellow Sea off Korea and the Black Sea between Russia and the Balkans. In fact, our assumptions are being challenged even by many of our allies, let alone our enemies.

General Ky, who is Prime Minister of South Vietnam—or anyway he was when this meeting started—said to me the other day in Saigon: "Don't talk to us about individual responsibility. Talk to us about rice and schools. We don't believe in individual responsibility. We believe the individual is precious only when he is part of the family, only when he sublimates himself to his parents and grandparents, and loses himself in the larger concerns of the people of his own blood."

It is, then, going to be difficult to deal with this kind of world. I do not think the big war is going to start or that the little wars are going to end in this decade or maybe even in this century. But different habits of thought are facts, too, and we are going to have to learn to think as steadfastly about them as those boys think when they bring down a jet at 135 miles an hour onto 200 feet of the deck of an aircraft carrier. In short, we are going to have to learn to live with disagreeable facts.

You may ask what all this has to do with you. What can you do about the distracting tumult of the world when you haven't yet adjusted to the distracting tumult of the campus? There are, I believe, a great many simple things you can do. You can park your prejudices at the door, or maybe even better, examine them and see where they came from, and whether they make any sense in the face of the stubborn facts of the present day.

You can put aside fifteen minutes a day to read a newspaper and get some idea of what's going on. I will not presume to tell you what newspaper to read. You can listen: that would be a remarkable innovation, and ask questions. I have learned in over thirty years of reporting that by far the most effective device is what I call the "dumb-boy technique," which is nothing more than refusing to pretend you know what you obviously don't know and saying honestly: "Sorry, I don't get it. I want to understand but I don't." You will, I think, be amazed at the possibilities of candid stupidity.

It is easy, of course, not to think consciously at all about these things, but simply relax and be carried along by the stream of others who seem to know where they are going. This is natural at first, but it would be a pity to let it go on for long. A university is not a few classes and teachers and a place to eat and sleep, with trees and pleasant walks in between. All the wisdom of the past has been gathered here on this fertile prairie. It can supply all the answers to all your questions except why a football bounces into the arms of the wrong man. But you have to know what is going on. A university is a vast catalogue of interesting events on the side: lectures, concerts, political, religious, and dramatic societies to suit every interest and taste. You cannot digest this whole smorgasbord. You will find that every teacher thinks you have nothing else to do except produce for him. But even so, you can look at the intellectual menu every morning in the Calendar of Events in the *Daily Illini,* and taste the fare from time to time.

Also, you can take a walk. This is a big place, but you can beat the bounds in an afternoon, and there's no telling what or who you may run into by suppertime. You may see somebody with a certain expression or a certain wistful smile that takes your fancy, and you may be pleasantly surprised to find out how easy it is to discover who she is and where she lives. I did, and it was the most important discovery of my life.

It is in these simple ways, by these practical small initiatives, that you come upon windows and doors into the wider world of the mind. Much more than my generation, most of you are going to live in the great clattering world of cities, where the enduring things of the human spirit—love and friendship and the association of lively minds—are not so easy to come by without an effort.

For a time here in this place, a comparatively brief intermission between leaving your father's home and starting your own, you will be free to discover who you are, and where you are, and what way you are going, and who's going with you. But it is a much more ambiguous world, much more complicated than following or defying the old man's orders at home. And it is, I think, better to paddle around and explore than just to drift, for if the privileged generation of educated young Americans do not learn to influence the revolutions of our time at home and abroad, the world is going to be in even worse trouble than it is.

The United States is now the most powerful nation-state, the latest, and if we falter, perhaps the last inheritor of Western civilization. We have avoided a big war for over twenty years, but we are still very new at the business, and we have to look to the men and women trained in these university repositories of our civilization, to understand what is at stake and how we can approach our problems.

For a long time, we denied that the disorder of the world was any of our business; for another period we thought that maybe it was our business but that we couldn't do anything about it; then in a spasm of presumption, we seemed to think that nobody else could do anything and that we could do everything. But now we are passing through a phase of intellectual revision, in which we see more clearly that we are neither helpless nor omnipotent, but that we need friends and allies, and above all clarity in ourselves about what we can do and what we cannot do.

In this situation, a bawling patriotism, relieved only by a whining moralistic criticism of other nations, is not very helpful. We need watchful minds and steady nerves to get through this period, and nothing, we may be sure, will come out as we would like, or even fit into those tidy intellectual patterns we adore. Nationalism is wrecking our policy of interdependence in Europe, but nationalism is the strongest force against Communism in Asia and Africa and may very well be our greatest hope on these two continents.

Above all, we must not be afraid of our enemies or make them so afraid of us that they will pull down the world. We thought there could never be an aggressor so wicked as Germany under the Kaiser, so we fought the First World War to the point of total surrender and in the process helped build up those two other more formidable enemies: Fascism and Communism. Fear and presumption are the great dangers to a steady course. The fear that Hobbes had in mind concerned men who were not absolutely brutish, and did not even want to be brutish, but were made brutish by fear and suspicion of one another and thus lurched into war.

Your generation did not invent anxiety. The world has always been unsafe and undoubtedly will be when your children are sitting where you now are. As Herbert Butterfield has pointed out, no nation can ever achieve the perfect security it desires without so tipping the power balance that it becomes or at least seems to become a menace to its neighbors.

The problem of this age is not so much insecurity as it is ambiguity. We are living in a time when change is the order of the day, when nobody but a fraud or a fool would pretend he had any perfect solutions, and when, above all, we need great integrity and flexibility of mind, not only to understand but to endure all this complexity.

This, at least, is my approach, my way of looking at this great university and the world. We shall have to develop a League of Minds, free and enquiring and respectful of fact, before we shall ever develop an effective League of Nations. And if we cannot look to the universities for this, I don't know where we can turn.

Science and Democracy

SCIENCE IS NOW PUTTING DEMOCRACY TO ITS SEVEREST TEST. PRESI-
dent Kennedy told the American people the other night that they
must face and understand the facts on the renewal of nuclear
testing in the atmosphere, but how do they do it?

Thomas Jefferson asserted, and President Kennedy apparently
agrees with him, that "there is no safe depository of the ultimate
powers of the society but the people themselves," but how can the
people understand a decision of this kind when the experts themselves do not agree on the facts and differ violently in their
interpretation of the facts?

Almost immediately after the President announced his decision to renew atomic tests, the British Government interpreted
the decision one way, William C. Foster, the U.S. disarmament
chief, interpreted it another, and a White House spokesman interpreted it in a third way. Part of the reason for this is that
scientists and other officials in the West must base their judgment
partly on facts, but mainly on what are now called extrapola-
tions.

"Extrapolation" is a seventy-five-cent word for an educated
guess. It is a calculation from a fact about what preceded that
fact or is likely to follow it. For example, if a good extrapolator
sees a boy wink at a girl, he may deduce (a) that the boy likes
that girl, or (b) that he likes all girls. Then, too, a bold or
romantic long-range extrapolator may look beyond the wink between the boy and the girl to their marriage, children, and grand-
children.

A great deal depends not on the facts at all, but on the inter-
preter, and this is why there is so much controversy over the
Soviet and American nuclear tests. Edward Teller, the doomsday
prophet, interprets them one way, and Hans Bethe, the optimist,

interprets them in another. As a matter of fact it is almost impossible to go to one of those interminable dinners in Georgetown, where the men disappear for forty-five minutes to solve the problems of the world, without running into the conflict between the Teller pessimists and the Bethe optimists.

Some distinguished scientists honestly believe that the Soviet tests of last autumn indicate great progress toward invention of an antimissile system, which, if perfected, would tilt the whole balance of world power against the United States. Others believe just as sincerely that while this is possible it is highly improbable, and that to renew American atomic testing on such an improbability merely puts the arms race into another upward spiral, increasing rather than decreasing the danger of world war.

This was the dilemma that faced the President when he had to make the decision about renewing U.S. nuclear tests in the atmosphere. Even for him, with all his expert scientific advice, it was an agonizing decision. One of his advisers, who spent many hours with him on the question, came away from it more impressed with the seriousness of the President's search for the right answer than with anything else.

For the most impressive fact of all in this field is that never in history has a President or any other head of government had to make such important decisions on the basis of so few dependable facts.

In the end, the decision to test came down not primarily to a scientific but, essentially, to a philosophic point. The President had to decide not on the basis of unquestioned facts but on informed guesses whether to assume the worst of Soviet motives or the best, and in the end he decided that he had to assume the worst.

It is hard to find anything in the historical records of U.S.-Soviet relations since the war to second-guess him. If he had assumed the best about Soviet motives and been wrong, the security of the Republic could have been at stake. But if he assumed the worst, at least he was prepared to meet his constitutional responsibility to defend and preserve the nation.

The reaction to his decision in the country has been sympathetic. Some troubled citizens have protested, but most have left it to the President, without either facing the problem or understanding it. And this raises Jefferson's question. He said he knew of "no safe depository of the ultimate powers of the society but the people themselves," and he added: "If we think them not enlightened enough to exercise their control with a wholesome discretion, the remedy is not to take it from them, but to inform their discretion by education."

This is what the President was obviously trying to do when he explained to the country his reasons for resuming tests, and he seemed to carry most of the people and the political opposition with him. But it would be overly romantic to believe that the Jefferson ideal prevailed. Even the press, which usually pretends to know everything, knew that it didn't and couldn't know the facts, and left it to the White House. But that wasn't what Mr. Jefferson had in mind.

MARION, MASSACHUSETTS

AUGUST 5, 1962

Brains and Politics

MAYBE WE'RE MAKING SOME PROGRESS AFTER ALL. NOT SO LONG ago the politicians of the states of the Union had nothing better to argue about than which state produced the cutest chicks, the roughest football teams, and the best clam chowder. But now, believe it or not, they're vying with one another on the quality and location of brains.

This is not necessarily a subject politicians know or care very much about, but the government of the United States will spend $12 billion this year on various research and development projects, and nothing makes a politician see the light like $12 billion.

Senator Leverett Saltonstall of Massachusetts, for example, is arguing that it now pays to be smart. His formula for economic growth in his state is superior technical education (by which he means Massachusetts Institute of Technology), plus good civic organization and salesmanship, plus modern scientific and engineering laboratories. This, says he, is what brings Government contracts to a state and guarantees prosperity.

Governor Pat Brown of California agrees. He feels that if you want to have a payroll to meet, the first thing you do these days is to get yourself (1) some Nobel Prize winners or other intellectuals who have never met a payroll and they in turn will (2) attract Government research and development contracts that will (3) attract industry that will (4) produce jobs which will (5) finally produce votes. It all starts, however, with brains, according to the Governor of California.

Senator Frank Lausche of Ohio does not argue with the principle of brains but dissents on the question of geography. He maintains that Ohio brains, fried or scrambled, are as good as anything produced in California or New England, and he wants the Government gravy train to stop more often in the neighborhood of Columbus.

The thing to notice, however, about all this agreeable nonsense is that, while each politician extols the intellectual virtues of his own region, they all agree that prosperity in the modern industrial society begins with well-qualified minds, and the official figures seem to bear them out.

In fiscal year 1961 the Department of Defense alone poured $120,400,000 into universities and nonprofit research in this state. Next highest was California with $87,500,000, and all the rest of the $431,000,000 in this category went to only ten other states.

The newly established Graduate Research Center (GRC) of the Southwest at Dallas explains what's happening as follows: "Management planners, in considering sites for new or expanded facilities, have found that the availability of trained minds overshadows even such factors as the labor market, water supply and power resources.

"The evidence is overwhelming: Route 128 encircling Boston,

the industrial complex around San Francisco Bay, that related to the California Institute of Technology and UCLA in the Los Angeles area and other similar situations are cogent examples of the clustering of industry around centers of learning."

In Massachusetts and California, the illustrious institutions attract the young geniuses, train them, and keep them. In most of the South, they don't train them, so lose them. But in the Middle West, they've been training them but losing them anyway. Maybe it's the weather, intellectual and otherwise.

Texas is coming up because what it has lacked in intellectual training, it has regained through political power. It hasn't produced an Einstein but it has produced a Lyndon Johnson, who helped bring the Space Agency to Houston and will establish one of the greatest scientific complexes in the world there before many years.

Nevertheless, the politician has finally discovered the intellectual—too late to gather votes for Adlai, but not too late to gather contracts for business. It was no doubt inevitable but it's all a little ironic. The fat contracts are avoiding the fatheads, and you can almost plot America's economic development in the future by locating the Nobel Prize winners in the natural sciences. There are seventeen of them in California, eleven in New York, five in Massachusetts, two in New Jersey, and seven in the Middle West.

Education and Integration

ON THE TENTH ANNIVERSARY OF THE SUPREME COURT'S PUBLIC-school-integration decision, the paradox and the tragedy of the American Negro are fairly clear. He is gaining legally but falling behind economically. He is slowly getting the rights but not the skills of a modern computerized society. He is getting a better chance at unskilled jobs, but unskilled jobs are being wiped out by the new bossman, the machine.

No doubt this ironical situation will pass in time. Already it has passed for many of the better-educated Negroes who have moved into the middle class. But even in those limited areas where the Negro revolution is advancing "with all deliberate speed," the scientific revolution is bounding forward with reckless speed.

This is the problem. History is both the Negro's friend and his enemy. In the public schools the Negro is no longer wholly separate but he is still not "equal." Even in the North he has often been integrated racially in the public schools only to be segregated intellectually. In short, ten years of progress scholastically and socially have not been enough to wipe out one hundred years of deprivation or to keep pace with the educational and scientific advances of the last decade.

Nobody recognizes this more than the best friends of the Negro. As Whitney Young, Jr., executive director of the National Urban League, sees it: "There are forces at work, such as automation, urbanization, and a host of others, that, on the surface, are indifferent to race. Unless we identify these problems, and take steps to meet them, we will find the masses of Negroes five years from today with a mouthful of rights, living in hovels with empty stomachs."

Basil O'Connor, chairman of the board of trustees of Tuskegee Institute, makes the same point: "As the formal barriers of prejudice and discrimination collapse," he says, "American Negroes will find themselves face to face with even more difficult and frustrating obstacles. The chief of these will be their collective educational deficit. . . ."

Fortune magazine's study of the problem reaches the same conclusion: "Negroes are on the verge of a major economic crisis, for the gap is widening between Negro education and training on the one hand, and the requirements of the labor market, on the other."

All the current agitation in Washington over the civil-rights bill will not deal with this deeper problem. Nor will the present efforts of the Federal, state, and municipal vocational retraining efforts, or the educational programs of the great foundations. No doubt all these things are necessary, but they are not enough to make up for a hundred years of poverty, neglect, and persecution.

After ten years of the Supreme Court's supervision less than 10 per cent of the Negro students in public elementary and high schools in the South and border states are now attending school with the whites. In the eleven Southern states, only 1 per cent of Negro students are now in biracial schools.

It will not do to wait for total racial integration to make substantial improvements in the schools still predominantly Negro. In the South, most Negro children will probably remain in segregated schools for at least another decade. In the North, because of segregated housing, most Negroes will still be segregated in their own community schools even if they are legally eligible to attend white schools.

Therefore, a vast and expensive new effort will probably have to be made to make the predominantly Negro schools "equal" even if they are still largely "separate." This is opposed by some Negro leaders in the belief that making the predominantly separate Negro schools "equal" will weaken the fight against keeping them "separate."

Yet it is fairly clear from the history of the last ten years that the fight for legal equality is insufficient. Educational equality must go with it, or at the end of another ten years we shall have a Negro generation with equal rights to jobs but few jobs, free access to restaurants and housing but no means to enjoy them, equal opportunity to vote but little understanding of the purpose of voting.

The progress of these last ten years in public-school integration is obvious, but the progress of science is even more obvious. The Negro has moved forward, but he had also moved into the modern urbanized world where the demands for progress are greater than the progress he has made.

One of the tragedies of the "abolitionists" one hundred years ago is that they spent all their energies on the legal abolition of slavery and did little to plan for the realities of victory. Ten years after the "integration" decision, the same ironical problem exists. The integrationists are winning, ever so slowly, but neither they, nor the country, nor the Negroes are prepared for the responsibilities of legal equality.

MAY 1, 1965

Students and Politics[1]

GRADUATION IS A SPECIAL MOMENT IN LIFE. IT IS THE INSTANT OF maximum freedom. Before graduation, there is the discipline of parents and teachers and the agony of youth: of not knowing where you're going to who's going with you. After graduation, there is the discipline of life itself: of love and marriage and children and work and bosses. But right now there is a period when you can choose, when the map lies before you and you face Robert Frost's intriguing question of the road taken, and the road not taken, which, as he says, makes all the difference.

All anyone can do at such a time is express his deepest convictions about the spirit of the age. We are in the midst of a great

[1] From the commencement address at the University of Michigan.

transformation of the world. The old empires are gone and the motherlands, proud and frustrated, are trying to adjust politically and psychologically to a lesser role. Decisive power has now passed out of Europe to the United States and the Soviet Union, which significantly are not only the strongest but the least experienced of the nations in the conduct of foreign affairs. The new nations are discovering, as you will soon discover, that independence and freedom are not the end of life's problems but merely the beginning. There is now a new class war developing in the world, between the rich nations and the poor nations. Europe is prosperous but is confusing prosperity with power. What Napoleon prophesied has come to pass: the sleeping giant of China has awakened, and is indeed trying to shake the world.

At home, we are in the midst of a great social revolution. In your lifetime the population of the United States has increased by 57,000,000 people, which is more than the population of Britain, or France. We are seeing, too, a convulsion of the races, and the automation of our industry, and a migration of our people off the land and into the cities that makes the old migrations of the nineteenth century seem like a weekend outing. . . .

If all this is true, it is clear, I think, that you are going to have to do hard things with your minds in the next twenty years. Prophecy is a risky business, and pious admonition from porky middle-aged characters is probably not your favorite diet—but we should at least be able to see some vague outlines of the world ahead, and come up with a few tips for the journey.

For the foreseeable future it will probably be a highly interdependent world in which the actions and philosophies of many different peoples will influence our lives: therefore we will have to learn a lot more than we now know about the languages and natures of men and women in other parts of the world.

It will be an increasingly crowded world: therefore the need for privacy, for some escape from singing commercials, for friendship, for love of family, for the most intimate things of the human spirit, will have to be sought and protected even more in your generation than in mine.

It will certainly be a world of high taxation: therefore a life devoted primarily to the acquisition of material things is likely to make even less sense in the last quarter of this century than it did before.

It will be a world of strenuous intellecual competition for you and even more for your children: therefore if you want to keep up rather than giving up, education will have to be a lifetime process.

Finally, it will, I believe, be a curious twilight world of neither total war nor peace, of alarums and rebellions and threats of violence: therefore, you will need some patience and perspective, some means of judging first and last things, and if possible some saving spirit or belief.

I have not come here to depress or pity you. In fact, I don't pity you at all. Your freedom of choice is wider than any American generation's of this century. Your parents were at your point of life around 1940, when the Second World War was already in progress. Their freedom of choice, therefore, was much more limited. Your grandparents were at your age around 1915, when the First World War was going on. That wasn't very easy either. In fact, you may be the first American generation in a hundred years with no personal memory of either a great war or a great depression, but you do face a new and highly complex set of circumstances which will require much greater flexibility of mind.

This is not a theoretical but a highly practical point. You may not want to go to the moon, or even to Washington, which I sometimes think is the same place, but even to be a good citizen or a good parent, you will have to grapple with the problems of your age . . .

The nature and location of war are changing. No rational nation can now think of total war as an instrument of foreign policy. The destructive consequences of all-out nuclear war obviously exceed any rational purpose. At the same time, there has been no change in the objectives of the major nations, and these are in fundamental conflict in many different parts of the world.

Therefore, the struggle will go on, probably for the rest of the century and maybe even for the rest of your lives. But it will go on with different means and for limited ends—particularly in the borderlands between the Communist and non-Communist worlds along the periphery of the Communist empire from Korea to Iran.

It is fairly obvious, I think, that if the United States succeeds in deterring a major nuclear war, which I am confident it will, but still does not master the art of limited war, which it has not yet done, it will face a terrible dilemma in the event of limited Communist aggression. On the one hand, that aggression, as in Vietnam, will not justify the use of nuclear weapons, but on the other, if the United States does not master the art of limited war, it could be faced with the unacceptable choice either of total war or ineffective resistance. The result of this would clearly be the piecemeal defeat of the Western powers, the paralysis of American diplomacy, and a steady disaffection of the neutral powers.

Limited war, of course, is not wholly new. It's what goes on on every campus every Saturday night. But learning the conduct of calculated limited war in the world will not be an easy exercise for Americans. In the first place, most of these wars will be fought in terrain unfamiliar and hostile to our soldiers—often in areas where many of our most effective conventional weapons are not effective at all. Also, it will require a transformation of popular American attitudes toward war. There is a curious paradox in the American character. On the one hand it has a strong aversion to war, but on the other, once war has started, it is violently pugnacious. Thus, many Americans regard bombing for anything but obvious self-preservation as wicked, while others regard halfway measures of bombing as timid, and maybe even foolish.

Accordingly, we are confused and divided when we use limited but still effective power for limited ends. We prefer our more comfortable concepts of either peace or war, and this is precisely what we are not likely to get in the next generation.

The present controversy over policy in Vietnam illustrates the point. I'm glad the university students of this country are getting involved in the argument . . . I'm all for demonstrations or debates or protest meetings or anything else except indifference. But this new kind of war confronts us all with the most careful problem of analysis if we are to reach sound judgments about the consequences of action or inaction. Nothing is going to be easier in judging policy in these limited wars than finding fault. There is literally no option open to us in the present situation in Vietnam, for example, that cannot be roundly condemned. The Communists are going to see to it that we are constantly embroiled in highly ambiguous situations, where the arguments are not clear but vague, and any decision is risky.

Students who want to "get out of Vietnam" or "stop the bombing" have every right to shout their views all night or petition the White House to follow their ideas, but the man who lives there has to take responsibility for the consequences of getting out of Vietnam or stopping the bombing.

The students may be right—nobody knows for sure what is the best answer—but I do not think it is asking too much to expect the academic community of the nation to lead the way toward the kind of mature democratic discussion we are going to have to develop in order to make our way through these highly complicated and delicate questions. It is easy to decide policy after a Pearl Harbor. But in this present and coming age there will be many courses, all of them chancy, all of them debatable, but all requiring debate of the most serious nature.

We shall not hold Asia with the oversimplified football-stadium mentality that thinks war is like football—a clear short violent clash ending with all the victors pulling down the goalposts. Wellington said the Battle of Waterloo was won on the playing fields of Eton. We could lose the Battle of Asia with the mentality of the football fields of America.

It is my deepest conviction that America will adapt itself to these new problems, partly because she must. She is now the only nation that has the power to defend the great central tradition of the Western world. Many others share her "love of law and liberty, of mercy and charity, of justice among men, and of love and goodwill," but only she has the power equal to the forces that are now challenging these things in the world.

It will not be prudent, I think, to believe that the United Nations, or the ancient allies of the Atlantic, or rising democratic nations of the Pacific will relieve us of this burden. My impression after a recent journey through these lands is that they are confusing prosperity with power and are not interested in reducing their prosperity to increase their power. I hope I am wrong, but for the time being at least they seem to be infected with the very materialism, nationalism, and isolationism they have so long charged against us. Maybe this is merely the justice of history: in the nineteenth century, we developed our continent behind their power; now they are primarily interested in developing the European continent behind ours.

Nevertheless, we are entitled to believe on the basis of the record that this country can hold the defenses of Western civilization until the older allies recover a larger sense of purpose and contribute more to the order of the world. In the time when this Class of 1965 was born, the Communists were confident that Western Europe would not regain its economic and political equilibrium and would be infested and maybe even captured by Communism. It didn't happen. They were even more confident that they would pick up the bleeding remnants of the old empires in Africa and Asia. That hasn't happened either. In the twenty years of our nation's primary responsibility for leadership in the free world, we have created a new balance of power and retained the peace. This is more than could be said about the period after the First World War—for, twenty years after that conflict, the world was again riven by the most vicious war in history.

As a result you are now able to plan your lives with much more assurance than your parents' generation, and this raises the question, What are you going to do with your lives? On this Commencement Day, what are you commencing? As you survey the map, you can take the easy way. You can choose the broad commercial superhighways that bypass everything, including, I sometimes think, life itself. Or you can take the byways, where your help is needed in the public service, in teaching, in making our cities and our country slums a more hopeful place, in any one of the many jobs that help create the conditions of peace in the world.

This kind of life will not only help your country but serve yourselves. The happiest men and women I know are not those who are providing the material things that clutter up our lives and dull our minds, or even those who escape from the struggle, but those who are engaged in the tasks that nourish and elevate the human spirit.

The problem of many generations has been that the average

man and woman felt helpless before the great questions of the day. They did not see how they could do anything practical to help. This is not true today. There is now a vast army of Americans working in the field—not only soldiers in Vietnam, or Marines in Santo Domingo, not only diplomats and journalists and doctors out in the world, but teachers in the slums, and artisans retraining the abandoned generation in Appalachia or bringing clean water to the villages of Africa and Latin America.

It is doubt about the usefulness of one's life and uncertainty of purpose and confusion of values that depresses man—a feeling of meaninglessness. Seldom, if ever, has there been a time when there were so many useful things to be done and so many opportunities for young people to do them.

I wish you well. If I am right in what I see, you are entering, not a period of decline and dereliction, but one of the great creative epochs of history. And even if I am wrong, an effort to make it so will be worth the struggle. . . .

JUNE 5, 1966

The Class of 1966

THIS YEAR'S GRADUATES FROM THE COLLEGES AND UNIVERSITIES OF the United States are particularly interesting. They were born of parents greatly influenced by the economic depression and the Second World War. They have come to maturity in a period of social and political revolution and economic prosperity, and if you listen to the psychologists, the periodicals, and the newspapers, they are a new breed of brilliant, hell-raising, loose-living, pill-swallowing, draft-dodging bums who have girls in their rooms until two thirty in the morning, and spend their time criticizing their parents, their teachers, and Lyndon Johnson.

There is something in this, but the psychiatrists, the periodicals, and the newspapers have probably changed more than most of this year's graduates. Everything and everybody is being analyzed in public these days, and the unusual is being confused with the usual. The New Left, the New Right, and the New Freedom make more news for the psychological editors, but is the vast majority of the university class of 1966 so different?

It is very difficult to tell. There are more of them: that is clear. Well over half a million undergraduate degrees will be given in the United States this month, and more than 140,000 master's and doctor's degrees. No such experiment in mass university education exists anywhere else in the world, but this is not new in the United States.

There is more of everything now in the class of 1966: more protestors against Vietnam, more complaints about early curfews and open dormitory doors, more cars and drinking and defiance of Puritanical parents and windmill political orators, but also more searching for a new philosophy, more graduates in the commerce schools and the technical and teacher schools, and more conformist organization men with their attractive wives than ever before.

It is dangerous to generalize, for despite the advanced and superior education of this year's restless and troubled university graduates, they have been singularly inept at defining what they want to put in the place of what they protest about. They are troubled about Vietnam, but who isn't? They want equality for the races, but are so affronted by President Johnson's style that they seldom mention his progress toward the equality they want.

The question is whether the protesting minority on the university campuses or the conformist majority will prevail. The protestors are getting the headlines. They are having some influence on Washington, but they are still a small minority, and after graduation their economic interests are likely to move them more than their philosophic convictions.

It is too bad. The young university radicals of the right and the left, no matter how much they differ about Goldwater and Johnson, are agreed on one thing. They both doubt the convictions of their parents, the material well-being which was the goal of the depression generation. And this is clearly an unsatisfactory goal in life for both the left and the right in the universities.

They want something else, but do not seem to be able to define what it is. They are skeptics, searching for faith, but rejecting the faith of the past. They have read Cardinal Newman and accept his goal but not his means. "Life is for action," he wrote long ago. "If we insist on proofs for everything, we shall never come to action; to act you must assume, and the assumption is faith."

This is now the problem: there is knowledge. There is protest, but the faith of the majority in the present system is probably greater than the faith of the minority in something new. The class of 1966 in the U.S. universities is probably not so different as it seems. Most of them are not protestors. Most of them are not relying on knowledge but on faith in the past—even if they cannot define what that faith is. The draft-dodgers, the perpetual students or academic bums are very small minorities. Most of the graduates are probably going on as before—searching for the right girl, the best job, and going into the Army and fighting well despite their doubts about both ends and means in Vietnam.

The radical students may be right in their yearnings, and they are now an influence on policy in Washington, but the conformist majority of the year's graduates are likely to prevail. Like other radical student generations before them, as Irving Kristol has observed, the present student radicals "are going to discover that their revolution too has been betrayed, that 'organized society' is what revolutions establish as well as destroy."

The faith or acceptance of the majority of university students today in the organized society as it is in the U.S. is still more powerful than the protests of radicals. This is not a radical class in 1966. It has a radical fringe and it has established a protest movement Washington will not be able to ignore, but it is not all that different from the majority of the classes of the last generation.

6

THE PRESS

The Press and Foreign Policy[1]

THE CONFLICT BETWEEN THE MEN WHO MAKE AND THE MEN WHO
report the news is as old as time. News may be true, but it
is not truth, and they never see it the same way. The first
great event, or "Man in the News," was Adam, and the accounts
of his creation have been the source of controversy ever since. In
the old days, the reporters or couriers of bad news were often put
to the gallows; now they are given the Pulitzer Prize, but the
conflict goes on.

The reasons are plainly that we are changing the world faster
than we can change ourselves, and are applying to the present
the habits of the past. We are imposing on a transformed world
the theories and assumptions that worked in another time at
home, and nowhere does this clash of past and present, theory
and reality, seem more dramatic than in the application of American constitutional theory to the conduct of American foreign
policy.

That theory is that the people know best. The first constitutional principle is that the success of any group of people in
dealing with their common problems rests on their knowledge
and understanding of the problems to be solved, and on their
intelligence, judgment, and character in meeting those problems.
The conclusion drawn from this is that the intelligence, judgment, and character of a majority of the people, if well informed,
will probably produce more satisfactory solutions than any
leader or small band of geniuses is likely to produce.

This is undoubtedly sound doctrine for sinking a sewer or
building a bridge or a school in a local community, but is it a
practical way to conduct foreign policy? Are the people getting
adequate information to enable them to reach sound judgments

[1] From the Elihu Root Lectures at the Council on Foreign Relations, as
summarized in Foreign Affairs, July 1966.

on what to do about South Asia, or the Atlantic, or the balance of payments, or China, or outer space? Is there any such information and any such people? And would enough of them pay attention to sustain a commercial newspaper or radio or television station that concentrated on these fundamental questions? These questions raise the old problem of the people's right to be informed and the Government's obligation to govern effectively, which sometimes means governing secretly.

Two contemporary situations illustrate the dilemma. Over 300,000 Americans, many of them conscripts, are now fighting a war in Vietnam. Most of them do not know how it started, and even many officials are extremely vague about how we got so deeply involved. It cannot be said that the people were well informed before their commitment to the battle, or even that their representatives in the Congress really debated the decision to wage this kind of war. On the other hand, the President is now conducting that war as Commander-in-Chief with television cameras on the battlefield recording daily for vast television audiences the most brutal and agonizing scenes of the struggle.

In the first case, there was so little information and so much executive authority that the President could do about what he pleased; and in the second case, the people have so much information about the violent incidents of the war that it is questionable whether the President of a democratic country can really sustain his policy over a long period of time while the public is being invited to tune in on the eleven-o'clock news and see Johnny killed. Something is obviously out of balance.

In analyzing the relationship between public opinion and public policy, it may be useful to try to understand the practical everyday conflict between reporters and officials and how it developed. General Washington went to his grave hating the press, and with good reason. Longfellow said, "This country is not priest-ridden, but press-ridden." I once had an argument about the press with a parson who referred me as penance to the first three verses of the 19th Chapter of the Gospel according to Luke: "And Jesus entered, and passed through Jericho. And behold there was a man named Zacchaeus . . . and he sought to see Jesus . . . and could not for the press. . . ."

The United States had a press before it had a foreign policy.

This is a large part of the trouble between its writers and its officials today. The American press was telling the country and the world where to get off before there was a State Department. The eighteenth-century American pamphleteers not only helped write the Constitution but thought—with considerable justification—that they created the Union. They believed that government power was potentially if not inevitably wicked and had to be watched, especially when applied in secret and abroad, and they wrote the rules so that the press would be among the watchers. In their more amiable moods, they no doubt conceded that the press should serve the country, but they insisted that the best way to serve it was to criticize its every act and thought, and something of this pugnacious spirit has persisted until now.

The natural and historical differences between the American diplomat and the American reporter are still the main cause of their present trouble. The American diplomat before the Second World War was trained in the days of our isolation to be a silent observer of world affairs. He was as discreet as a priest; he was supposed to know everything and to tell nothing. Even in America, let alone Britain, your ideal State Department man was handsome as Joseph Grew and as elegant as Dean Acheson, or vice versa. In contrast, the American reporter, circa 1930, was a very gabby and even rakish fellow who was usually trained in the police court, the county courthouse, or, as in my own case, the sports pressbox (where, incidentally, you had the consolation of knowing who had won at the end of the day). He was not discreet, but skeptical and often even impertinent. His general view of public officials was that they were probably up to something bad which the Founding Fathers had somehow appointed him personally to expose.

The American reporter of my generation was brought up to believe in the cocky frontier tradition of "publish and be damned," but the American diplomat of the same age quickly came to believe that if he helped you to publish the facts, *he* was likely to be damned, and this was only one of the conflicts that soon developed between the Government and the press.

The conduct of foreign policy is a process that never ends; the production of a newspaper or a television news program is a miracle that has to be accomplished somehow on the split second. The Secretary of State must think in generations and continents, but the reporter thinks in "stories," in "minutes," and often in "fragments." One profession is quiet, the other noisy; one slow, the other fast; one precise, the other imprecise. What makes their relationship even more difficult is that they are stuck with one another. They are married without the possibility of divorce, separation, or even an occasional period of quiet. The Government is always acting and the press is always blabbing and criticizing, and what makes this alliance even more galling is that it is unequal.

There are actually only a few hundred American reporters, editors, and commentators dealing primarily with foreign-policy questions all over the world, and those reaching the largest audience are not the well-known commentators but the news-agency reporters who serve most daily American newspapers and the radio and television stations as well.

Two points of history and geography are important to an understanding of the American news agency as the primary source of most foreign-policy news. Unlike Reuters in Britain, Havas in France, and Wolff in Germany, the original American news agency, the Associated Press, was created not for private profit or Government convenience but as a nonprofit cooperative association to serve newspapers that shared the costs. This had some significance, for since it had to serve editors of wholly different and conflicting views on domestic and foreign policy, it had to be as impartial, nonpartisan, and unbiased as possible. The result was that mutual distrust among American newspapers created the most accurate and trustworthy source of world news the world has ever seen, and with the advent of a second American worldwide news agency, now called United Press International, competition increased both the flow and the accuracy of the news.

The geographical point is more interesting and less encouraging. The American news agencies have to serve a vast continental country covering four different time zones, with some parts facing on the Pacific and some on the Atlantic, some looking north and some south, some living in arctic and some in tropical climates. Accordingly, news has to be written so that a news story on international trade could be filed at length for maritime cities interested in international commerce and briefly for agricultural towns concerned primarily with the price of corn. And vice versa. The news agencies had to devise a technique of writing the news so that each story could be adapted to the diverse needs and interests of widely varied communities.

Accordingly, they invented the "headline" or "all-purpose" agency news story which could be published at length in the large city papers or cut in half for the middle towns or reduced to a paragraph for the very small papers. This solution to a technical problem had results nobody in the AP or UPI intended and certainly nobody in the State Department wanted. It tended to sharpen and inflate the news. It created a tradition of putting the most dramatic fact in the story first and then following it with paragraphs of decreasing importance. Thus it encouraged, not a balanced, but a startling presentation of the news, based on what one of my irreverent colleagues calls the "Christ, how the wind blew!" lead. This was fine for the news of wrecks or murders, but was a limiting and distorting device as news of foreign policy became more and more complicated.

THE CONFLICT BETWEEN JOURNALISTS AND DIPLOMATS IS GETTING worse instead of better for a variety of reasons. The press corps in the major capitals is getting so large that it is often smothering the news rather than covering it. When I started covering the State Department for *The New York Times* in 1941, Secretary of State Hull saw the "regulars" every weekday in his office. He could explain his policies, often in the most vivid Tennessee mountain language, read from the diplomatic cables if he felt like it, and indicate, with full assurance that his confidence would be respected, what was on the record and what had to be off the record. A generation later, the Secretary of State has to meet the reporters in an auditorium where everybody is wired for sound.

The change in the nature of war has also complicated the problem of reconciling the traditions of press and Government. The nation is engaged in an underground war, an economic war, an intelligence war, in every continent of the earth. This requires a vast American secret-service operation in the armed services and the Central Intelligence Agency. What it costs and all that it does are not disclosed, and this is not only necessary, but it is something comparatively new in American life, at least on the present scale. The old tradition of the American press is that anything a Government hides, except in open and declared war, is wrong and should be exposed, but a press demanding unlimited freedom for this principle could in some cases risk the nation's freedom. Yet the problem cannot be solved simply by saying that the operations of the intelligence services of the Government are none of the public's business. I knew for over a year that the United States was flying high-altitude planes (the U-2) over the Soviet Union from a base in Pakistan to photograph military and particularly missile activities and bases, but *The New York Times* did not publish this fact until one of the planes was shot down in 1960. Was this a correct judgment? I think it was, but in other circumstances, the press is criticized for not printing intelligence and even military information.

The press, radio, and television help create the atmosphere in which the nation lives. It is not an atmosphere that encourages calm reflection or wide perspectives, and it makes little allowance for the limitations of human frailty. We have transferred into the capitals of the world the American police-blotter definition of the news—which is the news of violence and contention, of the unusual rather than the usual—given it the voice of the radio and the eyes of the television camera and added the insistent shouts of the advertiser and the singing commercial.

There are, of course, advantages. The American people are given more information about events that affect their lives than any other people in the world. More Americans now see their public officials and hear them discuss public questions on television than ever before in the history of any sovereign state, but there are disadvantages, too. Casual conversation about delicate diplomatic questions is necessarily imprecise, while the language of diplomacy is supposed above everything else to be precise. Officials find the television interview more dangerous but more alluring than the private interview, for though what is said on television must stand as spoken, they can reach millions by television in no more time than it takes to talk quietly and privately to a single newspaper reporter.

In times of high controversy over policy, this constant public thrust and counterthrust of criticism and defense, while inevitable in a democracy, has a serious effect on public officials. The more their policies are criticized, the more time they spend on defending their policies, until the words become as important as the acts and the defense of the policy takes on more meaning than the policy itself.

The energy devoted by the President and the Secretaries of State and Defense to the public-relations aspects of foreign policy is almost beyond calculation. When they are being criticized, they seem all the more eager to argue their case in public. If we really knew the cost of all this physical and nervous strain on the principal officers of our government, we would probably be appalled. The pressure merely of being agreeable to critics in the press and the Congress must by itself be a trial, and it certainly leaves little time for reflection on anything except the particular crisis in the headlines at the moment.

The obvious conclusion to be drawn from all this is that neither the press, nor the Congress, nor the Executive Branch has yet adjusted effectively to the new demands of the age. We are all following the procedures that were no doubt adequate when foreign policy was a secondary consideration. At the State Department, the men who are available to most reporters are not informed, and the men who are informed are usually too busy with the crisis to be available. On Capitol Hill, each committee is sovereign and assumes that Cabinet officers have nothing else to do but to repeat the same testimony three or four times to three or four different committees. And in the news-gathering agencies we go on doing more or less what we did a generation ago.

PERSONALLY, I DO NOT BELIEVE THAT THE CONSTITUTIONAL assumption that "The people know best" is a very reliable guide to the conduct of American foreign policy today. Similarly even the modern techniques for reporting foreign news are not yet adequate to the subject or to the need, but we should be careful about reaching the conclusion that the remedy lies with a less assertive press. It is not the press that is extending its power to the detriment of a sound balance between public opinion and foreign policy, but the President, whose power in this field is greater than that of any head of government in the modern world.

The question we have to ask is not about the President's interests, but about the public interest. No doubt both President and press will abuse their power from time to time, but where is the greater danger to the public interest—in the present power of the press or in the present power of the President?

I believe the power of the Presidency has been increasing steadily since the Second World War, particularly since the introduction of nuclear weapons, and that the power of the press and even of the Congress to restrain him has declined proportionately during this same period.

The Presidential power in the foreign field is in direct proportion to the size of the issue. The press can still embarrass him by premature disclosure of his plans, and the Congress can still oppose and even defy him on peripheral issues, but on the great acts of foreign policy, especially those involving the risk or even the act of war, he is more powerful in this age than in any other, freer to follow his own bent than any other single political leader in the world—and the larger and more fateful the issue, the greater is his authority to follow his own will.

As the leader of the worldwide coalition of nations engaged in constant contention with hostile forces in scores of different theaters of action or maneuver, he is virtually assured of support once he proclaims his intentions. The Congress, of course, retains its power to deny him the funds to carry out his plans, but it cannot do so without repudiating him in the face of the enemy and assuming responsibility for the crisis that would surely follow.

President Johnson's use of the so-called Congressional Resolution on Vietnam illustrates this point. The Congress did not initiate that resolution. It was written in the State Department and sent to Congress for approval on the morning after Communist PT boats made an unsuccessful attack on U.S. destroyers patrolling in the Gulf of Tonkin. It was not limited to the specific attack or even to the specific country at war. It asked the Congress to give the President authority to use whatever power "he" deemed necessary, not only in the Gulf of Tonkin or in Vietnam but anywhere in all of Southeast Asia against any Communist aggression.

Obviously, the Congress complied, with very little debate and with only two dissenting votes. It could scarcely have done otherwise. It followed the procedure initiated by President Eisenhower in the Formosa and Lebanon resolutions of the Fifties, and in similar situations in the future it is hard to imagine any Congress—even one dominated by the opposition party— doing otherwise.

The gravity of the issues since the advent of the cold war and atomic weapons has clearly enhanced the power of the President. In fact, I cannot think of a single major foreign-policy move any President wanted to make since the Second World War that he was unable to carry through because of the opposition of the press or of Congress.

President Wilson died believing that the balance of political power in America had swung so far toward the Senate that no President would ever be able to pass another major treaty. Yet President Eisenhower and his Secretary of State, John Foster Dulles, scattered treaty commitments all over the Middle East and South Asia with scarcely a dissenting voice in the Congress or in the press. President Kennedy waged one proxy war against Cuba, and risked a nuclear war with Russia over that same island without even asking the Congress. President Johnson sent more than 300,000 men to war in Vietnam despite some sharp criticism from many of the nation's leading newspapers and commentators.

I do not say this is wrong, but merely that it is a fact of the nuclear age. In the Cuban missile crisis of 1962, President Kennedy was free to blockade Cuba, or bomb Havana, or, for that matter, to do nothing, on the excuse that we had missiles in Turkey, so why not Soviet missiles in Cuba? Eisenhower was free to send his bombers to Dien Bien Phu in 1953 to relieve the French, or to refuse to do so, just as he was free to go to the help of Hungary when it was invaded by the Red Army, or to pass by on the other side. President Johnson was obviously free to bomb North Vietnam or not to bomb it, to negotiate with Hanoi or to blow it up, to mine the harbor of Haiphong or to leave it alone. No sovereign in history ever had such power or responsibility.

The press may report the news but the President makes it. If Senators are dominating the front pages with their protests against his foreign policy, and editors and professors are creating newsworthy disturbances on the university campuses and on the editorial pages, the President has a convenient remedy. He can divert public attention to himself. He can arrange a conference on an island in the Pacific, for example. Within seventy-two hours, he can bring the leaders of the nations on his side to a meeting that will arrest the interest of the world. Reporters and photographers will converge from all the capitals and fill the front pages with accounts of the proceedings, thereby overwhelming the less dramatic Senatorial mutterings.

This gives the President quite an edge. The reporters and commentators on the scene may see all this as an elaborate camouflage of realities and write their waspish critiques of the proceedings at his conference, but unless the great man is incorrigibly clumsy, which with the help of an experienced civil service he usually is not, the big front-page headlines will have much more effect than the witty chatter on page 32.

The two Roosevelts were the Presidents who first understood the primacy of news over opinion. Teddy Roosevelt used to joke that he "discovered Monday." He recognized that editors had little news on Sunday night and that if he held back his Presidential announcements until then, he got a better display on the front pages on Monday morning, even with secondary news, than he got on Wednesday with really important news. Franklin Roosevelt, who was elected to the Presidency four times against the overwhelming opposition of the American newspapers, was even better at dominating the news. He concentrated on the reporters and the front pages and vilified or scorned the commentators and the editorial pages.

Every President since then has understood the point. Europe has a press that elevates opinion; America a press, radio, and television that emphasizes news. The Lippmanns, the Krocks, the Alsops, have their audiences, and the brilliant young American satirists, Russell Baker of *The New York Times* and Art Buchwald of the *Washington Post*, tickle the intellectuals and often come nearer to the truth than all the solemn scribblers, but news is more powerful than opinion, and this is the point the politicians have understood.

Thus the President almost always has the initiative over both press and Congress if he chooses to use the instruments of power now at his command. He is no equal partner with the Congress in the conduct of foreign affairs, if he ever was. He and he alone is in constant communication with almost every other leader in the world. He can reach his own countrymen from his television studio in the White House whenever great events justify a request for network time. When the Congress is squabbling in the wings over Rule 22 or the intricacies of repealing Section 14-b of the Taft-Hartley Act, the President is constantly proclaiming the brotherhood of man, progress, generosity toward the weak, and the elevation of the poor and underdeveloped.

There is a theory, widely advertised at annual meetings of editors and publishers, that the modern Presidential press conference is a restraining influence on the Chief Executive. According to this notion, the reporters are representatives of the people, like members of the British House of Commons, who have the power to make the great man answer questions, usually about his shortcomings or failures. There is a shred of truth in this, but not much more.

President Johnson demonstrated his command of the press conference in a very simple way. He knew that the Washington press corps was full of specialists, some of whom had devoted most of their careers to the study of foreign affairs, or the federal judiciary, or science or military affairs, and therefore not only knew their subjects, but probably knew more about them than he did. If he announced his news conferences in advance, they would come running with their well-informed and awkward inquiries. So he simply did not announce his news conferences.

He called them when only the White House correspondents were around, and then usually on the weekends when only a few of them were on duty. He held them in his own executive office, where he was not on display before the cameras, but talking intimately with the reporters who travel with him all the time and are not only familiar to him but subject to his system of punishments and rewards, which can be embarrassing to a reporter on a highly competitive beat.

The point here is not that this is wicked, but merely that nobody need grieve too mournfully over the fiction of a poor, defenseless President badgered by a pack of insensitive and irresponsible barbarians. There is nothing in the Constitution that obliges him to conduct his office for the convenience of reporters. If he is experienced enough to get to the White House, he is usually nimble enough to handle the reporters who work there.

Every President develops his own defenses in this situation. Franklin Roosevelt scorned and ridiculed his questioners. He once pinned a Nazi Iron Cross on John O'Donnell of the New York *News* during the Second World War and ordered Robert Post of *The New York Times* to put on a dunce cap and stand in the corner. Asking President Truman a question was like pitching batting practice to the Yankees. He decapitated you and then grinned. President Eisenhower was amiably incomprehensible. President Kennedy, the real master of "the game," was a witty computer. He either overwhelmed you with decimal points, or disarmed you with a smile and a wisecrack. And President Johnson learned early to apply to the press conference the technique of the Senate filibuster.

President Johnson held only nine formal news conferences last year and has had only one this year. This, however, distorts the record and does not clarify his method. No President in the history of the Republic has ever devoted so much time to reporters, editors, and commentators. But he thinks of reporters in subjective rather than in objective terms, as individuals rather than as instruments of a free press in a free society; he sees them individually and at such length that the reporters themselves are often embarrassed to intrude so much on his other duties. It was not unusual last year for the President to sit casually in his rocking chair talking steadily to a reporter for a couple of hours, and sometimes even much longer than that.

This, of course, can be very helpful to the reporter concerned, but conversations of this length somehow imply, even if the President does not intend them to do so, a confidential, personal relationship that actually ties the reporter up more than it frees him to do his job. It is very difficult to sit and listen to a President explaining his terrible problems and narrow options without becoming sympathetic to the man and subjective about his policies. It is all the harder to remain detached about the range of topics discussed when he asks you what you would do in his place.

The power of the President to use the free press against itself is very great. If, for example, an influential columnist or commentator criticizes him for landing 25,000 Marines in the Dominican Republic to put down a rebellion, it is very easy for him to call in several other carefully selected commentators and give them the detailed argument for landing the Marines. He has all the vivid facts of the situation, and if he wants to put them out, he does not have to announce them himself. Other reporters will be perfectly willing to accommodate him, even though they know they are being used to knock down the story of a colleague.

The function of criticism itself has changed in an odd way during President Johnson's Administration. In the past, there has been a reasonable expectation among people writing political criticism that if they identified a problem, checked it out thoroughly, and proposed a reasonable remedy, publication of these things would be read within the Government in good faith and maybe even considered worthy of executive action.

This is still true today on questions of policy, but if the topic deals with individuals in the Administration, the chances are that the criticism will perpetuate the situation criticized. For example, if you write today that a particular Cabinet member has been exhausted by overwork, and should be liberated for his own and the nation's good, you can be fairly sure that you have condemned that man to stay at his grindstone until everybody has forgotten that you ever mentioned him.

Also, if you learn that the President is going to do something on Friday and print it on Tuesday, this is likely to be regarded as an impertinence and a presumption which the President will punish by changing his plans. I once saw the speech President Johnson was going to make at the twentieth-anniversary celebration of the founding of the United Nations and printed his plans for ending the financial crisis that was going on in the UN at that time. He was furious. He called in the Secretary of State the very night of the publication, ordered the speech rewritten to eliminate the reported plans, and made a different speech.

This is fair enough, but behind it there is a philosophic idea that has some disturbing possibilities. Bill Moyers, the White House press secretary, explained the President's view in these terms: "It is very important for a President to maintain up until the moment of decision his options, and for someone to speculate days or weeks in advance that he's going to do thus and thus is to deny to the President the latitude he needs in order to make, in the light of existing circumstances, the best possible decision."

No doubt this is true in many circumstances, but not in all. Is absolutely nothing to be printed about clandestine plans by the President to mount an illegal invasion at the Bay of Pigs in Cuba for fear of interfering with the President's option to humiliate the country? Are the people to be denied information about Presidential options that will involve them in a war they have to finance and fight? If all Presidential options are to be protected from speculation "until the very last minute," what redress will there be the next day after the President has opted to dispatch the Marines or bomb Hanoi, or publish a request to wage war as "he" deems necessary all over Southeast Asia?

These are hard questions, and the answers are not that the Commander-in-Chief must telegraph all his punches in advance. But at the same time, the doctrine of "no speculation" before action, even on nonmilitary matters, is something new in the catalogue of Presidential privilege.

In such a world, no doubt he needs all the advantages and privileges he can get. He has to take responsibility for his actions and we do not. He is the principal actor on the stage, but he did not write the script and may not even like the role. Therefore, he tries constantly to use whatever devices he can to ease the agony. He manages the news, as the heads of all institutions do, by emphasizing his successes and minimizing his losses. He has his own photographers constantly taking his picture and releases those that convey the impression of strong leadership or compassion or whatever other mood he wants to convey at the moment. All this is understandable, but we should not be fooled: the trend of power is running with the President, the danger of excessive use of power lies not in the newspapers but in the White House, and even the most casual look at the influence of reporters and commentators today makes this fairly obvious.

NEVER HAVE REPORTERS AND COMMENTATORS REACHED SO MANY people in America with their news and views as they do now, or had so little power to influence the direction of the nation's foreign policy. The television network "stars" reach as many as 26,000,000 viewers a night. They bring in their vivid reports on video tape from all the major capitals and battlefields of the world and occasionally even bounce them off man-made stars in transoceanic broadcasts, but the reaction of the public is quite different in the foreign field than in the national field.

A fundamental change has occurred in the attitude of the American people toward the Government's conduct of foreign policy. In the old days, the people tended to believe the Government was wrong until war was actually declared; now, confronted with torrents of ambiguous and often contradictory information about questions that could lead to war, the tendency is to assume the Government is right. I believe the American reporters were nearer to the truth than the published Government reports during the critical periods that preceded the indirect American invasion of Cuba in 1961 and the large American intervention in South Vietnam in 1965, but the people paid little attention to those reports and the Government was free to use its own judgment, which was not brilliant.

What influence the press has on the conduct of foreign policy often comes indirectly, not through the mass of the people, but mainly through the Congress of the United States. The relations between well-informed reporters in Washington and influential

Senators and Congressmen are quite different from the relations between reporters and officials of the Executive Branch of the Government. Officials in the White House, the State Department, and the Defense Department, though polite and often friendly, almost always regard the reporter with suspicion.

Congressmen are different. Unlike officials of the Executive, they live most of the time in the open. They think the good opinion of the press is important to their reelection, which interests them, so they see us and some of them even read us. Also, they are always making speeches and, like reporters, looking for mistakes to correct or criticize, especially if they are in the opposition. So the reporter and the Congressman are often natural allies. They exchange information in a discreet way, and sometimes in ways that are not so discreet. When the Administration comes to the Congressman for its money, it has to answer their questions and justify its programs and in the process it discloses a lot of information which interests the press a great deal. Also reporters gather a great deal of information in foreign embassies from some of the finest diplomats in the world, and when this appears in the press, Congressmen often want to question Cabinet members about it, and can do so much more easily than the reporters who published it in the first place.

This relationship between reporters and diplomats is not only widely misunderstood but underrated. Even well-informed and sophisticated Americans are often irritated by the toplofty pronouncements of American commentators, who seem to pass judgment on the Buddhists and Catholics in Vietnam one day, explain the mysteries of Southern Rhodesia, the Congo, and South Africa the next, psychoanalyze Senator Fulbright and Secretary of State Rusk on the third, and so on triumphantly through the week, without ever a doubt or a day of rest. It seems an impossibility and a presumption for any one man to know so much about so many things, but that is not the way it is.

Most of us are merely reporters of other men's ideas. Diplomats and reporters have one job in common: they have to report what is going on, the first to his Government, the second to his paper or station. All the influential people in Washington may be furious about France but they will be polite to the French Ambassador. They will tell a thoughtful reporter what they really think about President de Gaulle's policy but they will probably pull their punches with Charles Lucet. Knowing this, the French Ambassador will often talk to a well-informed reporter. He will exchange information, but on one condition, namely that the source of the information is not disclosed.

Therefore, if the reporter is passing on information gathered by the French in Saigon or by the Canadian member of the International Control Commission on Vietnam, he cannot disclose where he got the information. He must pretend that somehow in his infinite knowledge and wisdom, this is the way things are, for he is obliged to indulge in "compulsory plagiarism."

In the process a great deal of useful information and political analysis is gathered. The diplomats are the unpaid stringers for the reporters, the reporters the unpaid tipsters for the diplomats. Ideas that professional diplomats might hesitate to mention to the Secretary of State, and information and analysis which the reporter probably would not have gathered in any other way, thus get into the newspapers, hopefully without propaganda, and may sometimes even be read by the President—which may have been what the diplomat had in mind in the first place.

In such ways, reporters and commentators do no doubt have influence. They keep the debate on foreign affairs going. We can irritate the President, divert him from his tasks, stir up his enemies, excite the public and force him to calm things down, and sometimes even make a persuasive point which he may modify a policy to meet. But his power is at the center of action and we are at the edge, and my conclusion from this is fairly plain. We may be a nuisance but we are not a menace. And the way power is running to the President, it would be unwise, I think, to concentrate too much on weakening whatever influence we have left.

IN THE STATE DEPARTMENT, WHICH IS NOT UNDULY FRIVOLOUS, the Foreign Service officers have a fable. The grasshopper, worried about getting through the winter, sought advice from the cockroach, who seemed to thrive on cold weather. The cockroach was sympathetic. On the night of the first frost, he said, find a warm spot back of a radiator in a bakery, turn yourself into a cockroach, and stay there happily until spring. "But how," asked the grasshopper, "do I make myself into a cockroach?" "Look," said the cockroach, "I'm merely giving you policy guidance."

Most critics of the press and government give much the same kind of policy guidance: change and be saved, they say. Transform yourselves into something quite different from what you are. Stop giving the customers just anything they want—any amusement, any violence, anything that sells beer or cosmetics—and give them instead information they need to know to be good citizens in a democracy. You were not protected by the First Amendment in order to be a cheerleader for the status quo or your own social or economic class but to serve the general interest.

We will only fool ourselves if we think we are going to compete effectively for the mass mind against the voice of the hawker, or bring about vast changes in the present ways of making, reporting, and listening to the news, but some things might be done in some important places to reach and enlarge what Carlyle called the vital "remnant" of thoughtful citizens.

Newspapers are no longer the first messengers of the spot news, and television has deprived the newspaper of the great "picture" story. As a result, the modern newspaper is searching for a new role, or should be, and that role lies in the field of thoughtful explanation, which tends to make it more of an ally of the official than a competitor. We are no longer in the transmitting business, but in the education business. In fact, the mass communications of this country probably have more effect on the American mind than all the schools and universities combined, and the problem is that neither the officials who run the Government, nor the officials who run the newspapers, nor the radio and television news programs, have adjusted to that fact.

We are in trouble on the news side for a very simple reason: we have not kept our definition of news up to date. We are pretty good at reporting "happenings," particularly if they are dramatic; we are fascinated by events but not by the things that cause the events. We will send 500 correspondents to Vietnam after the war breaks out, and fill the front pages with their reports, meanwhile ignoring the rest of the world, but we will not send five reporters there when the danger of war is developing, and even if we do, their reports of the danger will be minimized, by editors and officials alike, as "speculation" and hidden back among the brassiere ads, if they are not hung on the spike.

I believe we in the news business are going to have to twist ourselves around and see these wider perspectives of the news, the causes as well as the effects, what is going to happen in addition to what Governments do. It is not Governments that are transforming the world today, but the fertility of people, the creativity of scientists, the techniques of engineers and economists, and the discoveries of physicians. Almost all Governments in the world today are merely rushing around trying to keep up with the consequences of what is happening outside their own official offices. What the Roman Catholic Church does about birth control, for example, is probably going to be bigger news than what the Indian Government does about it. The movement toward the unification of Europe did not start with Governments but with private citizens like Jean Monnet. And it is being carried on by European businessmen—who like the larger markets and the fluidity of labor across national frontiers—rather than by Governments.

Ideas are news, and we are not covering the news of the mind as we should. This is where rebellion, revolution, and war start, but we minimize the conflict of ideas and emphasize the conflict in the streets, without relating the second to the first. If the Secretary of Defense says, for the thousandth time, that the United States has enough hydrogen bombs on airplanes and submarines to wipe out both China and the Soviet Union, even after they have destroyed every major city in the United States, he is assured a big boxcar headline on the front page of every big city newspaper in America and a prominent place on the Cronkite and Huntley-Brinkley shows. But if some thoughtful professor makes a speech demonstrating that the destruction of the human race can be avoided, he may easily be ignored even in his home town.

What few practical suggestions can we make that may have some chance of acceptance in a few places? First, we are not likely to get more serious correspondence in the daily newspaper until we stop making analytical articles compete for space with spot news. There is always more spot news, much of it trivial rubbish, than any paper can print. It should not be impossible, however, to get the publishers of the big city newspapers to set aside a few columns of space every day for articles on the big issues. They do not make the recipes or the comics compete for space with spot news. They print them daily "for another reason," for a certain group of their readers, and the same thing could be done for their most thoughtful subscribers.

Second, the networks could do much more than they are now doing if they would put aside an hour each weekend to review the important news of the week and put it into some historical perspective. Congressional hearings which aim not to legislate but to educate have immense possibilities. Let the responsible committees of Congress explore the problems of population, of the Atlantic Alliance, of the balance of payments, of education and poverty—say one great issue every month or so—and let the networks carry the principal parts of the testimony for an hour at the weekend.

Third, much more could be done in the field of adult education on foreign affairs if the right kind of case studies were prepared and made available to study groups in the churches, service clubs and other non-Government organizations. Some of this goes on, but the method of study is vital to its success. The problem, I believe, is to present the great issues as a series of practical choices: to let the people look at the alternatives as the President has to look at them and try at the end to decide between the hard and dangerous courses. We need simple case-study outlines containing first a statement of the facts; second, a definition of one course of action, followed by arguments for and arguments against; and so on through definition of a second course, and a third and a fourth. The difficulty with the presentation of foreign-policy news to the people today is that it comes out a jumble of important and trivial things and personalities, so that the people cannot quite get the questions for decision clear, and end up either by giving up, or choosing up sides for or against the President. Even the Sunday newspapers might find room in their endless pages and sections for a syndicated case study of the issue of the month, but if not there, the foundations might take the project on.

Fourth, if I may engage in a little heresy, it may be that news and analysis of news in a democracy are too serious to be left to newspapermen. The United States has been involved in the world now for two generations. We have developed in the process a very large company of men and women in the universities, the foundations, international business, communications, and the Government who are well informed on world affairs—some of them better informed on many subjects than any other people in the world. Unfortunately, they are not sharing with their fellow countrymen a great deal of what they know.

The great opportunity of the daily newspaper is that it reaches people when they are paying attention. Galbraith can write a learned, amusing, and provocative book about his diplomatic mission in India, which would probably come out when everybody's mind was on the Congo or the sad decline of the New York Yankees, and if he was lucky, 50,000 people would read it, but if he took a day in the middle of the Indian-Pakistani war to analyze the conflict for the newspapers he could have an attentive audience of easily 20,000,000.

We need more open pages, preferably next to the editorial pages, where the best minds of the world could give their analysis of current developments; where the vivid passages out of the best speeches and periodical articles and editorials of the world could appear; where we could find the philosophers worrying not about the particular bill of the day but the issue of the decade. These could, if edited by thoughtful minds, be among the liveliest pages in the daily newspaper and bring some sense of balance and history to contemporary events. The "Letters to the Editor" columns of most newspapers—this is not true of New York— have been dominated by publicists and crackpots for years. We should be able to do better than that and make them into an exciting forum for the exchange of ideas and even for criticism of the papers themselves.

These modest suggestions for broadening and deepening the flow of serious news in America are not really beyond the capacity of the big papers and stations, and they are not, in my view, against their long-range commercial interest. Also, if we let our reporters use their minds as well as their legs on serious inquiries and then print their findings, we will undoubtedly attract and keep more sensitive and perceptive men and women. At the same time, we should attract more and more of the intelligent young readers who are pouring out of our universities in an ever larger stream and expecting from their newspapers a much more detailed and sophisticated account of world affairs.

On the official side, too, some improvements are desirable and even possible. The attitude of the President toward the reporters is vital. If he regards them primarily as a problem and therefore tries to manipulate them, they eventually convey their suspicion and even hostility to the people. If, on the other hand, he regards them as an opportunity and tries to explain his problems to them, they can be a valuable educational force. It is the President, however, who has the initiative and the capacity to define the rules and set the tone of public discussion. A revival of the calm philosophic talk of the quiet "conversation," as typified by Roosevelt's fireside chat, could help keep the public mind on the larger questions and minimize the capacity of others to divert attention onto narrow personal issues.

There has been a decline, too, in recent years in the relations between the experts in the State Department and the reporters. The reason for this is that the experts know the President likes to dominate public announcements and are afraid that they might disclose something that would detonate his temper. And since the most useful information comes, not from the top leaders, but from the men who brief the leaders, this chokes down a very valuable stream of information.

No Government in history ever received such a torrent of information from abroad as the United States Government does at present. Washington is inundated every day with reports on every imaginable problem. A good deal of this information is interesting and unclassified and could help nourish the flow of knowledge into the newspapers and periodicals of the nation, but it is not made available mainly because nobody thinks of making it available or because the idea has grown up that all this "belongs" to the Government.

It should be possible for officials and reporters to do much better than they have done in discussing these problems and opportunities together. There is a great deal of chatter about it with the White House Press Secretary on the Presidential press plane flying between Washington and Texas, but all suggestions for more formal committees to analyze and correct shortcomings, or alternatively for the press to establish some way of correcting itself, have usually ended in useless vapor.

"If there is ever to be an amelioration of the condition of mankind," John Adams wrote in 1815, "philosophers, theologians, legislators, politicians and moralists will find that the regulation of the press is the most difficult, dangerous and important problem they have to resolve. Mankind cannot now be governed without it, nor at present with it."

I am more hopeful. There is some reason to believe that the old conflict will diminish in time. Powerful forces are working for coexistence. In his own interest, the reporter is having to become an educator, and the more he concentrates upon explaining the news instead of being first with the news, the more the official will want to cooperate with him.

The Election of 1948

To the Editor of the New York Times

Before we in the newspaper business spend all our time and energy analyzing Governor Dewey's failure in the election, maybe we ought to try to analyze our own failure. For that failure is almost as spectacular as the President's victory, and the quicker we admit it the better off we'll be.

There were certain factors in the election that were known (and discounted) by almost every political reporter. We knew about the tradition that a defeated candidate had never been nominated and elected after his defeat. We knew that the national income was running at a rate of $210,000,000,000 a year, that over 61,000,000 persons were employed at unprecedently high wages, and that the people had seldom if ever turned against the Administration in power at such a time.

We knew also that this prosperity applied not only to the people in the industrial areas but to the people on the farms as well; we knew that the small towns of the country had, during the war, become industrialized and therefore more sensitive to the influences of organized labor.

We were, moreover, conscious of the fact that a whole generation had grown up under the strong influences of the Roosevelt era; that there were (and are) more poor people in this country than rich people; that personality is a force in American politics equally as strong as principle; and that the American people have always loved a fighter.

Yet while reporters on the Truman and Dewey campaign trains discounted all these points, each in his own way (including this reporter) was carried away by facts he did not verify, by theories he did not fully examine, and by assumptions he did not or could not check.

In a way our failure was not unlike Mr. Dewey's: we overestimated the tangible and underestimated the intangible; we relied too much on techniques of reporting which are no longer foolproof; just as he was too isolated with other politicians, so we were too isolated with other reporters; and we, too, were far too impressed by the tidy statistics of the polls.

What happens when a reporter goes out to "cover" an election? Usually he does one of two things: he goes on the campaign train or he goes out on his own to the various state capitals. If he goes on the train, he is usually so busy reporting what the great man says that he has no time for anything else. If he goes to the state capitals, he usually spends his time interviewing the political managers and the political reporters, all of whom usually get their information from somebody else and place enormous confidence in the so-called scientific polls.

In short, neither on the train nor in the capitals do we spend much time wandering around talking to the people. We tend to assume that somebody else is doing the original reporting in that area, and if the assumptions of the political managers, or the other reporters, or the polls are wrong (as they were in this campaign), then our reports are wrong.

The great tangible of this election was the political influence of the Roosevelt era on the thinking of the nation. It was less dramatic than the antics of Messrs. Wallace and Thurmond, but in the long run it was more important and we didn't give enough weight to it. Consequently we were wrong, not only on the election, but, what's worse, on the whole political direction of our time.

Harry Truman's Son-in-Law

CLIFTON DANIEL, THE POOR MAN'S PRINCE RAINIER, TOLD THE reporters in Independence, Missouri, yesterday that his working hours at *The New York Times* were from 9:30 a.m. to 5:30 p.m. but his bride had better not be deceived.

It is not a reporter's working hours that count, but the hours he works. These are regulated by the news, and the news is regulated by a very simple mathematical rule. This is that the news of the day, no matter how trivial or unimportant, always takes up more time than a married man has.

It makes no difference how many hours a man has to write a story or fix up a story for publication. That story, late or soon, momentous or frivolous, will develop a life of its own. It will kill time. It will refuse to go down on the paper. It will develop inaccuracies, and it will suggest historical parallels which the writer will not be able to run down in the library.

This is known, or will hereafter be known, as O'Neill's Law of Time Saturation. (Why?—Why not!) It is infallible, and can be reduced to a simple formula: News stories expand and time contracts, meeting inexorably each day precisely twenty minutes after a man is supposed to be home for dinner.

It is not difficult to understand why this is so. Anybody who has ever watched a careful reporter agonizing in the labors of composition knows that this cannot be done without a certain ritual. A man cannot sit down and bash things out unless he is already bang up against deadline and long past dinnertime. He must pay attention to the important things of life. Style is everything. He must, for example, be free to look out the window, go get himself a ham sandwich, find and light his tobacco, check on the progress of the ball games, dig out a fact, contribute to the topical banter that is always in progress in a newspaper office, and find himself a vivid active verb, and, if he happens to be the assistant to the foreign editor (or even if he isn't), visit with the latest correspondent back from the wars.

Also this 5:30 business is preposterous. John Foster Dulles never ends the cold war until well after six each day, and now that the politicians are on the loose in the Presidential campaign, the Republic is seldom saved before 10:30 or 11 o'clock at night.

If Miss Margaret will just think about this for a minute, the facts of newspaper life will soon be apparent. Suppose a Government official decides that he wishes to awaken an indifferent world with a vast pronunciamento, or stun the opposition with some verbal thunderbolt. What does he do?

He has somebody else write a speech and polish it. He gets it cleared by thirty-eight other officials, and when all the facts are arranged to suit his convenience, he issues it to the press. *He* then goes home at—5:30. His hoax for the day is finished, but when *his* day is over, the reporter's day is just beginning. Some inky wretch then has to take the spin out of the official announcement, and set it straight and in perspective.

When the Honorable Harry S. Truman retired as President of the United States and returned home to Independence, Missouri, a reporter asked him what he did on his first day home. Mr. Truman replied, in a statement that touched a responsive note in every husband's heart: "I took the suitcases up to the attic."

This illustrates the great difference between life with a politician and life with a newspaperman. No newspaperman ever has time to take the suitcases up to the attic. Few New York newspapermen ever manage to get a house with an attic, and those who do are almost always on the run and therefore leave their suitcases in the front hall.

Nevertheless, it will be fun. Daniel will not work from 9:30 a.m. to 5:30 p.m., and there isn't a man in the newspaper business less likely to be good at taking suitcases up to the attic. But when he does get home, eventually, he will have something to say, and, after all, few men who arrive home on the 6:22 train can do that.

Propaganda Tragedy

THERE ARE THREE WAYS TO DEAL WITH THE COMMUNISTS: THE best way is to play the diplomatic and propaganda game to the hilt; the next best way is to ignore them and concentrate on the unity of the West; and the worst way is to compromise between the two and lose the advantages of both. Unfortunately, the United States has chosen the third way. It has neither won the confidence nor attained the unity of the West nor mobilized all its diplomatic and propaganda instruments for the political war against Moscow. It has come into the propaganda arena with one eye, and, like Carmen Basilio, it has taken a terrible beating.

This was the tragedy of Washington tonight as it tried to deal with the announcement that Moscow was going to end all hydrogen and atomic weapons tests for the time being. Moscow acted, as it acted with its earth satellites, for propaganda purposes. Washington reacted with words, and found itself once more on the defensive.

If this were a well-informed world in which reason and logic prevailed, Washington could rely on the good judgment of mankind. But unfortunately, reason and logic are in short supply. The Soviet Union is telling the world what it wants to hear, and the element of wishful thinking is on its side.

Washington's two major proposals are perfectly simple:

Reliable arms limitation requires reliable inspection, and unreliable disarmament is criminal negligence.

Heads-of-government negotiation demands careful advance preparation.

There is not a single non-Communist diplomat in this city who disagrees with either of these positions. There is scarcely a well-informed individual in the world who knows the postwar record of the Soviet Government who regards these two points as unreasonable. Nevertheless, the propaganda tide is running against this capital. There are various reasons for this, among them the following:

The Soviet Government can control the flow of information out of and inside the Soviet Union and the United States cannot and does not want to do so. Moscow is exploiting Asia's hatred of the Western powers and Europe's suspicion of a resurgent West Germany.

The Soviet Union is telling the world what it wants to hear: that it can have peace by talking about it; that a top-level meeting will settle everything. Washington has never really mastered the art of repeating the truth, or mobilized its intellectual and economic resources to engage in the kind of political war Moscow has forced upon the world in the last fifteen years.

Finally, as the leader of the Western coalition, the United States not only has been outmaneuvered by the Communists but also has left its allies to wonder whether it really intends to throw all its resources into the unification of the Atlantic community, or for that matter, whether it will really support them if they get into serious trouble with Moscow.

So long as the "trumpet gives forth an uncertain sound," and so long as the United States holds back from bold action to create a stronger Atlantic community, economically and politically, the Western coalition is wracked with dissension.

The Opposition parties in Britain, France, and West Germany are all playing the United States off against the Soviet Union. The intellectuals who control the press of the West European and neutral worlds are overwhelmingly critical of the failure of the United States to define and articulate its purposes.

Meanwhile opportunities have been squandered here by the men responsible for United States action. They concede now that they developed the largest hydrogen bombs long ago to the point where they could safely have acted on their own, if necessary, to stop testing this particular kind of weapon.

Many of them believe, too, that it was possible for the United States to announce that it was prepared to do all its atomic-weapons testing underground where atomic radiation would not be scattered around the globe. But these things were not done.

What is even more surprising is that the United States, which pamphleteered its way to independence and elevated advertising and the other arts of persuasion into a national cult, should be unable to hold its own in a battle for the headlines of the world.

Everything the State Department said about the faithlessness of the Soviet Union today is true. Everything it said about the need for testing and for diplomatic preparation is true. The problem, however, is to make the world see that these things are true.

MAY 23, 1958

Great Voices Are Still

THE MEMORIAL SERVICES FOR ELMER DAVIS IN THE WASHINGTON Cathedral today were something more than a tribute to a great reporter. They marked, in a way, the evening of the remarkable generation of American editors and commentators who were prominently identified with the convulsive events that preceded and followed the two world wars. Last week the capital said so-long to Tom Stokes of United Features. Last month, it was Frank Kent of the *Sunpapers* in Baltimore, and these were only a part of a plain-speaking breed, now gradually disappearing.

In the last four years, the obituary list has included H. L. Mencken, the sage of Baltimore; Herbert Elliston, the editor of the Washington *Post*; Geoffrey Parsons, editorial page editor of the New York *Herald Tribune*; Anne O'Hare McCormick of *The New York Times*; and Bernard de Voto of *Harper's* magazine.

The events of these last four years have merely emphasized the loss of these remarkable journalists. It has been a time of great complexity, demanding the knowledge and wisdom of an Anne McCormick or a Geoffrey Parsons. It has been a time of sham and pretense, crying for the sharp and even cruel instruments of a gadfly like Mencken. It has been a period of conformity, requiring the courage of a Davis or an Elliston.

They differed from one another, this group, in manner, style, and political philosophy, but they resembled one another more than they resembled their successors. They were more outspoken than the modern breed. They were more reflective. They could write more vivid prose, and above all they had more wit and humor in their souls.

In his latter days, Elmer Davis became almost too violent a partisan to be an ideal reporter, but few men felt the pulse of the time more strongly or commented on it with more perception and vigor.

He was more than a reporter. He was a philosopher, novelist, essayist, and classical scholar. He mastered the whole range of his craft. He could write. He could speak. He could explain and describe, and he could expose hypocrisy more fairly and succinctly than Mencken at his best.

When he was writing politics for the *Times*, long before his flat Indiana twang became known to millions of radio listeners, Mr. Davis invented a mythical character, Congressman Godfrey Gloom, the last Jeffersonian, from Amity, Indiana. At national political conventions, Mr. Davis would pass on his own skeptical and wry comments through Congressman Gloom, who became such a well-known character that, when Elmer finally killed him at the 1936 convention in Philadelphia, the *Times* ran the story on the front page and Arthur Krock produced an appropriate obituary.

The accident of death in the last few years has, of course, hurt both major parties, but in the field of journalism it has undoubtedly hurt the Democratic party more than the Republican. Davis, Elliston, Stokes, and De Voto were all openly pro-Democratic, although Tom Stokes won the Pulitzer Prize for an exposé of the diversion of WPA funds into political channels.

Elliston, another Pulitzer Prize winner, was, like Davis, a scholar who knew how to put today's news into the perspective of yesterday and tomorrow. He often fought with the Democrats when they were in power, but on the whole teamed up with his close friend, the cartoonist Herbert Block, to support the liberal tradition. Frank Kent was on the other side, particularly in the days of the New and Fair Deals, but what was not generally known was that he wrote for years in the liberal *New Republic* under the initials "T. R. B."

It is scarcely surprising that most of the congregation at today's memorial service for Mr. Davis was composed of reporters who admired him, and former officials who had worked with him when he was the head of the Office of War Information. In mourning for him, the officials were, in a way, mourning for the political institutions and causes he supported, for no political party can easily replace in a few years the loss of Elmer Davis, Herbert Elliston, Tom Stokes, and Bernard de Voto.

They reported on the battles to establish social security at home and collective security overseas. They articulated the Democratic campaigns for conservation and public power. They scorned the isolationists and presided over the triumph of the internationalists.

Accordingly, while the liberals bemoan their departure, the conservatives have few regrets. That is the way it is in Washington, for in this fiercely partisan city, politics divide men, even at the grave.

The Mockingbird
and the Taxicab[1]

Walter Lippmann lives in the old former deanery of the Washington Cathedral at 36th Street and Woodley Road. He works in a second-floor study that looks out on the towering north

[1] From *Walter Lippmann and His Times*, ed. Marquis W. Childs and James Reston (New York: Harcourt, Brace & Co.; 1959).

transept of the cathedral. Books and newspapers surround him. Over his desk are steel engravings of the Right Honorable Charles James Fox and Right Honorable William Pitt, and between Pitt and Fox is a line drawing of James Thurber's man and woman, with the latter saying: "Lippmann Scares Me This Morning."

It is an appropriate setting: part intellectual, part political, with shadows of the spiritual in the background. It is quiet and orderly. Even his chimney is padded to muffle the melodic repertoire of a noisy mockingbird which he doesn't want to disturb and doesn't want to hear. But every Monday and Wednesday, precisely at 12:30, a Yellow taxicab from the Washington *Post* pulls up to his 36th Street door for his column. Later, at exactly 1:15, Miss Charlotte Wallace and Miss Jean Wehner, one reading and the other checking, telephone the column to Miss Bertha Rees at the New York *Herald Tribune*, and he emerges from the cloister to the clamorous world of Washington politics and journalism.

This has been the orderly method of Walter Lippmann for over forty years: half in the noisy pit and half in the quiet study, a duality of engagement in the world of public affairs and disengagement from the world of affairs into the world of books and political philosophy, of reason and meditation on ultimate values. He writes in *The Public Philosophy* about "The Two Realms." These are the realms of heaven and earth: "that of this world where the human condition is to be born, to live, to struggle and to die; and that of the transcendent world in which men's souls can be regenerate and at peace." He himself has lived in these two realms, but mainly he has dwelled in two parts of the realm of the earth: in the theoretical realm of the ideal society, and in the more practical and mundane realm of day-to-day political problems.

"I have lived two lives," he said recently. "One of books and one of newspapers. Each helps the other. The philosophy is the context in which I write my columns. The column is the laboratory or clinic in which I test the philosophy and keep it from becoming too abstract."

The remarkable thing about Walter Lippmann is that he has

lived these two lives simultaneously, that he planned it that way two generations ago, and that he is still going at it with extraordinary physical and mental vigor at 70.

As early as 1922, he placed on the title page of his book *Public Opinion* a quotation from Book Seven of *The Republic* of Plato.

"Behold! human beings living in a sort of underground den . . . they have been here from their childhood and have their legs and necks chained so that they cannot move, and can only see before them . . . At a distance above and behind them the light of a fire is blazing . . . This is a strange image . . . and they are strange prisoners . . . they see only their own shadows, or the shadows of one another, which the fire throws on the opposite wall of the cave."

Even then, Lippmann was clearly trying to turn men's eyes from the flickering shadows on the wall of the cave to the brighter and larger world outside. He was in the cave of shadows, the world of newspapers, but pointing to the light, the better world, outside. When he later had to name his column, he called it "Today and Tomorrow," again symbolizing the two worlds of the cave and the universe, and it explains why he has consciously lived as he has.

He could have lived the academic life at Harvard or Chicago or any number of other places, but this would have limited his participation in the lively world of political decision. He could have lived the life of a government official, but this would have chained him in the cave and violated his concept of disinterestedness, of nonattachment to governments or parties or specific policies, and thus limited his pursuit of the ideal society. And while he flirted briefly with both the university and government lives, he made his choice fairly early.

At 18, he wrote a review of a book (*The Privileged Classes*) by a Harvard English professor, Barrett Wendell, in the Harvard *Advocate*. When the review appeared, William James, the philosopher, who was then retired but living in Cambridge, walked across the Harvard Yard to Lippmann's room in Weld Hall and praised his spirit and writing. Thereafter, James inspired Lippmann in a series of Saturday-morning conversations at James's house on Irving Street to continue writing on political and philosophical subjects.

Lippmann did not hesitate long in rejecting the academic life as the means to this end. He took his degree at Harvard in three years and was just about to take the examinations for his master's degree when a new magazine, *The Boston Common*, was started. He passed up the degree to join the magazine.

No doubt Walter Lippmann, at 70, would prefer to be judged on his books of political philosophy, on the ground of his two mentors, George Santayana and William James. Even now he says: "James was the hero of my life." But while philosophy may be his love, journalism has been his mistress, and the amazing thing is that he has managed to be so faithful to both.

This has been done by applying to himself what he is always advocating for governments: a plan of action, a clearly thought-out set of priorities, a disciplined procedure that prevents secondary things from impinging upon primary things, and time for thought.

Governments may not follow Walter Lippmann's advice, but he follows it himself, and it has not been easy. Few Washington newspapermen, even those who analyze rather than gather the news, ever manage to reconcile their professional and private lives. They are the playthings of events. Just when they are in the midst of a paragraph, the ticker summons them to some conference or pronouncement, or somebody pops into the room with the latest political idiocy, and they take time out to run or listen.

Lippmann himself once described it in a lovely vignette on Mr. Justice Holmes's 75th birthday:

"The country's business at Washington," he wrote in 1916, "is conducted in an odor of dead and dying cigars suspended in steam-heat. Out-of-doors Washington is widely planned and men might move about it thinking for a nation. But in the halls of Congress, in the committee rooms, the air is warm and foul.

"It drags upon you till you wilt and your head swims, and the faces of men testifying grow hazy. In that mean atmosphere, so like the corridor of a cheap hotel, there is an invitation to relax and grow bored and cease to care . . .

"But there is at least one place in Washington where things have an altogether different quality, and no one, I think, comes away from it unmoved . . ."

Thereupon, he described the house of Holmes, whose "heart is with the laughing sad men." But he might have been contrasting the atmosphere and procedure of Washington today with the atmosphere and procedure of his own life.

Walter Lippmann is at least one newspaperman who gets home for dinner. His life is not commanded by events. It is a lively enough life, but it is lively in the way and with the people he and his wife want it to be. He guards and spends his time as a shrewd investor guards and spends his money. He is up to the minute with the news but he keeps his news ticker and his television in a closet, to be used like a broom or a razor for a specific limited purpose. As a result he is almost the only thoughtful man I know in Washington who never complains that he cannot find time to think.

At the beginning of a day, or a week, he knows precisely what he is going to be doing in that period. More surprising, if you ask him on New Year's Eve what he is going to be doing in the coming year, the chances are that he has a fairly detailed plan worked out. He knew at the beginning of this year, for example, that he was going to Europe on February 28; getting back on March 29; leaving for his Maine camp on June 7; returning September 9; and going to Europe again in October.

One day last March the ticker announced that the Big Four foreign ministers' meeting would be held in Geneva on May 11, and all the rest of us started booking our reservations, scattering our kids, and changing our private and professional plans to be there, but not Lippmann. He carried on with his normal program, which did not include Geneva.

This is typical. Consider the preparation of his column. He may meditate on it for days and fix his calipers between the State Department and the distant stars, but he writes it by the ticking of the clock. Mockingbird or no, the taxi is arriving at 12:30 and the long-distance call is going through at 1:15.

At nine o'clock, breakfast out of the way, *The New York Times*, the New York *Herald Tribune*, and the Washington *Post* read, he sits down to his desk with pencil and bond paper, and the count-down starts. He cannot stop the buses in Woodley Road, and the telephones may ring softly in the 36th Street side of the house, but on *his* side nothing is allowed to interfere with his task.

Nobody knocks on the door or runs the sweeper or hammers up a screen door for the next two and a half hours. If his two assistants, his research aide and his secretary, walk around, they must have on their gum-soled shoes, and if he doesn't emerge by 11:45, everybody in the house begins to wonder.

Such, however, is his concentration and discipline of mind that usually around 11:15 his voice is heard. This is a sign that he has finished writing and is dictating the column from his own tidy handwriting into the Dictaphone. In the process, he will edit the prose occasionally to improve the cadence or substitute a more vivid or simple word, and then an original and two copies are typed with wide margins. One is given to his research assistant—either Barbara Donald or Frances Van Schaick—to check. He reads over and may change the other, and after a brief conference with the researcher, it is retyped, checked again, and ready for the 12:30 messenger.

Only when he finishes writing will he look at the morning mail. While the column is being typed, he will dictate or write answers in reply, and shortly after 12:30, he will be dressed and off downtown to the Metropolitan Club for lunch, usually with a newspaper colleague or diplomat or official.

After lunch, he drives himself back home (he never drives after dark), and devotes most of the rest of the afternoon to recreation. If it is a good day, he and his wife Helen will drive up the Canal towpath by the Potomac, let the dogs out, and walk for an hour. Or they may golf at the Army-Navy Country Club, or if it is bad weather, go to the movies.

Between 4:30 and 6, he has a rest, reads the foreign newspapers, and makes notes of ideas for future columns. Then he usually goes out to dinner with friends in the embassies or the Government, or entertains at home.

This reflective and disciplined life has given his writing a scope and grace unmatched in American journalism today and probably not surpassed by any living political writer in the English language. His personal experience in government goes back to the days of Elihu Root and Henry L. Stimson and Woodrow Wilson in the First World War. He has steeped himself in the history of his country and its relations with the world. He has studied the great political philosophers. He has access to the best minds in the Western world, and has patiently written his political philosophy in a series of books that stretch over fifty years and still retain much that is fresh and useful today.

Nevertheless, I see him first, not as an original philosopher, but as a man and a newspaperman. He is a gentle person in the best sense of that term: extremely sensitive, easily hurt, even by noise, loathe to criticize anybody who does not have the means of counter-criticism: in short, the antithesis of what is widely regarded as the typical newspaper extrovert.

There is nothing more hazardous than trying to analyze a man who spends his life analyzing others, but what impresses me is that, before he analyzed others, he analyzed himself, and not only had the imagination to select a useful and high-minded life but the discipline and ability to live it in the noisy world of politics and newspapers.

Matthew Arnold made two comments about criticism almost a hundred years ago that summarize what I believe to be Walter Lippmann's special contribution to his time. He said (in *The Function of Criticism at Present Time*) that Edmund Burke was great because "he brings thought to bear on politics, he saturates politics with thought . . . His greatness is that he lived in a world which neither English Liberalism nor English Toryism is apt to enter: the world of ideas, not the world of catchwords and party habits . . ."

This is true of Walter Lippmann, but what is more important, I believe, is that he spent most of his life performing this function of criticism, not in philosophic tracts for the few, but in newspapers and periodicals which reached a wide audience. And he did it, first in a period of national contraction during the Twenties, and second in a period of revolutionary expansion of American influence, when old habits of thought and political action were in the process of unusual change.

Again Matthew Arnold defines his special role in his essay "Sweetness and Light" (1867): "The great men of culture are those who have a passion for diffusing, for making prevail, for carrying from one end of society to the other, the best knowledge, the best ideas of their time; who have labored to divest knowledge of all that was . . . abstract, professional, exclusive; to humanize it, to make it efficient outside the clique of the cultivated and learned . . ."

This is what Walter Lippmann has done: he has brought thought to bear on politics, and he has carried that thought from one end of our society to the other.

His critics, of whom there are many, say that he was wrong in his early estimates of Franklin D. Roosevelt, and Adolf Hitler, and John Foster Dulles, and many others; that he is better at analyzing a problem than finding a practical solution to it; that he has even violated his own ideal of "disinterestedness," as in his support of Alf Landon in 1936 when he was feuding with Roosevelt; and that he made appalling miscalculations about America in the Thirties and Germany in the Forties and Fifties.

Maybe so. The point is, not that he was never wrong, not that he did not change his ideas and even on occasion contradict his own theories, but that he provoked thought, encouraged debate, forced definition, and often revision, of policies, and nourished the national dialogue on great subjects for over half a century.

It is not easy, sometimes indeed it is presumptuous and even preposterous, to indulge in quick clinical analysis of speeding and complicated events to meet a newspaper deadline. Space as well as time is a problem, and while the human mind "hungers and thirsts after explanation," the effort to reduce diversity to identity often results in excessive simplification.

Therefore, even though Lippmann seldom employs blunt instruments and never tries, like Mencken, to "rattle his opponent's back teeth," he often annoys the policy-makers even when he is addressing their reason. For while they respect his experience and admire his style and clarity, they are constantly complaining, as one of them remarked, that "he is often clearer than the truth."

Nevertheless, it is precisely because he is their most experienced and learned critic, and because he is read so avidly by the political opposition and the learned community of the nation, that he commands their attention and is singled out for official complaint.

He annoys them too because, unlike Matthew Arnold, who thought "disinterested" criticism should "leave alone all questions of practical consequences and applications," Lippmann feels a moral duty to deal with the practical consequences, to parallel what he has criticized with his own alternative.

This sometimes leads him to propose solutions when even the men he admires the most in government life think the situation calls for "a little judicious leaving alone." Also, he occasionally seems to be searching for a *different* solution from everybody else, as though, like other newspapermen who are forever seeking information "scoops," he felt obliged to come up with an "intellectual scoop." Nevertheless, he rejects the view that it is enough to analyze a problem.

"It is not enough to criticize the official's policy," he says. "We must put ourselves inside his skin, for unless we have tried to face up to the facts before him, what we produce is nothing but holier-than-thou moralizing." This is Lippmann the young aide to Elihu Root and Colonel House talking. He has grafted onto the philosopher not only the journalist but the diplomat, and this explains another source of criticism against him.

Lippmann the philosopher would no doubt say that the forced division of Germany by the Red Army fourteen years after the armistice of 1945 is a wicked injustice. But Lippmann the statesman, putting himself inside his friend Christian A. Herter's skin, sets himself a different problem: not the philosopher's problem of right and wrong but the statesman's problem of how to get out of the mess.

To talk of war as a rational instrument of foreign policy when the destructive capacities of war now exceed any rational purpose seems to him a kind of madness—a particularly ominous shadow on the wall of Plato's cave. So his reason compels him to propose accommodations which his critics condemn as appeasement.

They condemn him, of course, because nations do not live by

reason alone—otherwise reason would have forbidden the American Revolution or the British decision to carry on the war after Hitler's conquest of all Western Europe. But nations do not endure either by ignoring reason in an era of atomic weapons, and it is part of his achievement that Walter Lippmann does have the power to compel debate between reason and instinct.

It is not that Mr. Herter, and Mr. Dulles, and Mr. Acheson before him are suddenly transported into new visions of truth by reading Lippmann at the breakfast table and rush forthwith to the State Department to mend their ways. More often than not, the Secretary of State is more annoyed than persuaded, but the point is that other powerful men in the Congress or the press or the universities—and some down at the pick-and-shovel level of the State Department—probably were persuaded and introduced Lippmann's ideas into the policy debate.

The curse of the average contemporary newspaper column, or as Lippmann prefers to call it, "signed editorial," is that it sounds like a stuck whistle. Most columnists never surprise you. Each day's news is either a dreary and undistinguished report of the obvious or merely a new peg for the old tired themes. But not Lippmann.

He always has something to say. He has an unusual gift of cutting through the underbrush to the core of the problem, and while he does not try to write in the vernacular—he rather deplores it—he uses the English language as it should be used.

When he returned not so long ago from Russia and later from Germany, his reports were part of the common conversation of the capital. Every embassy up and down Sixteenth Street and Massachusetts Avenue discussed them and reported them to their Governments. Members of the Senate Foreign Relations Committee read them and questioned the Secretary of State on his points. This is his multiplier quality that is so important.

Also, through the medium of the daily newspaper, he manages to address a vast audience while it is paying attention. The readers of his books on political philosophy are numbered in the thousands, the readers of his column in the millions. He talks to them when some particularly startling headline has startled them out of their normal preoccupation with family or professional life. This is an act of public education which few writers ever equal.

Others are better qualified than I to make an estimate of his philosophical contributions, but I know that he has given my generation of newspapermen a wider vision of our duty. He has shown us how to put the event of the day in its proper relationship to the history of yesterday and the dream of tomorrow.

It is a delight to pay tribute to him and to express, while he is still showing us the way, at least a small part of the esteem in which he is held by his colleagues.

NOVEMBER 29, 1966

How to Break the Rules
Without Getting Caught

IN HIS DEALINGS WITH THE PRESS, PRESIDENT KENNEDY HAS BROKEN every rule in the book and got away with it. His meeting and interview with Aleksei Adzhubel, Premier Khrushchev's son-in-law and editor of the Soviet newspaper *Izvestia*, is merely the latest illustration of the point.

Exclusive interviews with any individual reporter, let alone the editor of an official Soviet publication, were regarded around here under President Eisenhower as imprudent if not downright subversive, but President Kennedy does as he pleases and is creating a whole new set of ground rules in the process.

When he came into the White House, he was warned by his newspaper friends about all the wicked ways of the press, particularly their jealousy and their hostility toward anyone who gives special advantages to any individual reporter.

The President indicated how seriously he took this warning at the very beginning of his Administration. After his Inaugural Ball, he suddenly showed up at Joseph Alsop's house after midnight, much to the surprise of Mr. Alsop and the consternation of the neighbors. A few days later he drove around to Walter Lippmann's house for a talk, went to dinner at the home of Rowland Evans, Jr., of the New York *Herald Tribune*, and later had his old friend Charles Bartlett of the Chattanooga *Times* up to Hyannis Port for the weekend.

When some of the President's associates asked the President whether this was wise, he took the original view that reporters were also members of the Human Race, and added that he proposed to see anybody he liked and even some reporters he didn't like.

And so he has. He has not only allowed columnists to see him privately but has permitted them to publish his remarks. He has given television interviews on some networks and not on others. He has been the darling and collaborator of all budding biographers. He has started a round of luncheons with editors from the various states, authorized live television broadcasting of his news conferences, received foreign correspondents and their editors regularly, and permitted photographers to photograph his wife, not only in her latest gown and hair-do, but in slacks and even falling off a horse.

All this is new only in terms of the last generation. A hundred years ago, when the press corps was small and Washington was a sleepy little malaria-ridden Southern city, reporters camped out in the White House as cronies and advisers. Kennedy has not gone that far, but as he told an audience at a party there the other night, "It's hard not to get invited to the White House these days."

It was this atmosphere of informality, sensitivity to the importance of publicity, and willingness to break the rules that led him to pick up the suggestion of a reporter that he seek equal time in the Soviet press for the time and space given to Mr. Khrushchev in the American press.

This led to the interview now published in full in *Izvestia*, and while it is not a startling diplomatic document, it is certainly an effective presentation of the American case to an audience that usually gets only the anti-American side of every story.

Here is the President of the United States sitting in a rocking chair talking to Khrushchev's son-in-law, and how can you believe a man in a rocking chair is about to blow up the world? Here he is talking over and over again about the importance of raising living standards in both Russia and the United States, about the importance of peace for both countries, about the weakness and not the strength of Western Germany.

Not since former Vice President Richard M. Nixon went to Russia in 1959 has a top official of the United States been able to get his views over to the mass of the Soviet peoples. This was what President Eisenhower hoped to do just before his trip to Moscow was canceled in 1960, and this, of course, is what the Voice of America is constantly trying to do in its broadcasts beamed on the USSR.

There are, of course, many here who argue that this exploitation of modern mass communications unbalances the political system. There are others who think the high society around the White House is a little Frenchy, and maybe even frivolous in such serious times. But as a political instrument the new accessibility of the White House is undoubtedly effective.

Literally dozens of foreign politicians and statesmen have gone through the White House in the last year, all eager to have their pictures with Kennedy published in the newspapers back home, and now the technique is being applied to Khrushchev's in-laws. Anybody who doubts the political punch of all this need only check with the Chairman of the Republican National Committee. He spends most of his waking hours trying to figure out how to get equal time.

Who Says a Good Paper Has to Be Silly?

THE OFFICIAL SILLY SEASON IN WASHINGTON RUNS FROM Memorial Day to Labor Day and started this week with a particularly silly incident involving the White House and the New York *Herald Tribune*.

The *Tribune* has been doing a good aggressive job of reporting the Billie Sol Estes case, much to the annoyance of the Kennedy Administration. The *Trib*'s Republican heart has been in its work, and while its zeal has sometimes outrun its judgment, nevertheless it has been scalding the scoundrels and needling the Kennedys to move faster on the case.

So far fair enough. When, however, the issue of the *Tribune* that came to the White House the other day didn't carry a line about the copper company that got a windfall of $6,000,000 with the help of Government officials in the Eisenhower Administration, and the same thing happened when Bobby Kennedy, who has connections in the White House, defended the Government's handling of the Estes case, the order went out to toss Jock Whitney to the photographers.

Though the *Tribune* did report these incidents in its late editions, the President not only canceled his own subscription to the *Tribune*, but all White House subscriptions, including Pierre Salinger's, thereby not only cutting the President off from Earl Mazo, but cutting Pierre off from Art Buchwald and Red Smith.

Now, in the bad old days when newspapers thought their job was to print the news and raise hell, the *Tribune* would either have shut up or whooped with joy and told the President to go climb the Washington Monument. But alas and alack for old

Horace Greeley. The *Trib* gave over a quarter of its front page to a vaguely apologetic editorial all but pleading with the President to take them back.

It was, it said, "distressed." It told about all the nice things and some of the not-so-nice things it had printed about the President lately. It dismissed reports of a "feud" as "tommyrot" and concluded: "We hope the President will instruct his assistants to renew the White House subscriptions, and soon."

What is going on here? It used to be that newspapers didn't think they were doing their duty if they were read and tolerated in the White House. Tom Paine once wrote an open letter to George Washington saying that the father of our country was treacherous in private friendship and a hypocrite in public life. And Mr. Paine ended by wondering out loud whether G. W. had "abandoned good principle or whether you ever had any."

That was when the first cancelations of newspapers started in the President's house, and they went on steadily until President Eisenhower canceled the Washington *Post* and Kennedy bounced the *Tribune*.

Incidentally, there is nothing in the Constitution that obliges the President to read a certain paper, and very little in the public record to suggest that the failure to read newspapers in the White House is a political calamity. After all, President Eisenhower did not spend all his time memorizing the press and he was re-elected by 10,000,000 votes.

The surprising thing in the present Silly Season flurry is merely that the White House wanted it known that it had canceled out, and the *Tribune* wanted it known that it wanted back.

If Billie Sol Estes were a noble and misunderstood character hounded by a wicked press, and if President Kennedy had been suffering under hostile newspaper criticism since entering the White House, the thing might be understandable, but neither point is true. The Estes case is still an unexplained mess and the President has been getting a favorable press ever since he rode down the Avenue.

All the engines of publicity have been directed not on his Cabinet, which is a collection of competent but unspectacular technicians, but on him and his family. Never in recent American history has such a humiliating blunder as Cuba been passed over so lightly. Ninety per cent of the criticism has gone with him, but that other 10 per cent somehow ruffles his feathers.

Especially in the Silly Season. Then the soft winds come up the Potomac from Carolina, and Khrushchev begins to stir, and the Congress dawdles and complains, and Presidential aides, genuinely sympathetic about the burdens of the Boss, tell him about all those journalistic rascals prowling on the loose, and every day there is old Billie Sol.

It's a hard life, all right, but the thought here is that he'd still feel better if he read Buchwald.

DECEMBER 24, 1962[1]

A Letter to Santa

DEAR SANTA: ALL I WANT FOR CHRISTMAS IS *The New York Times*. I don't ask for any of these new fur bed sheets, or electric socks or automatic spaghetti winders, but a man is entitled to have old friends around at a time like this.

Somebody struck the *Times* in the belief that it's a newspaper, but that is obviously ridiculous. The *Times* is a public institution, like the Yankees or Barney Baruch. When everything else is changing, the *Times* remains the same—typographical errors and all.

Reading the *Times* is a life career, like raising a family—and almost as difficult. But I've become accustomed to its peculiar ways and can't break the habit. It is a community service, like plumbing. It will light more fires and line more shelves and cover up more rugs on a snowy day than any other publication in the

[1] Written during the long New York newspaper strike of 1962-3.

world, and I need it, Mister, especially at Christmas.

This is the season of peace and somehow—I don't know why —peace seems to have a better chance in the *Times*. Everybody else seems to be shouting at us and giving the human race six weeks to get out. But the *Times* is always saying that there was trouble in the sixteenth century, too. It never seems to think anything is quite as good or as bad as others make it out to be. It is always saying "on the one hand" and "on the other hand" and in the confusion it manages to give the impression that if things are *that* complicated, nobody will quite know how to start a war.

One of the great things about a newspaper, especially on Sunday, is that you can split the thing up and let everybody in the family settle into a quiet trance with the section he likes best. This cuts down on the noise. You can throw away what you don't want, and the ads don't sing.

The television makes newspapermen feel a little obsolescent once in a while, but it stuns the mind. It makes you listen to all the news you don't want to hear in order to get around to the news you do want to hear. You can't split up Chet Huntley or throw away part of Dave Brinkley—not at least without a fight.

This is one of the great advantages of the *Times:* you get so much more to throw away. It is impenetrable but indispensable. Other papers cover the news and the *Times* smothers it, but the reader benefits. People are always dying in the *Times* who don't seem to die in other papers, and they die at greater length and maybe even with a little more grace.

If a good professor is promoted to the head of the English department at Tufts, or even has the bad luck to be stuck with the presidency of Rutgers, the event is duly recorded—complete with ten-year-old one-column photograph—and is read with pride or sympathy on every campus in the land.

All this, Dear Santa, makes it hard, I know, to get the *Times* down the chimney, but striking the *Times* is like striking an old lady and deprives the community at Christmas of all kinds of essential information. If some recklessly beautiful girl gets married at the Waldorf this week, the television may let us see her gliding radiantly from the church and tossing her bouquet to some lucky member of the Hasty Pudding Club, but what about all those ugly girls who get married every Sunday in the *Times?*

Are they to be ignored just at their unlikely moment of triumph? The pretty girl may marry again, temptation and pretty girls being what they are, but the ugly girl hits the center aisle but once, and the event must be recorded then in the annals of human hope.

Without newspapers the procedures of life change. Tired men, sick of the human race after a long gabby day at the office, cannot escape on the train into the life story of Y. A. Tittle or the political perils of Harold Macmillan, but must go on talking to strangers all the way to Westport. Once home, they are bereft of excuses to avoid fixing that dripping tap or shoveling the walk.

Even history and geography seem different. Yemen was in deep trouble in the *Times* when the strike started, and things weren't very jolly in Afghanistan or Kashmir, but we never discovered how the thing came out.

So please do what you can to get the papers back. It's bad enough on the public but think of a reporter. I've been fielding the *Times* on the first bounce on my front stoop every morning for twenty-five years and it's cold and lonely out there now. Besides, how do I know what to think if I can't read what I write?

P.S.—Don't forget the *Herald Tribune*, too.

JANUARY 12, 1963

Publish and Be Damned?

THE PRESENT SYSTEM OF LABOR-MANAGEMENT RELATIONS IN THE New York newspapers is intolerable for the public, the unions, and the publishers alike. The President of the United States cannot censor the New York papers. The Congress of the United States is specifically forbidden in the First Article of the Bill of

Rights to abridge their freedom, but Bert Powers, the boss of the New York printers, can not only censor them but shut them down.

What is "free" about a press that can be muzzled on the whim of a single citizen? What kind of collective bargaining is it that permits a strike before there is any real bargaining, and postpones negotiation until a time when the publishers would be forced to surrender under the economic pressure of threatened extinction? This is anarchy in what is supposed to be one of the most reasonable elements of our society, and the unions and the publishers will have to end it either by making peace or preparing for war.

One way to make peace is to attack the problem of fear. The publishers are afraid they will be picked off one by one in selective strikes by any one of a dozen unions. The printers are afraid that new automatic machinery will destroy their craft and their security.

These are genuine fears but they are not unprecedented. Edgar Kaiser of the Kaiser Steel Corporation and Dave McDonald of the United Steel Workers have just used a technique to deal with the automation problem. They realized in 1959 that the old bargaining pattern was obsolete. Accordingly, they set up a "long-range committee" composed of three distinguished public members, three union members, and three company members to work out a plan to exploit modern machinery without destroying the security of the present generation of workers.

The Steel Agreement reached this week at Kaiser is not applicable to the wholly different problem of newspaper publishing, but the technique of the long-range committee is. Other unions have settled their differences over money by negotiating a long enough contract to enable the companies to concentrate on higher earnings rather than spending all their time and energy in fear of strikes to come.

If, however, peace cannot be achieved and maintained by these and other proven techniques, then there will have to be war. The papers will have to be published, in New York if possible, elsewhere if not; in union shops if possible, in nonunion shops if not. And they will have to be distributed, through the mails if necessary.

The present situation cannot be accepted in a democratic society. Consider the facts: The President of the United States has used his influence quietly to try to bring about a settlement. The Secretary of Labor has intervened with all the authority of his office. The Governor of New York State and the Mayor of New York City have tried to help—all without managing even to get serious negotiations under way.

So the flow of information in the nation's largest city is left to the play of sheer power, and the power struggle is wildly uneven. For the union is using all its power to stop publication and the owners are not using all their power to publish. This may be an acceptable situation in a meat factory or a steel mill, but newspapers are not pork chops or iron fences. Unless everybody from Jefferson to Mencken and Gerald Johnson has been kidding us, our job is to print the news and raise hell, with the kind permission of Bert Powers if possible but without it if necessary.

I know this view is not shared by all publishers, but reporters are part of this profession too, and if, failing to make an honorable peace, we acquiesce in the proposition that news is a dispensable commodity like soap, then we shall be treated like soap peddlers and deserve it.

Values and duties have become so confused that even the suggestion of publishing without the consent of the unions is now regarded as a declaration of war. How the old editors who founded our press would have hooted at that! This country was created by pamphleteers whose motto was "publish and be damned," and if the Government will defend the right of James Meredith to enter the University of Mississippi, surely it will defend publishers who carry the news through the mails.

This, admittedly, is a last resort. Peace, common sense, and honest collective bargaining are preferable, but if power is to be the only test, then it will have to work both ways. The strike is Bert Powers's "Gun Behind the Door." The mail is ours, and in the final extremity it will have to be used.

The Laggard Press[1]

SOMETHING SEEMS TO BE WRONG WITH THE NEWSPAPER PRESS. Everybody is either criticizing us, or what is worse, ignoring us. Arthur Schlesinger, Jr., told the American Historical Association in Chicago the other day that after working in the White House, he was convinced that newspapers were an unreliable guide for the historian. In Britain the courts have been tossing reporters in jail for refusing to tell where they got their news. In Washington Pierre Salinger is accusing us of managing the news and vice versa. In Cleveland and New York we have had a newspaper strike and lockout for over three months. And when you suggest that the duty to print newspapers in a democracy is more important than the right to strike or lockout, even newspaper folk look at you as if you were out of date and maybe out of your mind. . . .

I think we are in trouble because we have not kept up with the needs of the age. Change is the biggest story in the world today, and we are not covering it adequately; change in the size and movement of our people; change in the nature, location, and availability of jobs; violent change in the cities and on the land; change in the relations between village and town, town and city, city and state, state and nation; and, of course, change in the relations between the empires that are falling and empires that are rising, the old states that are going down and the new ones that are coming up. The population of the country was 97 million in 1913; it is over 187 million now. The labor force of the country has more than doubled—from 30 million to over 71 million—and the farm workers have dropped from 13.5 million in 1913 to 4.5 million now. We have gone in this time from a predominantly rural to a primarily urban society, from an iso-

[1] From remarks on the occasion of the 50th Anniversary of Columbia University Graduate School of Journalism. Published in *The New Republic*, May 4, 1963.

lated country with a defense budget in 1913 of $250 million to the most internationalist and involved nation in all history, with a defense budget of $56.7 billion. There were no radio or television stations in 1913, but 2,500 daily newspapers. This total has declined since then to 1,850. . . .

We are very good at reporting change when it is violent. When the bulldozers start to change property values at home or the guns produce change in Cuba or Vietnam, we are there. But we were not very good about reporting the economic and social conditions in Cuba that produced Castro, and we're remarkably indifferent to the unemployed in Pittsburgh and the social and economic conditions in Harlan County, Kentucky, and the Appalachian South.

What we have done in these last fifty years, I think, is to transfer the reporting habits of the police court and the county court house to the great capitals of the world. This was necessary. In fact, I wish we had retained a little more of the muckraking zeal of those days. But essentially we are—with, of course, notable exceptions—concentrating on the violence of the world as we concentrated on the violence of the police station, and this leaves a vast uncovered area of change.

It is not necessarily violent change that is going to transform the world. In fact, by concentrating on the violent troubles in Berlin, Vietnam, the Congo, Cuba, and elsewhere, we have created the impression that our overseas troubles are endless and maybe even insoluble, whereas the truth is that the United States has handled the violent changes of the past generation fairly well. It is not the earthquakes but the tides of history that are bothering us. It is the slow, quieter changes of the family, the scientific laboratory, and the electronic computer that are changing the fabric of the world, and it is the reporting of these changes that leaves so much to be desired.

The question here is merely one of degree. I am not suggesting that we leave spot news to the radio and television. I am merely saying that we should give as much space to this deeper strata of news as we do, say, to women's fashions. We do not make fashion news compete for space with Washington spot news. We say that we are going to allocate a few columns to fashions "for another reason." I think we should do at least as much for reports of these quiet revolutions in our cities, laboratories, factories, and farms. And the "other reason" here is fairly plain: for unless we report these changes, our people will not adapt to them, and every civilization must either adapt or perish.

When Woodrow Wilson called the reporters to his office for the first time in 1913, he said to them: "The news is the atmosphere of public affairs. Unless you get the right setting to affairs—disperse the right impression—things go wrong. . . ." The atmosphere of change was in the air in 1913 when Wilson made that remark, but we failed to make our people conscious of it, and a world war broke out the following year. We have been in four wars in these fifty years, and unless we adjust to change, we shall probably have some more.

Is the American newspaper doing all it can to make people aware of change? The answers, of course, vary a great deal, but in my view too many newspapers are not only underplaying change on their news pages, but are deploring change, inciting opposition to change, and perpetuating rather than destroying popular illusion on their editorial pages.

Part of the trouble, I believe, is that we have not really thought through a modern definition of news. Nobody questions that a splashy revolution in Guatemala is news, but file 1,000 words on the social and political conditions there that will probably cause a revolution next year, and see what happens on the desk of most American papers. Maybe you'll get it in if it's a dull day, and maybe you won't. Sometimes I think we'll do anything for Latin America except read about it. Things don't have to "happen" to be news. They can just be going on quietly, like the unemployment in Pittsburgh or the boom in Houston, or the allocation of most of our scientists to the Pentagon, the Space Agency, and the Atomic Energy Commission. Ideas are news, but they don't always get into the paper. Let Chairman Miller of the Republican National Committee say for the fiftieth time that we should blockade Cuba and tear down the wall in Berlin, and he will be sure to get in the press, but let some thoughtful but unknown professor suggest that we should have a peace plan for

Cuba in case one day Castro collapses—which is not a bad idea—and he'll be lucky to get a brief notice outside his home town.

I think we have to rethink not only our definition of news but the allocation of our reporters. We are not covering our own country as well as we should—maybe not even as well as we cover some other countries. Like officials in Washington, we suffer from Afghanistanism: if it's far away, it's news, but if it's close at home, it's sociology. You can get the cream of the graduation class at Columbia to go to Ethiopia for the Peace Corps or *The New York Times,* but try to get them to find out what's going on in the south side of Chicago!

This would change, I'm sure, if we gave men time to do a serious job of reporting on the south side of Chicago and let them move on from there to probe into other areas of poverty and unrest. Also, as this kind of material increased in our newspapers, the attitude of the public toward newspapers would change for the better, and the quality of the men attracted to our profession would improve. For unless I'm wildly mistaken, the people of this country would welcome thoughtful reporting of important changes in our society, and might increase their support and respect for the American newspaper as a result. . . .

7

THE U.S. AND THE WORLD

Christmas in London

BRITAIN TRIED HARD TO BE MERRY TODAY ON ITS FIFTH WAR-
time Christmas, but it tried so hard and failed so miserably
that it seems even a little grimmer tonight than it did before. The
plain truth is that this is an island of lonely people—American
soldiers standing around the Rainbow Club chewing the national
cud of discontent; lonely old couples evacuated from their familiar dwellings; lonely young women whose men have been gone
overseas for years; lonely parents whose sons are gone, many of
them forever, and whose daughters are in services in the factories
or on the land, far from home.

There is real hope in Britain this Christmas, which is something, and there is still gentility and goodwill, which are a great
deal, but the fifth Christmas is worse than all the rest on this
basic question of the break-up of family life. Now more than 90
per cent of the families on this island are broken up for one
reason or another. While this is necessary and the British people
can stand it 364 days out of this year and, if necessary, 364 days
out of next, on this one particular day it just knocks all the
merriness out of them.

Even the children, with that divine imagination and with all
those wonderful mysterious bombed houses to play in, are less
enchanted than before. Most of them, of course, do not miss the
shiny metal toys that other happier generations enjoyed. The
6,000,000 children less than 8 years old who never knew the
brightness of the old Christmases do not miss what they cannot
remember. But the children who have learned to believe in Adolf
Hitler cannot very well believe in Santa Claus, and that must be
considered one of the important minor events of the war.

The American invasion Army here tried to compensate for

their loneliness in many ways. In almost every camp they invited the children of overseas British soldiers to their camps and plied them with candy, cookies, and many other things, like oranges, that have almost departed from memory in this island.

As many soldiers as could find seats or standing room went to the thirty-two plays that are running in London. A number of boys from home were introduced to their first pantomime at the Coliseum, where *Humpty-Dumpty* was playing, and at His Majesty's Theatre, where *Cinderella* was on. But mainly they sat around their camps or went into the nearest town and indulged in the things in which soldiers indulge when they are on leave and bored.

On the whole, however, neither the British people nor the American soldiers solved that problem of loneliness. Despite all the promises of the Ministry of Food, the turkey and the beef did not quite go around, the whiskey was scarce, and the beer was weak. Even if all these things had been available in the right quantity or strength they would not have made up for the empty chairs.

In short, it was not a very happy Christmas, though perhaps it justifies a hopeful conclusion: In war, Hitler said, the people will come to realize that the State is the most important unit of society and the people will learn to cry out for the State. Maybe he was right about the Germans, but he was wrong again about the Americans and the British. Our men are looking to the family and not to the State, and this fact was never more apparent than in Britain on this Christmas night.

Siberia and Surprises

ONE PARADOX OF THE SOVIET UNION THAT THIS VAST, UNTAMED stretch of the country makes so clear is that it is talking about catching up with the United States before it has caught up with itself.

Siberia looks the way the American Middle West must have looked in its infancy. It is all big sky and boundless forests and prairies; unfenced, unconquered, and full of startling contrasts.

Vice President Richard M. Nixon flew here from Leningrad, more than 2,000 miles away, in four and a half hours this afternoon. When his party landed—so fast that the Soviet jets had to release parachutes to prevent them from overrunning the runway —there were fourteen new TU-104 commercial jets on the field.

Five minutes after Mr. Nixon left the airport, he was passing on the northern outskirts of Novosibirsk log cabins that might have been there in the days of Ivan the Terrible. Half an hour after weaving through an incredibly lovely sky in the descent through mountainous silver clouds from 35,000 feet, the Vice President was passing duck ponds and pony carts with old-fashioned halters over the ponies' heads, like haloes.

The main roads were cement in the town, but side roads were reminiscent of the old days in the American West, when there were signs reading: "Choose your rut carefully. You'll be in it for the next twenty-five miles."

This is a no-nonsense town, full of vitality and mud. On his way into the city, the Vice President saw many new apartment houses under construction next to some appalling slums collapsing under the merciless weight of the winter's snows. Yet when he got to a machine-tool factory here this evening, he was shown heavy machine tools of the most modern type for export not only to Communist China and Eastern European nations but also to Britain.

There was no soap when he arrived at his dacha and the towel was like a wire mitt. But he went to the Opera House and saw a superb performance of *Swan Lake* before an enthusiastic audience of more than 2,000, dressed as if ready for a football game. This is the way it has been for Mr. Nixon ever since he arrived. Nothing has quite fit the popular American image of the Soviet Union, just as the Soviet image of the United States is a vast distortion.

Mr. Nixon is essentially a political specimen, carefully in tune with the political winds on Capitol Hill. Accordingly, he has come here either believing or feeling that he has to pay attention to the popular political conceptions and prejudices of Capitol Hill. What he has seen, however, has not been the great, monolithic, single-minded, unified Soviet state, but a more diversified community of people, particularly in Siberia, than he had expected.

It is not that Mr. Nixon's basic conception of the Soviet Government has been changed in any important way. What has been changed, however, are those general surface impressions about people and places and popular attitudes of mind.

For example, Siberia is supposed to be a cold place, but Mr. Nixon would never testify to this on the basis of his reception here today. In all the many receptions he has had in his political life and may have in the future, it is unlikely that he will ever forget the warmth and friendliness of the people here.

Even the technical arrangements for his visit have been a great surprise. When he first proposed to Soviet officials that he bring nearly one hundred newspapermen into Siberia, the officials were appalled. At first they insisted that they could accommodate only fourteen. Mr. Nixon made an issue of this and finally it was agreed that despite communications difficulties and housing problems, the Soviet hosts would receive in this "closed" city their critical journalistic guests.

What has happened here has been quite the opposite of what was expected. It is true that in this city of 887,000 there is no commercial hotel. The reporters had to be housed on the edge of the city, four or five to a room, but other facilities were much better than expected. In fact, it has been easier and quicker to telephone this dispatch from Novosibirsk to London than to telephone previous dispatches on this visit from Moscow to London.

There has been a lot of talk about this being the Chicago of the Soviet Union. This is not an accurate image to an American, except perhaps in the sense of the vitality and spirit of Chicago. Novosibirsk, except for its purely modern aspects, is perhaps much more like Kansas City of seventy-five years ago.

In a sense the Nixon visit to Siberia illustrates the essential success of the United States–Soviet "people to people" program. The objective of this program was that it should help modify popular prejudices on both sides, and the Vice President's trip to Siberia has certainly done that.

APRIL 12, 1961

The United States and Cuba: The Moral Question

PRESIDENT KENNEDY IS NOW DEEPLY INVOLVED IN A MORAL AND political question that has troubled statesmen and philosophers ever since the days of Pericles. This is how to reconcile the nation's self-interest with its ideals and treaty commitments.

The self-interest of the nation undoubtedly requires the overthrow of the Cuban Government of Fidel Castro, which is providing a political and, increasingly, a military base for Communism in the Caribbean. But how far can the United States pursue this objective by secretly arming and training the anti-Castro refugees without misleading its own people and violating its treaty commitments under the Charters of the Organization of American States and the United Nations? For a democratic nation whose foreign policy rests on vast catalogues of treaties all over the world and on opposing the use of proxy armies and force by the Communists in Laos and elsewhere, this is a difficult question.

In fact, Presidents Jefferson, Monroe, and McKinley all discussed the dilemma of national self-interest and national ideals in relation to Cuba, and the surprising thing about it is that while the papers have been full of reports of U.S. aid to overthrow Castro, the moral and legal aspects of the question have scarcely been mentioned.

Thomas Jefferson was troubled about the conflict between the nation's interest in Cuba and international law as early as 1823. At that time President Monroe was drafting his Doctrine to oppose European intervention in this hemisphere and wrote to Jefferson asking him what he thought.

Jefferson replied: "I candidly confess that I have ever looked on Cuba as the most interesting addition which could ever be made to our system of states . . . Yet, as I am sensible that this can never be obtained . . . but by war . . . I have no hesitation in abandoning my first wish. . . ."

John Quincy Adams, then Secretary of State, expressed the same view that annexation of Cuba was in our self-interest, but in a letter to the U.S. Minister to Spain likewise drew back from proposing the use of force to achieve the end.

President McKinley, in 1897, disclaimed any intention of forcible annexation of Cuba, but before long was embarked upon the "capricious crusade" to free Cuba from Spanish "despotism, corruption, and cruelty."

These cases, of course, are not very similar to the present situation. The menace to the nation from Spain was certainly not comparable to the menace of Communism in the hemisphere today, but the moral dilemma of backing an invasion of a country to which we are treaty-bound under the American system nevertheless remains.

Maybe Jefferson and Adams were right in thinking that the annexation of Cuba was essential to the security of the United

States. It may even be that in taking the Philippines after the Spanish-American War we took the wrong islands, but at least in 1823 and 1898, despite all the noisy jingoism, the issues of right and wrong were debated in the Congress and in the country.

No such debate is going on now. President Kennedy and his advisers are discussing the question on an urgent basis, but the Congress is not talking about it, the press is ignoring the moral aspects of the question, nobody knows where the funds are coming from or where they are going, though Article 15 of the O. A. S. treaty, which we have signed, specifically declares: "No state or group of states has the right to intervene directly or indirectly, for any reason whatever, in the internal or external affairs of any other state."

Obviously, if this principle were followed in any and all circumstances, the Castro Government could build up an arsenal of missiles and missile bases which could threaten the security of the entire hemisphere. Accordingly, nobody here is suggesting that political realism be abandoned for a blind and legalistic idealism, but this country does depend on treaties being honored all over the world, and the defense of the West rests not only on physical power but on the moral and intellectual allegiance of peoples in the hemisphere and elsewhere.

It may be that overriding questions of national security are involved in Cuba and that, in these days of subversion and indirect aggression, these things justify the pursuit of national security without regard to national laws or international treaties. But if we have reached that point over the deteriorating military situation in Cuba, a government of laws should at least let the people know.

"To See Oursels As Ithers See Us"

IN TIME AND ENERGY PRESIDENT KENNEDY HAS PAID A HIGH PRICE for the personal friendship of world statesmen, but sometimes the results are equal to the cost.

This has been true of his conversations with Prime Minister Nehru of India, not because they agreed about the contemporary political issues of testing nuclear weapons or defending Southeast Asia—they didn't agree at all on these—but because Nehru emphasized things which Washington is sometimes inclined to minimize or forget.

For example, Nehru arrived in the capital at a time when Washington was preoccupied with military power and economic growth and other material things, but Nehru talked not about the power of America but about its spirit and philosophy. "Whenever I have come here," he said, "I have been deeply impressed not only by this great country, but, if I may say so, even more so by the popular goodwill and friendship that I met everywhere . . . The relationships of countries are more basic, I think, or should be more basic, than temporary political events that could happen."

In his private conversations at the White House and elsewhere here he has struck this same theme: that spirit is also power, that the imponderables of life are sometimes more important than the ponderables of politics, and that these things should not be forgotten in the savage controversies of the cold war.

Reflective foreigners have been stressing this point about the spirit of America even since the beginning of the Republic. What we take for granted, they have had a way of emphasizing since the days of Thomas Paine and Tocqueville. While we have been talking about being "bigger and better," they have been talking about American decency and equality, goodness and fairness and friendliness. This was the point Thomas Huxley made at the founding of The Johns Hopkins University of 1876, one hundred years after the founding of the Republic:

"To an Englishman landing upon your shores for the first time, traveling hundreds of miles through strings of great and well-ordered cities, seeing your enormous actual, and almost infinite potential, wealth in all commodities . . . there is something sublime in the vista of the future . . .

"Do not suppose that I am pandering to what is commonly understood by national pride. I cannot say that I am in the slightest degree impressed by your bigness or your material resources, as such. Size is not grandeur and territory does not make a nation. The great issue . . . is what are you going to do with all these things?"

Lord Bryce, in his monumental study of *The American Commonwealth*, asked the same question, but like Nehru he was even more impressed with America's spirit than with its material resources, and Jacques Maritain, a contemporary Frenchman, made the same point in his *Reflections on America:* "The supreme value in the American scale of values," he said, "is goodness; human reliability, goodwill, devotion, helpfulness . . . I am speaking of the accepted scale of values that people have in their minds and use in the conversation of ordinary life as well as in their external social behavior."

Nehru's point was that America was not alone now in having material power, but that, in the struggles of the contemporary world, it had a human power to add to its material power and that this should not be underestimated, especially in its relations with Asia.

For example, in his discussions here on the problem of Laos and South Vietnam, Nehru has emphasized that it was important to think, not only of opposing the power of the Communist invaders, but of the consequences of sending American troops into the front lines there. His view, right or wrong, is that American intervention would not only tarnish the American reputation in that part of the world, but give the Communists precisely what they need—namely, the argument that they were fighting "foreign intervention" by white troops from the West. He believes that the Soviet Union has intervened in Vietnam and Laos not to help the Chinese Communists there, but to prevent them from taking over the whole of Southeast Asia.

Whether this is right is anybody's guess, but Nehru's security is more at stake there than ours; he has his representatives in Peking; he knows more than anybody else in the free world about the immigration of millions of Chinese Communists into Tibet, and the pressure of China's rising population, now increasing by 16,000,000 a year, for living room in areas between Communist China and the Indian border.

Accordingly, Nehru's visit, coming as it does just when General Maxwell Taylor has returned from Vietnam with his report on what President Kennedy should do there, at least gives Washington a wider view of the problem. The Indian Prime Minister always divides Washington politically, but he gives the White House something to think about.

HAMILTON, BERMUDA

DECEMBER 22, 1961

What the Airplane
Did to Diplomacy

THE KENNEDY-MACMILLAN CONFERENCE IN BERMUDA WAS ALMOST the last in a disappointing year of personal diplomacy. In fact it is hard to remember a year in which there were so many splashy meetings of world leaders with so few tangible results. President Nkrumah of Ghana was President Kennedy's first major visitor of the year, and after what was billed as a successful conference Nkrumah went home and not only oriented his policy toward Moscow but established a kind of bush-league dictatorship at home. The Kennedy–De Gaulle meeting in Paris in May was proclaimed a triumph and was followed almost at once by one of the most quarrelsome periods of U.S.-French relations since the war. When the President met Nikita Khrushchev in Vienna early in June their talks were officially described as "useful," whereupon the President returned to Washington and called up the reserves. There were many others, now largely forgotten, which no doubt improved personal relations among the leaders for a few days, but the last of the really "successful" talks was with Prime Minister Nehru of India, who went home and ordered the invasion of Goa. Why, then, do these conferences go on? What do they achieve? And why do they raise hopes which are so quickly dispelled?

They go on for a variety of reasons: political leaders are restless and they have airplanes. The Communists have introduced the idea that nobody can reach big decisions except the big men at the top, and this dubious doctrine has spread to the West. Also this is an era of powerful personalities at the top and of technicians in the Foreign Offices. Kennedy, Macmillan, De Gaulle, and Adenauer are all to a large extent their own foreign ministers, and they are served by foreign secretaries who have neither commanding personalities of their own nor powerful political followings in their own countries: Rusk in Washington, Lord Home in Britain, Couve de Murville in France, Gromyko in the Soviet Union, and Schroeder in West Germany. Accordingly, personal meetings between the heads of Government have become a kind of status symbol of the governing trade, and they are self-perpetuating. For example, when President Kennedy goes to Europe and sees Khrushchev, De Gaulle, and Macmillan but not Adenauer, it is felt in Germany that somebody might think Adenauer is slipping. So Adenauer then goes to Washington, which of course proves that he is not slipping, but gives London the impression that maybe Macmillan is slipping. So here we are in Bermuda. These meetings soon create a feeling of disappointment because somehow the people expect meetings of the big men to do big things.

The truth of the matter, however, is that Kennedy and Macmillan are not dealing with the big question of the fundamental relationship between the United States and Britain in the future, though they should be, but with specific questions on nuclear testing, Berlin, and trade, which in the past would have been dealt with by their foreign secretaries and ambassadors. This does not mean that these meetings are not useful. Both the President and the Prime Minister will go away from here with a more accurate picture of the politicial problems facing the other, but they will not have time to sort out the complicated aspects of nuclear testing, Berlin, and trade, and they are not likely to come to grips with the big question of Britain's changing relationships with the United Nations, the European Common Market, and the British Commonwealth. Ever since the war the British have been trying to find a practical solution to the problem of what Sir Winston Churchill has called Britain's three intersecting policy circles with America, Europe, and the Commonwealth. This problem has now reached a critical phase. The British special relationship with Washington is now extremely vague. Macmillan has moved toward the Common Market, but is not yet in and may even have to fight an election before he knows whether it is prudent to go in. And the fight over British membership in the Common Market has confused London's relations with the Commonwealth. This is the kind of big question heads of government would have dealt with in the past, but the fashion today is to deal not with fundamentals but with the technicalities of other questions relating to other powers. No doubt Kennedy and Macmillan will have a lot to say about De Gaulle, Adenauer, and Khrushchev, but very little about this truly critical problem of the future of Anglo-American relations. This is why most of these big meetings produce small results. For they tend to deal with the immediate problems of the moment rather than the enduring relationships of the future. The modern heads-of-government conference is personal, ceremonial, and technical and is soon overtaken by events. Accordingly it is hard to remember what all those other conferences of 1961 actually accomplished, almost as hard as to remember what happened in the other Bermuda conferences of the Fifties.

The Senate and the UN

MANY OF THE CRITICISMS OF THE UNITED NATIONS IN THE U.S. Senate are true. Let us admit it: the UN has not achieved peace or justice. It has not ended the wars in Laos, or Vietnam or the Congo. It has soaked the rich to help the poor. It gives equal voting rights in the Assembly to small states and large states. It plays politics with great events. And darned if that is not precisely true of the United States Senate as well.

Senator Mike Mansfield of Montana complained the other day that it was unfair to have the same vote in the Assembly for the little countries as for big countries. Senator Richard Russell of Georgia pointed out yesterday that little Gabon had as much voting power as the United States, which has 433 times as many people.

Hard cheese, said the Senator (who did not rush to support the Supreme Court's recent reapportionment decision), but this, of course, is what happens in the U.S. Senate. Montana with 674,767 people in the 1960 census, Georgia with 3,943,116, and New York with 16,782,304 all have two votes in the U.S. Senate, and Mr. Mansfield of Montana is Majority Leader of the place, and a good one, too.

Life is unfair, as President Kennedy observed the other day. And unequal, too, but it is unequal and unfair and imperfect everywhere, including the U.S. Senate. The Armed Services Committee, which Senator Russell heads, hasn't stamped out war in Laos, Vietnam, or the Congo either, and Georgia hasn't rejected its share of Federal funds raised in those big states like New York.

The Senators who oppose bailing out the UN because of its failures are making some good points, but they don't go far enough. They liked the UN when the U.S. controlled the voting.

They approved bloc-voting in the UN when those two unlikely characters Nelson Rockefeller and Adlai E. Stevenson established the bloc-voting practice back there in the first UN meeting in San Francisco and London in 1945–6. But our blocs are not so large now and this is a problem.

We are in danger of losing control of the Assembly and even of seeing it used against the principles of the UN itself. The Senators are right in saying that the UN cannot deal effectively with direct confrontations between the great powers, that the Security Council is paralyzed in such cases by the veto, and that the General Assembly is an increasingly capricious and unwieldly political instrument.

But so is the U.S. Senate. Also, it was a United States Senator, Arthur Vandenberg of Michigan, who turned the UN General Assembly into "the town meeting of the world"—his phrase—and the United States Senate that rejoiced at the transfer of peace-enforcement power from the Security Council to the Assembly.

This transfer of power revolutionized the UN, but the U.S. did it, and it was no secret then that the colonial empires were being liberated and the size of the General Assembly increased. What is ironical, and even vaguely amusing now, is that Senators, of all people, should be complaining that the Assembly talks too much, that it trades votes, that it is untidy financially, and that it is not the answer to all the world's problems.

As Churchill said when the Germans got bogged down in the winter of the Soviet Union, "They should have known that it snowed in Russia." The Senators are no doubt justified in rebelling against the tiresome State Department and White House cliché that the United Nations is "the last great hope for peace in the world"—it is no such thing—but all parliamentary bodies tend to be oversold. Even the U.S. Senate is constantly being advertised, usually by Senators, as "the greatest deliberative body in the world."

What is "deliberative" about the present Senate debate on the UN and world affairs? It is talking as if the UN somehow had some mysterious power of its own, that it can stop aggression in Goa that Senators themselves don't want to send U.S. troops to stop, that in some curious way it is responsible for the world's problems instead of merely reflecting those problems.

The UN, however, is not wholly unlike the Senate. It is not responsible for friction in Berlin, any more than the Senate is responsible for unemployment in Detroit—probably not as much. Both merely mirror the problems placed before them and deal with them imperfectly in an obviously imperfect world.

Besides, Senators had better be careful about refusing to pay for political mistakes. For if this idea were to spread, they might soon be as broke as the UN itself. They voted $300 million for Laos, which vanished in the jungle fogs changing nothing. But they have to go on, and they will, because the alternatives are worse. Like the General Assembly, the Senators like to talk, but in the end they seldom have the courage of their prejudices.

NOVEMBER 4, 1962

A Nation Learns

a Lot in a Crisis

A NATION LEARNS A LOT ABOUT ITSELF IN A CRISIS. HUMAN BEINGS can adjust to almost anything except hanging, but they never know it until they are tested. Therefore, before everybody returns to the normal warfare of family, commercial, and political life, let it be noted that this country behaved very well in its first direct challenge from another atomic power.

There was a slight run on canned goods and the White House received a lot of calls and messages from the pacifist fringe, but on the whole, people went along about as before, unprepared and unafraid.

This troubles many sensitive men and women, who put it down to ignorance and are afraid that the human family will come to accept the idea of atomic war, not as any apocalyptic threat to the race but merely as something terrible that can eventually be borne like other wars of the past.

It is a serious point. In those olden days "before Man orbited and Woman twisted" survival depended on action. Success attended the ancient races of man who killed the most game, defied the unexplored seas, attacked the enemy before he was himself attacked, and used his power to the full. Thus, the impulse to sudden action was deeply ingrained and carried over into the atomic age when preservation does not necessarily depend upon action, but upon careful reflection about releasing uncontrollable power.

This is the idea behind the pacifist letters to the White House, and yet the American people, for all their affluence, are still greatly influenced by the frontier, still put action first when challenged on vital matters, and, despite all other differences or private concerns, support the President when he says the security or honor of the nation is at stake.

Here is where the leaders of the Soviet Union made their mistake on Cuba. They have swallowed their own baloney for so long that they think we are moved more by Wall Street than by Main Street, and forget how close we are in history to a frontier as harsh as their own Siberian plains.

The effect of all this on President Kennedy, now at the halfway mark in his term, has been profound. He and his associates are the instruments of the American spirit for the time being, and they have interpreted it in the last two weeks with remarkable sensitivity, accuracy, and skill.

In doing so, they did not have the guidance of a long tradition such as the British Cabinet system, but improvised as they went along. Two weeks ago they were a collection of highly intelligent amateurs, skilled in the arts of politics on Capitol Hill, of university life in Cambridge, Mass., and elsewhere, of making automobiles in Detroit, and of doing a lot of other things that had nothing to do with the mentality, the objectives, and the power of the Soviet Union.

Yet in the crisis they discovered that, whatever their background, they were able, under pressure, and almost instinctively, to reach a consensus, first, about the fundamental nature of the Soviet challenge; second, that the challenge had to be faced, whatever the dangers; and third, after very limited discussion about whether to bomb or blockade, what to do about it.

President Kennedy did not have to decide between one group of advisers who wanted to bomb the missile bases and another who wanted to blockade, though some started with one conviction and some with the other. The trend of policy was reached very quickly by one argument which moved everybody in the improvised "war council"—politicians, professors, professional soldiers, lawyers, and foreign service officers—namely (1) that the main objective was the removal of the bases, not the removal of Castro; and (2) that the history and philosophy of this nation required that the thing be done with a minimum loss of life.

Having gone through this experience, this is no longer a collection of amateurs in Washington, but a far more confident Government, not divided department from department, or party from party, but a much more united instrument of the spirit and purpose of the nation. In this sense Khrushchev has done America a favor by his challenge. He has enabled us to see what unites us, rather than what divides us; and we can only hope that he now sees it too.

De Gaulle Is Analyzed
by Uniquack

A PERPLEXED LADY IN CALIFORNIA WANTS TO KNOW WHAT UNI-quack thinks about the present state of the world, and since we have nothing else to do, we got the thing out and put some questions to it. Uniquack, for the benefit of any newcomers, is an electronic truth detector which, when seated in a comfortable room by a glowing fire and supplied with sufficient quantities of alcohol, can translate and decontaminate official documents, and even understand politicians.

QUESTION: All right, machine, let's start with an easy one. Please explain General de Gaulle.

ANSWER: Certainly. General de Gaulle, like vintage wine and Brigitte Bardot, is one of the great natural resources of France. He is a symbol of his country's regret and glory. He is unique among the statesmen of the Western world because (a) he knows what he wants, (b) speaks sparingly and eloquently, (c) doesn't give a damn for popularity, and (d) uses the word "no." He's sort of the opposite of that insular, seafaring type Mr. Micawber: he's always looking for something to turn down.

Q—Please don't be frivolous today, machine. The lady in California wants serious answers about the fight between Kennedy and De Gaulle.

A—Well, the difference between them comes down to this: Kennedy thinks the cold war is still serious, and De Gaulle thinks Kennedy has won it and doesn't know it. Kennedy thinks the problem in Europe is military and De Gaulle thinks it's political. The General is not worried about Russian soldiers taking over Europe but about British statesmen and American salesmen, generals, and politicians taking it over.

Q—I see. Coca-colonialism is the enemy.

A—Precisely. He sees time and history in another way. He tunes in the world on his private wavelength. He cannot forgive the Anglo-Saxons for the favors they have done him. Having lost an empire with the help of an army, he is determined to gain a continent without one.

Q—You mean he just doesn't like us.

A—No, it isn't that. He just doesn't want to marry us. Actually, in his own way he is paying us a tribute. He thinks we have saved Europe and split the Communist world and he doesn't trust his own people to stand up to our barbarian ways.

Q—So he would have us go away.

A—No, he merely wants American protection without domination, and no incineration without representation. What's wrong with that?

Q—He wants to have it both ways.

A—Certainly, and he'll get it because we can't hurt him without hurting Europe and ourselves. He thinks the centuries balance the books: in the nineteenth, America united and developed behind the sea power of Europe; in the twentieth, Europe will unite and develop behind the rocket power of America. It's all very simple.

Q—You are beginning to sound slightly Gaullist and subversive, machine. I suppose De Gaulle thinks he will unite Europe.

A—No, not precisely. He believes Europe will be united, not by De Gaulle, or Macmillan, Kennedy, or Khrushchev, but by Mao Tse-tung. He thinks the Chinese Communists will scare some sense into the Russians, and that the Russians will eventually come to terms with De Gaulle and Western Europe.

Q—It's all very tidy, isn't it? But when is "eventually" and how will the Germans like this French Rapallo?

A—"Eventually" in De Gaulle's mind is sooner than you think. He has already made a trade agreement with Moscow this weekend and even if the Germans don't like it, only Russia can put the two Germanys together. . . .

Q—What about Khrushchev's role in all this?

A—A very cunning and devious man. He has deceived the West. In the past, when the Western allies began quarreling with each other he has always made some violent lurch that has brought them back together. We have come to count on this. Fear is our ally. We need his hostility more now than ever, but he has double-crossed us. He is now talking peace and trade and sending messages of condolence on the death of Robert Frost. It is a very serious situation.

q—And the British?

a—They will never forgive De Gaulle. An Englishman can stand anything except being rejected by a club—especially when he thinks he's too good for it anyway.

q—And finally, what should Washington do?

a—Shut up. Tight.

q—An original idea, but how?

a—Any official who makes a speech, holds a press conference, peddles a Polaris submarine, mentions the words De Gaulle, Napoleon, or Joan of Arc, or talks even privately about Canada for at least a month should be fired.

q—And meanwhile?

a—Let them think.

q—Really, machine, you have the most preposterous ideas.

SEPTEMBER 4, 1963

How to Make Things Worse
Than They Really Are

This year's fashions in diplomacy, like this year's dresses by Dior, leave very little to the imagination. They disclose more than they conceal: naked diplomacy is now the fad.

President Kennedy, unhappy about the Government and policies of South Vietnam, simply goes on the television and says so.

President de Gaulle of France, displeased with both the Communists and the Americans in Vietnam, simply invites both of them publicly to get out.

The recent test-ban hearings dramatize the new style. Sign the treaty with the Soviet Union, the Administration told the Senate, because we are way ahead of them militarily and could wipe them out if they attacked us, and could stay ahead of them, even if they cheated, which they probably will.

This is at least original. The traditional diplomacy was private and discreet. Over a period of 300 years the nations developed an elaborate catalogue of cautious understatements which enabled them to speak frankly to one another without causing undue public excitement.

Diplomacy aimed at precision, and it was assumed that it was difficult to be precise in public. Diplomacy was the application of intelligence and, above all, tact to the conduct of relations between nations, and it relied upon what Sir Harold Nicolson called "that guarded understatement which enables diplomatists and ministers to say sharp things to each other without becoming provocative or impolite." Above everything, the old diplomacy avoided involving the prestige or self-esteem of another country and always sought to give the other side a graceful escape from an embarrassing position.

All this, however, is apparently old hat. President Kennedy involved the prestige of both the Diem Government and his own on the TV yesterday. He said bluntly that South Vietnam's repressions of the Buddhists were "very unwise." He added that the South Vietnam Government was "out of touch" with its own people. He invited Diem to make changes in the policies and personnel of the South Vietnam Government, said he didn't think the war could be won unless changes were made, and closed his lecture with the assurance that the United States would stay on there, regardless of whether Diem paid any attention to his advice.

Under the old diplomacy, the United States would have expressed its views and complaints privately, and left it to Diem to wonder whether he could both reject American advice and count on continued American aid. But that isn't what the President did. He both threatened and reassured Diem. He said: Change or we'll string along with you anyway. Now if Diem changes his policies and his Government, it will be said that he did so under public pressure from the United States; and if he doesn't change, the President will be charged with backing what he himself has called a losing policy.

Some open diplomacy in a democracy is desirable, or at least unavoidable. The test-ban treaty with the Soviet Union had to be ratified by the Senate. Not only the Senate but the country had to know why—after a generation of broken promises and savage controversy with Moscow—we were agreeing with them to a test ban which we could not verify on the ground.

This involved the Kennedy Administration in an awkward position. It felt obliged to argue that this was such a good thing for us that one wondered why the Soviet Union felt it was good for them. The hearings in some ways increased tension, though the purpose of the treaty was to reduce tensions. Yet this public controversy was probably inevitable and the surprising thing about it is that Moscow has said so little in rebuttal.

No such procedure was required, however, in the case of South Vietnam. The situation there is a mess recommending silence. Nobody quite knows who's in charge. The armed services are divided in their allegiance. No acceptable substitute for Diem has yet appeared, and the Kennedy Administration is not at all sure that it wants the army to get into politics instead of concentrating on fighting the Communists.

The situation was all the more complicated by the fact that Washington's main complaints are really against the powerful members of Diem's own family, so that Diem now either has to ignore Kennedy or turn on his brother and sister-in-law. It was like the head of a foreign government announcing publicly that President Kennedy was pursuing a losing policy, was out of touch with the American people, but might make amends by firing Bobby. Even General de Gaulle hasn't carried the new diplomacy that far.

Why the "Grand Alliance" Is Not So Grand

MUCH OF THE CONFUSION IN AMERICA ABOUT FOREIGN AFFAIRS comes from a tendency to think about allies literally as "friends," to personalize Britain into Macmillan, Vietnam into President Diem or even Mme. Nhu, and to assume that agreeable personal meetings with such political leaders will lead to common understandings and policies.

It is easy to understand how this popular idea developed. The American people like to believe that plain talk and open friendliness can solve almost anything. Eisenhower and Kennedy have both encouraged this illusion. And a whole new school of popular journalism has been built on the technique of explaining nations by telling the personal stories of their leaders.

Yet nothing is more misleading than this romantic and personal approach to foreign affairs. Kennedy's meeting with De Gaulle in 1961 was a triumph that soon developed into a disaster. His meeting with Khrushchev was a disaster that gradually developed into an accommodation. . . .

Some leaders may have the power to determine the policies of their countries by themselves. Maybe De Gaulle can do it for France, but nations usually act in accordance with their own selfish interest regardless of what they have said in some tête-à-tête with Kennedy. Thus, our Democratic "friends" are kicked out as leaders of Honduras and the Dominican Republic, not because those countries are against the Alliance for Progress but simply because the military in those countries are thinking first about themselves.

The United States is bound to have trouble with its allies

because only at the point of imminent war do they all have a common interest in following common policy. And the less the chance of war, the more the allies tend to follow their own devices, which may be what Khrushchev had in mind by reducing tension in the first place.

Also, the United States, facing on both the Atlantic and the Pacific, must have a worldwide policy, while Britain, France, and Germany do not. If Washington allows the Communists to break out anywhere in the world, its policy of containment is in jeopardy elsewhere. So it fights in Vietnam, but the French and British, who are also obliged by treaty to help in Southeast Asia, do not feel that Vietnam is vital to them, so they do nothing there but scoff at our mistakes.

On the other hand, Britain and France felt that they had to fight in Suez to defend their interests, and the United States, opposing the use of force as an instrument of its worldwide policy, refused to go along and even opposed them.

The obvious truth is that the allies differ drastically in power and responsibility; their interests may be common in some places and under some circumstances but not common and even contradictory in others; and the result is, no matter what statesmen say to each other in the glow of private conversation, their geography, history, ideology, and commerce prove to be more powerful than treaties or private personal understandings.

Adenauer and Macmillan are just the first of the old generation of statesmen to leave the stage. Nehru, Chiang Kai-shek, Salazar, Franco, and even Khrushchev, Mao Tse-tung and Tito will follow in due course. Thus, it is not too early to begin thinking about alliances in terms of quality instead of quantity, and of adjusting these relationships to power, responsibility, and common interests, rather than to personality.

Moscow in December

FOR ABOUT A THOUSAND DOLLARS THESE DAYS YOU CAN GO TO Moscow and gather impressions that are probably not worth a dime. But it is a bracing experience and for people who like a long, cold, and expensive trip in the middle of the winter, it really cannot be matched.

Moscow is a city of contrasts. It has one foot on the moon and the other stuck in the mud. It has a new glass and neon-lighted airport where you can buy cut-rate vodka and fur hats. Both are essential in these latitudes for internal combustion.

Downtown there are now over 10,000 taxis, all of which seem to charge from every traffic light, like the kickoff at a football game, and defy pedestrian traffic for all but the most expert broken-field runners. At GUM's department store, they have three fashion shows a day, and at the fancy restaurants, the waiters wear tails and scowl at tips just as they do in New York.

Yet in the freezing suburbs, the old women are still drawing water from outside pumps and carrying it to tipsy old wooden houses that look as though they had been "frozen in the act of collapse." They look like figures in the Grandma Moses pictures that are now showing here at the Pushkin Gallery.

Sometimes the new and the old are combined in charming ways. The place is full of vending machines, and on Gorky Street you can buy a caviar sandwich by putting a coin in the machine and waiting for an old woman to peer out at you and nod. She then makes the sandwich and drops it into the slot. Very good too.

In the last five years Moscow has changed in many subtle ways. Essentially it is the same, but like the country girl who went to town, it has put on a little more rouge, a little more weight, and a few more airs.

Some of the women are now tinting and lacquering their hair in accordance with the latest Paris outrage, and others are wearing flashes of color around their heads. But in the main it is a city of silhouettes, of funereal figures shuffling through the snow against the savage wind, or waiting, always waiting for buses, for newspapers, for groceries, or something else.

I first came here in 1942, when Moscow was under siege from the advancing German Army and the only route of travel from Washington was southward to Brazil, across the South Atlantic to Ascension Island and Accra, and thence across the heart of Africa to the Sudan and northward to Cairo, Teheran, and Moscow. It is an easier and more rewarding journey now.

The progress since then is startling. The ragged ghosts in the dim night streets of those heroic days have disappeared. The people are comfortably and sensibly dressed. They are much better housed than even five years ago, and the Government has completed between the center of the city and Moscow University on the upland fringe what must be the largest and ugliest complex of apartment houses in the history of human habitation.

There is much more money, much more food, and much more vodka around than in the days of Dick Nixon's political invasion of Siberia in 1959. Accordingly—though I did not take any measurements personally—I have the impression that the girth of the Soviet people, calculated at the beam, is increasing at an alarming rate. And in a misspent life around football games, press club bars, political blow-outs, and other alcoholic establishments in America, I have never seen more boozy befuddlement in so short a time.

Yet at other times and places, the Soviet crowds are much better disciplined than our own. At the ballet or theater, for example, they have achieved two remarkable things: they have eliminated that bane of the Broadway theater, the noisy latecomer, and even more commendable, they even seem to have abolished the common cough. How this is done without chloroforming anybody whose nose twitches is not quite clear, but it is obviously one of the great achievements of theatrical history.

What a Westerner misses here is variety, spontaneity, and laughter. It is not merely that the clothes are dark and uniform or that the shops all look alike—this is understandable—but that the faces are uniformly shut and frozen. If they are marching to the New Arcadia, they don't look very happy about it. One almost longs for precisely what they are determined to stamp out: the cult of personality; some sign of individuality or originality; some indication that the human spirit can cry out here in the dim light and be heard.

Moscow is a brooding city, though starkly beautiful in the powdered snow. It is changing all right, but changing this vast continental country is a little like trying to change the Atlantic Ocean. Nevertheless, these are not people to be taken lightly. Any race that can survive the bitter cold of these northern winter nights could conceivably conquer the human race and populate the frozen face of the stars as well. If only they smiled, the prospect for the future would seem more tolerable.

SAIGON, SOUTH VIETNAM
AUGUST 26, 1965

The Alien War

THE WAR IN VIETNAM IS SO ALIEN TO THE AMERICAN EXPERIENCE and such a tangle of conflicting cultures, interests, memories, religions, and personal, regional, and tribal ambitions that it defies precise definition and is almost beyond comprehension. Even the words normally used to describe a war are misleading here. This is not a war in the usual sense. It is a series of violent actions, some rather like Al Capone's gang raids in Chicago, some like the frontier skirmishes in the French and Indian War, still others like the savage encounters between the Americans and the Japanese in the Pacific island caves of twenty years ago—all this with the Strategic Air Command, of all things, bombing guerrillas, of all people, in tunnels in the Vietnamese forests, of all places.

This war needs a new vocabulary. Vietnam is not really a nation but a physical and strategic entity, broken into conspiratorial families, clans, sects, hamlets, and regions by many generations of Mandarin, French, Japanese, and now American influence.

The Prime Minister here in Saigon is not prime. Buddhists and the Catholics bear little relation to Western notions of either Buddhism or Catholicism, and we even have some Chinese mercenaries fighting on our side, one of whom is a bodyguard for Ambassador Henry Cabot Lodge. In this situation, it is almost impossible to perform the reporting function of reducing diversity to identity. All you can do is try to illustrate just how complex human political and military relations are in this part of the world.

The squabbling disunity and suspiciousness of the members of the central Government, for example, are hard to believe. It is not unusual for one member of the South Vietnamese Cabinet to warn the American Ambassador against the dangers of confiding in other members of the same Cabinet. And the presence of two American Ambassadors here has apparently convinced some Vietnamese leaders that one Ambassador was sent here to do business with the Catholics and the other to negotiate a settlement of the war with the Communists through the Buddhists.

Even at this critical point in the war, some important groups here are pressing Ambassador Lodge and General William C. Westmoreland, the United States commander here, to train and arm their private armies outside the command of the South Vietnamese Government.

The Montagnards, for example, are powerful in the Vietnamese highlands. There are about 700,000 of them. The Vietnamese regard them as *moi*—savages—and this only adds to the Montagnard's resentment against the Vietnamese. So the Montagnards want their own army of 50,000 men, and while they do not like the Vietcong, they are threatening to stop fighting unless their demands are met.

The Catholics are both more pliable and more ambitious. The Rev. Hoang Quynh, the 65-year-old leader of the Catholic Citizens Alliances, wants an army of 100,000 Catholics, whom he promises to recruit and lead in an invasion of North Vietnam. Father Quynh is a spare blunt man with short gray hair and a gray bristle beard, who sat in his fortified Phatdiem parish office in Saigon today gurgling on a water pipe and giving his views on the war.

The South Vietnamese, he said, lost more than 60 per cent of the agents they sent into North Vietnam—which is true—because they were not trained properly and not chosen from the districts they were ordered to disrupt. He would do it better, he promised, and he knows where to get the 100,000 men.

The one thing that seems about the same in this as in other wars is that soldiers are interested in women, and this is an increasing problem between the growing American force and the civil population. Father Quynh was interested in this, but his order of priorities was even more interesting.

We must face realities, he said. The Communists would certainly take advantage of the problem. Therefore, he said, it is important to "arrange secure, sanitary, and private conveniences for the comfort of the troops." The Vietnamese are not alarmed by the problem of dealing with Americans, he added. "We dealt with the French," he said.

A day in the country here is equally illuminating about the Vietnamese attitudes toward the war. Haunghia Province lies thirty miles northwest of Saigon. It has a population of 228,000 and not a single doctor. Most of it is under the control of the Vietcong. Even the roads out of Baotrai, the capital, are mined by the Vietcong at night. But the biggest sugar refinery in the country lies in the middle of guerrilla territory, and the Vietcong permit it to operate freely and allow it to ship the sugar to Saigon, no doubt at a price that Al Capone would have admired.

Accordingly, it is a little difficult to tell where the accommodations with the Vietcong end and the war begins, when a man is in the South Vietnamese Army and when he is not. Yesterday's hero is tomorrow's deserter, and war and peace go on in the same village at the same time with astonishing equanimity.

The American bombing in North Vietnam may be an issue in the United States. But the bombing and artillery fire here in South Vietnam are even more remarkable, certainly more casual and, therefore, probably more dangerous.

For example, there was a rumor of a Vietcong unit of some fifty men in the area the other morning when I was in Baotrai. Back of the dusty main street, where the Americans are startling the population by building sidewalks, there was a South Vietnamese Ranger battalion, equipped with 105-mm. and 155-mm. artillery guns, which were firing away in the general direction of where the Vietcong were supposed to be.

Maybe the Vietnamese Rangers had sent out a patrol to make sure that the Vietcong were there, and maybe they had not. The American military advisers thought they had not. We sat in their hut, with the blasts of the guns rattling our back teeth, and talked about what was going on.

"This is yesterday's operation," a serious young American captain said. "We really knew that the Vietcong were out there last night and called for an air strike, but there were no planes available. Now the planes are available, and I just hope the Vietcong are still around, but we don't know."

While he spoke, fighter-bombers were attacking an area about a mile out of town, and life was going on in the street as if nothing more alarming than a fire truck were coming round the corner. Nobody took cover. Actually there was no cover to take.

The women walked along in the dust, resigned as usual to the inexplicable stupidity of the noisy masculine world. The children, some of them no more than 2 and 3 years old and naked as the day they were born, watched the real thing with that same solemn and startled wonder of American kids staying up too late watching violence on television.

None of this gets into the communiqués. It happens sporadically here and there all over the country every day—unreported bombings and unobserved shellings of unchecked enemies in uncertain locations—and what the cost of all this is in human death and suffering and resentment against America or the Vietcong, nobody knows.

And yet this picture of irresponsible violence is also misleading, for while it happens and is true, it is only part of the truth in this complicated world, where the feelings and assumptions of the Western world are so different from the feelings and assumptions of the Oriental world.

"I have been here for a long time," said U. Alexis Johnson, the Deputy American Ambassador, who is returning in a few days to the State Department, "and all I have learned is that no generalization is true, including this one. I cannot make any positive statement about Vietnam that I cannot honestly contradict with another statement. But it is different from anything else in the experience of our country. At least I am sure of that."

SEPTEMBER 12, 1965

The United States and Asia

THE WORLD AT THE MOMENT SEEMS EVEN MORE PERVERSE THAN usual. It is blazing hot in Washington when it is supposed to be cool. India, which invented nonviolence, is at war. Berlin, the flashpoint of Europe, is calm, and the imperious New York Yankees are in sixth place in the American League. It is all a little odd. The Communists are vilifying one another like Eastern and Midwestern Republicans. The Western allies are staggering, blundering, and squabbling like schoolboys. Asia is using the techniques of the West to destroy the dwindling influence of the West, and for the moment a tornado of angry voices dominates the Asian majority of the human race.

All this noisy disorder of little men in big jobs sends a shudder through the rest of the world, and suggests a vast and irreparable breakdown of organized society.

Yet bad as it all looks and sounds—and is—two qualifications probably ought to be made. There is still a great difference between the words and the actions of all these bawling patriots, and there is less military power involved in their dangerous adventures than the headlines seem to suggest.

The Vietcong, for example, are carrying on their war against half a million South Vietnamese and over 100,000 Americans in Southeast Asia with about ten tons of supplies a day from North Vietnam. This amounts to little more than four two-ton trucks full of arms and ammunition every twenty-four hours, and gives some idea of how much trouble can be caused with a little gunpowder, and how hard it is to stop such a trickle of supplies in so large a peninsula.

India and Pakistan have more power, but certainly not enough to wage serious war for a long time over the vast subcontinent of India. They do have the capacity and apparently the irresponsibility to risk the slaughter of a religious war among their peoples, but they are both short of oil and ammunition, and this may limit the consequences of their action.

This is an awkward and disturbing period, but nations no longer resort to total war because of the murder of archdukes. They still talk as if they would bring down the world if they don't get what they demand on Monday morning, but on the whole they do not seem to take their own threats quite as seriously as the headline writers for whom their threats are obviously intended.

The world is naturally horrified by the outbreak of yet another war—this last one between peoples who have lectured the human race on the virtues of philosophy and passive resistance —but even the moral monsters of the world outside the Indian subcontinent seem to have learned to put some limits on the use of military power since the advent of nuclear weapons.

What is surprising in this immense struggle for influence over the unredistributed areas left over from the last world war is not that so much power is being used to control these borderlands of the Communist empire, but that so much power is being held back in the fighting.

The United States may not be prevailing in Vietnam, but it is limiting its war power and limiting its war aims; and China is retaliating mainly with words. Even Sukarno in Indonesia is not acting as viciously as he is talking, and it can be taken for granted that this comparative restraint is not due to any moral scruples on his part.

At least one reason for this is that American power is a restraining influence—from Berlin to India, Pakistan, Vietnam, Korea, and China. Despite all Washington's mistakes of the past in dealing with the postwar redistribution of power and influence in Asia, the influence and power of the United States in that part of the world is still considerable.

Without it Vietnam and probably the rest of Southeast Asia would probably have been taken over by China already, and without the threat of U.S. intervention in the Indian-Pakistani conflict, China would be sorely tempted to intervene in that war in order to expand its influence if not control over the whole Indian subcontinent.

China may still do so. It is too early to tell. People hope vaguely and fear precisely, and for the moment they are fearing a great many alarming things. But other factors are at work for restraint and sanity if not for peace, and the greatest of these is the power of the United States.

Peking's Upside-Down Diplomacy

CHINA SEEMS TO BE TRYING SOMETHING NEW IN THE FIELD OF diplomacy. What she does is the opposite of what she says. What she fears she brings about. What she desires she blocks. It is all a little odd.

"The Chinese people are ready to make the supreme sacrifice," Foreign Minister Chen Yi announced this week, while inviting the United States and its allies to invade China.

"We welcome them to come, to let the Indians come with them, to let the British imperialists come with them, to let the Japanese militarists come with them, and to let those [Soviet] revisionist leaders coordinate the attack. But even then, we'll win victory, for the U.S. and their puppets to send a few million troops to China will not be enough."

This is very interesting coming from a Vice Premier of Communist China and a Marshal of the People's Liberation Army. For it not only scorns about a quarter of the human race but links together the United States, the Soviet Union, the British, the Indians, and the Japanese—all of whom China is hoping to divide.

China wanted to prolong the Indian-Pakistani war, but by the very violence of her ultimatum to India, helped bring about precisely the kind of cease-fire she didn't want. China wanted to weaken the United Nations and split the United States and the Soviet Union, but actually managed to bring Moscow and Washington together on the Indian question and bring most of the world to the support of the United Nations in that conflict.

Not since Stalin frightened Western Europe into the North

Atlantic Alliance and brought into Europe the American Army he wanted to stay at home has there been such a dramatic demonstration of how to bring about precisely the opposite of what was intended.

Peking has been saying for months that the United States and the Soviet Union were working together in world politics—this at a time when the differences between Moscow and Washington over Vietnam had stopped almost all cooperation between them. But China's threat to help Pakistan by coming over the Himalayas into Sikkim and Ladakh actually did bring Moscow and Washington together and didn't even help Pakistan, for the threat was never carried out.

Under this form of upside-down diplomacy, China's words are not a guide to China's actions, but a substitute for them. Peking has been unrestrained in its threats to wipe out American power in Formosa and Vietnam, but has actually been highly restrained in its military response in both places.

There are three places, *The Economist* of London remarked this week, "where China has promised not to stand idly by, and then done just that—the Formosa front, Vietnam, and now the Himalayas. For the coiner of phrases about paper tigers, it is embarrassing . . ."

Chen Yi's comments about the United Nations and nuclear weapons were equally erratic. He called together journalists from countries that are sympathetic to bringing China into the United Nations and harangued them for four hours with arguments and demands that made China's entrance into the UN almost impossible. He virtually branded the British, the Russians, the Indians, and the Japanese as "puppets" of the United States just at the time when sentiment in those countries for seating China in the UN was high. And on the spread of nuclear weapons, he said that he hoped more Afro-Asian nations would produce them, but that there was no hurry about this because "if you are cold you cannot wear an atom bomb; if you are hungry you cannot eat an atom bomb."

Washington has been reading all this with dismay, but not with any compliance. The whole thing seems so irrational to officials here that they are not prepared to believe this is all bluff or that China will not act just as irrationally as it talks next time.

Thus, it can be taken for granted that officials here will be strengthening their air and naval power in South Asia over the coming months precisely because they may yet be called upon to provide air power in defense of India at some future date. This, too, can be put down to the peculiar antics of Peking. The last thing China wants is to increase American power in Asia—even Washington is not eager for larger commitments in that part of the world—but the Chinese are bringing it about.

Peking may not be acting as she talks, but officials here cannot be sure that she will remain as contradictory as she sounds. In the face of a great nation talking in such an erratic manner, Washington has to be ready for anything, and China's odd diplomacy is assuring that the U.S. Government will do just that.

FEBRUARY 9, 1966

Ships Passing in the Night

THERE IS A GREAT DEAL OF MOTION ON VIETNAM THESE DAYS, BUT the central figures in the action seem vaguely unrelated to one another, like ships passing in the night.

The Administration's diplomacy at the United Nations was designed to arrange a peace conference at Geneva, but the Administration's diplomacy at Honolulu seems to have committed the United States more completely to the Saigon Government and therefore reduced the chances of a peace conference with Vietcong representatives. The Senate Foreign Relations Committee is holding open hearings in the hope of clarifying the issues in Vietnam, but the Administration seems less interested in the

Senate chamber than in drowning them out.

Meanwhile the one clear fact is that the military build-up is proceeding steadily on both sides. Present plans here call for doubling the American manpower commitment in the present calendar year, from 200,000 to 400,000, and going up to 600,000 in 1967. President Johnson, it is understood, has not committed himself to carry through this entire program, but he is going along with the scale of reinforcement on a month-to-month basis.

Everything in the Johnson strategy seems to be done in twos —something for the hawks and something for the doves: bomb North Vietnam and go to the UN Security Council; step up the military forces and increase the pacification program and send Hubert Humphrey to Saigon at the same time; criticize the Saigon Government in private and commit American power and prestige to it in public; assert that America cannot police the world but proclaim simultaneously that tyranny in the jungles of continental Asia is just as much America's concern as tyranny and subjugation of the peoples of Europe.

Do these policies complement one another or cancel each other out? Does half a war offensive, and half a peace offensive, excluding the enemy doing most of the fighting, add up to a whole policy or no policy? Will an American commitment to win a military victory in Vietnam and oppose tyranny almost anywhere in the world really encourage the South Vietnamese and the other allies to fight harder or will it encourage them to leave more and more of the struggle to Uncle Sam? These are some of the questions that are still troubling Washington, especially since the recent moves by the President give some impression of impulsive improvisations inspired in part by domestic political considerations.

The appeal to the Security Council was made before there was a detailed exploration of the problem in the capitals of the members of the Security Council, and only a short time after our own and the UN officials were saying a debate there would merely increase the divisions. The Honolulu conference was called on such short notice that even the normal security arrangements for a President crossing the ocean could not be made. And the

Koreans, the Australians, and the New Zealanders, who also have troops in the battle, were not even invited.

The new thing here on Vietnam is not the policy but the process of deciding policy. The Administration cannot disclose all the information that leads to its decisions without helping the enemy. The critics of the Administration cannot be sure they have all the facts, but they are entitled to feel that the Administration is reaching its decisions in a careful, orderly, unemotional way, with some relationship between Vietnam and other world responsibilities, and this is precisely the feeling they do not have.

On the contrary, the President has recently been giving the impression that he is not following a clear strategic policy, but that he is thrashing about, rejecting peace offensives and then trying them, stopping bombing and then starting bombing, rejecting the UN and then appealing to the UN, sending Vice President Humphrey to brief Asian leaders on the Honolulu conference which he did not attend—all in an atmosphere of restless experimentation and self-righteous condemnation of anybody who differs with him.

Even his handling of the Senate, usually so effective, has recently been clumsy and scornful. At Honolulu his public statements left the impression that all his critics were "special pleaders" who counsel "retreat," and that "only the callous or timid" could ignore the cause of the Vietnamese, which is a bold statement since most of the allied world is ignoring them.

In short, he is leaving little room for the possibility that his policy may be wrong, and this attitude, far from silencing his critics, is merely adding to their uneasiness.

The Alliance for Progress?

THE PARADOX OF AMERICA IN THE WORLD TODAY IS THAT IT CAN fairly claim to be making progress almost everywhere, yet finds that its problems are outstripping its gains. We have come to the end of the first half of the ten-year Alliance for Progress in this hemisphere, for example, with some encouraging results to report, but with little real hope of achieving the objective of self-sustaining growth by the end of the 1960's.

The reason for this is not that the republics of the hemisphere have not made gains, but their gains have been very uneven from country to country, and they find that their economic growth must increase faster and faster just to keep pace with their population growth.

Psychologically, the atmosphere is much better. The cruel gap between the very rich and the very poor remains, but there is visible evidence of change and improvement in many places. There is more help from the advanced countries of Latin America—Brazil, Mexico, Argentina, and Chile—to the poorer countries of Latin America than ever before, and the new generation of pragmatic technicians is appearing with little interest in the old economic myths and political feuds of the past.

Nevertheless, the statistics now being published to mark the progress of the Alliance's halfway mark are somewhat misleading. The goal of the Alliance was an economic growth rate of 2.5 per cent per capita a year, and after a slow start this was achieved in 1964 and 1965, but only about half of the Latin American republics achieved this growth rate, and most of the countries actually had a lower growth rate in 1965 than in 1964.

It is the trend of the economic growth rate in relation to the trend of the population growth rate that is most disturbing. The population is now increasing in Latin America as a whole at a rate of 2.8 per cent; in Costa Rica, where the economic growth rate was 0.9 per cent last year, the population growth was 4 per cent; and in Central America as a whole, the population is now growing faster than in any other part of the world.

Dr. Sanz de Santamaria, chairman of the Inter-American Committee on the Alliance for Progress, estimates that the present Latin American population of 220 million will more than double to between 500 million and 600 million by the end of the century, and there is nothing in the present economic trends to compare with this perplexing prospect.

There are some hopeful signs in some countries. Brazil, Argentina, and Chile, whose gross national product amounts to almost 56 per cent of the total gross product of all Latin America, have finally managed to make some progress against their inflation. Mexico, Venezuela, Peru, and Colombia have had an average economic growth rate of well above 4 per cent for the last few years, though the per capita growth rate declined last year in all of these four countries except Peru.

According to the Inter-American Development Bank, the social progress in the region as a whole has been discouraging. Because of the increase of the population and the vast migration of the peoples in the hemisphere from the land to the cities, there is a housing deficit in Latin America, according to the Inter-American Bank, of between 15 million and 19 million units. To eliminate this and provide for the rising population the bank estimates that eleven to twelve units per 1,000 inhabitants must be built each year, but no more than two units per 1,000 inhabitants are in fact being built, so that the housing deficit is expected to increase this year once more.

Land reform and social reforms are proceeding slowly, the experts at the bank concede. But agricultural production has actually slowed down over the last five years and the educational reforms are not keeping pace with the mounting school population. Of every 100 children enrolled annually in the first year of school in Latin America, only eight complete their secondary education, and in 1964 the university population of the entire region was only 4 per cent of the university age group.

This is the kind of situation that causes rebellions and wars. It is true that in any ten-year program of reconstruction the progress always tends to be slow in the first half, but there is very little in this picture to justify the current official optimism here about achieving the 2.5 per cent per capita growth rate. It is the over-all trend that counts, and the trend is not running toward President Kennedy's objective of self-sufficiency by 1970, but is actually running against it.

MAY 1, 1966

The Arrogance of Power?

THIS IS A GREAT COUNTRY FOR WORRIERS, GRUMBLERS, AND PRO-testers. No great nation in history ever had so little to worry, grumble, and protest about at home, or did so much of all three. It is hard on the nerves, but probably good for the soul.

"Gradually but unmistakably," Senator J. W. Fulbright said the other day, "America is succumbing to that arrogance of power which has afflicted, weakened, and in some cases de-stroyed, great nations in the past. . . . It is showing some signs of that fatal presumption, that overextension of power and mission, which brought ruin to ancient Athens, to Napoleonic France, and to Nazi Germany. . . ."

Worriers on the other side abound. Joe Alsop and Bill Buck-ley, who usually worry about each other, are united on the prop-osition that the timidity of power rather than the arrogance of power is America's danger. And so it goes.

America is a big word. It is not going along with either Ful-bright or Alsop—and probably doesn't know either of them ex-ists; it is taking care of the kids and going to work and the supermarket. It is neither arrogant about power nor timid about the use of power. It is not pushing the President to step up the war in Vietnam, as Fulbright fears and Alsop wants, but admitting it doesn't know what to do and doing whatever it is asked to do, which, in a way, justifies the worriers.

There is a problem here—a serious problem if the American people will go along with either expanding the war or abandoning the war—but it is not merely a problem of what to do but of deciding how to decide what to do, and the people who are worrying about this are probably closer to the heart of the problem than anybody else.

The main problem is that the leaders of America—not only in Government but in the universities, the churches, the big corporations, the newspapers, and the television networks—are so overwhelmed by the problem of doing things that they have little time left to think about what they are doing. Operations dominate purposes. The practical men have taken over from the ideological men, and this has many advantages, but pragmatism may be misleading us.

The Under Secretary of State, George W. Ball, defined the problem the other day before the American Society of International Law. "Pragmatism," he said, "is the course of least resistance. It is easy, and tempting, to become absorbed in the operational aspects of foreign relations and to ignore the longer-term implications of policy. But if America is to survive as a civilization, if in fact the world is to survive as a healthy environment for human beings, then we do have to remind ourselves of the larger framework of policy—something better than the habits, the improvisations, the expedients of years gone by—or we shall find ourselves repeating old mistakes in a world where mistakes by great nations can mean world destruction."

John W. Gardner, the Secretary of Health, Education, and Welfare, was making the same point long before he came into the Johnson Cabinet. "Very few of our most prominent people," he has written, "take a really large view of the leadership assignment. Most of them are simply tending the machinery of that part of society to which they belong. The machinery may be a great corporation or a great government agency or a great law practice or a great university. These people may tend it very well, indeed, but they are not pursuing a vision of what the total society needs. They have not developed a strategy as to how it can be achieved and they're not moving to accomplish it."

This is precisely the problem in the American Government today, though Mr. Gardner was not directing his remarks at the President. But it is true. He is worrying, as is Under Secretary Ball, about the main thing, and two points should be made about this. First, all the other worriers, though they differ about policy, would agree about this confusion of purpose in Washington, and, second, very little is being done here about it.

As a matter of fact, the question in Washington is not why the President doesn't listen to Fulbright or Alsop—both may very well be wrong—but why he does not get down to this vital question of purpose defined so sharply by his own men whom he respects and trusts.

It is not only that there is confusion here between operations and objectives, between ends and means in Vietnam, between going for "victory" in Southeast Asia or for a negotiated settlement, but that there is a confusing gap within the Government between what is said and what is done. Speeches are speeches and policies are policies; one is often quite different from the other; and it is not at all unusual for the President to congratulate an adviser on what he says and then ignore the man's main point.

Pray silence, then, for the worriers and the grumblers. The problem is not to silence them or even to follow them, or to appease the hawks one day and the doves the other in the hope of "consensus," but to listen and decide the larger question, not of operations but of objectives. And this is precisely what is not being done.

The American Economic Invasion

THE REMARKABLY SUCCESSFUL AMERICAN ECONOMIC PENETRATION of foreign markets is becoming a major issue in world politics.

In October the Liberal party policy conference in Ottawa was asked "to do something to halt the spread of United States control of Canadian industry." It settled for a compromise encouraging "Canadian ownership without discouraging foreign investment."

Last month the Western allies meeting in Paris were complaining about the unfair advantages of American capital investment and technological skill. This week the Prime Minister of Britain, Harold Wilson, sounding vaguely like General de Gaulle, said that "However much we welcome new American investment here as in other parts of Europe, there is no one on either side of the Channel who wants to see capital investment in Europe involve domination or, in the last resort, subjugation."

What is happening here is remarkably interesting and significant. American big business, through its vast multinational companies based in the U.S. but operating extensively in other countries, is not only running into economic and political resistance abroad but also forcing foreign competitors and even foreign countries to combine in order to meet the American competition.

It has been the political policy of the United States for almost twenty years to encourage the economic and political unification of Europe. What is ironical is that the big American corporations, which have ventured abroad since the war with nothing more in mind than making money, seem to be having more influence on the European unity movement than the officials in the State and Commerce Departments.

The extent of the American economic penetration abroad is

understood far more clearly there than here. At the beginning of last year the book-value investment of U.S. companies in foreign branches and subsidiaries amounted to $44.3 billion of which about $35 billion was in manufacturing, petroleum, mining, and smelting.

American firms control over 45 per cent of all Canadian manufacturing, over half of its mining and smelting, and nearly two thirds of all Canadian petroleum and natural gas. American direct investment in United Kingdom commerce and industry was estimated at $502 billion in 1965, up $600 million from 1964; and it will increase by another $760 million in the present calendar year.

Thus, while these vast investments bring new industries, new employment, and new managerial and technological techniques to these countries, we are beginning to hear more and more cries of American "economic imperialism," more and more complaints about Europe's "technology gap," and more and more charges that America's vast resources of capital are not only dominating many foreign markets, but also running poorer and older foreign companies out of business and attracting many of the best foreign scientists, engineers, and other technicians into American companies.

Secretary of the Treasury Fowler, while praising the record of these U.S. multinational companies, has recognized that what is best for General Motors is not necessarily always best for Britain, Germany, and France. He has called on them to adopt what he calls a Code of Good Corporate Citizenship, and urged them to adapt their commercial interests to the national interests of both the United States and the countries where they are operating.

This, however, is not so easy. For if an American company, operating, say, in Canada, sells trucks to Communist China with the consent of the Canadian Government, its parent company in the United States can be prosecuted for violating the U.S. Trading with the Enemy Act.

This is just one of the many complications of reconciling commercial and national interests, and the problem will get infinitely greater as the Johnson Government tries to expand the activities of these multinational companies into the state-controlled Communist countries of Eastern Europe.

Nevertheless, these pressures are having their advantages. They are expanding the exchange of technicians and techniques throughout the industrial world, helping in the development of the new nations of the world, and even forcing Harold Wilson to grapple at last with the idea that only by getting into the European Economic Community can he become part of a large enough economic unit to compete on equal terms with the U.S.

8

SPOOFS

A Uniquack That Talks Views the Campaign

GOOD MORNING, MACHINE. PLEASE IDENTIFY YOURSELF.

ANSWER: I am the 1960 model of the electronic truth detector, Uniquack. The new feature this year is that I can talk.

QUESTION: What a pity. Please explain.

A—When plugged in near a fireplace and filled with alcohol, I can tell nothing but the truth.

Q—That must be very awkward. Republican or Democrat?

A—Independent: transistorized mugwump.

Q—Who's going to win the election?

A—Kennedy.

Q—How do you know?

A—Every President in this century has had a double letter in his name. William McKinley—two l's in William. Theodore Roosevelt—two o's. Then there were William Howard Taft, Woodrow Wilson, Warren Harding, Calvin Coolidge, Herbert Hoover, Franklin Roosevelt, and of course Harry.

Q—What about Eisenhower? Wasn't he President?

A—We must await the judgment of history on that. And anyway, his initials are D. D.

Q—So you rule out Richard Milhous Nixon, Adlai Ewing Stevenson, Hubert Humphrey, Lyndon Johnson, Stuart Symington, and Chester Bowles?

A—I don't rule them out. I merely state the facts as reported by Huntington Cairns and the *Scientific American*. The Republicans might have won with Rockefeller, but they insisted on defying the teachings of history.

Q—Do you have any other brilliant observations?

A—The human race is nuts.

q—That is not brilliant, and please don't use slang in the *Times*. What do you think of the candidates?

a—They all seem determined to prove that they are what they aren't and vice versa.

q—Please go on.

a—Kennedy, who is young, has bobbed his hair in order to look old. Johnson, a Southerner, says he's a Westerner, Stevenson, a statesman, pretends he's a politician. Nixon, a politician, pretends he's a statesman. Symington, a conservative, votes like a radical. Rockefeller, a rich man, is the poor man's friend. It's all very unscientific.

q—I take it you don't think much of human logic.

a—I haven't seen much of it lately. The President says everything's dandy, and takes another trip. Everybody knows everything's not dandy, but they say it's nice to see the President getting around like that. Dozens of committees study defense, education, and housing, and issue millions of words saying we'd better pull up our socks. The President says our socks are just where they ought to be. He adds that he knows more about socks than anybody else, having worn them all his life. And everybody says that's absolutely true.

q—You have a wicked tongue, machine. Is there any little knob or screw I can turn to tone you down?

a—Please don't monkey with the machinery. Where is the logic? An election is a judgment on the future and everybody talks about the past. Rockefeller could have clobbered any Democrat in the race, so the Republicans bet everything on Nixon. You ask what Nixon believes, and they tell you he likes Ike.

q—And the Democrats?

a—They are five times as illogical as the Republicans because they have five times as many candidates.

q—You don't think much of their campaign?

a—It's not a campaign but a civil war. Johnson passes the first civil-rights bill in eighty years. He blocks the open war against the Supreme Court in the Senate. He maneuvers the censure of McCarthy. So the liberals scorn him as a conservative.

q—What do you see ahead, machine?

A—I see a great ceremony on October 14, 1960, the President's seventieth birthday. I see the President with his arm on the Vice President's shoulder, I see the passing of the mantle and I hear the President's voice appealing for continuity, peace, and prosperity.

Q—Anything else?

A—I see the American people crowded around their television screens. I see the Vice President accepting the mantle and looking very young and appealing, and I can't help thinking what a pity it is he doesn't have a double letter in his name, like G. Mennen ("Soapy") Williams.

JANUARY 20, 1961

Something for the Girls

PRAY SILENCE FOR THE NEW WIVES WHO HAVE COME TO WASHington, the sidekicks of the big shots who are about to become our masters. They are important, these ladies of the new Administration leaders, because it is a rare man who can survive the pace and power of the town without a sensible woman at home to remind him who he is and where he came from.

Right now most of the new Cabinet appointees are all right. They are duly impressed with the grace of this lovely city and modest about their new responsibilities. Some of them have even helped with the house-hunting, or at least taken the suitcases up to the attic.

In a few days, however, the atmosphere will begin to work on them. A chauffeur will pick them up every morning in an automobile as long as a freight car. Parking spaces will open before them as if by magic. They will have offices as big as the Grand Central Terminal with wall-to-wall carpets as thick as mattresses. Everybody will call them "Mr. Secretary," and get out of their way, and stop talking when *they* want to talk, and agree with their most preposterous banalities. It is a ghastly prospect, and do they love it!

Meanwhile back at the charming old Georgetown house, rented at three times its worth, the little woman is already having just the slightest twinge of doubt. The original plumbing, installed personally by Benjamin Franklin in 1793, drips and gurgles. The new servants, if any, can't find a thing. The kids are moaning about their lost pals back home and whimpering about the fiendish teachers at the new school.

Also, five unremembered old schoolmates have called up and insisted on bringing Mr. Secretary to dinner "just any time in the next month." Invitations for nineteen cocktail parties, most of them from somebody named Kennedy, are on the hall table, and dinner is already forty-five minutes overdue when who should arrive but Mr. Secretary himself, full of the latest dope on Laos and Lumumba.

Here, then, is the first great crisis of the Kennedy Administration. If she says, as usual, "Where have you been?" or "Let's get one thing straight at the beginning: I'm not going to any cocktail parties even for the Kennedys," everything may work out all right for a while. But if she is impressed, if she runs and gets him a drink and shushes the children and sits adoring the wonderful, handsome, successful man while he drones on importantly about Lumumba, the whole free world at that moment may be in mortal danger.

This is not, gentle reader, entirely a spoof. The greatest danger in this city is that civilized, intelligent men do forget in this heady atmosphere who they are and where they came from. More important, if not deflated once a month by a loving wife, they fall victim to the most deadly habit in Washington, which is that they begin to think they actually are what they merely represent.

No doubt this is what Woodrow Wilson had in mind when he divided the men who come to Washington into two classes: those who grow and those who swell. Behind every one who swells— every pompous stuffed shirt—there is a timid woman. This is known here, not very widely, as Reston's Law No. 1. And Law

No. 2 is like unto it—namely, that every official who grows undoubtedly has a wife who loves him just enough to tell him off when he begins to be a bore.

The official establishment in Washington, of course, works against the plain-speaking, spontaneous woman. It is always fencing her off, and cutting her down, and knocking all the stuffing out of her, so that eventually she retreats and suffers the old man or humors his vanities.

This is a great pity, for if the press is not going to slap the great men down, the wives must. Not every night, you know, but just often enough to keep them loose and respectful. This does not, of course, apply to great men who marry ninnies, who chatter and scold too much, but I wouldn't know about them.

FEBRUARY 12, 1961

Aesop Updated

ONCE UPON A TIME ALL THE CREATURES IN THE ANIMAL KINGDOM got to lying around drinking Olde Mead (120 proof) and making goo-goo eyes at every cute chick in the forest. All, that is, except the Bears.

The Beavers wouldn't cut down trees unless they had power saws, and the Rabbits wouldn't eat anything except icebox lettuce with Thousand Island dressing, and pretty soon the Bears started going around gobbling up all the other animals.

After a while, a horse named Gallup took a poll which showed that 97.3 per cent of the animals left were against being gobbled up so the American Buffalo called them all together and made them a big speech about the need for sacrifices.

"Ask not what the forest can do for you," he said, "but what you can do for the forest." Everybody from the Elephant to the

Jackass was deeply impressed and began asking exactly what. "What can we do to help?" asked the Chief Worker among the Ants.

"The trouble with you," replied the Buffalo, "is that you need more incentives. You are not getting paid enough for your labor. I'm going to see to it that your minimum wage is raised from a dollar an hour to a dollar and a quarter an hour right away."

"But it is jobs we need more than anything else," said the Chief Ant.

"I know," replied the Buffalo. "It is a terrible thing to be an unemployed Ant, so I'm going to increase your unemployment compensation and stretch it out over a longer period."

"What about us?" asked the Fat Cat. "What can we do to help?"

"Produce," replied the Buffalo. "Production is what we need, and I promise that your depletion allowances will be maintained at a high level so that you continue to have more cream than anybody else."

"And what about us?" asked the farmer Jackass. "What shall we do?"

"Don't produce," said the Buffalo. "Farm production is what we don't need. Please don't produce any more and we'll pay you well. We'll do anything, but please take it easy."

Up then strode the Tiger, who had been watching the Bears from a missile gap on the fringe of the forest. "Give us your orders," said the Tiger. "We have seen the enemy and we want to help."

"I want you to be happy," said the Buffalo. "I know how it is out there without your womenfolk and your cubs. Go back to your post in peace and I'll send them all out to you at Government expense."

At this point, there was a ghastly roar from the Bears in the forest. "Harken to that," said the Buffalo. "We have never been in greater danger. The outcome of this struggle is very much in doubt. Where are the volunteers?"

First to step up was a very old British Lion. "We must be sensible about this," he said. "We must talk things over with the Bears. It is all very tiresome, but we must not be rash or beastly in our attitude."

Next came the French Giraffe, who said he hated Bears but pointed out that the Giraffes were all fighting among themselves and did not really have time to watch the Bears.

Finally, a German Police Dog offered to watch the Bears but complained that he could not afford to do very much and besides did not trust himself to get too close to the Bears. Whereupon the Buffalo called once more for volunteers.

"Let us help," said all the female animals. "You treat us like a bunch of useless ninnies while all the female Bears are working over there like mad."

"This is a male's world," said the Buffalo. "You are consumers, not fighters. You must consume more useless things, so that the workers can produce more useless things."

"What about us?" said all the young Oxen. "We are strong and willing."

"But you are dumb," roared the Buffalo. "You must educate yourselves. Everybody who is not dumber than an Ox must have a college education."

"But I am poor," said the Church Mouse.

"Don't give it a thought," said the Buffalo. "I'll get you a scholarship at Oberlin, or a Government job in Washington under the Harvard faculty."

So saying, the Buffalo lay down with the Lamb, and the Bears laughed and laughed, and the wise old Owl flew off in search of a safer perch.

Moral: Ask and ye shall receive; ask not, and ye shall receive anyway.

A Bill to Amend the Human Race

WHEREAS THIS DATE IS APRIL ONE, A CELEBRATED DAY FOR FUN, when even Congress takes it ease and fools may gambol as they please;

Whereas the winter is a bore (to which we all say "nevermore") and wintry men and wintry things give way at last to flowering springs;

Whereas the scene in Rock Creek Park now boasts a soaring meadow lark, and daffodils on every ridge, and herring by the Q Street bridge;

Whereas the kids along the Mall are flying kites and playing ball, and lovers wander quite unheeded through misty glens marked "Newly Seeded":

Then surely this is just the time to legislate—of course in rhyme—as A. P. Herbert[1] taught us to (and stealing here a verse or two):

SECTION 1. Be it enacted by the House, and by the Senate, its lofty spouse, that every single tiresome bill ever committed on the Hill be stricken from the Federal stacks, beginning with the income tax.

(a) The Congress shall forthwith repeal all excise laws that make men feel that everything that's warm and nice must bear a tax like common vice. (This Act applies to wine and booze and everything that makes men snooze.)

(b) The Congress may, by joint decree, reward a man in Schedule C, with extra special tax rebates for asking ugly girls for dates, or otherwise relieving life of painful, silent human strife.

[1] A. P. Herbert: "The Spring (Arrangements) Bill" (New York: Doubleday, Doran & Co.; 1936).

(c) Penalties shall be hard on him who does not follow every whim to scrutinize the cherry trees or bumble with the humble bees, but talks incessantly of Laos, of Castro, Khrushchev, Congo Chaos.

SECTION 2. It shall be lawful after this for Democrats to give a kiss to any pretty little Vixen, or even Richard Milhous Nixon, so long as every day at dusk, the GOP backs Mr. Rusk.

(a) From now until the First of June, the President shall be immune to savage threats of Communism, and all the walls of Journalism (especially dreary cries of gloom and pessimistic sighs of doom). He may cut down or climb the trees, say "yes" or "no" and take his ease; dress as he likes, however fancy; do what he wills, however chancy: Provided that, in this connection, the Congress raises no objection.

(b) For members who remain in town, the President shall provide a crown of multicolored morning glories (white for Dems and pink for Tories). And all shall dance, by Speaker's rule, each noonday round Reflecting Pool.

(c) "There shall be banks of maidenhair arranged about the Speaker's Chair"; (subsection 1 of section 4 of Herbert's Act, see heretofore) "and roses white and roses red shall hang above the Speaker's head; like some tremendous window-box, the galleries be gay with phlox."

(d) Meanwhile from now until July, new rules of conduct shall apply:

(1*d*) Bills to improve our education shall shun religion and integration.

(2*d*) Liberal Senators shall relax while Tories argue "spend and tax."

(3*d*) Congress shall reward the man "who modestly does all he can,"[2] bearing in mind, when it is able, to try to keep the dollar stable.

SECTION 3. If any student feels he must get out of classes now or bust, but hasn't finished all his themes because his head is full of dreams, it shall be proper for the same to give the Registrar his name, and say "I want to be excused because I'm feeling

[2] *Ibid.*

quite confused," and there shall not be any fuss, concerning students acting thus. (His grade, by law, must be B-plus.)

(a) The order of the day declares that anybody selling wares, shall cut the price at least in two, especially in the case of brew; and barbers, under Section 3, shall cut boys' hair, as well, for free.

(b) It shall be lawful every place, for citizens to slow their pace, to walk on "red" and smoke in bed, or even read all night instead. And it shall not be indiscreet to park cars anywhere in the street.

(c) "All citizens who choose to ride on taxi-tops and not inside, and those who do not use their votes because they're busy painting boats, and any miscreant who hums, instead of doing dismal sums; whoever does a silly thing need only answer 'Tis the Spring,' and this shall be a good defense in any court with any sense:

(d) "Provided that, in late July, this act, of course, does not apply."[3]

FIERY RUN, VIRGINIA

JUNE 25, 1961

The Standard Khrushchev Speech by Uniquack

FOR THE BENEFIT OF READERS WHO DO NOT HAVE TIME TO MEMOR-ize seven speeches a week by Nikita Sergeyevich Khrushchev, the following all-purpose Khrushchev speech has been summarized by Uniquack, the electronic truth detector:

[3] *Ibid.*

Comrades: As is well known, capitalism is a worn-out mare while socialism is new, young, and full of teeming energy [prolonged laughter]. Our epoch is the epoch of the triumph of Marxism-Leninism [prolonged cheers]. I will refer to Stalin and Mao Tse-tung later [prolonged boos and throwing of chairs from the balcony].

How should a Marxist-Leninist view the present time? We must learn to think in centuries, regarding the whole story of mankind. Thus it is clear that from the beginning of time conflict has been the inevitable lot of the human race. Adam was a good Marxist who wished to see the equal distribution of the world's goods. Eve was the first usurer and exploiter of man, a monopolist and imperialist who did not understand "peaceful coexistence."

During the entire period between Adam and Marx there was no hope for mankind, but since Marx history has been divided into three phases: 1. From the 1848 Revolution to the Paris Commune of 1871; 2. From the Paris Commune to the Russian Revolution of 1905; and 3. Since the Russian Revolution.

When I say this is now the epoch of the triumph of Marxism-Leninism, what do I mean? [Cries from the audience: "Yes, what *do* you mean?"] I mean that after the triumph of socialism within the USSR we won the last war despite the activities of the American imperialists and started the great worldwide movement toward socialism. Prior to the second World War the USSR was the only Socialist country in the world. At present the Socialist countries cover about one fourth of the territory of the globe, have one third of its population and one third of its industrial production. [Tumultuous cheers and cries of "Good old Nik," and "When do we bury them?"]

We must be patient. The capitalists are crumbling, but they are still strong. They have vowed to "stand firm" in Berlin, but as Lenin said, "Those who stand firm get a sore back." Our major problem is to wipe out the vestiges of the last war we don't like, such as the Western presence in Berlin, but to solidify the vestiges of the last war we do like, such as the great Socialist Government of East Germany.

For this purpose we have devised the "doctrine of the three

wars." World wars we rule out, for while we would obliterate the German militarists and revanchists, and wipe out the American monopolists, millions of our own people would also be killed and we would be left with over 700 million of our dear Chinese brethren on our borders. I need not say what that would mean [prolonged boos].

Therefore we rule out world wars. We also rule out limited wars like Suez, but wars of national liberation are totally different and we must be clear about this distinction. If the British and French invade Suez, that is an important war and therefore inadmissible. If, however, we help our comrades invade Laos or South Korea, that is a war of liberation. Similarly, if Castro in Cuba rises against Batista, that is a war of liberation, but if the American imperialists help other Cubans to fight Castro, that is counter-revolution. Is this clear? [Cries of "No!" and scuffling in the balcony.]

What we must do, therefore, is to persuade or intimidate Kennedy into accepting our idea of what is an admissible and what is an inadmissible war. The distinction is perfectly clear: an admissible war is one which benefits us; an inadmissible war is one that benefits them.

This brings me to the question of our internal situation, and particularly to the question of food. [Storms of applause and prolonged shouting and whistling.] As is well known, we will pass the United States in the production of grains and meat on October 9, 1973. [Cries of "Meat! Meat!"] However, here again we must see this internal problem in historic terms. The first phase of socialism (1905–30) was the phase of No Meat. The second, or Stalinist phase, was the phase of Some Meat, not much but some. As I said in Kazakhstan on June 23, we are now entering another phase, the phase of Horse Meat. This is progress which no capitalist country can claim.

Comrades: Down with the imperialists! [Cheers.] Down with Hitler and Adenauer! [Prolonged cheers.] Down with war! [Tumultuous cheers!] On to Berlin! [Dead silence.]

A Happy New Year
and All That

WELL, 1961 WAS DIFFERENT, ANYWAY. IT WAS THE YEAR OF THE Wall, and the Twist, and the Shelter, and the electric toothbrush, obviously the greatest invention since the double bed.

There were new styles in almost everything: girls, politics, art, houses, and hair-dos. For some reason things suddenly seemed to get turned around this year. The natural girl went out of fashion for the first time in 1,000 years, and took the curl out of her hair with glue and put black shoe polish on her eyes. Nobody knew why, but men seemed to like it anyway. The male, on the other hand, went plain, narrow, and soft in 1961: soft shoulders, plain vests, narrowed lapels, trousers, ties, and minds.

It was a hard year on big shots and big nations. Khrushchev exploded a fifty-five-megaton bomb and everybody in America was supposed to be scared to death, but the Americans produced more babies and more glass houses than in any other year in the history of the Republic.

Some little country was always telling some big country to go climb a tree. Cuba defied the United States, Albania defied the Soviet Union. Algeria defied France, Formosa threatened to invade China, and Katanga thumbed its nose at the whole United Nations.

In fact, nothing in international politics followed the usual script. The weaker France became, the more it provoked Russia and its own allies. The Russians built a wall in Berlin, not to keep the invaders out of heaven but to keep the angels in. Nehru gave the world a new definition of passive resistance by invading Goa, and Khrushchev, of all people, said publicly that it was sometimes possible for him to be wrong.

Art had a big year in America—under President Kennedy. Pablo Casals and William Shakespeare replaced Ike's old friend Fred Waring and his Pennsylvanians in the White House. People who, in the 1950's, didn't listen to good music on regular hi-fidelity records, didn't listen to it in 1961 on stereophonic records.

The English language made a comeback this year. The President of the United States, for the first time in eight years, was heard to arrange a subject, verb, and object in proper order in a single sentence.

At Harvard, President Pusey dropped Latin and substituted English on the university's diplomas. This naturally produced a student demonstration and a charge by the Harvard *Crimson* that Pusey was changing *alma mater* to "foster mother." But Pusey had the last word. He said: "What's pat in the Latin/or chic in the Greek/I always distinguish/More clearly in English."

The United States was never more affluent or resourceful than in 1961. Saks Fifth Avenue sold a Mark II after-shower cologne in a solid gold splasher and a rosewood box for $2,500; Black Starr & Gorham took a two-column ad in *The New York Times* to advertise a "flawless blue marquise diamond," nicknamed the Vega, for $123,000; and Nieman Marcus in Dallas offered "his" and "hers" airplanes for $176,000 apiece.

It was the shelter craze, however, that brought out the true genius in the American entrepreneur this year. Hammacher Schlemmer in New York, the Tiffany of civil defense, displayed a $20,000 "shelter for living" which was "comfortably furnished with various decorative and functional . . . creature comforts."

Of course there were some "extras" for the shelter—a cordless electric television with an eight-inch screen ($249.95), presumably to catch all those late late late night shows during the Soviet air raids, and a transistor clock-radio ($68.00) guaranteed to help you survive on time.

This was not all that happend in 1961, however. Piracy spread from ships to jet airplanes, and those perennial pirates, the politicians, of course were extremely active. The Right Wing replaced the Left Wing as the most prolific pamphleteers in America and, as if this was not hard enough on the Republican party, the GOP produced the Ev and Charlie television show, which was often funnier than Jackie Gleason. The Democrats, not to be outdone, agreed to replace Sam Rayburn with John W. McCormack of Massachusetts as Speaker of the House of Representatives, and this was widely regarded as the worst trade since the Kansas City Athletics sent Roger Maris to the New York Yankees.

So all in all, it was quite a year—a little goofy, maybe, but original, anyway.

MARCH 23, 1962

Dear Uncle

GENTLE READER, THE GOVERNMENT OF THE UNITED STATES LOVES you. It cares. It wants you to know that, if you have a problem and Dear Abby can't help, all you have to do is get in touch with kind old Uncle Sam.

President Kennedy has personally taken out after tradesmen who sell air with their cornflakes or put water in their booze, and he has instructed the Postmaster General to make it easy for the consumer to buy all those how-to-do-it pamphlets issued by the Goverment Printing Office.

These include everything from the treatment of chiggers to the trapping of bobcats. Before long, all you'll have to do is go down to your post office and ask for Pamphlet No. A. 1.35:403/2 (5 cents) "Chiggers, How to Fight Them," or 34D "Hints on Bobcat Trapping" 10 cents, and J. Edward Day, the Postmaster General, will do the rest.

The notion that you get nothing for your income taxes but a lot of bad news is totally wrong. Take the problem of a citizen whose automatic dishwasher breaks down or one who gets stuck with 158 melting sirloin steaks when his home freezer konks out. Old Uncle Sugar has the answer in "What to Do When Your Home Freezer Stops" (A. 1.35:321 . . . 5 cents) and "Methods of Hand Dishwashing" (FS 2.6:713/3 PO.5 . . . 5 cents).

In either of these cases, however, the citizen would have to have the pamphlet on hand in advance. Otherwise his steaks would turn green and he would not know which method of hand dishwashing to use while the dishes piled up in the sink.

The Government is particularly good on children's problems. If, for example, you are having a baby, or if you've already had one and the darn kid won't stand up straight, Washington is ready with practical and cheap advice in "So You're Having a Baby?" (FS 3.210:1 . . . 10 cents), and "Good Posture for Boys and Girls" (FS 5.7/A:P 847 . . . 5 cents).

Hunters and fishermen seem to be a particular favorite of the Federal Government, probably because the hunting and fishing vote is so large. Official pamphlets tell them "Definitions of Body Dimensions Used in Describing Tunas," "How to Catch Frogs in Southeastern Brazil," "How to Palpitate Domestic Rabbits to Determine Pregnancy," "The Age and Growth of the Redfish (Sebastes Marinus) in the Gulf of Maine," and how to attract birds and cook crabs almost anywhere.

Ralph Waldo Emerson said once that "The cheat and bully and malefactor we meet everywhere is the Government," but that was before the Government took a personal interest in its citizens and their cares. Now an ever thoughtful bureaucracy is ready with official information on how to cook apples in appealing ways, how to "Eat a Good Breakfast to Start a Good Day," how to preserve leather bookbindings and prctect home-cured meat from insects, and how to track a hurricane and prevent a gully.

In order to humanize its advice, to give the voter a feeling that he has a warm-hearted pal or two in Washington, the officials have created some fictional characters named "Butch" and Sam and Sue. "Butch" is apparently the handiest character around the house since Tom Swift. There is one pamphlet called "Let's Save Soil with Sam and Sue," but "Butch" has at least five, including "Butch Blows a Fuse" (anybody can do that), "Butch Learns to

Lift," and, what is harder, "Butch Learns Good Housekeeping."

Many of these pamphlets are reminiscent of life on the old frontier, and they certainly are not written in the iambic pentameter of the New Frontier, but some also aim at solving contemporary problems.

For all those citizens who sit around longing to recall what Dick Nixon did say when he was around here, there is one book of his collected speeches and another of his debates with John F. Kennedy. These are in the political-science catalogue along with the letters of Theodore Roosevelt, entitled, for some mysterious reason: "No Political Influence Will Help You in the Least."

The most popular pamphlet of all is one called "It's Good Business to Know Your Man," but the women were apparently intrigued by the title and this is now out of print. There is, however, little demand for "The Golden Eagle and Its Economic Status" and even less for "The Bald Eagle and Its Economic Status," which for some reason costs a nickel more and 15 cents more than one on having a baby.

Incidentally, the last time these pamphlets came into the news there was a thunderous response from the citizenry. At that time, during the early Thirties, Senator Pat Harrison of Mississippi demanded to know why the Government was printing a pamphlet on "The Love Life of the Bull Frog." The immediate reaction was a demand from the country for over 10,000 copies. The Secretary of Agriculture went on the air and denied the existence of any such pamphlet, whereupon the public ordered over 100,000 copies. The thing never died down until the outbreak of World War II, but maybe Kennedy will be luckier.

The Lion's Letdown

ONCE UPON A TIME (THIS WAS AWAY BACK IN 1962) ALL OF THE free animals of Europe got together to decide whether they would let the British Lion join them to help defend the forest against the Bear.

All the little animals were for it. They said that the Lion, though old, was wise and very good in a fight. But the old Fox was doubtful and the tall Giraffe was jealous.

This was a very special Giraffe. He was proud. He was taller than the Washington Monument, and he thought he could see farther than all the other animals. Also he believed the Bear was too worried about the Tiger in the far eastern part of the forest to be a menace to the rest, and he didn't like the Lion—partly because it was called the King of the Beasts, partly because the Giraffe wanted to be the King of the Beasts himself.

If the Lion came in, the Giraffe said, it would make a deal with the American Buffalo that was defending the forest against the Bear at that time—and between them they would tell all the other animals what to do. So the Giraffe devised a scheme he thought would keep the Lion out.

If the Lion wanted to help defend the forest, the Giraffe said, it would have to give up all its cubs, all its claws, and all its teeth and not have any side deals with the Buffalo and it would also have to agree to do only what the Giraffes, the Foxes, and the small animals directed.

This did not amuse the Lion, who didn't have any teeth or claws anyway, but who was very proud of his cubs, and while he thought the Buffalo was a clumsy beast, he also regarded him as being potentially useful, so he refused to accept the Giraffe's terms.

For a time all this was kept secret and the chief Buffalo sent his mate to plead with the Giraffe to be reasonable (the chief Buffalo's mate spoke French in those days), but the Giraffe refused to compromise. He said he would allow the Buffalo to help defend the forest at the Buffalo's own expense provided the Buffalo recognized that Buffaloes were a strong but uncultured breed, who were debasing the standards of the animal kingdom. But the Buffalo told him to go climb the Eiffel tower.

When the news of this crisis finally got out (it was leaked by a mouse to Sydney Gruson of *The New York Times* in the Bavarian part of the forest) there was a ghastly row. The Lion finally refused the Giraffe's terms and the Buffalo got mad and sailed away across the seas, leaving the defense of the forest to the Giraffes and the Foxes.

So long as the tall Giraffe and the old Fox lived, all the animals were happy and drove around in Volkswagens and went to the Folies Bergère every night. But one day the old Giraffe, by some oversight, got a terrible sore throat and died, and not long after so did the old Fox, and the young Foxes, being stronger than the young Giraffes, took over.

Now this worried the Bear. He thought Giraffes were funny, but he thought young Foxes were not only unfunny but mean and cunning. So he got on the Trans-Siberian Railroad and went to the far eastern part of the forest for a conference with the Tiger. He told the Tiger he didn't like him, and the Tiger told the Bear it was mutual. But they agreed that they disliked Foxes more than they disliked each other.

Thereupon, after a little underground testing, they started back west together with all the other Bears and Tigers, and one night when the Foxes and the Giraffes were busy drinking and dancing the Twist, the Bears and the Tigers ate them all up (except a few which they kept for a Communist zoo), and the Buffaloes were too far away to do anything about it.

Meanwhile the old Giraffe had been buried, but when he tried to return to earth again to save the forest, as he had promised he would do, somehow he never did quite make it.

Moral: Never trust a Giraffe with a sore throat.

The Imprudent Man's Tax Deductions

SECRETARY OF THE TREASURY DILLON HAS BEEN WORKING ON A new tax law, and is going around asking for suggestions about how to close the biggest tax loopholes. Actually, there are only three ways to get rid of the biggest loophole of all—the 27½ per cent deduction for depletion and depreciation of oil and gas wells.

The first is to get rid of Texas, which may be difficult. The second is to shoot Senator Robert Kerr of Oklahoma, which is illegal. And the third is to apply the principle of tax deductions for depletion to all natural resources.

Part 1 of Section 611 of Title 26 of the Internal Revenue Code deals with "natural resources" and is based on the idea that if you have a natural resource which is used up or "depleted" with the passage of time, you are entitled to a tax deduction.

Mr. Dillon's mistake has been in trying to persuade Texas and Senator Kerr to give up this bonanza. They want to be paid for the oil they sell and paid again for not still having what they have sold. What Mr. Dillon could do, however, is to apply the depletion principle across the board.

Take pretty girls. Nobody would deny, certainly not Senator Kerr, that they are a "natural resource." Also, feminine beauty, like oil, is a wasting asset. Nothing depletes a gal more than having a flock of kids, yet the present law does not apply to her. This is clearly an injustice. Section 611 of the Internal Revenue Code says: "There shall be allowed as a deduction in computing taxable income a reasonable allowance for depletion and for depreciation . . . according to the peculiar conditions in each case."

Admittedly, it might be difficult to calculate the value of depleted beauty, especially since there would indeed be "peculiar conditions in each case." Some women, for example, depreciate fast and would therefore be entitled to a quick write-off or depreciation allowance.

Also, if oil wells are entitled to a depletion allowance, what about prizefighters? Nothing depletes a man quicker than a hard punch in the nose. It takes longer to bring in a good heavyweight than a good oil well, and the supply of natural prizefighters is short.

Thus, the American prizefighter is at a disadvantage. He has no protection, like glass and carpet manufacturers, from foreign competition. Ingemar Johansson, the Swedish meteor, has a tax haven in Switzerland and got out of this country with more dubious foreign-aid funds than Chiang Kai-shek. But the poor American pug is stuck. He blooms and fades like the morning glory, and while Section 611 of the tax code protects the "operating mineral interest" of lead and zinc—the Senate Majority Leader, Mike Mansfield, comes from a lead and zinc state—nobody protects the "operating mineral interest" of bone and gristle.

Novelists are another American natural resource with a high depletion rate. They deplete themselves gathering enough experience to write a novel, and then deplete themselves further in the writing. The Treasury Department recognized this fact for General Eisenhower when they let him consider his memoirs as a life work and write them off as a capital gain. But most novelists shoot their whole story in a single volume and usually end up without either capital or gain.

Secretary Dillon ought to put these points to Senator Kerr. He cannot remove the depletion allowance in the tax structure without removing Senator Kerr, who has almost as many oil wells in and around Oklahoma as he has votes. But the Secretary might be able to appeal to the Senator's sense of humor, if not to his sense of justice.

If this cannot be done, Mr. Dillon is in trouble. For he cannot recommend a general tax cut without tax reform, and he cannot get a fair tax reform without doing something about the biggest tax loophole of the lot. In fact, the oil and gas depletion allowance has become the symbol of tax inequality, and Senator Kerr the personification of the problem. His political influence is not depleted but enhanced with the passing of time, so Mr. Dillon has to find a new approach, no matter how silly.

JULY 22, 1962

The Prudent Man's Tax Deductions

Gentle Reader, get thee Prudence. For the Senate Finance Committee has just proclaimed a new doctrine for the new expense-account age. It is the doctrine of "The Prudent Man," and it lets you deduct from your income taxes any business or entertainment expense that might be incurred by "a prudent man in the exercise of his sound judgment."

This obviously has possibilities. Suppose a citizen of the Great Republic absolutely has to go to Paris on business, or to New York, or anywhere else where the women are recklessly beautiful. In this situation a Prudent Man, in the exercise of his sound judgment, would obviously take along his wife and write her off as a prudent deduction.

Webster's New International Dictionary defines Prudence as "practical wisdom . . . the wisdom that conduces to moral virtue." No doubt this is precisely what the Senate Finance Committee had in mind, for nothing conduces to moral virtue in a traveling salesman more than having his wife along on his travels. The same dictionary also defines Prudence as "skill or sagac-

ity in the management of practical, especially business affairs—
sometimes with an implication of self-interest."

This opens up to the artful tax-dodger golden opportunities
for legitimate chiseling. It shifts the emphasis from the tax col-
lector's interest to the taxpayer's "self-interest," and provides a
means of solving many modern problems heretofore regarded as
insoluble.

Consider the agony of living in the same world with both
Nikita Khrushchev and Mortimer M. Caplin, the new Commis-
sioner of Internal Revenue. No less an authority than President
Kennedy has told us that this is a dangerous time. Khrushchev
has said that he now has an intercontinental ballistic missile that
can hit a "fly in the sky" and cannot be brought down by anything in the arsenal of democracy.

In such a world, equipped with such ghastly fly-swatters, a
Prudent Man would surely provide some means of escape for his
family—say a yacht well stocked and lubricated with provisions
capable of maintaining life for a considerable period of time. Or
a hideaway in the mountains equipped with a large deep pool of
water for protection against radiation. And these would, of
course, have to be maintained and kept in running order by
periodic use, say on weekends.

President Kennedy does not favor the Prudent Man doctrine.
He prefers the doctrine of the Honest Man. His tax bill would
have ruled out all general business deductions and then permitted, maybe, some specific exceptions. The Ways and Means
Committee of the House of Representatives was a little more
lenient, but it insisted that deductions had to be demonstrably
related to the business activity of the taxpayer. It was then that
the Senate Finance Committee came along with this lovely loophole of the Prudent Man.

Every age has its fashions in men. There was, for example, the
Forgotten Man of Herbert Hoover's time, whose "chief business
in life is to pay." Then there was the Common Man, so dear to
the heart of Franklin Roosevelt, but these are now out of style,
and the coming thing is clearly the Prudent Man.

If he has business associates who love good wine and food
(and who doesn't), he will be prudent about having an adequate
supply of same always on hand. If he has a lovely wife, and

especially if he doesn't, he will certainly be prudent enough to see that she does not go out with him on what the Finance Committee calls "business-oriented occasions" looking as if she had been slipcovered, but will instead fit her out like Jackie, and care for her gently as a Prudent Man should, and see that she gets a good, long, business-oriented rest both winter and summer.

Finally, if "an ounce of prudence is worth a pound of gold," no Prudent Man will kill himself with work at the office or imagine that the country has a brain tumor every time the stock market develops a little fever—not when, "in the exercise of his sound judgment," he can take a good, long, prudently deductible rest with a couple of agreeable business associates and their wives.

Of course, the Congress has to approve the doctrine and somebody has to make the provision for the Prudent Woman, and President Kennedy, if the bill passes, must not veto it. But he wouldn't dare. He's in enough trouble already.

FEBRUARY 15, 1963

Washington's Brains and Feet

PRESIDENT KENNEDY IS A PUZZLE. ONE DAY HE PLEADS WITH THE country to sacrifice, and the next he pleads with it to accept a tax cut. One day he venerates brains, and the next he tries to popularize walking.

Trying to popularize walking in America is like trying to popularize prohibition in Kentucky. Asking a citizen to walk instead of ride in America is like asking a Frenchman to drink milk instead of wine. And the last French premier who did *that*, Pierre Mendès-France, was booted out of office.

President Kennedy himself is a living symbol of the dangers of exercise. So long as he concentrated on history, literature, and politics, he was all right. But the minute he picked up a spade and started digging a hole for an Arbor Day tree in Canada, his back buckled and he's been a rocking-chair case ever since.

There are great advantages to the sedentary life, particularly around the White House. President Franklin D. Roosevelt survived and succeeded in office at least partly because he was a victim of polio. He wasn't always mounting his horses or airplanes or promoting fifty-mile hikes. He had to sit still and think, and he survived four Presidential elections and lived 63 years 72 days, whereas Theodore Roosevelt, the champion of the strenuous life, only got through one and a half terms and died at 60.

This is very dubious advice, living on Metrecal and hiking for publicity into the Blue Ridge mountains. Look at President Taft. When they sprung him from Yale in the class of 1878, the average weight of his classmates was 151 pounds. Taft weighed in on graduation day at 225 and kept going up from there to around 300. Meanwhile, he endured long sentences in the War Department, the Philippines, Cuba, the Presidency, the Yale Law School, and the Supreme Court before he finally died here in Washington at the age of 72. In contrast, Calvin Coolidge, that skinny symbol of austerity, died at 60, probably because after he left the White House, he took up the reckless and strenuous craft of writing a newspaper column.

The political implications of this walking binge could be even more serious than the physical. President Kennedy survived the anti-Catholic vote in the election of 1960, but the anti-walking vote in America is infinitely larger.

For example, as soon as the President started urging people to take to the hills, an anti-exercise organization in Washington, previously partial to President Kennedy, held an emergency protest meeting here in Hall's saloon. The name of the organization is Athletics Anonymous. It is composed of men who have previously suffered from exercise, most of them heart cases, and it works roughly on the same principle as Alcoholics Anonymous. Only in Athletics Anonymous, when a member hears about somebody who begins to get a compulsion to walk or ride a horse, or run around the Lincoln Memorial, he goes to the poor fellow, puts a drink in his hand, and talks him into staying home.

Bobby Kennedy, of course, is the villain of this whole silly business. Bobby is an athletic delinquent. He bats his kids over volleyball nets from birth just to toughen them up, and it was no surprise that he was the first New Frontiersman to hike the fifty miles. He should study the life of Winston Churchill, the greatest man of the age. Winnie trifled with exercise in Africa during his youth and later built brick walls, but later he reformed and most of the time thereafter preferred smoking and drinking to hiking.

What this capital needs is not the fifty-mile hike but the fifty-minute "think." It could easily be arranged. The National Security Council, for example, could have been summoned to think for fifty minutes before doing or saying anything.

Even Theodore Roosevelt, who is being blamed for the official hiking craze, wasn't all "Rough Rider." He made his daughter Alice learn something new out of a book every night before she went to bed, and tell him what it was at breakfast every morning, no matter how late she was out the night before. The device worked too. She has been following his advice ever since, and bless her, she was 79 this week and is the most interesting lady in Washington.

SEPTEMBER 1, 1963

Nonsense on the Hot Line to Moscow

THE EMERGENCY "HOT LINE" FROM THE WHITE HOUSE TO THE Kremlin opened this week:

WASHINGTON: Testing . . . testing . . . testing . . .

MOSCOW: Chairman Khrushchev wants to know why you are

testing. As is well known, the test ban has just been signed. What is this provocation? Who is . . .

WASHINGTON: Please be patient, Moscow. We are not testing bombs, we are merely testing these new communications machines to see that they work. . . . The quick brown fox jumped over the lazy dog's back . . . the quick brown fox jumped over the lazy dog's back. . . . Do you get it, Moscow?

MOSCOW: We do not get it at all. We received something about animals. Are you calling us "lazy dogs"?

WASHINGTON: Please listen carefully. There are no lazy dogs and, honest, there are no quick brown foxes jumping over them. These are words, meaning nothing. Let's begin all over again. We are going to send some new words to make sure that all the keys are working. Ready?

MOSCOW: Ready.

WASHINGTON: Now is the time for all good men to come to the aid of their country . . . now is the time for all good men to come to the aid of their country . . .

MOSCOW: Why?

WASHINGTON: What do you mean, why?

MOSCOW: Why is this the time for all good men to come to the aid of their country? Is something happening over there? Why are you calling up your citizens to come to the aid of the country? Is there an emergency?

WASHINGTON: We are going to try again, Moscow. Please confirm the following numbers: 1 2 3 4 5 6 7 8 9 10. Over.

MOSCOW: 10 9 8 7 6 5 4 3 2 1. Why are you sending us a countdown? Chairman Khrushchev is very upset.

WASHINGTON: Please put him on the line. We want to talk turkey to him about this.

MOSCOW: This is Khrushchev. I do not understand what Turkey has to do with this line. The Turks are lackeys of the capitalist warmongers. They have your missiles on our border. What do they have to do with this line?

WASHINGTON: Please observe carefully. When we say we want to "talk turkey" on something, that is merely a popular expression which means that we want to talk straight and truthfully about it. Do you understand now?

MOSCOW: Certainly not. As is well known, the Turks are

notoriously crooked and untruthful, and if they use this line to make any moves against us, our rockets will wipe them out in an instant.

WASHINGTON: The purpose of this line is not to wipe people out but to keep from wiping people out. Please test the machine from your end, Moscow. Say something nice.

MOSCOW: Peace and Friendship.

WASHINGTON: That's better. President Kennedy wants to say a word to you, Mr. Chairman.

MOSCOW: Where is he?

WASHINGTON: In Hyannis Port.

MOSCOW: What's he doing there?

WASHINGTON: Running away from Washington.

MOSCOW: Hello, Mr. President. This is Khrushchev. How's your back?

HYANNIS PORT: Sore. We've had a busy week. You know how it is: People fighting over the budget. Cutting foreign aid. Wanting to test everywhere. Trouble in Vietnam. Trouble on the railroads. Everybody wanting everything—now! But it's pleasant here—nice and sunny. How's the weather there?

MOSCOW: Why do you ask about the weather? You know the weather is a military secret. All this talk about the weather on this line, and Turkey, and mobilizing people to come to the aid of the country, and lazy dogs, and countdowns—instead of peaceful coexistence—worries me.

HYANNIS PORT: You are too suspicious, Mr. Chairman. You always assume the worst. You see things that don't exist. You misunderstand our words. We merely want to use this line to keep in touch, but we don't want to harry you.

MOSCOW: You couldn't bury us if you tried.

HYANNIS PORT: I didn't say "bury" but "harry." That's what I mean. You're too suspicious.

MOSCOW: What about the lynchings in the South?

The Fable of the Pygmies

ONCE UPON A TIME TWO YALE MEN[1] SET OUT TO RESCUE THE GREAT city of New York from a plague of pygmies. Handsome John and Witty Bill, they were called, and both were members of the Grand Old Party.

The pygmies had been running the city for years and it was a mess. Scoundrels and in some cases even ruffians terrified the citizens. Young mothers had to take their babies to Central Park in armored cars. Old women went to the theater in tanks, and no pretty woman would venture forth after dark unless convoyed by a regiment of troops from Governors Island.

In the outlying or underdeveloped regions of the city things were even worse. Some neighborhoods had been subjected to guerrilla warfare for years. The police wore bulletproof underwear and were armed with mortars and 15-inch howitzers. The streets were full of chuckholes as big as swimming pools, and the air was so full of soot that the setting sun could not penetrate across the Hudson River any farther than Sixth Avenue.

"This is not a wholly satisfactory state of affairs," said Witty Bill.

"We must kick the midgets out," said Handsome John.

"But first," said Witty Bill, "we must purify the people and cleanse the Grand Old Party. We must be worthy of victory. If the people were good we would not need to worry about scoundrels or even ruffians. If the people were self-reliant, they would live clean lives and move out of Queens into penthouses in Manhattan, and send their sons to Yale and their daughters to Radcliffe, or vice versa."

"If you go on like this, you'll wreck the party," said Handsome John.

[1] John Lindsay and William Buckley.

"But we'll own the wreckage," said Witty Bill. (He stole that line from Boise Penrose of Philadelphia who was also a very funny man in a very funny way.)

So saying, the two Yale men fell out.

Meanwhile, back at City Hall the pygmies were busy. When they first heard about Handsome John, they were scared, and the top pygmy resigned and ran off and got married, leaving the leadership to the smallest pygmy of them all.

"Unite," cried the smallest pygmy, and Bobby Kennedy and Hubert Humphrey—the noble defenders of good government and promisers of better things—rushed to his side.

"Unite," cried Handsome John; and Ike went West and peddled his books.

"Divide and perish, Republicans," shouted Witty Bill.

"Isn't he clever," said the press.

Well, a lot of mud and filth flowed under the Brooklyn Bridge between September and November. The East River was the color of Manhattan clam chowder, speckled with garbage, and things went, to steal one of Witty Bill's favorite phrases, from bad to worse. The newspapers closed down. The Yankees finished in sixth place in the American League. Thirty thousand cops had to be mobilized to get the Pope from Kennedy Field to St. Patrick's, and the moral climate of the city became so bad that Adam Clayton Powell had to rush back from Puerto Rico and pronounce his benedictions on the pygmies.

Then an odd thing happened. One night just before the election, there was a terrible storm in the city and everything stopped. The subways were flooded. All electric power went off. Every street in the city was choked with cars or streaming with water, and everybody had to stand still.

High in the great skyscrapers, suddenly black against the driving rain, the people were stranded without elevators, or television, or noise, and had nothing to do except think. That, apparently, is what did it.

By Election Day, the city was normal again, the polling booths were open, and the candidates were still at it. "Pygmies forever," cried the Democrat. "Divide and perish," said Witty Bill. "Kick the midgets out," shouted Handsome John.

But the voters simply passed by the polls. The Liberals came to their senses and abandoned the pygmies and the Republicans decided that one Yale man was enough. In the end Handsome John won, 156 to 93, and turned out to be a pretty good Mayor, or anyway, bigger.

Moral: When in doubt, sometimes it's better to stay in bed.

FIERY RUN, VIRGINIA

DECEMBER 30, 1966

The Old Virginia

Farmer's Almanac

THE OLD VIRGINIA FARMER'S POLITICAL ALMANAC FOR 1967:

January: Big Wind out of Texas hits Washington. President Johnson declares 1967 "peaceful bombing year." . . . Green Bay Packers put Kansas City through meat grinder in Super Bowl. . . . President says State of the Union is great. "Transcendental moonshine," says Senator Everett McKinley Dirksen. . . . Administration postpones decision on tax increase: waiting for more guidelines, President explains. . . . Berkeley students strike for abolition of midterm exams.

February: Storms buffet the capital, uprooting the beautification tulips. . . . Seventh Fleet bombs Harrison Salisbury of *The New York Times*, claiming he is a military target. . . . Representative Adam Clayton Powell moves entire House Education and Labor Committee to Puerto Rico, gives wife $5,000 raise. . . . Kennedys buy *Look* magazine and Harper & Row publishing house.

March: Abnormal calm settles over world. All officials give up public speaking, columnists give up Lyndon Johnson for Lent. . . . Forty-Day self-denying Moratorium on Meanness ensues. . . . Hawks and Doves have egg-roll on White House lawn. . . . General de Gaulle says that some Anglo-Saxons are not barbarians. . . . Bobby Baker stops tapping J. Edgar Hoover's telephones. . . . Senator Dodd of Connecticut praises Drew Pearson as "a fearless and geometrically accurate reporter." . . . President Johnson says Washington press corps is "tired," proposes unconditional truce discussions at Credibility Gap.

April: Turbulent weather breaks out again at equinox. . . . Representative Gerald Ford of Michigan proposes "safe, inexpensive victory offensive" in Vietnam. . . . Senator Mansfield proposes truce in Vietnam war, President counters with truce in war on poverty. . . . LBJ ranch defies high interest rates, adds three more counties to holdings in Texas. . . . New York knocks down last hotel in Manhattan, turns city over to the plumbers. Kennedys settle suit of Manchester book, hold philosophic seminar with 323 prominent book reviewers at Hickory Hill.

May: April showers bring May flowers. Outdoor sports begin. Yale moves to Poughkeepsie for on-the-spot inspection. . . . Justice Department demands particulars on Yale-Vassar merger. What kind of merger is planned? How far will it go? Are Princeton and Bryn Mawr involved? . . . President denounces both inflation and deflation; asks for more guidelines. . . . Walter Reuther demands three-day week and guaranteed annual wage. The new president of General Motors, Ralph Nader, says Reuther is unsafe at any price.

June: Summer thunderstorms spread. Colleges graduate largest class in history. . . . Secretary Rusk tells them we have turned the corner in Vietnam. General William Westmoreland says we have *not* turned the corner in Vietnam. Senator J. William Fulbright of Arkansas says there are no corners in Vietnam, only blind alleys.

July and August: Everybody goes away for the summer to think about it. John Chancellor appointed new White House press secretary.

September: Governor Ronald Reagan moves capital of California to Hollywood. . . . Georgia votes to do without a Governor, fifteen other states applaud the decision. . . . Supreme Court returns to Washington, abolishes cry of "God save the United States and this honorable Court" on ground it might violate Court's prayer decision. . . . President Johnson confers personally with each of the heads of the 500 largest corporations on advisability of tax increase, asks for patience and moderation. . . . Ray Shearer appointed new White House press scretary.

October: Los Angeles goes through World Series without a single hit, loses again to Baltimore. . . . Berkeley students strike for two-day week and guaranteed annual grade. . . . Austin, Texas, radio and television station praises President's policy in Vietnam. . . . Kennedys buy NBC and CBS. . . .

November: Governor George Romney of Michigan announces in East Lansing that if he decides to run for the Presidency, and gets the nomination, and is elected, "I shall go to Saigon." Edward P. Morgan, the new White House press secretary, says President Johnson was there way back in 1966.

December: President Johnson puts an end to the criticism of his Vietnam policy, appoints Bobby Kennedy Secretary of State, David Rockefeller Secretary of the Treasury, Walter Lippmann Ambassador to France, and Senator Fulbright Ambassador at Large. *Time, Look,* NBC, and CBS all applaud the decisions. Secretary Rockefeller says he is considering a tax rise.

9

FIRST AND LAST THINGS

The Things That Unite[1]

THE THINGS THAT UNITE THE PEOPLE OF THIS COUNTRY ARE
stronger than the things that divide them. That is why the original thirteen states compromised their differences and formed this
nation. That is why, in the last analysis, the will to preserve the
Union triumphed in 1865 over the dividing issue of slavery. . . .

The cause of this war lies in the failure of the peoples of the
Western world, who were bound together by Christian principles,
to put those principles into effect in their relations with each
other and with the rest of the world. Nobody but the most cynical scoffer will deny that our materialistic outlook in the past
twenty-five years has contributed greatly first to the wild boom of
the 1920's, then to the economic depression, and finally to the
Second World War. We have, in other words, lost sight of the
great uniting force of the Christian ethic which started this country and was the heart of its strength in the nineteenth century,
and have concentrated on materialistic issues which have divided
us section from section, class from class, and nation from nation.

It is not enough to say that God is on our side and to sing
"God Bless America." Take it from an old Presbyterian back-
slider, the question is not whether God is on our side but whether
we are on God's. God has blessed America. It's our turn now. . . .

"America," said Woodrow Wilson, "is not anything if it consists of each of us. It is something only if it consists of all of us;
and it can consist of all of us only as our spirits are banded
together in a common enterprise. That common enterprise is the
enterprise of liberty, justice and right." There is a lot of work to
be done in every community in this country in finding out again a
little more about the common enterprise of liberty, justice and
right. . . .

[1] From *Prelude to Victory* (New York: Alfred A. Knopf; 1942). Paper-
back edn. published by Pocket Books, December 1942.

The essence of the dynamic, progressive, American unity we must have in this war is tolerance. It is remarkable that anyone should have to stress that, but if you will look at our affairs in recent years or even in recent months you will see that there has been very little tolerance between labor and capital, between the New Dealers and the Old Dealers, between the young daring minds and the "traditional" minds, between the nationalists and the internationalists, and between the planners and those who want to let things ride. Somehow we have got into the habit of thinking that a man must be a whole-hogger: everything is either right or wrong, black or white, everybody is a New Dealer or an Old Dealer, a Roosevelt follower or a Roosevelt hater, isolationist or Utopian, Tory or Red. It is an unfortunate trend . . .

This same tendency to see everything as all good or all bad, all hopeful or hopeless, has plagued our thought and hampered our progress for a hundred years. Until the outbreak of the last war we suffered from what John Haynes Holmes has very well called an "optimistic fatalism." As one reads the history of the latter half of the nineteenth century, it seems that the majority of the historians and writers of those days were convinced that there was something in the nature of the universe, or in the economics of supply and demand, or in the balance of nations, or in the principles of democracy that assured the steady progress of mankind. Some attributed it to one thing and others to another, but until Marx came along with his great doubts there was general agreement that man's destiny was to go forward and upward and that no sin of omission or commission—and there were many, as we now know—could prevent that inexorable upward surge. Men spoke then of the "Golden Age," and of the "Stream of History," and of the "Law of Progress" as if there were indeed an inevitable movement of events toward the ideal as there was the inevitable movement of water to the sea, or as if there were a law of progress as certain and unavoidable as the law of gravity.

The result of that was that our "optimistic fatalism" made us unaware or indifferent to the need of fundamental change in the relations between men and their employers, between men and their governments, and between the great nations of the world.

And when that era of opportunity and indifference ended in the catastrophic war of 1914, the trend of men's thought suddenly shifted to the opposite extreme, and we have seen in the years since 1929 a wave of pessimism that has denied the law of inevitable progress, declared that the Century of Hope was dying from the moment of the first machine, and even questioned man's ability to determine his own fate. Look anywhere in the literature of the Western world in the dim era between the wars and you will find variations on this same theme. Spengler (*Decline of the West*), Berdyaeff (*The End of Our Time*), Keyserling (*The Travel Diary of a Philosopher*), Huizinga (*In the Shadow of Tomorrow*), Drucker (*The End of Economic Man*), De Reynold (*L'Europe Tragique*), Voigt (*Unto Caesar*), Dawson (*Beyond Politics*), and Wells (*The Fate of Homo Sapiens*) all declare that we have reached the end of an era. Man, it seems, is definitely behind the eight-ball. Liberal democracy, they say, is finished (Dean Inge defines it as "the artificial equality of unequals"). Their theme is that a dark and unpredictable future is before us, a period of "spiritual decadence, of loneliness and dereliction." A "cycle of catastrophes and collapses has begun." This, says Huizinga, is the pragmatic age; nothing is right or wrong, true or false. Even our taste has been degraded and "we are turning work into play and play into work." Somehow, Berdyaeff figures out, democracy, liberalism, socialism, and Communism are as out of date as Toryism; all these belonged to an age that has passed and we can merely look forward to a new dark age like that which followed the fall of the Western Roman Empire. We cannot win, it appears, no matter what happens. By the time we get a useful idea and finally understand it, behold, it is out of date!

So goes the theme, and you do not need to read a lot of bad translations of European pessimists to hear it. In a more moderate form you will see it in the pages of the *Congressional Record* for 1941 and 1942; you will see it in the columns of our press; you will hear it on any train. And the worst of it is that it is still competing with the "optimistic fatalism" of the late nineteenth and early twentieth centuries. On the one hand we have those who think we cannot lose this war; on the other we have those who do not see how we can prevent unprecedented collapse even if we win. On the one side we have those who said before the war: "It isn't necessary!" and on the other side we had those who said: "It's no use!" And the astonishing thing about it is that sometimes the same people said both.

The passage of time has shown us, however, that we were far too optimistic about the era between the Civil War and the first World War, and the events of this war have shown us that we were far too pessimistic about the ability of the British and the Russians to resist the Axis hordes. We have seen that both extremes of optimism and pessimism have prevented us from taking vital action in our own interests; we have seen that undue optimism led us to assume that action was not necessary, and that undue pessimism prevented us from taking action which we thought would do no good. But while we have had the opportunity to observe this basic fact we have not learned the lesson it contains.

Nobody has expressed the need for cooperation among "all of us" any better than Geoffrey Crowther in an editorial in the London *Economist* entitled "Wanted—A Prophet." "The need is," said Mr. Crowther, "not for a break with the past but for a return to the native tradition of clear thinking and courage, of lucidity and daring, of bold action for moderate ends. . . . The task of the Prophet is to fuse agreement into faith. He must take from each side not what is most inoffensive, but what is most effective and dynamic, and from the marriage of principles as opposite as male and female breed a new birth with life of its own.". . .

Obviously, these great and fundamental changes we have had to make to save our lives demand a new conception of each man's relation to his government, his business, and the rest of the world.

St. Albans School
Baccalaureate Sermon[1]

MY TEXT IS A SIMPLE ONE. IT IS TO BE FOUND IN THE FIRST VERSE OF the 21st Chapter of Revelation: "And I saw a new heaven and a new earth, for the first heaven and the first earth were passed away."

My theme is that, in the life of every young man and every young nation, there is a time when the first earth passes away; that this is true of you young Americans and that it is also true of America; and that this is a melancholy time only if young men and young nations cannot see the new heaven and the new earth of maturity.

In the space of one short generation, between your fathers' and your own, it is true that America's first heaven and earth have passed away. The era of the physical frontier is gone. The century of detachment from the world has passed. The time of America's youth is over, and now our lives and our ideals are no longer protected adequately by older civilizations in other parts of the world. You are not, therefore, the only ones who are graduating. America is going through its own commencement. Like you, it is passing into the era of responsibility.

If America does so like a young man, strong and eager for new responsibilities, well grounded in the moral philosophy on which it was founded, I have no doubt that it will succeed against any odds. If, however, it does so reluctantly, always looking backward and longing for a world that is gone, constantly looking outward at the defects of other people instead of searching in its own soul, it will not succeed and it will not realize its possibilities.

Last summer, my wife and I were on assignment in Europe. In

[1] The Cathedral Age, Autumn 1948.

Holland, we met a remarkable women, and she told us a story which illustrates my point. One of her sons had been killed in the war, and another was a prisoner in Germany. In a mood of depression one day, she wrote a letter to this second boy, reflecting on the sad fate of her country and her family. But the boy did not share her sorrow.

He wrote her a letter in which he said this: "I understand how you feel, but I do not agree. I have thought a lot about this and I have come to this conclusion: that if a man or a nation does not complain about fate, but seizes its fate willingly and clasps it eagerly, as the will of God, nothing in the long run can prevail against that man or that nation."

I cannot prove that the Dutch boy's philosophy has always been true of all men and all nations, but I believe that it is true of young men in this country today, and that it is profoundly true of America. I commend it to you, therefore, as an approach to your own problems and as an approach to the problems of your country.

It is not surprising that old men look back. They have always done so, and for many excellent reasons they must continue to do so. But a backward approach, especially at this time, has its limitations. It would have been convenient for us if the British security system had lasted for another generation or so. It would have been good if France had developed a sense of political responsibility equal to the principles of 1789. It would have been wonderful it our own achievements in the field of morality and social responsibility had kept pace with our scientific developments. It would have been pleasant if the Russians had remained in isolation for another century . . . But facts cannot be dismissed with wishes. The British security system is weak; the French have neither power nor political unity; the Russians do have a birthrate of forty to the thousand and will probably increase their population by over 40,000,000 in the next two generations. And these facts cannot be dismissed by longing for the day when they were not true.

There have been generations in this country which enjoyed the luxury of merely carrying on the work of their fathers more or less as it was done before, but yours is not one of them. You are going to have to experiment and pioneer again. You are going to have to re-examine, with objective openmindedness, many things that have been taken for granted by your fathers.

For many years, we have believed that human rights came before all other rights, that democracy was the political expression of great religious ideals, that the state existed for the individual, and that generosity, kindness, and pity were among the essential attributes of civilized men and nations. We still believe these things and I hope we shall always do so, but we must not assume, as we have in the past, that these things are self-evident to all other men. Today, the foundations of our philosophy are being challenged all over the world, and many men believe not only that these things are not true, but that we do not even believe them ourselves.

Another phenomenon of our time is the widespread belief that America's greatness rests primarily on its physical power. Woodrow Wilson, seeing the development of this idea in another time, argued against it: "America," he said, "is not ahead of other nations because she is rich. Nothing makes her great except her thoughts, except her ideals . . ." He was expressing an old and noble idea. . . .

"We must remember," the Younger Pitt told the House of Commons before Waterloo, "that it is not for ourselves alone that we must submit to privations. We have for ourselves the great duty of self-preservation to perform, but the duty of the people is now of a nobler and higher order. Amid the wreck and misery of nations, it is our just exultation that we provide not only for our own safety, but hold out a prospect to other nations . . . of what the exertions of a free people can effect; [and that, simultaneously] we demonstrate that at least in this corner of the world, the name of liberty is still revered, cherished, and sanctified. . . ."

You will notice that Pitt not only used the word "duty" but spoke of the "exultation" of the task. In the crisis of his time, England's first heaven and its first earth were passing away, but he had enough imagination to see a new heaven and a new earth in the challenge.

The time and place are different, and the instruments of tyranny are far greater than in the time of Napoleon, but the challenge to liberty is very much the same. Whether we like it or not, we are the inheritors of a great cause, and I am suggesting that we should not rail against this fate, but should, like the Dutch boy, clasp it eagerly, as the will of God.

APRIL 10, 1955

"Destitute of Faith but Terrified of Skepticism"

IN LINCOLN'S DAY, IT WAS SAID WE WERE "DESTITUTE OF FAITH but terrified of skepticism." It is more true today. The tragedy of official Washington is that it is confounded at every turn by the hangover of old political habits and outworn institutions but is no longer nourished by the ancient faith on which it was founded.

It clings to the bad things and casts away the permanent. It professes belief but does not believe. It knows the old words but has forgotten the melody. It is engaged in an ideological war without being able to define its own ideology. It condemns the materialism of an atheistic enemy, but glorifies its own materialism. It is searching for answers, not perceiving that the answer lies in the true meaning of Easter.

For the answer to Washington's fears lies in the hope of the Easter story, in the triumph of the spirit, which Easter symbolizes, in the faith that distinguishes us from our enemies and gives meaning to our society.

Washington is restless today because it wants an explanation of everything. It wants proof and reasons and total solutions, and it has forgotten what the Easter story tries to tell us, that man has always lived by hope, by his belief in the power of good to triumph over evil, a belief symbolized by the Festival of the Resurrection.

For us, on this newspaper, the meaning of Easter will always be defined by that saintly woman Anne O'Hare McCormick, who wrote just before she died last year: "In recent years, it has been necessary to emphasize the message of Easter—proof for the believer of his immortal destiny, evidence for the unbeliever of nature's constant renewal of life . . .

"Whatever happens, the earth will continue to renew itself and mankind will find reasons for living in the 'constants' that survive wars, Governments, revolutions and all the historic changes . . .

"Everywhere the things that last are more astonishing than the things that pass; they last because they are part of the spirit and nature of man, proofs of the divinity that shapes our ends, and also because they are kept alive by man's faith in himself and his hope of carrying into the future."

These ideas are not dead in Washington today. Indeed, they are our hope in the conflict that is proceeding here within the hearts and minds of the men who have the power of decision in the momentous question of peace or war.

Dwight D. Eisenhower, President of the United States, has recently fallen into the habit of talking about the use of the tactical atomic bomb as if it were merely another "conventional weapon," but he is still the son of Ida Elizabeth Stover Eisenhower of Augusta County, Virginia, and in the Far Eastern crisis, which is almost sure to come before another Easter, he is not likely to forget her religious training.

The same, fortunately, is true of John Foster Dulles, who in recent days has also been discussing the tactical A-bomb almost as if it were an instrument of mercy. (It knocks out military targets so much more effectively than the old bombs, he recently observed.) For Mr. Dulles, when he was not so harassed by the terrible urgencies of world politics, expressed the true nature of our dilemma not in terms of Capitol Hill but in terms of the traditional Easter story.

"As a nation, although still religious," he wrote in *War or*

Peace, "we have lost the connection between our religious faith and our practices. We keep religion and practices in separate compartments. We no longer see that our faith is relevant to modern conditions . . .

"We are in a dilemma, and it is a grave dilemma. Because we have not resolved it, our spiritual influence in the world has waned and we are tied down to the area that we can reach and influence by material things—guns and goods . . .

"Our greatest need is to regain confidence in our spiritual heritage. Religious belief in the moral nature and possibilities of man is, and must be, relevant to every kind of society . . . Great material power is dangerous in an age of materialism. It is not dangerous in an age of spiritualism . . ."

Against these ideas the appeals of political pressure and military strategy compete for supremacy, the issue comes to focus in the rocky islands of Quemoy and Matsu, and in the end the outcome of this conflict of moral, political, and military considerations within the minds of these two men may very well influence the whole course of history. This is the relevance of the Easter story in Washington today.

FEBRUARY 16, 1958

A Stronger Light

THE TEXT OF THIS MORNING'S SERMON IS TAKEN FROM AN ADDRESS by Mr. Lincoln to a young men's lyceum in Springfield, Illinois, on January 27, 1837. "At what point," he asked, "shall we Americans expect the approach of danger? By what means shall we fortify against it? Shall we expect some trans-Atlantic military giant to step the ocean and crush us at a blow? Never!

"All the armies of Europe, Asia, and Africa combined, with

all the treasure of the earth (our own excepted) in their military chest, with a Bonaparte for a commander, could not by force take a drink from the Ohio or make a track on the Blue Ridge in a trial of a thousand years.

"At what point then is the approach of danger to be expected? I answer, if it ever reach us it must spring up amongst us; it cannot come from abroad. If destruction be our lot we must ourselves be its author and finisher. As a nation of freemen we must live through all time or die by suicide."

This is, if one may say so during the Lincoln Birthday celebrations, almost as good as anything ever written by Bryce Harlow for Sherman Adams, and it is as topical as *My Fair Lady*. For while missiles, rockets, launching sites, and military affairs in general still dominate the headlines and the debates in Congress, the unresolved crisis of our times, underlying all other crises, is not primarily military but ideological, not external but internal, not mechanical but cultural.

The point, of course, is relative; the military threat is real and grave; nobody denies it. Mr. Lincoln did not have to worry about transatlantic rockets or atomic power in the hands of an enemy. But the country is aware of the military threat: it is taking steps to deal with it. The same cannot be said with equal assurance about our internal defenses in the fields of education, philosophy, or diplomacy.

Congress will give the Pentagon all it wants for missiles, and probably more, but what it will do about scholarships, teachers' salaries, school construction, the foreign service—what lead it will give the people on how to meet the crisis at the personal and community level—is another matter.

"There is no ill," Thoreau wrote, "which may not be dissipated, like the dark, if you let in a stronger light upon it. . . . If the light we use is but a paltry and narrow taper, most objects will cast a shadow wider than themselves." The light cast here this week has once more been on military objects, on political campaign contributions from the gas lobby in Texas, on influence peddling in the FCC on unsubstantiated McCarthy-like charges against Federal officials.

"I hope I am over wary," Mr. Lincoln said to his lyceum

friends in Springfield. "But if I am not, there is even now something of ill omen amongst us." His appeal, 121 years ago, was not to the Federal capital in Washington, but to individual men and women in their communities. He was not asking what Washington could do to help the people, but what the people could do to help Washington, and fortunately the same need is felt today.

Nothing is clearer here now than that the Federal Government is not going to solve the education problem, and could not, even if the men at the top thought in terms of ideas and brains, which they do not. They will make some money available, no doubt, but they will not set a national standard for high school graduation, badly as it is needed, and they cannot set standards of study in the home.

The trouble in the land, said Robert Oppenheimer recently in *Foreign Affairs*, is that the American people have no clear image of the good life or the Government's place in it. One wonders. The trouble is that we do have such a clear image of the good and easy life that nobody even debates it. It is based on the assumption that the production and consumption or enjoyment of material things guaranteed by the Government is in itself the good and easy life, and the crisis is that this assumption has failed us.

In past national crises there was little that ordinary citizens could do to help. They could not produce missiles. They could not get the Vanguard off the ground. They could not pierce the Soviet mystery.

But they can sit on school boards. They can inquire into the state of education in their local schools. They can demand standards of study. They can influence their children to prepare for and serve the nation, and they can listen to Mr. Lincoln: "Passion has helped us," he said, "but can do so no more. Reason— cold, calculating, unimpassioned reason—must furnish all the materials for our future support and defense. Let those materials be molded into general intelligence [and] sound morality . . ." Here, as the man said, endeth the lesson.

"The Strong, Central Role of Simple Fairness"

"I SOMETIMES THINK," SAID MR. JUSTICE CARDOZO IN 1921, "THAT we worry ourselves overmuch about the enduring consequences of our errors. They may work a little confusion for a time. In the end they will be modified or corrected or their teaching ignored. The future takes care of such things." This was written in a day when reflective men were more confident than they are now about the inevitability of progress, and yet the stabilizing influences in American life have been at work this week.

In the generation since the depression of the early Thirties, the executive and legislative branches of the Government have combined, often with the acquiescence of the judiciary, to strengthen the authority of the central government in dealing with the anxieties of war and economic distress. This has been done often at the expense of individual liberties, but now the Supreme Court has stepped in to redress the balance and to remind us of what Mr. Justice Holmes proclaimed in 1897: that "the law is the witness and external deposit of our moral life: its history is the history of the moral development of the race."

In the series of opinions handed down this month, and particularly this week, the high court has simply been serving once more as the moral conscience of a people drugged by the uncertainty, perplexities, prosperity, and diversions of the past two decades.

It is not saying that the representatives of the people cannot use the investigative power of the Government to gather information and pass laws in defense of the Republic. It is merely saying that these things should be done with due respect for the Constitution and the Bill of Rights. It is reminding us of what we are and what we stand for, and despite the torrent of legal language, it is really saying some very simple things.

It is reminding Government officials that Government employees are also citizens who are covered by the Bill of Rights. It is saying that teachers must not be harassed by the state just because some officials or legislators don't like their teaching. It is questioning Government's right to compel men to squeal on other men and to convict them on evidence they cannot see or evaluate.

And what is so surprising and significant about all this is that these proclamations of "liberty through all the land" have created such a stir. For what they are saying is merely what was once taken for granted—namely, that there must be a fair balance between liberty and authority in a government of laws. Thomas Wentworth, Earl of Stafford, summed it all up in his defense against a charge of high treason in 1641: "God, His Majesty and my own conscience . . . can bear me witness: that the happiness of a kingdom consists in a just poize of the King's prerogative and the subject's liberty: and that things would never go well till they went hand in hand together."

Men will always differ about what is a "just poize" between authority and liberty, as Mr. Justice Clark's dissents this month illustrate, but as Bernard Schwartz has pointed out in an excellent book on *The Supreme Court,* published this week, it is the high court that is entrusted under the American system with securing that "just poize."

The central question is whether in the light of the trend toward economic centralization in the United States and in the face of the clear and present danger of the Soviet menace, the pendulum has swung too far in recent years toward the side of Government authority.

Mr. Justice Jackson went to his grave in 1954 believing it had. "In this anxiety-ridden time," he wrote just before his death, "many are ready to exchange some of their liberties for a real or fancied increase in security against external foes, internal betrayers or criminals.

"Others are eager to bargain away local controls for a Federal subsidy. Many will give up individual rights for promise of collective advantages. The real question . . . is whether, today, liberty is regarded by the masses of men as their most precious possession."

The court, this week, has reflected Justice Jackson's parting anxiety. It has not only revived the ancient traditions of the sanctity of reputation, and the rights of privacy and academic freedom, but has summoned the rest of the Government to redeem Chief Justice Hughes's promise that "in the forum of conscience, duty to a moral power higher than the state has always been maintained."

Whether that duty will be maintained now remains to be seen. The court does not make the laws, and people do not always follow their conscience. But it has invoked what John Lord O'Brian calls "the irresistible moral power exerted by conscience," and argued that the strength of the nation demands "a strong and central role of simple fairness."

FIERY RUN, VIRGINIA

APRIL 17, 1960

Twilight of Evening, Twilight of Dawn?

THE HUMAN RACE, TO WHICH SO MANY READERS OF THE NEW YORK *Times* belong, has made another journey round the sun. Despite Mr. Khrushchev and the Presidential candidates, Fiery Run is once more charging through the green coves and valleys of Virginia to the sea. It is Easter again, with its message of the new beginnings of life, and even the Washington Senators are dreaming of getting out of the American League cellar.

Where, then, do we stand? Are the pessimists right that this is the twilight before the darkness? Or are the optimists right in seeing our age as the twilight before the dawn? In the larger terms beyond petty politics, there is something to be said for the optimistic view.

All the politicians—Republican and Democratic American, British, French, and Russian—are overwhelmed by the dangers of the age. In our own country there is a growing debate on fundamental things: on the education of our children, on the relations of the white man and the colored man, on the condition of our old people; in short, on the faith, purpose, and values of our society. Nobody on the national scene seems to have any clear answers, but everybody in the Presidential race is at least dealing now with the basic questions.

Vice President Nixon may be right in saying that the Federal Government should not play a larger role in the allocation of our national resources. Governor Stevenson, and Senators Kennedy and Humphrey, on the other hand, may be right in arguing that the Federal Government must give a stronger lead and more money if educational standards are to be raised, hospitals are to be built, and slums are to be cleared. But at least they are all dealing with the same fundamental problems of the purpose and security of the American people.

Most politicians have the same problem: their shortcomings are usually visible on the surface and their virtues concealed. With President Eisenhower, however, it has been the other way around: his virtues have been more apparent than his shortcomings. His optimism, his generosity of spirit, his faith in compromise, his general cheerfulness have all been more obvious than his determination to avoid trouble.

As a result, the country has been dreaming. One hundred years ago, the population of the United States was 31,000,000. In the last ten years alone, which have been a decade of social, military, and political revolution all over the world, the population of the United States has grown by 30,000,000.

This is not a situation that can be handled effectively by half measures, and fortunately the new Presidential candidates of both parties realize it. Even the Democratic candidates of 1960 are different from their predecessors of the New and Fair Deals. Franklin D. Roosevelt and Harry S. Truman taught the country to expect the benefits of the welfare state. The new men are beginning to teach the country that it must also pay for these benefits.

We are, then, at least at the beginning of a new beginning. It may be true, as the philosophers, the divines, and some politicians say, that there is no sense of purpose in the country. But how does a vast, continental nation of 180,000,000 get a sense of purpose without assertive political leadership? It can get it in a shooting war; sometimes purpose rises out of a great religious renaissance; but neither exists in America today.

Accordingly, political leadership, bringing the intellectual and political communities of the nation together to define the new problems of a new age, is necessary. This will not produce faith, but it can produce purpose, and the chances are that if the destiny of the nation were expressed in moral terms from the pinnacle of the government the people would follow it.

Maybe the pessimists are right: Easter in American may be just a new hat or the beginning of the major-league baseball season. But religion, if it is no longer a powerful faith, is at least still a powerful symbol, especially when it speaks hopefully, as it does at Easter, of new beginnings.

CAPE CANAVERAL, FLORIDA

FEBRUARY 25, 1962

Is the Moon Really Worth John Glenn?

THE EXAMPLES PLACED BEFORE A NATION ARE VITAL. WHAT WE constantly observe, we tend to copy. What we admire and reward, we perpetuate. This is why John Glenn himself is almost as important as his flight into outer space, for he dramatized before the eyes of the whole nation the noblest qualities of the human spirit.

Outside of the morality play of our cowboy movies, where the hero always gets the girl and the villain always gets slugged behind the saloons, courage, modesty, quiet patriotism, love of family, and religious faith are not exactly the predominant themes of our novels, plays, TV shows, movies, or newspapers these days. Yet Glenn dramatized them all coast to coast and around the world. This was no insensitive robot who landed here from the heavens yesterday morning, but a warm and thoughtful human being: natural, orderly, considerate, and, at times, quietly amusing and even eloquent.

His departure from Cape Canaveral in a blaze of orange fire was a technical triumph, but his return was a human triumph. When he came back and saw his lovely wife, Annie, he put his head on her shoulder and cried. Thereafter nothing ruffled him, not the President, or the clamorous press, or the whirring cameras, or the eager shouting crowds.

This memorable performance, of course, may not stamp out juvenile delinquency overnight, but the models of the nation— not the uncovered cover girls of today but the larger models of human character—are probably more important than this age believes.

When Walter Bagehot, the English editor and scientist, made his famous study one hundred years ago of why some nations progressed, he concluded that what a nation admired and despised was almost as important as its military power. "Slighter causes than is commonly thought," he said, "may change a nation from the stationary to the progressive state of civilization, and from the stationary to the degrading."

It all depended, he insisted, on the model of character emulated or eliminated. If the enduring qualities of nobility, intelligence, perseverance, and courage were uppermost, then he felt all was well. For then, he asserted, "a new model in character is created for the nation; those characters which resemble it are encouraged and multiplied; those contrasted with it are persecuted and made fewer.

"In a generation or two, the look of the nation becomes quite different; the characteristic men who stand out are different; the men imitated are different; the result of the imitation is different. A lazy nation may be changed into an industrious, a rich into a poor, a religious into a profane, as if by magic, if any single cause, however slight, or any combination of causes, however subtle, is strong enough to change the favorite and detested types of character."

If this was true in the middle of the nineteenth century it has even more validity in this age of instantaneous communication. Only a few hundred people heard Lincoln's Gettysburg Address. New models and styles are now set by television every day, but most of them are models of cars and styles of dresses and hairdos. What transcontinental television did for the nation on the Glenn story illustrates the wider application of the idea. It almost made up for what it does to us the rest of the time, but not quite.

Meanwhile, the question remains: how many more John Glenns and Al Shepards are hiding in this country? Outer space is a long way to go to discover a new generation of leaders of men, but if we have to recruit them there, why not? Human weightlessness is almost our major problem in Washington and, since these astronauts know more about it than anybody else, maybe a couple of them should be transferred to the thin hot air of the capital.

After all, Glenn is 40 and even if he looks like the freshman football coach at Muskingum College he can't go off spinning around the earth without his Annie forever. Once Christopher Columbus had discovered America, Ferdinand and Isabella didn't insist that he go back every Tuesday.

Besides, is the moon worth John Glenn, when we need him so badly on earth?

APRIL 18, 1965

The Capital and the Easter Story

THE OLDER THE WORLD GROWS, THE MORE IT NEEDS AND DENIES faith. This is why Easter and the Passover, the great religious symbols of hope and belief, are still relevant.

We protest against it, but we cannot escape it. What the astonishing modern mind creates, the normal mind can neither understand nor disprove and must therefore reject or accept on faith. Nothing important that we begin is sure to turn out as planned; therefore, we must hope. Nobody who leads our affairs is perfect; therefore, we must believe in somebody or something.

Easter was not a popular nationwide celebration in the early days of the Republic. Louisiana and other non-Puritan states accepted it. The Lutherans and the Episcopalians did, too. But the Puritan mind rebelled against the excesses that often followed the Lenten period, and it was not until the Civil War that the majority of the Protestant churches, seeking to console the bereaved in the war, chose to celebrate Easter, with its promise of victory of life over death.

The present age is caught up in the same dilemma. It lives in uncertainty. It is searching for guidance. It has created a world it cannot understand. It does not believe, but it believes in believing; therefore, it relies on faith, without knowing what its faith is.

Nothing illustrates the tug of America's religious past better than the Johnson administration. The President is always quoting Isaiah: "Come let us reason together," though no President in this century was ever so allergic to other men's reason. His most intimate staff member, Bill Moyers, is a deeply religious man who cannot write a Presidential speech without quoting the Good Book.

The more the President gets involved in the complexities of the present-day world, the more he is confronted with conflicting advice, reason, and logic, and, therefore, the more he falls back on his own intuitive judgment. He is not himself a religious man, but he feels the tradition of the past and acts on it when in doubt. In doing so he is not far from the spirit and tradition of a country whose political institutions are a reflection of religious principles.

The liberties all the spokesmen at the White House, the State Department, and the Pentagon talk about defending today, after all, were established by that remarkable group of eighteenth-century American political leaders who took their conception of Man from the West's central religious tradition. They insisted that the individual man belonged to his Creator, and, since he was an immortal soul, he was entitled to certain inalienable rights which no government had the right to deny.

On the ethical or religious concept that each man is important and should have an equal chance, American constitutional government was founded. If there has been a decline of decency in the modern world and a revolt against law and fair dealing, it is precisely because of the decline in the belief in each man as something precious.

American policy since the last war has been guided, almost unconsciously, by this principle. On the home front, the war on poverty, the education bill, and Medicare are merely illustrations of the point. Overseas, no doubt, the defense of democratic principles all over the world served American national interests, but Washington has nevertheless been operating more than most capitals on an ideal.

It has not, like the British, the French, the Dutch, and the other colonial powers, been defending an empire. It is the first source of power in the world that has tried to maintain peace all over the globe, not primarily for its own commercial interests. Whatever may be said, for example, about the moral ambiguities of American policy in Vietnam, it cannot be said that the United States is fighting there for Wall Street or the rubber industries of Akron.

The United States had no major commercial interests in defending Greece and Turkey, in protecting Berlin, in going to the defense of Korea, in risking nuclear war with the Soviet Union over Cuba, in helping put down the threat to the Congo, in defying the Chinese Communist bombardment of Quemoy and Matsu, or in trying to maintain the peace in Cyprus.

In many of these crises, the United States has made mistakes. Often it has overreached itself, and sometimes it has presumed, not only to do God's work but to replace Him. But, in general, it can be said, twenty years after the last war, that it has acted for the common good.

None of this, however, could be done without some kind of faith. Sometimes it has been the kind of faith in "believing what you know ain't so," sometimes, as in the Cuban crisis, it has been what Wordsworth called "the faith that looks through death." But most of the time it has been an instinct from the past, and that instinct comes, whether we accept or deny it, from the religious tradition of the past.

The Johnson Administration prides itself in creative pragmatism. Johnson is its political genius, McNamara its resident human computer, but both of them are in the old tradition. On the big decisions they go back to instinct, and that instinct is not one of reason or pragmatism alone but of the old faith which is the Easter story of "things hoped for, the evidence of things not seen."

10

AMERICA

DECEMBER 8, 1941

America Goes to War

THE UNITED STATES WENT TO WAR TODAY AS A GREAT NATION should—with simplicity, dignity, and unprecedented unity. The deep divisions which marked this country's entrance into the wars of 1776, 1812, 1861, 1898, and 1917 were absent. Overnight, partisan, personal, and sectional differences were shelved. The atmosphere of the Capital was grave, but for the first time in years there were no doubts.

It was clear from early morning that historic events were afoot. By sun-up workmen were pounding great stakes into the ground and straining a wire cable around the House wing of the Capitol to keep the crowds back. At the same time, barricades were being moved into place at the main entrances to the Capitol and attendants were tacking up signs reading "Show Your Passes."

By 11 o'clock, Marines with fixed bayonets and Metropolitan and Capitol police were swarming all over Capitol Hill and guarding the White House. Streets leading to and from these two buildings were blocked off. By 11:30 two open cars full of Secret Service men had rolled up under the pillared portico of the White House with riot guns rigged along the sides.

Meanwhile, the whole tempo of the city had changed. There was very little of the sense of impending physical damage which dominated London on the outbreak of the war, but there was a sense of hurry. More cars were on the streets than at any time since Inauguration Day; everybody was evidently trying to do a great many things all at once; jammed telephones caused delays of as long as three hours on calls to New York; crowds were rapidly gathering at the White House and the Capitol.

Promptly at noon the big glass doors at the White House swung open, six limousines drew up, and President Roosevelt came out on the arm of his eldest son, Captain James Roosevelt, who was wearing the uniform of an officer of the Marines.

Mr. Roosevelt descended the steps without a word. The car, bearing the White House insignia, started at once for the Capitol. Mrs. Roosevelt, Mrs. James Roosevelt, Mrs. Dorothy Brady, Mrs. Stephen Early, Grace Tully, the President's acting secretary, and General Edward M. Watson and Captain John Beardahl, the President's military and naval aides, were in the official party.

The crowds at the Capitol cheered as the official cars rolled up to a special entrance. Mr. Roosevelt went at once to the Speaker's entrance, where he waited for a few minutes before entering the chamber.

Meanwhile, the Army and police officials were taking elaborate precautions at all entrances. At every door stood a soldier of the Regular Army or a Marine. As each person approached, the soldier snapped to present arms, blocking the door. Credentials were examined twice more at special barricades before anyone was permitted to enter the chamber.

Even the Chinese Ambassador, Dr. Hu Shih, for whom this was an especially important occasion, was held up at the door until Senator Connally of Texas interceded for him, but he finally got in to join Dr. A. Loudon, the Minister of the Netherlands, and Viscount Halifax, the British Ambassador.

As the President waited in the Speaker's office, members of the Senate marched down the long corridor and through the rotunda to the House side and entered the chamber behind Majority Leader Barkley of Kentucky and Minority Leader McNary of Oregon.

As soon as the Senators were seated the members of the Supreme Court entered in their black robes and sat along the edge of the House on the left of the rostrum. At 12:23 the members of the President's Cabinet arrived, in time to hear Speaker Rayburn rap for silence and announce: "The President of the United States!"

The members of both houses, their guests in the rear of the chamber, diplomats in the gallery, officials of the Government, a handful of soldiers, and the people who had managed to get seats in the galleries immediately rose to their feet. For an instant there was silence and then suddenly there was an ever-increasing round of applause, which terminated suddenly as Speaker Rayburn rapped with his gavel.

At that moment the President appeared. Then he received an ovation unmatched in his eight years as Chief Executive. Applause broke into cheering and lasted over a minute. Then, after a brief prayer by the chaplain, Mr. Roosevelt began to read his message while the movie lights blazed down on him from the galleries and the cameras whirred.

Seldom, if ever, in a message to the Congress has the President judged the temper of the representatives of the people better than he did in this speech. Two facts seemed to impress this gathering more perhaps than the simple words of the speech. By not the slightest inflection did he suggest that the facts of the world situation had finally justified his policy, as even his opponents were admitting today he might very well have done.

When he said that the United States would always remember the character of the Japanese attack, everybody stood and applauded, and he was interrupted repeatedly by cheering. Only at the end did he acknowledge this greeting. Then he looked up and smiled and waved his hand.

The Young Man from
the Upper Middle West

THE DEATH OF SENATOR JOSEPH R. MCCARTHY RAISES AN INTRI-
guing question about the politics of the Upper Middle West, particularly of Wisconsin and Minnesota. What is it about the
politics of these two states in the depression and post-depression
era that has produced so many startling young politicians who
have faded in early middle age?

Old Bob La Follette and George Norris came out of the
Populist movement of the early 1890's and managed to stay the
course on the national scene. But what of young Phil La Follette,
whose star shone so brightly for a time and then suddenly flick-
ered out? And what of young Bob La Follette, who lasted much
longer, won the respect of the Senate, but was finally defeated by
McCarthy and ended in suicide?

Other parts of the country have produced similar cases of
prominent young men who rose to national renown and then
faded fast, but Wisconsin and Minnesota seem to have reproduced the pattern more than most.

Harold E. Stassen was Governor of Minnesota at 31, the
youngest and most promising Governor in the Union. At 35, he
was temporary chairman and keynoter of the Republican Convention and floor manager of the late Wendell Willkie's successful fight for the 1940 Presidential nomination. But his political
fortunes have steadily declined, though the liberal Republicans
whom he supported are now in command of the party.

Governor Floyd Olsen of Minnesota was the darling of the
young liberals of the Upper Middle West during the depression,
but like McCarthy, he died unexpectedly in his forties. Joe Ball
of Minnesota was appointed by Stassen to fill the unexpired term

of the late Senator Ernest Lundeen in 1943, made a great splash as a liberal maverick in the upper chamber, then turned conservative and disappeared into free-lance journalism and business.

Governor Luther Youngdahl of Minnesota gave promise for a time of emerging on the national scene as another brilliant young liberal, but chose to return to the comparative obscurity of the bench just when he was beginning to attract attention. To a certain extent even Senator Hubert Humphrey of Minnesota has followed the pattern. Nobody in the Senate works harder, covers more ground, or masters the intricacies of complex legislation more than Humphrey, yet he has not realized the hopes and ambitions of his early years in Washington.

No generalization is intended here, and certainly these men are not to be compared with McCarthy except in this one sense of sudden prominence followed by disillusion. And yet there is something in the post-depression political record of these two states that differs from the pattern elsewhere.

Almost all these men were fierce advocates, with a vast capacity for exciting both devotion and sharp opposition. Almost all were, or are, deadly serious. Stassen is as determined now to make a new political career in Pennsylvania as he was when he started in Minnesota. And he is deterred neither by the failure of his "dump Nixon" movement last year nor by his lack of support in Pennsylvania.

The political atmosphere and ground rules of Wisconsin and Minnesota help explain the early rise of young, individualistic reformers. This politically restless country is less rigidly tied to the two great parties and often more radical than the other areas of the Middle West.

Populism, championing the revolt of the farmers, was more formidable in the Nineties in Kansas, where "Sockless Jerry" Simpson—"the Moses of Medicine Lodge"—and Mary Ellen Lease exhorted the poor farmers to "raise less corn and more hell." It produced more successful national figures in William Jennings Bryan and George Norris in Nebraska, more striking personalities in Benjamin R. ("Pitchfork Ben") Tillman in South Carolina and Tom Watson, "the sage of Hickory Hill," in Georgia.

But these states reverted to party discipline, with its rigid rules of political apprenticeship and slow political promotion, while Minnesota and Wisconsin remained for many years under the influence of the experiments with farmer-labor politics.

The economic depression of the Thirties, too, kept alive the spirit of Populism and political irregularity in Minnesota and Wisconsin to a degree not evident in other states. The depression and post-depression politicians from this area—or at least many of the young successful ones—have all been in a great hurry, believing, somehow, that their particular reforms, if defended with endless advocacy, could quickly change what they felt was wrong.

On the larger stage of national politics, however, young men in a hurry have their troubles, especially in these days of full employment and general prosperity.

OCTOBER 30, 1963

Those Standard-Setters
Along the Potomac

THE CAPITAL OF THE UNITED STATES IS INVOLVED ONCE MORE IN official scandal, and no wonder. The work and atmosphere of the place breed it, and the surprising thing, given the opportunity and temptation, is not that there is so much of it, but so little.

At the upper levels, this is an expense-account town. More money is available here to entertain and influence a few hundred people than in any other city in the world. More officials, ambassadors, lobbyists, and legislators are living beyond their salaries here than in any capital on earth, and this is not designed wholly to promote happiness and culture.

Politics is in many ways the art of exchanging favors. A Congressman's votes win Government contracts for his district. An ambassador's entertainment often gains special consideration for his country's political or financial interests. A lobbyist's campaign contributions often gain him access to officials who influence Government grants. This is useful but sometimes awkward.

A conflict of interest is more than merely an Internal Revenue agent auditing his own income-tax return. For a Congressman, it may be a genuine conflict between his district's interest, between his friends and his constitutents, and sometimes even between his own country and some other country that may be retaining his law firm at an inflated fee.

Almost everything is inflated here more than most places, beginning with the language. Exaggeration is the instrument of political life. The Administration inflates its budget on the assumption that it will be cut by Congress. Congress inflates its attack on the budget on the assumption, usually correct, that the bill was padded in the first place. Candidates, as we know, are either infallible or insufferable, depending on who's talking, and after a while, nobody quite believes what the other side is saying.

This, of course, has always been true. President Washington was charged with placing the capital here in the first place in order to benefit from the sale of his private lands, but lately four things have contributed to the cult of petty chiseling. These are the high cost of living, the high cost of TV campaigning, the high rate of taxation, and the high level of Government spending at home and abroad.

Many Congressmen who have trouble meeting their expenses here and in their districts pass judgment on billions of dollars' worth of appropriations, often without conviction that all the money is being well spent. Most of them live in terror of being defeated and of going broke to avoid being defeated.

Increasingly, the success or failure of many politicians depends on their getting Government contracts for their areas, and when they are successful these contracts are so large that the companies concerned are lavish with campaign contributions, or legal fees, or favors of other kinds.

Meanwhile, some officials have access to ships for their private pleasure (former Secretary of the Navy Korth), some are intimate with key Senators or Pentagon officials (Bobby Baker), and there are always trips abroad offered by foreign governments, or private companies, or financed by the Congress itself with counterpart funds piled up in some foreign country.

In this atmosphere of waste, favors, and expense-account entertainment and travel, a kind of moral indifference develops about petty corruption. Most men in both branches of the Government are as honest and sensitive to conscience as men elsewhere. In fact, judging by the splashy larcenies of the old days, the current breed of politician is probably an improvement, but with all this money, all this conniving, and all this temptation around, it is not always easy to stay out of trouble.

Nor has it been made any easier by year-round antics of the Congress. When the right honorable gentlemen finished their work by Labor Day or before, their women were able to keep them right and even make them gentlemen, but now many of them are loose on the town for weeks at a stretch, and this has not added much to their moral grandeur.

A shorter and more efficient Congress, and particularly a sensible way of raising money for political campaigns, would help all this, but more conflict-of-interest laws would probably do little good. Everything depends on the standards that are accepted or at least tolerated, particularly among those who presume to set standards for the nation. And the standards around here are under severe strain.

They have been debased by power and money, by the pressure of politics, and by the most fatal weakness of Washington, which is that, after a certain success, men here begin to think that they really *are* what they merely represent.

Who Will Investigate
the Investigators

THERE IS A MESS IN WASHINGTON AGAIN, AND VERY LITTLE EVI-
dence that either the White House or the Congress is going to do
very much to clean it up. The improprieties of Secretary of the
Navy Korth in carrying on his private business on Navy stationery
and on his official yacht are widely condemned in the capital, but
he will be given an honorable farewell by the top admirals of the
Navy when he leaves tomorrow. And he leaves with the assur-
ances and even praises of the President himself.

This is the man who wrote to his former and future associate,
G. E. Homstrom, at the Continental National Bank of Fort
Worth about his plans to "have a little party aboard the *Sequoia*
[the Navy Secretary's official yacht] primarily for my Texas
friends. . . .

"I am just wondering," Secretary Korth's letter of August 13,
1962, continued, "whether you and some of my other friends at
the Continental may be coming through; likewise if you have
some extra good customers that it would be nice to have."

This and much more evidence of misuse of the Secretary of
the Navy's office came to the attention of the Congress, and
shortly thereafter Korth resigned, but the President took the line
today that the Secretary had not acted improperly and, while
vaguely regretting his letter-writing, praised his contributions to
the nation's security.

The "Bobby Baker" case illustrates the same casual attitude
toward charges of improper conduct. Ever since Baker, former
secretary to the Democratic majority in the Senate, resigned after
charges that he was using his position to amass a private fortune

on the side, this city has been full of ugly rumors about illicit relations between Baker's girl friends and prominent Senators and officials in the Administration. Every vigilant newspaper office in Washington has a list of names of those implicated with Baker and his lobbying friends and his girls. And the gossip feeds on itself to such an extent that it has already poisoned the atmosphere of the whole Government.

The only way to deal with this kind of material, much of it deeply disturbing and a lot more of it probably malicious trash, is to investigate it thoroughly, objectively, and in private. This may yet be done. It is in the hands of the Senate Committee on Rules and Administration, but that committee is operating under a Senate resolution which instructs it to look into the conduct only of Senate employees and former employees (not Senators), and it is refusing to provide outside legal counsel for both the Democratic majority and the Republican minority of the committee. The result is that there is absolutely no confidence here that the Rules Committee will really investigate their own Senate colleagues or that the permanent Senate employees will really be in a position to investigate their bosses.

The main problem in both the Korth and Baker cases is not illegal or criminal action. In fact, all the talk about Korth and Baker tends to obscure the main thing, which is the loose system in Washington that encourages these personal improprieties. It is the system of trading favors and using influence and yachts for the purpose that is the cause of the trouble. Baker and Korth, whose indiscretions were quite different, are merely the result.

The yacht *Sequoia* is merely a flashy symbol of this system. It costs the Government far more than Baker or Korth is ever likely to make in a lifetime. It plies up and down the Potomac with a crew of two officers and eight men and is primarily a floating restaurant and bar for the entertainment of Senators and Congressmen.

Baker allegedly peddled influence to lobbyists and managed to buy houses and motels where he could give and get more favors. But the *Sequoia* is the Pentagon's own official instrument for influence peddling—for encouraging generous defense appropriations—and under such a system it is scarcely surprising that

Korth used the old tub occasionally for his own purposes.

The mess, in short, is not going to be cleaned up by concentrating on Korth and Baker, but by overhauling the system. Baker couldn't peddle such influence on his own; his influence came from his close association with Senators and with officials who knew he was close to Vice President Lyndon Johnson and others. Korth wasn't crooked; he was morally insensitive and stupid, but the President insists Korth wasn't fired, which raises the question: Why not?

How is the system to be changed if the President praises a man with judgment like Korth's, and the Senate won't conduct an objective investigation of its own shortcomings? The official reaction here to Baker and Korth is more of a problem than they are, for they are gone and the system that produced them remains.

MAY 6, 1962

How to Reach Agreement
on the Wrong Thing

LABOR AND MANAGEMENT ARE ACTING THESE DAYS LIKE A QUARRELsome old married couple. They have been hurling pots and pans at each other for twenty-five years, often at the peril of the whole neighborhood, but just as soon as somebody steps in to restore order, they turn on the interloper and demand to be left alone to fight in peace.

Big Labor and Big Business disagree on almost everything else, but on this they are united. They want the Government to stay out of the collective-bargaining process. They don't say the "public interest" is not important, but each wants to define it for himself. Maybe they can make this stick, but if they do they will be about the only centers of power in the world today that can exercise such a degree of freedom. Everywhere else in an increasingly complicated and interdependent world, power is being scrutinized and limited.

Kennedy and Khrushchev have more physical power at their command than any two potentates in the history of the world, but their freedom to use it is more restricted today than in the days of Teddy Roosevelt or Alexander the Great. The more atomic bombs they gather the more the world demands their control. Each has the power to end the war in Vietnam tomorrow but neither dares use it.

Every action increasingly produces a reaction. Russia demands the freedom to test its bombs and the United States follows, but the exercise of that freedom does not increase their security. If Washington raises tariffs on glass and carpets, the Common Market countries retaliate. If London raises its interest rates, Wall Street is affected.

It would be surprising in such a world, then, to find two such enormously powerful entities as American Big Labor and Big Business achieving the kind of freedom from Government supervision and even intervention that they are now demanding.

What labor does about wages and what business does about prices inevitably affects the nation's ability to compete with other democratic industrial nations, to maintain a population that is growing by 3,100,000 a year, to deal with the 4,500,000 unemployed, to find the 2,500,000 new jobs required each year as a result of automation and the growing labor force, to sustain a $50 billion annual bill for the armed forces, and to help the free world maintain itself.

It is not a corporation's or a labor union's primary function to fend for the national interest. If the steel industry satisfied its stockholders at 50 per cent of capacity production or the electrical and other construction workers gouge their employers and the public, then somebody has to look to the national interest, and that is clearly the President's job.

The remedy, however, is not to try to apply old concepts of

Government intervention to new problems. The tidy cure-alls of the Left are probably as outmoded as the hands-off slogans of the Chamber of Commerce. The theories adequate to the industrial revolution do not necessarily apply to the conditions of the new scientific revolution. Look, for example, at the large group of economically significant and technologically advanced industries that depend for their existence and growth, not on the open competitive market but on sales only or primarily to the United States Government.

The thing is changing all the time. The Federal Government put $1.1 billion into research and development in the fiscal year 1950; in fiscal 1963 the total is expected to be $12.4 billion. In the past the Government utilized profit-making industry mainly for production, engineering, and the manufacture of final products. But in the current scientific period the older industries have declined as suppliers of the Government and the newer research-and-development-oriented industries—such as those in aircraft, rockets, electronics and atomic energy—have come to the fore.

All this is producing a social and political crisis the dimensions of which are not widely understood. Maybe the Chamber of Commerce is right in longing for a simpler day, but the country wants the benefits of modern technology. It has to have them for its security, and it is not likely to deal with the problem merely by telling the Government to "get lost."

The Problem of
Succession to the Presidency

A FEW MINUTES AFTER PRESIDENT KENNEDY WAS ASSASSINATED THE defense forces of the United States all over the world were informed and instructed to be on the alert. No "emergency defense condition" was ordered. No additional atomic bombers were flushed, as during the Cuban crisis, but in this day of instantaneous attack nobody could be quite sure whether the assassination was the end or merely the beginning of the agony.

The nation has had too much of death lately to want any ghoulish speculation now, but this urgent signal to the troops even before Lyndon Johnson was sworn in as President indicates just how critical the problem of Presidential succession can be.

Has the Congress prepared the Presidency adequately for the possibilities of a violent age? Is the rule of Presidential succession satisfactory for these days of human madness and scientific destruction? Or do not the men in line for the Presidency—all of them, not just one or two—have to be selected and instructed much more carefully than in the past?

Lyndon Johnson, of course, was no problem. He had been schooled for years in the mysteries and complexities of emergency defense action. Also, the "powers and duties" of the President transferred to him automatically on the death of President Kennedy, even before the new chief was sworn in.

But after what happened in Dallas, it is not too difficult to imagine that the assassin might have taken Johnson too, in which case the Presidency would have passed to Speaker McCormack, a man 71, who was not prepared for the normal pressures of the Presidency, let alone the emergencies, and who still isn't.

The Congress has been remarkably casual about this succession problem from the start of the Republic. From the beginning of the nation until now, it has never really dealt effectively with the problem of serious incapacitating illness in the Presidency, and—as we now see—it has consistently put men into the line of succession for the Presidency without ever considering whether they had the capacity to do the job.

The second Congress of the United States voted in 1792 to make the President *pro tempore* of the Senate and the Speaker of the House heirs apparent after the Vice President in that order. This act remained in force for almost a hundred years, despite the fact that on several occasions Vice Presidents died when there was neither a President *pro tem* of the Senate nor a Speaker of the House.

Finally, in 1886, the Congress voted to make members of the Cabinet, beginning with the Secretary of State, next in line for the Presidency, and this was changed again, in 1947, to make the Speaker next in line after the Vice President, to be followed by the President *pro tem*, and the Secretaries of State, Treasury, and Defense, the Attorney General, the Postmaster General, and the Secretaries of Interior, Agriculture, Commerce, and Labor, in that order.

The Speaker of the House was moved up in the order in 1947 at least partly, and perhaps even mainly, because a remarkable and highly qualified man, Mr. Sam Rayburn, sat in that chair at the time. But Mr. Sam is gone now, and while there were many who felt Mr. McCormack was not the best man to succeed him as Speaker, certainly nobody even considered the possibility that he would, for almost thirteen months, be first in line after President Johnson.

The tendency now, of course, is to do nothing but pray for the President's health. Johnson has enough problems ahead in Congress without instigating a battle to unseat the Speaker, but there is perhaps another way.

The Speaker himself could propose a solution. If he will not resign as Speaker, he could propose legislation that would name another person first in line for the Presidency. This could be done in several ways. For example, he could propose a bill which stated that in the event of the Vice President succeeding to the Presidency, both houses of Congress should then by majority vote select someone from the President's party to be next in line.

This is not intended as a personal unkindness. Mr. McCormack is an industrious and in many ways a competent Congressional servant. But he would be the first to concede that it was not the judgment or intent of the Congress that he should ever be first in line for the Presidency of the United States. He was chosen by seniority for one job and thrust by an appalling accident into line for a totally different job. This raises not a legal or political, but a moral, problem—namely, whether a man wishes to remain in line for a job the Congress never intended him to have.

In normal times (whatever *they* were) maybe it would have been all right to count on luck and avoid raising embarrassing personal questions, but these are not normal times, and lately our luck has not been very good.

JUNE 27, 1965

The Tendencies of News

NEWS HAS AN ODD KIND OF MATHEMATICS OF ITS OWN. THE WHOLE is not the sum of its parts, but often something quite different. The news of racial conflict in America has been a downward spiral of violence for years, but the tendency has been upward toward greater social justice. It is the tendencies of the news that are often the most important, and it is conflict that often produces progress.

The first half of 1965, for example, has been a remarkable period in the development of the American nation. All the old differences between North and South, labor and management, black and white, city and country, rich and poor, remain; but there has been a easing of tensions among all these contending forces during the last six months and a definite progress on the home front toward "a more perfect union."

Nothing has been solved but many things have been improved. A start has been made in the battle against poverty in the city and rural slums. The state-church issue, long a barrier to effective Federal aid to education, has been modified by the ingenious compromises of President Johnson's education bill. The old and the sick, long abandoned by a restless society, are now to get some relief under the modified Medicare legislation, and the disenfranchised Negroes will have a better chance under the new voting-rights bill.

Meanwhile, the states have made substantial progress toward a more equal distribution of voting power under the Supreme Court's order redistricting the state legislatures, and the national economy is booming along, with occasional spasms of doubt, toward higher levels of productivity and employment.

Ironically, the very poor, while better off now than at the beginning of the year and considerably better off than at the start of the 1960's, are steadily falling behind the rate of economic progress of the rest of the nation. But the over-all trend is nevertheless upward, the middle class is growing, and the divisions over economic policy and theory are not as bitter or emotional as they were at the start of the tax debate only two short years ago.

This trend toward compromise and cooperation on the home front has been blurred and sometimes even overwhelmed by a contrary trend toward contention, division, and violence in the nation's relations with other countries, but this is all the more reason for recognizing the progress where it exists.

There seems to be a growing realization in the nation that no one class or region or race can achieve its objectives in isolation from the rest, and that modern science, technology, and education are challenging all institutions to adopt, in their own interests, a new spirit of interdependence.

Neither the Democrats nor the Republicans, for example, now

think that they can win a majority of the nation by appealing to sectionalism or factionalism. Goldwater tried it in the Presidential campaign of 1964, and his monumental failure produced the Democratic majority that is now putting through the domestic social legislation Goldwater opposed. Thus, Johnson is now wooing Republican big business, and John Lindsay is running for Mayor of New York, not as a Republican but as a fusion candidate. Meanwhile the trend toward compromise is going beyond either Goldwater's ideology or Johnson's "y'all come" invitation to "consensus."

For example, the state Governors, long the symbol of states' rights and state pride, are now forming regional compacts and working together on regional problems that transcend state boundaries. The churches too, long in contention over the "true faith," are now minimizing their theological and denominational differences and concentrating on the things they agree upon rather than the things that divide them.

Universities and colleges are following the same trend. They are engaged in all kinds of new cooperative experiments: working together on common regional development programs, exchanging students and members of the faculty, and permitting their teachers to spend time serving the Federal Government which the teachers then protest against when they return to the campus.

In short, there is a kind of roving experimental inquiry going on in the United States today. Things are changing so fast that nobody seems to be quite as confident or dogmatic as he used to be about his inherited ideas and prejudices; so everybody is shopping around for new answers to new problems.

Fortunately, this new spirit of pragmatic experimentation on the home front happens to fit precisely the temper of the presiding officer of the nation. Lyndon Johnson would not have been comfortable in a period of vicious ideological warfare because he is not a doctrinaire man, but when everybody is searching and all factions are vaguely mixed up together, his political genius is most effective.

It would, therefore, be difficult to find another six months since the war when more progress was made at home than since the beginning of 1965. Maybe at the end of the decade Vietnam will still stand out as the historic issue of the Johnson Administration, but maybe not.

More than likely the transformation of the domestic scene—the acceptance of the new New Economics, the redistribution of political power in the South and the cities, the progress in education and social legislation, and the overall movement toward greater discussion between the races and religions and classes—will take on a larger significance than they are given today.

OCTOBER 13, 1965

Prosperity for What?

THIS IS THE TIME OF YEAR WHEN THE ADMINISTRATION BEGINS forecasting the economic prospects for 1966 and drafting and redrafting the Federal budget to be presented to the Congress next January. It is now, then, that the vital questions of priority arise. How much for defense? How much for education? How much for the moon? How much to limit farm production or lift it to help deal with starvation in the world?

Fortunately, the economic outlook is good. The official estimate is that the gross national product for 1965 will reach $670 billion. This is up by one-third since 1960 and represents a "real" rate of growth of 4.4 per cent a year over this period.

But growth for what? What are the ends to which this fantastic accumulation of wealth is to be directed? This is the question which officials are now debating in the privacy of their offices and to which so little public attention is paid at the time of decision.

On the home front, officials are thinking hard about this. "Economic growth," said Gardner Ackley, chairman of the

Council of Economic Advisers, the other day, "is not the ultimate objective of our society. We want a strong and productive economy, so that we can better achieve our objectives as individuals and as a nation. . . . We have undertaken a war on poverty. We have begun to face up to the ugliness and the social disorder of our cities. . . . In short, we have begun to build a society that one day will be called great."

All this is true, but despite the generous contributions of the United States to human needs beyond our frontiers, the gap between the rich nations and the poor nations increases spectacularly every year, and this, in turn, is helping create a new kind of class war between the very rich countries and the very poor.

Will the budget now in preparation take this situation into account? The cost in this decade of our moon explorations alone is estimated at over $35 billion. The total appropriations to alleviate world starvation and misery are still only the smallest fraction of the sums used for atomic and rocket research, yet the main battlefields in the cold war are increasingly among the starving peoples.

This is a question of perspective and proportion, and it is interesting when viewed against the perspectives now coming out of Communist China. The Chinese Minister of Defense and Vice President of the Chinese Communist party, Marshal Lin Piao, recently took a look at the planet as a whole and concluded that North America and Western Europe were the "cities of the world" encircled by Asia, Africa, and Latin America, which he described as "the rural areas of the world."

"In one sense," Marshal Lin observed, "the revolutionary movement presents us with a picture of the cities encircled by the rural masses. In the final analysis, the whole cause of the global revolution depends on the revolutionary struggles of the peoples of Asia, Africa, and Latin America, who comprise the overwhelming majority of the world's population."

This has the misleading simplicity of the vast geopolitical dreams that carried the Nazis to their destruction, but there is enough truth in it to make us consider more seriously than we have in past budget-drafting days whether we are giving a high enough priority to the human war that is now going on and too high a priority to the big military war of our nightmares.

Time and again, President Johnson has talked eloquently of the dangers of overrating our own national prosperity while underrating the dangers of poverty and hunger in the rest of the world. But the budgets of the past have not reflected his rhetoric.

The budgets have been generous beyond the contributions of all the other nations of the northern industrial lands, of the rest of the advanced world of cities, but they have not begun to deal with the rising misery of the swollen populations of the world of the rural nations.

As Georg Borgstrom has written in his new book, *The Hungry Planet*, "The victory in the fight for world supremacy may not go to the one who has accomplished the most spectacular celestial fireworks, but rather to the party which does something to alleviate the distress among peoples of the earth." This is at least worth considering when the budget-makers allocate $4 billion to American farmers for limiting their production of food.

DECEMBER 1, 1965

The Quiet Disasters

THE CRITICAL PERIODS OF THE VIETNAMESE WAR HAVE OFTEN BEEN the quietest. These have been the times when some official has come back from Saigon and persuaded the President, usually in the privacy of the White House, to increase the American commitment.

In such ways the Americans changed from a small force of 700 noncombatant "advisers" to a fighting expeditionary force of 165,000, and it is one of the oddities of the war that even many well-informed people cannot remember when these decisions were taken. They know where we are now, but they do not know how we got there.

The answer is that we got there by stages in these quiet periods: the advisers in Vietnam became "assistants"; the "assistants" flew the planes but did not man the guns; then they manned the guns but used them only when attacked; then they "retaliated" against attacks on our own bases; then against attacks on the South Vietnamese bases; then they engaged in deep patrols to keep the enemy away from our bases; and finally, they were ordered to "search and destroy," to "find, fix and fight the enemy."

This is relevant now because General Westmoreland, our commander in Saigon, has asked for more troops, and Secretary of Defense McNamara is home from Saigon, preparing for another of those quiet talks with the President. Mr. McNamara has defined the problem as he sees it quite succinctly: despite the U.S. victories of recent weeks and the severe losses of the enemy, the size and ferocity of the Communist forces have increased and, says Mr. McNamara, we will send whatever forces "are required" to deal with this situation.

A kind of melancholy fatalism seems to be taking over. The pattern of the war is becoming clear: more Vietcong, more Americans, more violence, more casualties, more replacements for the casualties, again more violence, and finally more replacements for the replacements. This is now the vicious spiral of Vietnam. When we are winning, we will negotiate but the enemy won't, and when he is winning, the roles are reversed, and it is clear that we are now on the verge of another new commitment.

Maybe it is unavoidable, but at least this time it should be explained. Is it our policy now to commit anything and everything to win that ground war in Vietnam? Are our commitments of ground troops to be determined by the Communists, who have unlimited manpower for this kind of war? How many more men and planes can we send there without turning the war into an American war and destroying the country we are trying to save?

The original American policy in Vietnam was far easier to understand than the present one. We could help, we said, but the South Vietnamese themselves had to win the war and pacify the country. We can still help with bases and supplies. We can hold

our bases without unacceptable casualties. We can bomb North
Vietnam, but a strategy of searching for the enemy in the jungles
is a formula for a permanent war which will increasingly divide
the country and the alliance, divert the nation from its constructive purposes at home and abroad, and leave the Chinese free
eventually to dominate the peninsula.

If this is wrong and victory is essential to "the vital interests"
of the United States, then let us organize and live and fight the
way men must when their "vital interests'" are at stake. We are
certainly not living today like a nation engaged in a "vital"
struggle. The contrast between prosperity at home and sacrifice
in Vietnam is startling, and Secretary of the Treasury Fowler is
almost apologizing to the people for not giving them another
tax cut next year. In fact, the people who are telling us it is going
to be a "long, hard war"—the same people who were telling us
we were going to bring a lot of the boys home by this Christmas
—are now planning another business-better-than-usual budget,
and warning the Federal Reserve not to raise interest rates.

So something is out of kilter. A policy of more troops and
more profits, draft the poor and reward the rich, more Social
Security at home and less security in Vietnam is not easy to
explain, but somebody who knows ought to try.

Either the war is "vital" or it is not. Either this is essentially a
Vietnamese war or essentially an American war. The impression
is gaining that everybody is trapped by events and not quite
sure of what to do, and it is this sense of stumbling deeper into
the bog that is frustrating and dividing the people.

A Date to Remember

THE 200TH ANNIVERSARY OF THE DECLARATION OF INDEPENDENCE will be celebrated ten years from this week, and while Americans are not normally enthusiastic about ten-year plans, July 4, 1976, is a date worthy of some serious and sustained planning.

The pursuit of happiness, which lately has been exceeding the speed limit, may get in the way, but if some of the creative minds here have their way, a national movement will soon be under way, not only for a big blowout ten years from now but for a record of local and national achievement that is worth blowing off about. The generation of Americans that is alive and kicking on the 200th anniversary of Thomas Jefferson's famous document ought at least to do a little better in 1976 than the generation that celebrated the 100th anniversary in 1876.

When we look back on the main events of that year, about all we find is that Wild Bill Hickok was shot dead (from behind) by one Jack McCall in Deadwood, South Dakota; that General George A. Custer and 264 soldiers of the Seventh Cavalry were killed in the Sioux Indian War at the Battle of the Little Big Horn; and that Rutherford B. Hayes, Republican, was given the Presidency over Samuel J. Tilden, Democrat, after a fishy election settled by a party vote in the Congress.

This level of achievement should not be hard to beat. On July 4, 1976, Bobby will just be finishing his first term in the White House and preparing his nomination for a second term, so there will be some competition; and advance preparations are, therefore, all the more important.

Anniversaries, rightly used, are the benchmarks of history. The third quarter of the twentieth century has seen the rapid disintegration of the old empires, the emergence of the United States and the USSR as the two most powerful nations in the world, the stirring of China, the reconstruction of Europe, the birth of a whole catalogue of struggling independent and impoverished nations, and the doubling of the human race.

The vast convulsion is still in process, and whether it moves gradually toward some kind of cooperating order in the world, or loiters down into misery and chaos, will depend in large measure on the wisdom, wealth, and leadership of the United States in the next ten years.

The Johnson Administration is just beginning to think about all this. Government committees to prepare policies to be completed by the 200th anniversary of the Declaration are being established. Robert Bowie of Harvard, the newly appointed counselor of the State Department, has been asked by the Administration to prepare an ambitious projection of "the world of the seventies," and some officials here are watching the Soviet Government's plans for the fiftieth anniversary of the Soviet Revolution in 1967.

Outside of Philadelphia, however, all this is still little more than an idea in the minds of a few officials. The 200th anniversary, however, is providing a new target date for those who are concerned with the reconstruction of the central cities of the nation, with the war on poverty and the pollution of the air and rivers, with equality of educational opportunity and with the development of rapid transportation in the populous areas of the country.

The Governors of the states, the Mayors of the cities, and the leaders of the professions will all have to be brought into this project, however—and fairly soon—if plans are to be made and coordinated, funds found and appropriated in time to reach goals worthy of such an occasion.

It is not beyond the capacity of this vigorous and booming country to transform the Harlems in New York, the Wattses in Los Angeles, and the other slums that are now infecting the cities of the country. The Roman Catholic Church has in the last few years given the world an example of what can be done when an institution engages in a serious attempt to analyze and modernize its work in a time of great change.

The United States is probably better organized than any other modern society for a similar inquiry among all its institutions and professions. The political parties, the churches, the press, the radio and television networks, the commercial and professional associations are all trying to adapt to change today, all criticizing and analyzing their methods and purposes.

The 200th anniversary of the Declaration provides an opportunity to bring all this scattered analysis into focus—not only through Government action but through broad private action in all the communities and institutions of the country.

JULY 24, 1966

"The Shame of the Cities"

THE NEGRO PROTEST MOVEMENT IN AMERICA IS FOLLOWING THE normal pattern of most revolutions. It is not waning with the first signs of Negro progress, but getting bolder and more demanding. It is not sticking with the moderate leaders who helped achieve its legal aims, but tending more and more to follow the militants who are demanding larger and quicker economic and social gains.

This is not a unique Negro reaction, but a typical reaction of most American protest movements. The American industrial workers in the cities and the farmers on the land may have rebelled out of despair, but their rebellion increased with the first hope of success. The violence of the American labor protest movement was not as great at the beginning as in the middle when the more militant leaders began to see the possibilities of violent opposition.

Likewise, the revolt of the white American farmers increased in the early stages as it succeeded. This is the norm: Revolution feeds on itself. Mary E. Lease became the authentic voice of inland American populism in the 1890's, not because she counseled patience and reason, but because she advised the farmers to "raise less corn and more hell."

There are great dangers for the American Negroes and the nation as a whole in the notion that violence gets better results than patience, but there are probably greater dangers in assuming that the American Negro will now be patient just because the white folks think reason is making progress and is therefore preferable to violence.

This is not the way human nature, white or black, behaves, and unfortunately, it is not the way governments and communities behave. The facts of life in Harlem in New York, Watts in Los Angeles, and Hough in Cleveland were well known to the governments of those cities. All officials there knew that the conditions in their slums encouraged violence, but they did not or could not react to reason as well as they could react to violence.

It is the same the world over. Most of the time, just grievances are removed only after the aggrieved resort to the uses of power. The American Government has always known about the strategic importance of Cuba—Mr. Jefferson wanted to annex it because he feared it might be used by our enemies—but officials here did not really worry about it until Castro turned it into an instrument of Communist power.

The United States did not get deeply involved in the affairs of Europe until Europe dragged us into two world wars. The Johnson Administration did not really deal with the Buddhists in Vietnam until their "struggle movement" threatened to interfere with our whole war effort in that country. The old imperial empires did not deal effectively with "black power" in Africa until it resorted to violence and compelled London, Paris, and Brussels to do so.

The will and the machinery for peaceful settlement of disputes and the adjustment of just grievances are defective and out of date, and the American Negroes are merely following the lessons of history. They have learned that "it's the squeaky wheel that gets the grease," and they are likely to demand more and more grease, like everybody else.

The conservatives of the American South understood this perhaps better than the liberals of the North. They knew that one Negro demand would lead to another. They were undoubtedly wrong in thinking that they could hold the line by opposing all Negro demands, but the Northern liberals were probably equally wrong in thinking that they could contain the Negro revolution by legal concessions.

President Johnson, who has done more to produce legal remedies for the American Negro than any other President of this century, tried to deal with the recent outbreaks of violence in Chicago, Cleveland, and Brooklyn by reminding the Negroes that they cannot remove their grievances by violence because they are only 10 or 11 per cent of the total American population. But this is a conclusive argument only if the large majority of "white power" is used against the 10 per cent minority of "black power," and this is obviously out of the question.

A violent confrontation of "white power" against "black power" in America is civil war. Violence can compel reason but cannot replace it. It can force people to look at the facts, and the facts now, as in Disraeli's time in England, are that we have today "two nations"—a nation of the rich and a nation of the poor, many of which are black and separate, with their own values and torments, their own schools, largely segregated in the South by tradition and prejudice, and increasingly resegregated in the Northern cities by prejudice and economics.

The Federal Government has identified all these problems but the scope of the problems is larger than the scope of the remedies. The revolution is moving faster than Washington, and Washington is not in control of local police, local housing codes, local school boards, and local jobs—the latter being one of the main problems.

For the moment, the outcry in the United States is merely against the violence of the cities, and not against the causes of the violence. This is quite different from other urban crises in the American past, when the moral indignation of the progressives was directed, not against the protestors but against the conditions that produced the protests.

When Lincoln Steffens wrote *The Shame of the Cities* in another time, he uncovered the graft and corruption of governments, but he did not blame them as much as he blamed the people themselves. He dedicated *The Shame of the Cities* "to the accused, to all the citizens of all the cities in the United States." His conclusion is not wholly irrelevant today. We are still blaming the Negroes and the violence, but not the causes of the violence, which are more serious in our own time than they were in Steffens's.

JANUARY 1, 1967

The Last Third of the Century

THIS IS NO ORDINARY NEW YEAR. WE HAVE NOW SLIPPED INTO THE last third of the twentieth century, and if its first two thirds are any guide, the outlook is for a cataract of surprises that will transform the universe.

The first third of the century brought America out of her political isolation; the second third handed her the leadership of the Western world; the final third will determine whether she can guide the blind forces now threatening the human family.

The first third of the century gave us the automobile, the airplane, the First World War, the Soviet revolution, and the great economic depression. The middle third destroyed the old empires and the old political and religious order in an even more savage World War, and gave us atomic power and the intercontinental rocket, the Chinese revolution, and a wholly new map of fantastically rich and miserably poor nations.

Prophecy is a risky business, but some things we know. No matter whose babe is first born in 1967, all or almost all of this new generation from now on will live most of their lives in the twenty-first century. By 1970, over half of the American people will be 25 years old or under. The vast majority of the human race will not be white, and they will be hungry, and a quarter of them, despite the Joint Chiefs of Staff, will be Chinese. If you put all this into your computer it is bound to come out trouble.

By the end of the century, our present political preoccupations and assumptions are likely to look unimportant and even silly. If we cannot explain Vietnam to our children now, imagine trying to explain it twenty years from now.

The major conflicts in the world now, as in the middle third of the century, are discussed in ideological, almost in theological terms. We are blocking the "spread of Communism" in Asia, we say. We are opposing the Marxist-Leninist theory of property and the state. We assume, despite these ideological assertions, that the Soviet-Chinese conflict is "irreconcilable."

Yet in the last third of the century we may very well see as many switches of allies and enemies as we saw in the middle third. President Charles de Gaulle of France, for example, once told this reporter that the conflict at the end of the century would "not be ideological but racial," not between the democracy of the West and the Communism of the East but between the poor agrarian nonwhites of the underdeveloped nations in the south of the world and the rich industrial overdeveloped white nations of the north.

The ideological struggle between Moscow and Washington has already changed substantially in the last few years. It is still carried on in the American press and in American politics, but the U.S. Government is no longer pursuing the crusading anti-Communist militancy of the days of John Foster Dulles.

The present assumption in Washington is that the conflict between Moscow and Peking is "irreconcilable," but after the dramatic changes in the relations between the major nations in the middle third of the century, who can be sure that this conflict will continue? If Stalin is followed by a moderate Khrushchev in the Soviet Union, who can say that the militant Mao Tse-tung will not be succeeded by a moderate in China? Or by some Chinese leader who will revive the Moscow-Peking alliance and open up an even more formidable Communist coalition against the West?

At the beginning of 1967, nobody here knows the answer to these questions. The only valid assumption officials have is that the changes in the last third of the century are likely to be at least as dramatic as the changes of the first two thirds. What Washington would like to do—but for the present is prevented from doing by the Vietnam war—is to open up a discussion with the allies, with Moscow, and eventually even with Peking about this last third of the century.

There is a growing feeling here, at least among those few officials who have time to think, that the present conflicts over Vietnam and trade are secondary, and that the great issues of food and population, of arms limitation and particularly the control of nuclear weapons, of the rising conflict between the rich nations and the hungry nations must take priority in international relations if these coming three decades are not to be disastrous.

This is the real tragedy of Vietnam. It is carrying the ideological conflicts of the middle third of the century into the last third. It is blocking progress on the issue of arms control and the fundamental problem of the overpopulated, hungry, and frustrated new nations.

Midcentury is now gone, but its problems are still with us. The problem of the New Year and the years to come is to liquidate the old issues and get on to the new: not the East-West but the Rich North and the Poor South problems; not the war in Vietnam but the war on poverty; not the agrarian problems of the past but the urban problems of the present and future; not the ideological problems of the middle third of the century, but the practical problems of the last third; not the questions that are in old men's minds, but the questions that are in the minds of the young.

11

JOHNSON

Yodels for a Texan

WHEN THE LEADERS OF WASHINGTON, REPUBLICAN AND DEMO-
cratic, executive and legislative, start yodeling in unison about
the virtues of a single Senator, it is fair to conclude that the
Senator has (a) just died, or (b) retired from the Senate, or (c)
won a very special place for himself in the capital. This is what is
now happening in the case of Senator Lyndon B. Johnson of
Texas. The Democratic Majority Leader has not died or retired;
he is merely coming to the end of another Congressional session
in which he has managed to win approval for a lot of controversial legislation without making anybody angry.

Other Senate leaders with large majorities and powerful Presidents have pushed through more legislation, but it has seldom, if
ever, happened that so much controversial legislation has gone
through a divided government with so few cuts and bruises.

When the second session of the 84th Congress started last
January, the Administration's foreign economic program was in
serious trouble. Mr. Johnson himself feared that the Reciprocal
Trade Agreements Act and the foreign-aid appropriations would
be cut to pieces. Both have come out, *not* precisely as the Administration wanted them, but solidly intact.

Much the same was true of the Pentagon reform bill, but it,
too, has survived the interparty and interservice rivalries. Of all
the really major objectives, only the labor bill is still in trouble,
and House Speaker Sam Rayburn, who taught Johnson much of
his parliamentary skill, may save that at the last minute.

All this, of course, is not Senator Johnson's doing alone. He
has developed a strange but genuine partnership with the Senate
Republican leader, William F. Knowland of California. He
worked closely with Mr. Rayburn and the House Republican
leader, Joseph Martin. On the tariff, he had intelligent support

from C. Douglas Dillon, Under Secretary for Economic Affairs, who is one of the few good things that has happened to the State Department recently, and on Pentagon reorganization, he established a firm and even affectionate alliance with Neil H. Mc-Elroy, Secretary of Defense.

Nevertheless, everybody from President Eisenhower to Senator Everett Dirksen agees that Senator Johnson is primarily responsible for the record and nobody quite knows how it was done. Even Under Secretary Dillon, who followed the tariff bill for the State Department, cannot explain even yet how Senator Johnson disentangled the bill from a number of complicated personal and parliamentary difficulties.

It is impossible to have a conversation with Senator Johnson on the subject. Nobody has a conversation with the Texan. He does all the talking all the time and his talk is as detailed and complicated as his tactics. As a strategist, he is the best quarterback to come out of Texas since Slingin' Sammy Baugh. He seldom originates legislation himself, but he can take complex human beings and ideas and select or invent ways and means of winning consent for effective compromise legislation.

His assumption is that the Senate is not a seminar in theoretical political ideology but a workshop for passing laws, and while this emphasis on parliamentary skill has earned him the reputation of a political mechanic, it is probably significant that even the theorists in this city are beginning to join in his praise.

Next to his gift for dealing with complicated details and cantankerous human beings, vitality is his great strength. This is one of the odd paradoxes in a very complex man. He has had a severe heart attack and yet burns up more energy than a tank. Washington is very conscious of this quality at the moment. The heart of the trouble in the Executive Branch of the Government is the lack of sustained energy at the center. It is not that there are no ideas or programs but that there is very little driving force in the White House to carry things through.

Senator Johnson, like President Eisenhower, has political power. But in addition, he allies immense energy to skill and ideas. The ideas may come from other men, but he will work eighteen hours a day putting the thing over and, because he has both political power and physical energy, he achieves objectives other men cannot reach.

He has his weaknesses, like other mortals. The major defect in Congress is that everybody is working on a few trees at a time, and few manage to see the whole forest. Senator Johnson does not escape this episodic and narrowing aspect of the Congress, yet even here, his record is better this session than last.

Part of the reason for this is that he has developed an excellent staff in his office. He discovered during the civil-rights debate in the last session that the intellectuals of his party outside and inside the Congress could be useful in defining goals and devising compromise legislation, and he is now using them more than ever before.

As a result of all this, he will go home at the end of this session with broader support within the Democratic party and the press than he has ever had before. For his cheering section now runs from John Foster Dulles to Dean Acheson, and from Hubert Humphrey to Herman Talmadge, and that is quite a distance.

JUNE 22, 1960

What Kind of Prejudice Are You For?

THERE IS AN INCREASINGLY AGGRESSIVE AND EVEN BITTER NOTE IN Senator Lyndon Johnson's campaign for the Presidency. The Texan is doing what he rarely if ever does: he is attacking his Democratic opponents personally. In particular, he is trying to stop Senator Kennedy by arguing that the New Englander is too young for Presidential responsibility: an argument beginning to replace religion as Kennedy's major handicap.

At the same time, he is saying that Adlai E. Stevenson is just not the type to carry the politicians with him in the election and that Mr. Stevenson cannot carry Texas and some other Southern states.

This is not typical of Johnson, but it is understandable, for he is being rejected for the Democratic nomination because of prejudices he does not share and because of things he can do nothing about: his Texas origins, his tough-guy appearance, and, oddly, because of the recent rise of black Africa as a major factor in world politics.

The African situation is secondary, but it illustrates how events beyond our frontiers increasingly influence domestic political decisions. In the last four years Africa has been very much in the news, with one predominantly Negro nation after another gaining independence. This has had some effect on the thinking of Negro leaders and students in the United States. They have seen these new African nations take on new importance in the United Nations. They have observed the leaders of these nations welcoming world leaders in their capitals and visiting the capitals of the West.

Inevitably, this has been a source of considerable pride to Negroes in this country and of resentment against everything and everybody who has seemed to stand in the way of equality for this country's Negro. Accordingly, the nomination of a Southerner, even one who has put through the Senate the only civil-rights legislation since the Civil War, is repulsive to many Negro leaders in the large cities of the North, and whether it is admitted or not, the fact is that Negro leaders, like labor-union leaders, have great influence in the choice of any Democratic Presidential nominee.

This is hurting Johnson personally and handicapping his campaign, for even those professional politicians in the North who admire his political skill, absolve him of prejudice against the Negro, and even think he would be the best President of the lot are saying candidly that they are not prepared to risk losing Negro and labor-union votes with Johnson at the head of the ticket.

It is true, of course, that many Democrats reject him because he has had a heart attack, because of what they regard as his emotional temperament, and because they think he is too conservative on economic questions. Nevertheless, despite all these considerations, many of those who reject him for one or all of these points concede that the Democratic convention would undoubtedly nominate him if he were from the North or from a border state.

Thus, while he has argued against religious prejudice when that seemed to be hurting Kennedy early in the campaign, he is himself the victim of regional prejudice. And, ironically, this is coming from the North, which is always complaining about the regional prejudice of the South.

What makes this all the more galling to Johnson is that religious considerations are now helping Kennedy defeat him. The decisive point for Kennedy and against Johnson in the large urban areas of the North is that the New Englander, partly because he is Catholic, will bring out a large Democratic vote in the areas that are strongly Catholic, while the Texan will lose votes among those who assume that any Southerner, even if he does not share the segregationist sentiments of the Deep South, is a handicap on the Democratic ticket.

Johnson is enough of a pro to recognize the force of this argument, though he deeply resents its injustice. Why should religious preference help nominate one man while regional prejudice eliminates another? What are we against—all prejudices or just Southern prejudices?

The Office and the Man

It is part of the mythology and even the history of the Presidency that no man is ever the same once he walks through the portals of the White House. Right or wrong, this pleasant fancy seemed already to be working on Lyndon Baines Johnson today. By the time he faced the Congress, he had taken on the gravity of the hour and the office. In his old Senate days, he slouched and mumbled, or when aroused raced his engine and whooped and bellowed, but shock and sorrow and responsibility have already toned him down.

He sounded for all the world like Mr. Sam Rayburn today, ever so slow and serious, but with repressed emotion always behind the deep strong Texas voice. It would have been so easy in the emotion of the moment for him to have gone too far today, or, being deeply moved, to have choked on the lovely cry "America, America" at the end. But he was both bold and restrained and never read a speech better in his life.

The new President of the United States obviously has a lot going for him on Capitol Hill, and this is not only the general sense of tragedy about the assassination of President Kennedy, or the natural sympathy for a man suddenly assuming such awful responsibilities under such tragic circumstances.

Presidents Truman and Kennedy were also Capitol Hill men, and their first Presidential speeches to the Congress were also a kind of homecoming. But Johnson is something different in the Congressional mind. He ran the place, and without his special magic and cunning, his urgent energy, and his bag of tricks and treats, nothing has quite seemed to run as well on Capitol Hill since he left.

Truman and Kennedy were minor figures in Congress by comparison. The legislators were comfortable with Truman but never in the same way with Kennedy. His gifts of cultivated speech, his graceful form and elegance, aroused their admiration and sometimes even their envy, but he was never a leader of the Congress in the Johnsonian sense.

Also Johnson talks in their own idiom; he is, to use his own inelegant phrase, "a gut fighter," a nonstop talker, and a parliamentary tactician with few equals. Congress did not always like him—often it hated him—but it never trifled with him. . . .

Congress does not adore intellectuals, and vice versa. But Johnson is not an intellectual, not a man of thought but of action, not a critic but a champion of the Congress—and when he came down the aisle today, a big rangy bony man with a loose rolling stride, they clearly recognized him as one of their own.

These human changes in the political equation—of manner, appearance, age, and origin—are important on Capitol Hill, probably more important than they should be.

Skipping President Wilson, who skipped the South when he was young, President Johnson is the first Chief Executive from the South since the last President Johnson in 1869, and this is probably not without some significance. For Lyndon Johnson's most severe critics in Congress are among the Northern liberals, who are going to vote for his civil-rights and tax bills anyway, and his closest friends on Capitol Hill are among the Southerners, who have opposed these bills and will now have to tell Johnson personally why.

This will not be an easy or a pleasant exercise. President Kennedy had a way of seeing all sides of a question and respecting an opponent's vote. President Johnson has a way of concentrating on his own side of a question, and of invoking Southern loyalty to a Southern President in a way that no man from Massachusetts could hope to do. "I know how you feel, but can I count on you?" he says, and when the thing is put that way, upstairs in the White House, with Lyndon's long arm on a man's shoulder, voting suddenly becomes slightly complicated.

Besides, John F. Kennedy is in his grave, but he was never more alive as a political force on Capitol Hill than he is right now. He is very much on the memory and the conscience of the Congress, and President Johnson clearly intends to keep him there.

The whole psychology of the capital city, therefore, has been changed by the cruel events of the last week. The program is the same. President Johnson did not alter a single line in it today, but the mind and spirit of the city have been transformed. This is the terrible paradox and tragedy of the moment, for President Kennedy apparently had to die to create a sympathetic atmosphere for his program.

JANUARY 8, 1964

The State of the President and Other Matters

THE PRESIDENT'S STATE OF THE UNION MESSAGE IS USUALLY FORmal and useful, like a report card from the headmaster, but the reader or viewer should not be misled. It is not the whole story. It is the beginning and destination of the journey without a road map, and it tells little or nothing about the State of Lyndon Johnson.

This is an important omission. The only way to get a complete State of the Union message from President Johnson is to wire him for sound and cut him loose without a text in the well of the House of Representatives. But since this is unlikely, the only alternative is to give a few personal impressions of the man from the sidelines.

He is going into the big battle with Congress like a football coach going into the big game. He is exhilarated but vaguely apprehensive, and like all prudent coaches he is constantly talking about the remarkable powers of the opposition.

The balance of political power is probably much more favorable to him than he says. He is going to have a savage fight over taxes and civil rights in the Congress, but in the Presidential election campaign his Republican opposition is deeply divided, and he benefits greatly from the prospect that the American people are not likely to be wildly enthusiastic about having three different Presidents in little more than a year.

In the first seven weeks of his Administration the President has done a remarkable job of maintaining a line with the Kennedy Administration while putting his own personal stamp on the Presidency. The other day, walking around his ranch in Texas, he said, "The best fertilizer for a piece of land is the footprints of its owner," and he applies this doctrine not only to the LBJ Ranch but to the conduct of the Presidency.

It was widely assumed when he took over that he would not have much time to do anything more than make a few minor changes in the Kennedy budget, but he has been working eighteen hours a day ever since to make it reflect his own personal mixture of liberalism, conservatism, populism, and political pragmatism.

He carries around in his left hip pocket, for example, a slip of paper showing how he cut about $10 billion from the budget requests of the major Government departments and how he used some of the savings to increase the budget of the Labor and Health, Education, and Welfare Departments.

He is fascinated with the idea of using surplus food as an instrument of foreign policy and at the same time cutting the cost of storing food at home. He is constantly talking about the problem of the teen-age dropouts from school and studying the possibility of cutting down teen-age unemployment by expanding the high schools into junior colleges, and transforming obsolete military bases into special schools for critically poor neighborhoods.

Mr. Johnson's qualities are energy, boundless confidence in his intuitive judgment about what men will and will not do, a shrewd gift of anticipating trouble ahead, and a tireless, almost nagging persistence in following things through to a decision.

This is true whether he is blocking and tackling the Joint Chiefs of Staff or trying to buy a piece of land. He was driving along Texas Highway No. 1 last Sunday when he passed a farm across the road from his own. With one hand on the wheel, he picked up his radio telephone, called his ranch manager, and told him to look into buying it. But that wasn't enough. He wanted to know where the manager was, how many minutes it would take him to get to the farm, how long to get back. He demanded —and got—a report at 2:45, fifteen minutes before he flew to Austin to see the Governor. Meanwhile, in less than an hour, he had lunch, said goodbye to the staff at the ranch, and gave specific orders about who was to fly in helicopter No. 1 and who in No. 2.

President Kennedy's eloquence was designed to make men think; President Johnson's hammer blows are designed to make men act. He is not concerned with the fastidious refinements of speech. He is a vivid, earthy talker who either persuades or stuns his hearers.

The preparation of a Kennedy budget or speech was a calm and sophisticated debate; the preparation of a Johnson budget is a wrestling match. Intellectual Europe and America preferred the Kennedy style, not because it was typically American, but because it wasn't. President Johnson, on the other hand, is a representative American, one who represents our popular characteristics. In this sense he is now starting out on a journey that will test not only him but the efficiency and temper of the American character and system.

Maybe he will do more with his program in Congress than Kennedy did with his, and maybe he won't. But if he doesn't, it won't be because he has any doubts about the system or any lack of knowledge about how to make it work.

The Man Who Knows the Deck

PRESIDENT JOHNSON'S ABILITY TO GET HIS PROGRAM THROUGH THE Congress is recognized by both political parties here, but there is still much confusion about how he does it. One explanation, to use Tommy Corcoran's phrase, is that the President "knows the deck." He knows the value of every card. He knows the players intimately. And he works at it night and day.

All the popular notions of Johnson the "arm twister" and the "wheeler dealer," while partly true, debase and distort a much more intricate, delicate, and positive art. The problem is to know where the wires of power lie, who are the key men, what one group wants that another opposing group can be persuaded to accept and a third group is likely to tolerate, however unwillingly.

This involves a whole lot more than "twisting arms" and "knocking heads together," though these political gymnastics help. It involves mastery of the details of a vast variety of bills. It requires great knowledge of every parliamentary rule and trick in the book. It demands an intuitive understanding of human nature and enough experience to know what arguments will move one man but not another, and precisely when to speak or be quiet.

John Kennedy did not "know the deck" and, frankly, he did not like the Executive-Congressional game. It irritated him to spent hours wheedling votes out of the proud and powerful chairmen of the committees. He was not really an insider in the "club" even when he was a member of the House and Senate. He was a back-bencher, who never quite lost the new boy's deference for the elders of the Congress.

Johnson, in contrast, was an insider in the Congress, almost from the first. For nearly thirty years he has been talking and drinking with the senior members, campaigning for them in their districts, visiting with them and their families. Unlike Kennedy, he loves "the game." It is not a part of his life—it is his whole life; his work and his sport. He doesn't separate politics from policy or even from family, but mixes them all up together.

Ironically, even Johnson's success in getting things done perpetuates the illusion that he is a political manipulator who somehow lacks interest in things of the mind. Yet the intellectual requirements of mastering the political art are enormous. He not only has to master legislation and men, but he has to know their districts and states, their strengths and weaknesses, their supporters and opponents back home, their ambitions and their fears.

President Johnson knew that he had to have Harry Byrd's cooperation if not his vote to get the tax bill out of the Finance Committee. He soon learned that the thing could not be done if he didn't agree in advance to keep his budget below the $100 billion mark, so he cut the budget in Byrd's presence and got the bill out on the floor.

He was not at all satisfied with the poverty bill as it came to him from his executive advisers. He knew instinctively that he would lose one group of voters unless he eliminated some parts of the bill and another group if he didn't add something else. Accordingly, he directed the changes before he let it go to the Hill and wrote some of them himself. This is what is meant by "knowing the deck."

President Kennedy was a detached man. He talked to the legislators too, but his way was his own. He would call a Senator to his office. He would explain his purpose clearly and precisely and express the hope that the Senator could go along with him.

President Johnson does it differently. He takes time for such adventures. He stage-manages them. He is likely to invite to the White House not only the Senator but the Senator's wife, and while she is going through the house with Mrs. Johnson, the President will "visit" with the Senator on a dozen topics for hours before getting to the point.

Then he will argue his case. He will know it by heart. He will defend it until any opposition from the Senator will seem like treason or worse. Then he will expound on all his troubles from Vietnam and the Congo to Cuba and Mississippi, and finally ask the poor exhausted man on his way to the door: "Can I count on you?"

By such tactics and many others he got his tax cut and his civil-rights bill, his poverty bill, and a lot more. A year ago the political scientists were wondering whether President Kennedy was going to be overwhelmed and broken in a kind of civil war with the Congress, and they were writing ominously about paralysis of the American system of divided powers.

In ten months Johnson has changed all this. Now the pedagogues are analyzing his victories, speculating about his domination of the convention, and wondering how the poor Republicans are going to get enough seats in Congress to keep him from unbalancing the whole two-party system.

JANUARY 17, 1965

Lyndon Baines Johnson

THE INAUGURATION OF A PRESIDENT OF THE UNITED STATES STARTS with a prayer and ends with a dance. This is not a bad combination. Most of the great occasions in life involve a little intermittent laughing and crying, and the installation of a new President is clearly a great occasion. It is a kind of birth or wedding in the nation's family life.

By some curious combination of intuition and caprice, it lifts one fallible mortal from among the millions and says: Go guide half the human race. No wonder the people pray. It asks the man in the Big White House to govern a vast, almost ungovernable continental nation, to "preserve, protect and defend" a Constitution which his fellow countrymen interpret in different ways, to lead a worldwide coalition of proud, independent, and competitive nations, and to preserve the peace in a rebellious and revolutionary world. In the face of such a preposterous challenge, the people naturally look around for whatever heavenly help or earthly escape they can find. They kick up their heels and they pray—some for the President, some for the country, and many for both.

Who, then, are we praying and dancing for? Who is this Lyndon Baines Johnson of Texas who will be installed on Wednesday as the thirty-sixth President of the United States? What is the explanation of this extraordinary man?

Lyndon Baines Johnson is to the politics of America what the State of Texas is to the other states. He is a gargantuan figure; he is a whopper. Measuring him for history is like measuring an active volcano with an inch-tape. He barbecues people who try and eats them for breakfast.

When you interview him, he ends up with your life story. He does not want to be analyzed or classified; he wants to be loved. Anything you say he said, he can usually neutralize with something else he said on the other side. If you say he's liberal, he can prove he's conservative, or vice versa. If you suggest he's from the South, he will insist he's from the West, or the other way around. If you don't tell the precise truth about him, which is almost inevitable, he thinks you are dishonest, and if you do, he feels you are disloyal.

This, however, is the caricature of Mr. Johnson and, like all caricatures, it magnifies one feature and minimizes all the rest. It is amusing, but it is unfair. The big slouching Texas Ranger on the ranch, the master politician on the telephone, the restless, sleepless "arm-twister," trading favors for votes in the smoky back room—all so dear to the cartoonists—are all true, but misleading.

He is more than that—far more. It is too early to say that he is a leader of men in the classic sense of being "quick to know and to do the things that the hour and his nation need," particularly in the foreign field. He has not yet proved that he can get and keep and inspire the best men in the nation to serve him, or even that he has mastered the art of using his staff and his time effectively. But he is a shrewd and knowledgeable man, an elemental force of nature who commands respect and even a certain amount of fear.

"When you come into the presence of a leader of men," Woodrow Wilson observed, "you know you have come into the presence of fire—that it is best not incautiously to touch that man—that there is something that makes it dangerous to cross him." Johnson conveys this feeling and it is both his strength and weakness. His technique works but it hurts. He can make men do what he wants them to do but he does not make them like it or him in the process. There is a kind of intimidating shamelessness about him that makes men feel that if they don't go along there may be the most frightful and embarrassing row. But he is a highly intelligent man who is not to be dismissed as just another brilliant political operator.

He is far more complex than the boys in the back room. The master politician on Capitol Hill and in the White House is not the same as the *Last Hurrah* types out of Tammany, Boston, or Chicago, though Johnson has been hurt by the popular confusion of the two. The political leader in the capital has to deal not only with the masses of men but with a highly intelligent Cabinet, an expert civil service, and a staggering catalogue of problems and ideas.

This is not, by any fair test, an unintellectual process. It involves a great deal more than physical strength, tactical skill, personal acquaintance, and a telephone. It requires immense concentration on the facts of a great many issues at the same time, a quick knack of identifying and absorbing the essence of complicated and critical questions, and a limitless memory for those intimate personal and political facts that will move men to compromise.

There is much confusion on this point. Lyndon Johnson is not Dean Acheson, with a clear vision of the world and a carefully worked-out plan of the role America might play in the human story. But he clearly did not get where he is on a bag of tricks alone.

He does not concentrate on thinking programs through but on

getting them through. He does not believe in "inevitable conflicts," or think in terms of tidy programs imposed or manipulated from the top. He is one of those old-fashioned, small-"d" democrats who think that the People and their representatives, if presented with the facts, will find reasonable solutions. He sees politics as an exercise in adapting oneself to all sorts of people and situations, of discussing and bargaining with legitimate groups in search of a consensus.

His university really has been Capitol Hill, his classroom the committee hearings. He retains the memory of his experiences in Texas and in the Congress, but it would never occur to him to try to organize them into a system. Life to him is full of surprises, more so as the tempo of change increases, and he would no doubt support H. G. Wells's dictum that "to be honest, one must be inconsistent."

This, of course, only adds to the caricature of Johnson the manipulator. But there is another side to it. He is an incorrigible believer. He believes in everything that works. He shares all the popular ideals, assumptions, and illusions of the nation. Kennedy was troubled by what he called the "myths" of the American past. Johnson loves them. Kennedy came to the White House wondering out loud whether a country governed such as ours could endure. Johnson could no more think or say that than he could denounce Lady Bird or the flag. He believes in the American system. He accepts it as he accepts the weather in his hill country of Texas: a little irritating and even cruel at times, but inevitable.

Similarly, he accepts the Congressional system the way it is—warts and all. Kennedy was in the Congress, Johnson is of it. He struggled to the top through the system and therefore thinks it's all right. He is not a critic of the elders of the Congress but their companion. He has lived with them for thirty years, spoken for them in their elections, stood up with them at their family weddings and christenings and funerals; drunk whiskey with them in Mr. Sam Rayburn's "board of education" hideaway in the House.

The pessimism and complexity of the modern world, accordingly, do not bother him. Unlike many of his intellectual critics, he is not paralyzed by excessive contemplation or doubt. He is all for the businessman making a pile, having made one himself. He believes in Horatio Alger's triumphant ragamuffin (who, after all, is Johnson). He believes in the hard doctrines of John Calvin and individual responsibility, and now that the planned deficit and the tax cut have increased prosperity, he even believes a little in John Maynard Keynes. He is fiercely patriotic. He genuinely believes that God looks out for Uncle Sam. He has no doubt that this nation was set apart to achieve good and noble purposes; that America is indeed the New Arcadia, or will be if he has his way.

This highly political, highly pragmatic, and ceaselessly industrious approach, however, irritates a lot of people. Mr. Johnson is a hard, inconsiderate man, especially with his personal staff. He thinks of his staff as members of his family. At his ranch they eat all their meals with him, including his colored secretary. He showers them with presents, but he dominates their lives. He works night and day himself and he expects them to do the same. His personal considerations are not permitted to take precedence over the job; theirs are not expected to either.

It is interesting that the men of his own generation, who were his associates in the New Deal days, and whom he respects and consults on many of the most imtimate questions of policy and personnel—Abe Fortas, Clark Clifford, James Rowe, and other friends such as former Secretary of the Treasury Robert Anderson and Donald Cook, the utilities expert in New York—have not joined his Administration. There are no doubt many reasons for this—maybe he wants it that way—but even some of these men prefer to work with him as outside advisers rather than under him as government servants.

This is not surprising. He is blunt and intolerant of mistakes, like his father, whom he strongly resembles. Sometimes he is in a rush and will not take time to listen. Sometimes he will give hours to people who are embarrassed to use up so much of his time. On one occasion he may listen attentively and say very little. On another he may carry on a monologue which stuns rather then persuades the visitor.

This torrent of activity is deceptive. It gives the impression that he is impulsive, but nothing could be more misleading. All the talking, all the telephoning, all the expenditure of energy are generally part of an elaborate system of checking and double-checking to be sure he knows all sides of the question before he moves. He has a catalogue of persons with whom he talks on each subject, some in and some out of government.

He knows these people extremely well and has them catalogued precisely in his mind. Each of them fits into a kind of Johnsonian political spectrum. "I know he regards me," explains one of his intimates, "as pessimistic and a little left of center and he judges what I say on this basis." If the answer given by the pessimistic and left-of-center friend conforms to that pattern, the President will probably not spend much time talking to him. But if, for whatever reason, the answer comes back "optimistic" or a little conservative, the President will pay attention and start re-checking. He may go back over the list entirely to clarify this one point. But one way or another, he will pay attention to that surprising answer, like a scientist exploring some odd chemical reaction.

He has a horror of making mistakes. He is highly conscious even now of Franklin Roosevelt's Court-packing blunder after the election of 1936. President Kennedy's fiasco at the Bay of Pigs in Cuba is a nightmare to him. "Never move up your artillery," he says, "until you move up your ammunition." Like a majority leader who does not like to call up a bill until he is sure he has the votes, he does not easily make decisions as President without being reasonably sure of victory. This is why he has been so restrained in responding to the Communist pressures in Vietnam, and this, of course, is why he is under attack from those who think a President must sometimes move without being sure of victory and without being certain of popular acclaim.

Lyndon Johnson is not to be explained in the newspaper clippings of today but in the writings of the past. He came to the Presidency with more Government experience than any man in this century, but personally, he is a throwback. He is a link between the Old Frontier of the days of William Jennings Bryan and the New Frontier days of John F. Kennedy.

When Frederick Jackson Turner came to the end of his long study of the influence of the American frontier on American character, he put himself to the task of defining the dominant human characteristics produced by frontier living, and in the process drew a word portrait of Lyndon Johnson. He defined the frontier characteristics this way:

"That coarseness and strength combined with acuteness and inquisitiveness; that practical, inventive turn of mind, quick to find expedients; that masterful grasp of material things, lacking in the artistic but powerful to affect great ends; that restless, nervous energy; that dominant individualism, working for good or evil, and withal that buoyancy and exuberance which comes from freedom—these are the traits of the frontier or traits called out elsewhere because of the existence of the frontier."

In his attitudes toward his Government, likewise, Johnson retains a faith that was once more popular than it is today. The political critics of the present time wonder whether a man so preoccupied with political tactics can conceive of the programs essential to the well-being of a complicated modern society. They see the leader, or so it seems to me, in Churchillian or even in Gaullist terms as a man with a sharp vision of the world and his place in it, and with a precise plan for leading the nation toward his goals. This is not Johnson's way.

He retains the old faith that the *total society* will find the answers to its problems, not the President alone. "A President does not shape a new and personal vision of America," he said in his first State of the Union message after his election. "He collects it from the scattered hopes of the American past." Lord Bryce, in his monumental work *The American Commonwealth*, summed up this attitude seventy-seven years ago.

The American people, Bryce wrote, "have unbounded faith in what they call The People and in a democratic system of government . . . hence a further confidence that the people are sure to decide right in the long run. . . . If you ask an intelligent citizen why he so holds, he will answer that truth and justice are sure to make their way into the minds and consciences of the majority. This is deemed an axiom, and the more readily so deemed, because truth is identified with common sense, the quality which the average citizen is most confidently proud of possessing."

President Johnson believes in this today. He was brought up on it. He loves to tell of the days when his grandfather and uncle campaigned together in the same horse and buggy for a seat in the Texas State Legislature, one on the Populist ticket and the other on the Democratic ticket. His mother, who was a great influence on his life, gave him a scrapbook in 1954, four years before she died. On a scrap of lined paper inside, she wrote: "May he find in the lives that have gone into the making of his life fuller understanding of his traits of mind and heart, deep appreciation of his ancestry, and continuing stimulation and incentive to a rich and rewarding life."

From this background has come that deep sense of home and country, which Tocqueville noticed in so many Americans when he came to this country in the 1830's. "There is," he remarked in *Democracy in America*, "one sort of patriotic attachment which principally arises from that instinctive, disinterested, and undefinable feeling which connects the affections of a man with his birthplace. This natural fondness is united with a taste for ancient customs and a reverence for traditions of the past; those who cherish it love their country as they love the mansion of their fathers."

President Johnson approached his first full term in much the same mood of nostalgia. The Presidency, he said, in his State of the Union message, brings no gift of prophecy or foresight and the President's hardest task is not to do what's right but to know what's right.

"The answer was waiting for me in the land where I was born," he said. "It was once a barren land . . . but men came and worked and endured and built. . . . There was a dream . . . a dream of a continent to be conquered, a world to be won, a nation to be made. . . . Remembering this I knew the answer. . . ."

This connection between Johnson and the concepts of the frontier is startling, but is it relevant to the present time? The young intellectuals do not seem to think it is. The university and diplomatic worlds are dubious. Who, they ask, is to lead and articulate the new American Idea, so casually called the Great Society? Where will we get the synthesizing intelligence that will rally the Government and the nation and reduce diversity to identity? The President represents the popular characteristics of the ordinary people, but paradoxically, is not wildly popular, maybe because the people want to be represented by qualities better than their own.

This hurts Mr. Johnson but it does not change his mind, and it clearly cannot change his character. He thinks the concepts of the past are relevant to the present day. He believes we are still on the hard frontier of a wicked world, where men are bound to get hurt and sensitivities overrun. He does not feel that it can be won without faith, and the faith he sees and hopes to nourish is the faith of our fathers. He does not think it can be done without a vast collective effort and without unity. And this is not feeling and sentiment alone.

He believes in an apparent paradox—namely, that the very complexity, mobility, and menace of the world today, which are causing so many problems, are also affecting all regions, and classes and nations, and therefore making it a little easier to bring about reconciliations between North and South, labor and management, rich and poor, the Congress and the White House, and even between the squabbling nations of the world. Accordingly, he feels that he is not trying to impose the past on the present, but merely trying to use the symbols of the past to create popular support for the essential innovations of the future.

Since his spectacular victory in November he has seemed more calm, as if he had tamed his inner demons at last. He is not a deeply religious man, and his attitude toward life was little changed by his heart attack in 1955, but it would be surprising if he were not now affected by the startling change in his fortunes.

At 45, he was convinced that he was as well prepared for the Presidency as any man in his party. At 52 he was denied the nomination because of what he regarded, with some bitterness, as prejudice against his Southern background. At 55 all was changed by the assassination of President Kennedy, precisely when Mr. Johnson had finally concluded he would never reach the White House. This is the central paradox of his story. The things he planned and manipulated in pursuit of the Presidency failed, and the thing he did not plan—he took the Vice Presidency for the sake of the party and against the opposition of his wife—carried him in the end to the top.

He does not talk about the election now; he doesn't even analyze the results, as he analyzed the polls before the vote. He merely talks unity, and who is to say at this moment that he is wrong? "The art of free society," wrote Alfred North Whitehead, "consists first in the maintenance of the symbolic code, and secondly, in the fearlessness of revision. . . . Those societies which cannot combine reverence to their symbols with freedom of revision must ultimately decay."

This is Johnson's theme and method. He does not study these things; they are in his bones. Kennedy's purpose was to make men think; Johnson's is to make men act. Both were reformers but went about it in different ways. Kennedy demanded reforms by challenging the conformists; Johnson got Kennedy's reforms by seeming to be a conformist himself.

So let us pray. He may back into the future but he will do so consciously, for he believes there is a spirit of wisdom in America's past that will guide her wherever she goes.

NOVEMBER 28, 1965

His Attitude Toward Criticism

THE OFFICIAL WHITE HOUSE LINE IS THAT LYNDON B. JOHNSON loves dissent, and in theory this is absolutely true. Johnson will defend to the death a man's right to oppose him until the man actually tries. Then, brother!

All Presidents resent their critics but react to them in different ways. Franklin Roosevelt scorned them. Harry Truman denounced them. Dwight Eisenhower ignored them, and Lyndon Johnson has his own way. He confounds them by perpetuating what they condemn.

The Johnson system is the most intricate of the lot. He takes criticism as a personal affront. If you write that it is foolish to keep Sargent Shriver in charge of both the poverty program at home and the Peace Corps overseas, he will keep Mr. Shriver in both until poverty is abolished from the face of the earth.

Arthur Schlesinger assured Dean Rusk's tenure as Secretary of State by attacking him and reporting that President Kennedy intended to fire him. When the press predicted that Mr. Johnson would get rid of all the Kennedy men in the White House, he invited them all to stay, and when he was later praised for doing so, he gradually let almost all of them resign.

It does not follow from this that he does not listen to criticism or adjust to it. He will change policies that are attacked but seldom people who are attacked. He has been responsive to those who wanted him to offer to negotiate a peace in Vietnam and also to those who wanted him to step up the war in Vietnam. In fact, he tried to placate both the hawks and the doves and wound up in the middle.

Yet this suggests a capriciousness that is not quite fair. Arthur Schlesinger says of President Kennedy in *A Thousand Days*: "No doubt he [Kennedy] realized that Vietnam was his great failure in foreign policy and that he had never really given it his full attention." No such charge can fairly be directed at President Johnson. When he faced the decision to bomb North Vietnam, and again the question of sending a large American expeditionary force to that country, he took elaborate precautions to see that the opponents of these policies within his Administration had plenty of time to define their positions. . . .

His feeling, however, is that when a decision of this magnitude is made in a difficult, intricate, and dangerous situation overseas, the President should be given the benefit of the doubt. Again, in fairness, this was the attitude he took when he was the Majority Leader in the Senate and President Eisenhower was in the White House. He would differ on domestic questions, but when Eisenhower acted for the nation overseas, he not only went along, but used his influence to try to persuade the other Democrats in the Senate to do the same.

That other men may, with equal sincerity, have a different view of the purpose of criticism in a democratic society does not seem to impress him. . . .

JANUARY 26, 1966

HIS DIFFERENCES WITH THE CHAIRMAN OF THE SENATE FOREIGN Relations Committee, J. W. Fulbright, tell quite a lot about his concept of his job.

This is not a personal feud. The President likes the Senator. Their families were close when the two men were in the Senate together. Their wives have been on the friendliest terms throughout Mr. Johnson's stay in the White House, and when President Kennedy was looking for a Secretary of State in 1961, Mr. Johnson recommended Senator Fulbright for the post.

In fact, the intimacy of the Johnson-Fulbright relationship in the past helps explain the present difficulties, for personal loyalty takes priority over personal conviction in Mr. Johnson's catalogue of political virtues. He can forgive his enemies, particularly when he thinks they are wrong, but not his friends, especially if he fears they may be right. There is a difference, too, in the President's attitude toward private and public criticism. No President of this century has sought more private advice from more people than President Johnson, but public criticism of his policies from a friend is another matter.

Senator Fulbright, in contrast, has been extremely careful not to exploit personal associations with the President to press his own foreign-policy views. He has stated his opinions when they were requested. But he has purposely not discussed with the President statements he was going to make in the Senate on foreign policy for the simple reason that he did not want to involve the President in his opinions.

Their difficulties started last year over precisely this point. Senator and Mrs. Fulbright spent a pleasant Sunday evening with President and Mrs. Johnson in the White House and a day or two later the Senator criticized the Administration's foreign policy. The President simply could not understand the Senator's impersonal and detached view of the duty of a Chairman of the Foreign Relations Committee and acted as if he had been betrayed. Similarly, Mr. Johnson was irritated by the Senator's long critique in the Senate of the Administration's military and political actions in the Dominican Republic crisis last September and has been fussing privately about Fulbright ever since.

What the President has done is to transfer to the White House the personal attitudes and political techniques he used as Majority Leader in the Senate cloakroom. He operated on Capitol Hill through a system of punishments and rewards and highly personal arrangements, and his system worked. It worked again at the White House on domestic policy, but the foreign-policy issues are proving too serious for personal manipulation. On questions of war and peace, the President's critics are not responding either to social blandishments or isolation.

This is especially true of Fulbright. . . . For example, the President, who is required by the Constitution to seek the advice of the Senate on foreign policy, and the Senator differ about what consultation means. When the President calls in the Congressional leaders, as he did tonight, and has the directors of the Central Intelligence Agency and the Pentagon tell them about the North Vietnamese sending new men and supplies to South Vietnam, he calls that "consultation." Actually, he is not "consulting" them, but "briefing" them. He is not mainly seeking their advice, but giving them his. . . .

THUS, THE PRESIDENT DOMINATES THIS TURBULENT CITY BUT HE doesn't persuade it. He overwhelms both his own party and his opposition, but he doesn't convince either; he manipulates but alienates the press, and he does all these things so naturally that he genuinely believes all the above statements are outrageous if not libelous lies. . . .

The price he pays is doubt. He has no effective opposition but himself in Washington. Few people here question his objectives. He genuinely wants peace and freedom and a negotiated settlement in Vietnam; and equality and good wages and high profits and even nobility at home; but he surrounds all this with such cunning political techniques that, even when he wins, he gets in the way of the things he wants.

What he wants is worthy of the faith and confidence of the nation, but this is precisely what he does not have, because his techniques blur his convictions. He is confusing what men say to the pollsters with what they say to their friends. He is mixing up news and truth. He knows what his aides say to him personally but he does not know what they say to their wives.

He is confronted, in short, with a crisis of confidence, and it is important not because it will defeat him but because he will go on winning and have to live with it, and this will not be easy. The chances are that he will have the political power to go on until 1973 against a weak opposition party, but increasingly his power will depend on his ability to persuade, to make people believe rather than merely to go along or knuckle under, and this is what he has not yet managed to do.

On Presidential Power

THE POWER OF THE PRESIDENT TO DO WHAT HE LIKES ON QUESTIONS of war or peace has seldom been dramatized more sharply than in Lyndon Johnson's conduct of the Vietnam war. He has done almost everything in Vietnam he vowed publicly not to do. He has done it all legally, and in the process he has demonstrated that the American President now exercises personal power in the field of foreign affairs unequaled by any other political leader in the world.

He was against taking the Vietnam issue to the United Nations Security Council for judgment, but he presented it to the UN this week nevertheless. He opposed bombing North Vietnam when he ran for the Presidency, but he ordered the bombing after he was elected. He was at first against defining his war aims publicly, against committing his troops to an offensive strategy of seeking out and destroying the enemy, and emphatically against risking a major ground war against superior numbers on the Asian continent—but he has done all these things in the face of sharp opposition within his own party and the nation.

This decisive Presidential power is best illustrated by his main argument for renewing the bombing in North Vietnam. His central argument was that the enemy was building up its forces during the bombing pause, and that unless the bombing was renewed "the cost in life—Vietnamese lives, American lives, and allied lives—will only be greatly increased."

In saying this, he made no reference to the much greater build-up of allied power during the pause, and implied that unless the United States renewed the bombing and stopped the flow of enemy arms, the balance of power would be changed in favor of the enemy, and the American command would be put in danger. On this basis, obviously nobody could challenge his thesis.

The facts before the Senate, however, do not support this proposition. The Vietcong, it is true, get most of their arms from Communist North Vietnam. They have gone over to a new weapons system that gets all its ammunition from China, and cannot be supplied by capturing supplies from the U.S. and South Vietnamese forces, whose ammunition does not fit their new weapons. But the Vietcong are fighting mainly with small arms, and can keep up the present level of fighting with no more than twelve tons of supplies a day.

The official line in Washington is that the Vietcong need 200 tons of supplies a day, which is a lot, and therefore that bombing them will cripple their operation. But 200 tons a day is an estimate based on the assumption that every Vietcong unit will be engaged all the time, and this never has happened in the Vietnamese war and is not likely to happen in the foreseeable future. Nevertheless, when this picture of North Vietnamese trucks delivering 200 tons of arms every day to attack our positions is presented as a factual situation, the opposition to President Johnson does not know what to say.

The President's legal argument is equally difficult. He says that the Congress authorized him to take any action "he," the President, deemed necessary, not only in South Vietnam but in all of Southeast Asia, to oppose the aggression of the Communists, and in this he is absolutely right. But the President asked for this power in the midst of the crisis over the Communist attack on American ships in the Gulf of Tonkin last summer, when the Congress really had no choice but to give him whatever he requested publicly or repudiate him and thus help the enemy.

The President may be right in what he has requested and what he has done, but the constitutional point is perfectly clear. The system has changed dramatically in the last generation. The President is now able to get the legal authority he wants if he chooses the right time to ask for it publicly, and he is able then to exercise that power to bomb or not to bomb, to commit 100,000 men or 500,000 men to the battle to carry out his policies if he so chooses.

Even in the midst of this week's controversy between the President and the liberal Democratic Senators of his own party over whether to bomb or not to bomb North Vietnam, the President's power was overwhelming. He sought their "consent," but did not really seek their advice on the things he eventually did.

Once the decision was made, the power of the Presidency began to appear. General Eisenhower, not by accident, supported it publicly. John J. McCloy and Allen Dulles and the other elder statesmen were brought into the White House and gave their support.

The President went on television to announce the results, and went on again to repeat it for the Columbia Broadcasting System, because Walter Cronkite happened to be launching his news show in color that night, and that was not all. Secretary of State Rusk, Secretary of Defense McNamara, and White House Assistant McGeorge Bundy were all suddenly available to explain the reasons for the bombing to waves of reporters representing the big columns, agencies, papers, and syndicates.

All of which is quite legal and even convenient. But it underscores the main point of all this. The balance of power has shifted in America to the Presidency. Wilson in Britain and even Kosygin in the Soviet Union never had such freedom of action in foreign affairs. Something important has happened in America since Woodrow Wilson went to his grave believing that the President of the United States was paralyzed in the foreign-affairs field by the overwhelming power of the Congress and public opinion.

His Dreams and Ideals

WHEN HE IS IN TROUBLE, LYNDON JOHNSON GOES BACK TO HIS OLD dreams. He was formed on the hard land of Texas and came to political power in the Depression and the early days of the New Deal, and when he talks about Franklin Roosevelt, as he did here this week, this link with the struggles of the Thirties is perfectly clear.

His speech to the Freedom House audience at the Waldorf-Astoria was a symbol of the tragedy of his Administration. He started out to express the continuity in American aspirations. He talked about Roosevelt's Four Freedoms—freedom of speech and expression, freedom of religion, freedom from want and fear—and when he talks about these things, even the glass teleprompters and his monotonous voice could not cover up his obvious sincerity. But then there was Vietnam.

Always Vietnam. He wanted to say there was something else going on in the world, but he couldn't leave it alone, and even if he had tried, the picketers outside and the protesters in the opulent ballroom would not let him or the audience forget it.

Yet it is clear that, in his own mind, whatever his critics say, he believes he is carrying on a noble tradition. Vietnam has never really known freedom of speech or religion, or freedom from want and fear, but all the more reason, he feels, that he should do what he can to bring these blessings to them.

His remarks on Vietnam were full of contradictions. He was angry with his critics but eloquent about the right of dissent. He was fighting for limited objectives but promised General Westmoreland whatever power was necessary to wage the war. And yet, though his reach may exceed his grasp, it has to be said for him that he is a yearner after great ideals.

Roosevelt was a cautious and even cynical man compared

with his protégé, Lyndon Johnson. F.D.R. talked eloquently about "quarantining" the enemies of freedom, but let France fail and Britain stagger before he made war after Pearl Harbor. Johnson, however, is bolder and far more melodramatic. He makes the New Deal seem like a grudging handout. Before he came to New York, he went to Andrews Air Force Base and greeted his Vice President as if Hubert had brought peace to the entire Pacific basin. Earlier in the day, he sent a message to Congress calling for the purification of the air and streams of the nation.

Nothing is beyond his aspirations. Roosevelt's Vice President, Henry Wallace, was condemned as a visionary because he wanted to give every Hottentot a quart of milk. Humphrey came back talking as if he wanted to send them all to college, and the President's message in New York was that the Four Freedoms can never be secure in America if they are violated elsewhere in the world.

This is not mere speech-making to Lyndon Johnson. His language sounded unrealistic to many in the audience, and the passages on Vietnam overly optimistic and even sentimental to many others, but he remains a believer in an unbelieving and cynical world.

His programs illustrate the point. He is out to eliminate poverty in America. Without any doubt, he feels he can bring adequate education to the multitude, and his confidence goes beyond the boundaries of the nation. Never mind that the British and the French let him know this week that they were reducing their commitments in the world; he sees a combination of American power and generosity dealing somehow with the problem.

Has Malthus become as great a menace as Marx? Are the death rate and the birth rate too high? He has programs for them all—containment for China, birth control and surplus food for India, a program to wipe out disease and another to deal with illiteracy beyond our frontiers.

Yet it is not fair to criticize him without acknowledging his aims. He wants everybody to have the Four Freedoms. He wants to reassure both Walter Lippmann and Joe Alsop. He wants to carry on for Franklin Roosevelt, unify the Atlantic and make up with General de Gaulle, and strengthen the Germans without worrying the Russians.

He looked troubled and sounded hurried in New York, and no wonder, for he is bearing all the dreams and lost causes of the century.

JULY 3, 1966

More War to End War

PRESIDENT JOHNSON SAID IN OMAHA THAT WE SHOULD COUNT TEN before we dissent from his policy in Vietnam. Okay: 1 2 3 4 5 6 7 8 9 10; but it doesn't work. On the Fourth of July, a man is still entitled to a stifled cry, for the Omaha speech is a mishmash of bad history and dubious logic.

"What happens in Vietnam," the President said, "will determine—yes, it will determine—whether ambitious and aggressive nations can use guerrilla warfare to conquer their weaker neighbors. It will determine whether might makes right."

This is quite a proposition. If Vietnam will really determine this ancient dispute about right and might, which goes back to Plato in 370 B.C., every porky middle-aged character in the country will surely want to volunteer for Saigon, but it will settle this or anything else? Here is the basis of the dispute between Mr. Johnson and his critics.

The President sincerely believes it will. Increasingly he is talking as if Vietnam were one of the decisive battles of the world: stop the enemy there and we've stopped him everywhere. Defeat the guerrilla technique now and we have convinced the enemy and reassured our uniting Asian allies, and for such historic ends, no matter what the cost of sacrifice, "We will see this through; we shall persist; we shall succeed."

Mr. Johnson is escalating his speaking as well as his bombing.

He is applying the do or die sentiments of the Alamo (which, after all, was not a glorious success) to one of Walt W. Rostow's latest theories. This is that President Kennedy's stand against Khrushchev in the Cuban missile crisis was the "Gettysburg" of the cold war, and that Vietnam is the Wilderness Campaign—a difficult, untidy mopping-up exercise before the end.

Maybe so, but it is hard to look ahead to the end of President Johnson's Administration and imagine this stable, free, cooperative Asian world that will, in his view, be established by the sacrifices of Vietnam.

If President Johnson told us bluntly that we were in a power struggle to establish a decent order in Asia—which we are—and intended to establish American military bases at Kam Ranh Bay and elsewhere to maintain in Southeast Asia what he calls the "vital security interests of the United States," that, at least, would be a policy. But he has not said that.

He has said that we want to prove to the Communists that guerrilla warfare does not pay, and after they have seen the light and come to the conference table, the United States wants no bases in Southeast Asia and will go away leaving the future of Vietnam to the converted Democrats in Saigon and the defeated and intimidated Communists in Hanoi and Peking.

This, with the best will in the world, is hard to believe. It is not a policy but a myth. It is possible that American power will finally smash the main units of the North Vietnamese Army in the South and disperse the Vietcong guerrillas—after severe casualities on both sides—but it is highly unlikely that this will produce either a democratic order in Saigon or an acquiescent Communist order in Hanoi and Peking.

The struggle will go on. China will still represent a quarter of the human race. Rhetoric will not change geography. Mr. Johnson may get his "honorable settlement" and get past the election, but what will he have settled, and what will he have achieved that will justify the lives that will be lost between now and then?

The President has already proved to the Communists that guerrilla warfare is an expensive business. He has a chance now to influence the constitutional convention in Saigon so that it will bring in a representative government that will negotiate peace with all the enemies in the field, including the National Liberation Front, but he is not doing this.

Either now, before more and more killing, the Communists are going to participate in a compromise settlement; or later, after our "victory" and departure, they are going to participate in such a settlement anyway. The President, however, does not see it this way. It is awkward politically. It involves a compromise with the Communists which is harder to explain than letting them force a compromise after we are gone. But the cost of fighting on until Hanoi, Peking, and Moscow agree to an American conquest on the battlefield is likely to be very great, and the end result, after we leave, not much different.

The President talked at Omaha about fighting for the "will of the people" in Vietnam, but the will of the people there, so far as it can be determined, is for peace, while the will of the generals, whom the President is supporting, is for war.

He defended bombing Hanoi and Haiphong on the ground that it was necessary to halt the large-scale infiltration of arms which the previous bombing was supposed to control. He tells us that instead of diminishing the flow of Communist supplies by bombing, the flow of supplies has been increased; instead of human supply trails through the jungle when the bombing started, "the trails turned into boulevards," which seems a little odd; instead of small weapons carried on the backs of human beings, "they built all-weather roads . . . they began sending troops in by trucks rather than on foot . . . they shifted over to heavy weapons using imported ammunition, most of it coming from Communist China." And the President's conclusion from all this was that there must be more bombing "at the source," which will probably mean China if the supplies at Hanoi and Haiphong are destroyed.

Something happens to Johnson when he crosses the Appalachian Range. He drops the restraint of the Capitol and picks up the idiom of the political stump. Our soldiers in Vietnam, he says, are not going to fail us; the question is whether the critics are going to fail them.

Count ten, he says, before you let me and them down, before you "hurt." But something is wrong. We count and we don't want to "hurt," but somehow it doesn't work.

12

EISENHOWER

The Two Candidates

SOMEBODY IS GOING TO HAVE TO WRITE A NEW BOOK OF POLITICAL rules, for the Chicago stockyards never saw a slaughter to compare with what happened to the old political maxims, assumptions, and clichés here this month.

In opposition to most of the ideas by which American politics are supposed to be governed, victory in both conventions went:

Not to the pros but to the amateurs;

Not to those who shouted the most but to those who said the least;

Not to those who sought the nomination the hardest but to those who shunned it almost to the end;

Not to the extremist of the left or right but to the moderates;

Not to those who spent and promised the most but to those who spent and promised the least;

Not to the old-timers but to the newcomers;

Not to the men who concentrated on the things that divide the American people but to those who emphasized the things that unite them; and

Not to the men who were longing for the world as it used to be, but to those who are prepared to grapple with it as it is.

These things are bound to have a profound influence on the forthcoming campaign. It will not be a struggle between the Taft-Hoover-MacArthur conservatives of the Republican party and the Humphrey-Lehman-Harriman wing of the Democratic party. These two extremes of right and left made strong bids for control of both conventions and lost. Accordingly, though there will still be a great deal of campaign oratory about the Old Dealers and the New Dealers, the issue has been narrowed by the selection of

General of the Army Dwight D. Eisenhower and Governor Adlai E. Stevenson.

General Eisenhower is instinctively to the left of the men who have controlled the Republican party in Congress and in the national committee for the last eight years, and Governor Stevenson is to the right of the New Dealers and the Fair Dealers. The General may be to the right of center and the Governor to the left of center, but if they can dominate the campaign, it will be fought not from the extremes of the gutter but on the higher ground in the middle of the road.

Neither the General nor the Governor got into this campaign because he was opposed to the main lines of the present United States foreign policy. When the primary election campaign started there was a basic difference between the leading candidates of the two parties.

It is not easy to define this difference accurately, but in general terms, it was a difference between those—such as Senator Cabot Lodge, Jr., of Massachusetts and Paul G. Hoffman, the former Marshall Plan director—who believed that it was imperative to defend America through alliances and cooperation with other countries and those—such as Senator Robert A. Taft of Ohio—who placed far more emphasis on America's defending itself and far less emphasis on alliances.

The nomination of Governor Stevenson and General Eisenhower reduces if it does not eliminate this basic difference of approach. Both are convinced and enthusiastic believers in the Atlantic, Pacific, and hemisphere alliances and in the United Nations. Both are positive men, more interested in planning for the future than in raking over the mistakes of the past, and both are in the campaign because of a sincere conviction that serving the cause of world peace is worth a man's life.

As a result, the forthcoming campaign is likely to concentrate far more on domestic issues and on the struggle for control of Congress than was thought likely a month ago. This was already apparent in the speeches before the Democratic convention. The emphasis was not on personality but on policy, not on foreign policy so much as on the social and economic policies of the New Deal.

In this field, the gap between General Eisenhower and Governor Stevenson is likely to be wider. Both favor more emphasis on the rights and responsibilities of the states and municipalities than the past few Democratic Administrations, but Governor Stevenson has dealt with the economic and social problems at the state level; he knows the importance of Federal aid and the difficulty of getting the states and the communities to assume responsibility on their own. Consequently, he is likely to tolerate and even to support a larger degree of Federal influence in the states than would General Eisenhower.

The real difference between the two men, however, is in character and personality. If one can generalize about these things, General Eisenhower is the classic man of action, Governor Stevenson the man of reason. Each has the qualities the other lacks. Although General Eisenhower has wobbled from left to right in his political speeches, his military career shows him to be a man of decision; while Governor Stevenson is not noted for this quality.

Governor Stevenson is distinguished for the intellectual content of what he says; General Eisenhower's speeches since he returned lack precisely this quality; General Eisenhower is tough-minded, simple, and direct in his approach to questions, Governor Stevenson more complicated and introspective, much more inclined to brood and worry over his problem.

Their approach to the problem of Presidential nominations illustrates these things. Both were doing jobs in which they believed—General Eisenhower the command of the North Atlantic Treaty armies, Mr. Stevenson the Governorship of Illinois. Both were under extreme pressure from one set of friends to stay on the jobs they were on and from other friends to run for the Presidency.

Neither felt that he was particularly fitted for the job, but as soon as it became apparent to General Eisenhower that the time had come to make a decision, he made it. He listened to the arguments on both sides; he said publicly that his calculations had gone wrong and he decided to come home and run for office.

Mr. Stevenson, however, never really did make up his mind.

He did not decide to get in and he did not decide to get out. He merely worried the question until events took command of him and forced him into the nomination. And this was not a calculated strategy as some people still suspect. From beginning to end, the process was one long personal anguish. Even after the bandwagon started to roll this week and everybody was in agreement that he was going to be nominated, he still talked privately about trying to find excuse for pulling out.

Once he got in, however, once he started grappling, not with personal questions, but with ideas, he was both decisive and courageous. He promised his party nothing. He avoided the weary platitudes, the half-truths, the cheap debating points that have dominated the political atmosphere here and in Washington for the last two or three years.

"Sacrifice, patience, understanding and implacable purpose may be our lot for years to come," he told the convention. "Let's face it. Let's talk sense to the American people. Let's tell them the truth that there are no gains without pains; that this is the eve of great decisions, not easy decisions, like resistance when you are attacked, but a long patient costly struggle which alone can assure triumph over the great enemies of men—war and poverty and tyranny."

Stevenson is a Wilsonian figure, highly literate, idealistic, and urbane. He is not regarded as a good Administrator out here, and he has something of Dean Acheson's weakness for satirical wisecracks, but his gift of expression, his knowledge of who we are and where we are in history, and his transparent sincerity cannot help but elevate our public life.

It is a long time since the Republican and Democratic parties were both led at the same time by men who will be appealing to the noblest qualities in the electorate. The leaders of both parties for the past few years have managed, either by their narrow views or their lack of eloquence, to reduce the great experiments and projects of the era to the level of street-paving debate. Eisenhower—when he speaks out of his heart and not out of a ghostwriter's file—and Stevenson have the capacity to lift the whole project and give it some dignity and perspective.

It is not to be expected that Senator Joseph McCarthy of

Wisconsin, Alger Hiss, Chiang Kai-shek, Owen Lattimore, Ambassador Phillip Jessup, and all the other leading characters in the debate of the past three years will suddenly vanish from the canned campaign speeches written by the paid ghosts of the Democratic and Republican national committees. Nor is it likely that the voters will be spared more apoplectic harangues about Yalta, Teheran, Potsdam, the 80th Congress, the "Hoover depression," and all the rest of the historical whipping posts, but things seem to be looking up.

The two candidates—if not their supporters—are already talking more about the future than the past; both have appealed for a campaign that will not affront the intelligence of the voters. Both see our problems, not primarily in terms of personalities, but in terms of the vast upheavals of the age, and while this will produce all the old cries, particularly in this vicinity, that both parties have abandoned Colonel Robert R. McCormick, this need not necessarily destroy the republic.

Between Stevenson and Eisenhower there is still room for plenty of debate. They are vastly different men. Neither has yet met the test of a great political campaign, and attractive as they both are personally, neither is more important than the institutions they represent. In the last analysis, the battle for the Congress may prove to be more important than the struggle for control of the Executive branch of the Government.

Eisenhower's Special Gift
at the Summit

THERE IS A SHORTAGE OF NEW IDEAS, ROOMS, AND TAXIS AT THE summit, but otherwise everything has been arranged. The President is in. The Alps have been wired for sound. Fifteen hundred reporters are here from all the great engines of information, and droves of tidy officials have arrived with briefing notebooks that trace the history of Germany from Charlemagne and Luther through Bismarck and Henry Morgenthau to Chancellor Adenauer.

Now it is up to Eisenhower. Churchill, who started it all, is in retirement. Roosevelt and Stalin, the other members of the last heads of Government meeting at Potsdam, are dead. The foreign ministers are deadlocked on Germany, the central issue, and if the deadlock is to be broken, President Eisenhower will have to do it.

The reason for this is that the heart of the problem is to convince the Russians that the H-bomb, the A-bomb, the guided missile, and the jet airplane have so revolutionized warfare that the old concepts of defense and the old methods of containing the Germans are out of date.

Eden and Faure, Dulles and Pinay can talk all they like about "the new Germany," but they will never convince the Russians that the Germans have changed. Eisenhower, however, might be able to convince them that the world has changed, and that is the main hope of this conference.

History has taught the Russians that there is safety in space. Big land armies, vast stretches of geography, and cruel weather enabled them to beat Napoleon and Hitler. This is why they are so eager for their deep belt of satellites between their western frontier and the Germans. This is why they cling to East Germany. Like all continental powers, like the Germans who minimized sea power in the First World War and air power in the Second, the tend to overestimate military power on the ground. The hope is that Eisenhower can persuade them that, in their own interest, they must develop new concepts of defense in general, and new ideas for containing the Germans in particular.

If anybody can do this Eisenhower can. He collaborated with them in the defeat of the Germans ten years ago. They respect his abilities as a soldier. He has been the most moderate American politican in his discussions of the Soviet problem. And he has arrived for the Big Four conference precisely at the moment when the Soviet military leaders seem to be in the ascendant.

There has always been a kind of international fraternity of soldiers. More than diplomats, the generals seem to be able to talk to one another about military power, if not about politics, in understandable terms. Two of the three Soviet leaders here— Bulganin and Zhukov—are soldiers, and while Bulganin has been primarily a political general, Zhukov is not only a professional soldier but a man who respects and is respected by President—formerly General—Eisenhower.

Consequently, it is just possible—no more than that—that Eisenhower may be able to induce the Russians to try a new approach to the German problem. They want to detach the West German Federal Republic from the West. The President's theme will be that security for Russia depends not on keeping Germany out of the Western alliance but in getting her involved in and controlled by that alliance, not in alienating Germany but in reforming her, not in dividing Germany and nourishing her grievances but in uniting her and removing those grievances, not in geographical devices designed to win a war against Germany but in new political and military relationships that will prevent that war from breaking out.

Eisenhower is not the only man here who knows what the new weapons have done to weaken the traditional "defense in depth" strategy of the Russians, but his military judgment on these questions is likely to be listened to more than anybody else's. Nobody here thinks that the President will produce any spectacular reversal in the Soviet position in Geneva. In fact the President may say very little about these strategic and logistical problems in the formal meetings, but in the private meetings with the Soviet leaders he may have some influence.

SEPTEMBER 11, 1955

Not a Political Movement but a Love Affair

THE POPULARITY OF PRESIDENT EISENHOWER HAS GOT BEYOND THE bounds of reasonable calculation and will have to be put down as a national phenomenon, like baseball. The thing is no longer just a remarkable political fact but a kind of national love affair, which cannot be analyzed satisfactorily by the political scientists and will probably have to be turned over to the head-shrinkers.

Very much against his will, the President is suddenly being presented as the answer and solution to everything: war, juvenile delinquency, the decline in farm prices, parental irresponsibility, the division of Europe and Germany, polio, death on the highways, the school shortage, and all the rest.

When the Republican state chairmen met here this week, they went over all these things and came to the same conclusion about everything. Ike was the answer. To a man they agreed that if he should refuse to stand for re-election next year the confusion in the party would be indescribable, but even in their private sessions with one another they refused to consider an alternative.

Whatever the President does now is automatically wonderful. If he goes to Geneva and cries peace, even when there is no peace, he is proclaimed throughout the world. If he counters the optimism of Geneva six weeks later with stern warnings to the Communists, nobody asks why he didn't think of that before but hails him as a scourge of the appeasers.

When he reminds his party that he is a mortal man and that no institution should place so much reliance on a single individual, nobody pays any attention. When the farmers think about the decline in commodity prices they don't blame the President but Secretary of Agriculture Benson. When people have complaints about foreign policy, they turn on Secretary of State Dulles. When they worry about polio, they blame Mrs. Hobby; about taxes, Secretary Humphrey; and so on.

It is a remarkable psychological situation. Roosevelt at the height of his popularity never had it so good. The Democrats were just as single-minded when they based all their hopes on the re-election of F.D.R., but they were much more cynical about it, and even when they backed him many of them criticized him openly.

Eisenhower today not only commands the overwhelming support of his party, but the affection as well. There is something very personal about his following. The mail coming into the White House is full of personal items. It isn't only the amateur philosophers seeking his support for their special solutions to the world's ills but the men and women with personal problems who turn to him for help.

This sense of personal identity with the President is especially noticeable within his official family. Roosevelt's Cabinet and White House staff always included at least a few individuals who were not only critical of his policies but who were openly critical of his aggressiveness, his divisiveness, and his methods of dealing with people.

No such criticism is heard today. The President's associates vie with one another in praising his fairness. And even those, like Air Secretary Talbott, who have left the Administration with what they regarded as a just grievance have nothing to say against the President personally. . . .

It is now almost precisely three years since the late Senator Taft and General Eisenhower met at Morningside Heights and

Mr. Taft issued the famous communiqué which was interpreted as a capitulation by the General to the Senator. Since then, as this week's meeting with the Republican state chairmen illustrated, the former supporters of Senator Taft have been won over to his support, partly for political, but also partly for personal reasons.

He is, indeed, a symbol of the atmosphere of the time: optimistic, prosperous, escapist, pragmatic, friendly, attentive in moments of crisis and comparatively inattentive the rest of the time. What America is, at this moment of her history, so is Eisenhower, and the Democrats don't know what to make of it. They are trying to criticize him, but as "Peck" Trussell of the *Times* said this week, "In politics, you can't kick a man when he's up."

MARCH 4, 1956

The Human Drama in the White House

THE HUMAN DRAMA OF THE EISENHOWER STORY HAS NOT YET BEEN told. The reporters have done their best and, thanks to Jim Hagerty, they have told a great deal, but the novelists and the historians will have to take it from here.

Maybe even they will never get at the whole truth, for the real drama lies where truth can scarcely be pursued with assurance: in the innermost thoughts of the President's mind, in the reactions of his dutiful wife, and in the actions of his doctors and associates who created between November and March a political situation from which he could hardly escape without serious injury to his party.

What is clear is that somewhere along the way his thinking changed. He wrote in his book, *Crusade in Europe,* after a four-day illness: "I learned a lesson I did not thereafter violate: A full measure of health is basic to successful command."

Better than any other President of the century he expressed with great eloquence last August his convictions that no President was "indispensable" and that the party should think of other younger Republicans for the Presidency. Until this week his public utterances emphasized the dangers to the Republicans of risking a second term after a heart attack and at an age beyond any other second-term candidacy. Yet he took the risk.

One exchange in his Wednesday-morning press conference adds to the plot:

Hazel Markel: "Mr. President, can you tell us: Had you made up your mind previous to your heart attack that you would run for a second term?"

The President: "You know, Miss Markel, that is one secret I don't think I will ever tell anybody. Possibly in my papers that can be opened twenty-five years after I have passed on, why, it will be told."

In his broadcast that same night, he said he was "undecided" before the heart attack, and yet this fascinating exchange remains. If his decision had been "yes" before the attack, or if he had been "undecided," why the reference to the "secret" which could not be disclosed until a quarter of a century after his death?

The President did give some reasons for his decision: the work he had set out to do four years ago was not finished. Beyond that, he said, "I have, first of all, been guided by the favorable reports of the doctors." He went on to say, in a remark that has fascinated many observers here, that "some" of his doctors thought the dangers to his health would be "less in the Presidency than in any other position I might hold."

This, however, merely raises the other fascinating question about the philosophy of Dr. Paul Dudley White. I rode to the airport with him the morning after he made his final report that the chances were that the President could continue as he was now for "five or ten years." He is a charming man and clearly a philosopher. He explained his philosophy about advising heart patients. The primary question he asked, he said, was about the state of a patient's mind. If you could contribute to a man's happiness, he observed, you could probably add to his life.

Therefore, he continued, a man's spiritual foundations and his work were the main things to be considered. It was important to a patient to feel that he was "carrying on," Dr. White said, preferably in the work he had been doing. Dr. White added that, of course, it was also important to see that in "carrying on" a patient did not submit himself to too much strain, but that, he concluded, was secondary.

The novelists and the historians will be interested in Dr. White and his philosophy. They will want to study, too, the role of Jim Hagerty, his influence on Dr. White, and the silence of the press and the medical profession on the merits and implications of a second term during the period when the President was making up his mind.

More than anybody else, Mr. Hagerty and Dr. White created the situation which the President recognized by saying "yes" this week. Dr. White made the reports which conformed with his honest diagnosis and his philosophy and Mr. Hagerty dramatized those reports in one of the most brilliant public-relations jobs in history.

This is normal human behavior, which will not surprise the novelists. White House aides almost always develop a fierce loyalty to "the boss," as Jim Hagerty has. Doctors usually think of their patient and not of history. And men of action never like to quit at any age, especially if they can retain power (see Roosevelt, Churchill, Adenauer, Rhee, and Chiang Kai-shek).

But the Eisenhower story is still a great novel, for we do not know whether he was aware of the situation that was being created by the passage of time. We do not know who or what really changed his mind.

The Eisenhower Era

PRESIDENT EISENHOWER HAS NOW COMPLETED HIS OFFICIAL FARE-
wells and will retire tomorrow as the most popular and the most
criticized American of the day.

In a generation or so, the historians may be able to agree on
his place in history; but meanwhile, it is fairly clear why this
paradox of criticism amidst popularity exists. He was popular
because he was in tune with the spirit of the nation, which,
during his eight years in office, was generous and optimistic, but
not militant or experimental. He was criticized because he was
not in tune with the worldwide spirit of the age, which was
convulsive and revolutionary.

This contrast between the spirit of the nation (which he
helped to create) and the spirit of the world is the heart of the
Eisenhower story. He was a good man in a wicked time; a con-
solidator in a world crying for innovation; a conservative in a
radical age; a tired man in a period of turbulence and energetic
action.

In President Eisenhower's own terms—which are important at
the point of a man's retirement—he has had a successful Administration. He is not a glory merchant. He never thought he was
the answer to the world's problems, but he had certain limited
goals that he feels he has achieved.

He stayed the course, despite three terrible illnesses. He upheld the dignity and honor of his office. He avoided war and
depression, the two things he feared most. He broke the isolationist tradition of his party, which is why he sought the Presidency in the first place, and he presided over an era of prosperity
and good feeling within the nation.

No doubt he would have liked to secure the peace he did so
much to win as a soldier, but he never thought he could stamp
out human folly or human misery. Accordingly, he thinks it is a

little silly to blame him for not taming Khrushchev, Castro, and Lumumba, since he didn't invent them in the first place.

Popular opinion accepted this attitude, which is why the American people are now bidding him an affectionate farewell. They like him because they shared so many of his feelings. They were not yearning for unlimited goals. They were not trying to influence the course of events in all the continents. After the upheaval of change, war, and depression from 1940–53, they were reassured by the figure of a renowned soldier optimistically calling for agreements at home and abroad without demanding too much sacrifice or painful thought.

Critical opinion in America, however, was not satisfied with this test of the Presidency. His critics saw him not merely as an attractive human being with decent instincts and sound objectives, but as a leader of the free world who was confronted by a unique and cunning challenge, which he underestimated from the beginning of his Administration.

President Eisenhower came to power in 1953. This was the year when Stalin died, when the Russians decided to give first priority to producing a missile-delivery system, when Moscow exploded its first hydrogen bomb, when the Chinese Communists started their first Five-Year Plan, when the Russians launched their trade and political offensives in the underdeveloped nations, and when Khrushchev gradually began working toward a more flexible system of decentralized power after the death of Stalin.

President Eisenhower was aware of all these things, but he was preoccupied with other considerations closer to home. He had a Republican Administration to form, the first in twenty years. Though he had won the Presidency in a savage fight against the conservative Taft wing of the party, he turned over to the conservatives the key power roles in the Cabinet: Treasury, Defense, and Budget.

Accordingly, he started his Administration not with his eyes on the new situation in post-Stalin Russia but on the Republican objectives of reducing the budget, cutting the nation's commitments overseas, increasing the deterrent of atomic weapons, wiping out inflation, and reducing the authority of the central Federal Government.

Even before he entered the White House, but after his election, President Eisenhower went to Korea and, on the way back on the cruiser *Helena*, worked out with the principal members of his Cabinet what Charles J. V. Murphy of *Fortune* magazine, who had access to the official documents, called "the great equation" of the new Administration.

The objectives then defined were to curb excessive credit, to remove controls as soon as possible, to reduce the cost of the Federal Government, get it out of competition with free enterprise as much as possible, and to balance the budget as soon as possible and as near as possible to Senator Taft's goal of $60 billion. Coincidentally, the strategic goals of "the great equation" were to end the Korean War immediately and to revise the strategic concepts of the armed forces so as to rely more on the new atomic weapons and thus cut the costs of the defense establishment.

As Walt Whitman Rostow of the Massachusetts Institute of Technology summarized it: "Eisenhower as President was imprisoned by the initial political and strategic dispositions he made—from the time of the Republican convention [of 1952] down through the Morningside Heights meeting with Senator Taft, to the selection of his cabinet, the days on the *Helena*, and beyond through the first year in office."

The Eisenhower Administration was greatly influenced, too, by the President's concept of political leadership and staff organization, both of which were to a large extent the result of his military experience. He thought of his Cabinet as many theater commanders who should have a wide latitude of decision within a general policy set by the President himself. He looked to his Cabinet and staff to produce agreed decisions, which he usually followed. If the staff could not reach a consensus of what to do, he did not hesitate himself to decide.

He was deferential to the Congress, as most general officers are, having in mind that the Congress holds the pursestrings. He opposed the idea of regular talks to the nation. He even put the agreed judgments of the Cabinet in many cases above his own instinctive judgment. He decided, in short, only when his subordinates could not agree, and he addressed the nation not as part of an educational process, but mainly in some crisis when it was imperative to speak. Again this system was based on personal qualities that were popular in America. They reflect not a tendency to Caesarism, which the Democrats threw at him in the first campaign of 1952, but modesty and even a kind of self-abnegation. He was orderly, patient, conciliatory, and a thoughtful team player—all admirable traits of character.

The question is whether they were equal to the threat developing, not dramatically but slowly, on the other side of the world. This was debated throughout the eight years inside as well as outside the Government. As early as 1953, a movement developed within the Administration to tell the people the startling facts of the new world of rocketry and nuclear weapons, to spell out the challenge and seek consent for much greater efforts and sacrifices. This, however, was rejected.

In the second Eisenhower Administration, the gap widened between the intellectual community of the nation and the political Administration on what was needed to meet the political and military and economic policies of the Soviet Union.

Thus the Gaither Report, ordered by the President, called for much greater exertions, but was never made public. The Rockefeller Brothers' report did the same, not only in terms of military but political, economic, and education policy. The Administration rejected most of the conclusions of these reports, however, even after the startling Soviet scientific achievements in outer space.

There were many reasons for this. The Administration was convinced that it had sufficient power at hand to deter the Communists from making war. The President and particularly the Treasury felt that inflation was a serious menace to the stability of the nation and had to be curbed.

Also, the President, by swift action, had blocked the Communist thrusts in Guatemala, and in Lebanon, had helped end the Suez war, and avoided intervention in the Hungarian revolution. Thus he was satisfied that a middle course was the true path to the avoidance of war, and this was strongly favored by a prosperous nation in no mood for overseas adventures.

Accordingly, the Eisenhower Administration has come to a

close with a series of truces in Korea, Indochina, the Taiwan Strait, and Berlin. Nothing has been settled but nothing vital to the free world has been lost. On this compromise, the American people if not the critics are willing and eager to praise President Eisenhower for a job well done.

He has been the President of the transition from Republican isolation to Republican involvement in the world. He has consolidated the New and Fair Deal policies his party fought against for a whole generation. This was not enough to satisfy the national interest, which has no doubt suffered as a result of the expansion of Communist power in Asia, the Middle East, Africa, and Latin America, but it is something.

President Eisenhower at least maintained enough power to deter the big war, and the big depression, and that was his important if limited objective from the start.

13

KENNEDY

Kennedy Looks to 1960

SENATOR JOHN F. KENNEDY OF MASSACHUSETTS IS QUIETLY BUT diligently building support these days for the 1960 Democratic Presidential nomination. Though the voters are not even showing much interest as yet in the 1958 election, the handsome young New Englander was here today helping the West Virginia Democratic candidates in the hope that they will in turn help him two years from now.

This is not a new adventure for Senator Kennedy. Ever since his strong bid for the Deomcratic Vice Presidential nomination in 1956, he has been methodically going from one state to another, meeting the party leaders, speaking at party rallies, and getting himself better known. There is no doubt that this is paying off in experience if nothing else. He has always been an effective performer on television and in small gatherings. Now he is a much more effective platform speaker.

He looked a little self-conscious today riding down the main street of Parkersburg in a scarlet Cadillac convertible with his attractive young wife. Somehow he seemed out of place in a parade with a Democratic donkey and the Parkersburg High School Band, especially since few people on Main Street seemed to know who he was or what the noise was all about.

When one bystander discovered that it was a politician signaling the start of the biennial autumnal madness, he expressed indifference and cynicism by remarking: "It's just some politician riding down the street on the taxpayers' money. When you get one party in power you get war, and when you get the other you starve to death."

The Democratic party workers, however, were less indifferent, and once he got on the platform Senator Kennedy made his points with an assurance he did not have two years ago and with a clarity and brevity not usual in political oratory. He has an excellent New England voice: cultivated, yet strong and full of vitality. His clothes and hair-do are a masterpiece of contrived casualness. He hits hard on foreign policy and labor, which he knows best, lacing his speech with learned quotations from Shakespeare, Justice Holmes, Woodrow Wilson, and the Founding Fathers.

But primarily this is an exercise in the display of a personality, and it seems to go over fairly well. The politicians like him, the audiences are respectful, if not enthusiastic, and even with Mrs. Kennedy on the platform his influence on lady politicians is almost naughty. The effect, in short, is of a serious and personable young man with a fresh personality. He has at least got far enough already so that the party workers come out to see and hear him, and they went away today obviously impressed.

He said nothing particularly new or arresting. He remembered all the names of the state and local candidates on the platform— a considerable achievement—and concentrated, somewhat wistfully, on the good old days when, as he saw it, we used to have leadership in the White House. His main target, however, was not President Eisenhower but Vice President Richard M. Nixon, whom he scorned at every opportunity. And his main theme was that the foreign policy, labor policy, and social-security policy of the nation were in bad shape due to the sloth and shortsightedness of the Republican party.

The young Senator's strategy is fairly clear. He is trying to exploit a situation in which no Democratic candidate has a clear advantage and he is trying to do it early. Every trip he makes gets him in the papers, and on television locally. Every Senator or Congressman he helps get elected in 1958 is a potential Kennedy delegate at the 1960 convention.

He was in Delaware and New Jersey yesterday, in West Virginia and Maryland today, flying with only his wife and his executive assistant in a chartered airplane. No reporters follow him on these trips, which are taking place while his own campaign for re-election in Massachusetts is in progress. But he is building carefully in the hope of getting a considerable lead before Adlai E. Stevenson and the other candidates get going.

Kennedy's Nomination

JOHN F. KENNEDY WON MORE THAN THE PRESIDENTIAL NOMINA-
tion tonight. For he won the right not only to represent his party
as its youngest nominee, but to represent his generation, and to
represent himself. This last, ironically, is important to Kennedy.
For he is free at last to be judged for what he is. The focus will
now be on him as a human being, not on his father, or his
church, or his money, or his attractive young wife, but on his
personal qualities of mind and character.

These outside considerations have been important to him and
he would be the first to admit it. Without them, he would probably not be his party's Presidential nominee tonight. He has
benefited greatly by his family, his money, his church, and his
wife, but he reached a point about halfway through this campaign where these assets overwhelmed everything else and turned
the individual candidate into a tribe and even, according to his
political opponents, into a kind of conspiracy.

This was, and still is, a major problem for Kennedy. He has
reached a pinnacle of success unknown to any man of his age in
this party, but he is also the victim of the political and public-
relations attributes that have helped him succeed. For the popular assets that helped him get where he is tonight fit so neatly
into the shorthand of modern journalism and television that they
have obscured his own personal qualifications for the high office
he seeks.

It is early yet to pass judgment on these deeper qualities of
character and ability—the campaign will soon provide an adequate test—but the primaries and the convention have already
indicated what these qualities are.

It is obvious that aside from all the help he has had, he is a
remarkably gifted young man: experienced well beyond the nor-

mal expectation of his years, at home in both the intellectual and political institutions of the nation, articulate particularly in the give and take of modern television discussion and debate, industrious, energetic, and above all courageous. Four times in the last few months he has been confronted suddenly by challenges from his opponent, and every time he has come through under circumstances where he was on his own.

The first of these was last November when the Roman Catholic bishops of his own church took a position against the dissemination of birth-control information by the nation to other nations. He took an independent line on this at once and declared that he would not only decide the point on whatever was best for the nation, but that he would put his constitutional oath of office above every other obligation spiritual or temporal. Reflective men are still debating this point.

The second test came in the West Virginia primary election, when he was up against charges that he had won the Wisconsin primary with the aid of a "Roman Catholic vote," and when he was faced with agitation among the predominantly Protestant West Virginia voters to retaliate by taking a position against him. Kennedy immediately dramatized this issue by carrying it publicly before the American Society of Newspaper Editors in Washington. He gambled on exposing and challenging the issue. He accepted Senator Hubert Humphrey's challenge to a television debate on the issues of the campaign, and in the process reversed the adverse trend against his candidacy and won the election.

The third challenge came from former President Harry S. Truman of Missouri, who suddenly and sharply criticized Kennedy's youth and invited him to withdraw in favor of more experienced men. Kennedy responded to this challenge with courtesy and serenity. He refused to withdraw and turned the issue of his youth into an asset in one of the most brilliant statements of the campaign.

Finally, this week here in Los Angeles he was challenged to a debate by his leader in the Senate, Lyndon B. Johnson of Texas, who apparently acted on the assumption that he could blow his young opponent out of the water. Kennedy accepted the proposal and again demonstrated his ability to articulate the issues of the campaign under extremely difficult circumstances.

Kennedy has in short shown the capacity not only to mobilize the considerable material physical and institutional assets at his command, but has demonstrated firm nerves and a more determined purpose than any other man in his party. He was nominated tonight not only because he had won the primary elections of New Hampshire, Wisconsin, West Virginia, and Oregon, but because he had a more solid foundation with all the major elements of the Democratic party than any other candidate.

He had strength in every region of the country with the exception of the South; he had support among the party's intellectuals; he had strength among labor union leaders and Negro leaders; he had delegates in the rural areas as well as the urban areas; and last but not least, he had strength among that extremely important section of the people who do not normally vote unless they are attracted into politics by an unusually magnetic personality.

Thus while a great deal of attention has been paid in the last six months to Kennedy's subsidiary opportunities and qualities it has become increasingly apparent that in his individual right he is one of the most remarkable young men to come into American politics in a long time.

There is no doubt that he has matured in the struggle of his long pre-convention campaign. He knows a lot more about this country and its problems today than he did when he started touring the states of the Union shortly after his unsuccessful bid for the Vice Presidency in 1956.

He is infinitely more confident than he was a year ago or even six weeks ago. In fact, in these last few weeks he has not only shown a willingness and eagerness to engage in combat with men much older and more experienced than himself, but has recently been displaying a toughness and even a touch of arrogance in the process.

He was elaborately courteous in his reply to Mr. Truman a couple of weeks ago, but he did not hesitate yesterday to tell the Texas delegation that he thought Lyndon Johnson was a fine Majority Leader who should stay where he was. When Senator Homer Capehart of Indiana challenged one or two of his points in a foreign-policy speech on the floor of the United States Senate in mid-June, Senator Kennedy was scornful and sarcastic in reply.

In the battle here in Los Angeles for the nomination, the Kennedy organization has been imaginative, tough, and efficient. Of all the candidates in this convention Kennedy was the one whose organization knew better than anybody else's where the votes were, the one whose men were in touch with one another in cars, on the floor, in the downtown headquarters, and in the Kennedy model house outside the Sports Arena by shortwave radio and wireless telephone.

Tonight, however, Kennedy himself rather than his organization or anything else is the primary consideration. He has won the nomination. He has earned the right to be tested on his own merits, and there is not a man in this arena tonight, even among his opponents, who will not concede that his merits are considerable.

JANUARY 22, 1961

President Kennedy's Inaugural

THE REACTION TO PRESIDENT KENNEDY'S INAUGURAL SPEECH WAS even more remarkable than the speech itself. Everybody praised it, from the conservative Republicans to the Communists in Moscow, which is quite a distance. The question now is whether it was a speech or a policy.

Even as a speech it was remarkable, and maybe we ought to settle for the revival of the beauty of the English language. The evangelical and transcendental spirit of America has not been better expressed since Woodrow Wilson, and maybe not even since Ralph Waldo Emerson. But all those who have praised it cannot possibly be so enthusiastic as they sound, unless they are merely reacting to its style and music.

For, like all true expressions of the American ideal, this was a revolutionary document. It was not only eloquent, but moralistic and even religious, and if it is taken at face value, it is a proposal, not merely that we "get going," but that we begin transforming our national life, our relations with the allies, and our relations with the Communists.

Many such speeches have been made in the past eight years, perhaps not as good, but in the same noble spirit. There is a difference, however, between the faith and zeal of youth and the weary aspirations of old age. The yearnings of America influence both, but when these young new leaders say America will pay "any price" to assure the success of liberty; that we will help the underdeveloped nations not because of our differences with Communism, but because it is "right"; that we will convert our "good words into deeds" in the Western Hemisphere, they say it with the seriousness of youth.

Kennedy is not a flaming missionary, but he is not a cynic merely engaged in a theatrical performance. Accordingly, it might not be a bad idea to assume, at least for the time being, that Kennedy means what he said yesterday—that American idealism has now been allied to American power, that those who now speak for America mean to act for America—and if this is true, then his inaugural address must be seen as something more than a graceful television performance in the snow.

He was careful to say that his goals could not be achieved in 100 days or 1,000 days, and maybe not even in a lifetime, but if he does no more than make a start toward these goals, the nation, and the allies, and the Communists, will have to review their assumptions of the past.

To the nation, he said, "Ask not what your country can do for you; ask what you can do for your country."

To our "old Allies" he offered a new partnership "in a host of cooperative ventures," which can scarcely be interpreted as a proposal for lowering the budgets here or in Bonn, Paris, or London.

To the UN he offered more cooperation in an effort to establish international law, which is presumably not a suggestion for greater national control over our foreign policy.

To the new states of Africa and Asia, "to those people of the globe struggling to break the bonds of mass misery," he pledged "our best efforts," which can scarcely foreshadow a cut in foreign-aid appropriations.

It would be interesting to know whether all the people who praised all this are willing to go along with the sacrifices implied, particularly those who praised him in the United States.

Before President Kennedy spoke, Robert Frost, the poet, read his old familiar lines:

> Something we were withholding left us weak
> Until we found out that it was ourselves
> We were withholding from our land of living
> And forthwith found salvation in surrender.

This presumably was what Kennedy was talking about. He was asking us to get engaged in the struggle. To find salvation in surrender to the nation's needs. Later on he will present the bill to carry this out, and then we will find out who was for his speech and who was against it.

MARCH 17, 1961

The Kennedy Press Conferences

THE PRESIDENTIAL PRESS CONFERENCE IS GETTING BIGGER AND noiser all the time, and under Kennedy has turned into an exercise in physical fitness. Every time the President stops to take a breath in one of these question-and-answer games at least forty-seven reporters shout "Mr. President," thereby cutting the poor man down in midflight, and perpetuating the popular idea that reporters are not only unreadable but unspeakable.

Of course, we are actually as refined and gentle as Whistler's mother, but since these conferences have been going out over the television networks, the TV audience, apparently unaccustomed to violence, has been complaining that we act like a pack of district attorneys working over a criminal.

There is a problem here, but it is primarily one of mathematics, and not of manners. Outside of the Government itself, the newspapers and periodicals are the biggest employers in Washington. There are more reporters here than lobbyists or even preachers, and they no longer cover the President: they smother him.

Woodrow Wilson, who started the Presidential press conference with a cry for "pitiless publicity," could seat the whole White House press corps of those days around his fireside. Franklin Roosevelt stood them up around his desk in the Executive Office of the White House. Harry Truman and Dwight D. Eisenhower had to move them to the comparatively small if hideous Indian Treaty Room of the old State Department Building, but now the mob has got so large that Kennedy has them in an auditorium almost as big as Carnegie Hall.

This is a dandy place for a movie or a Patterson-Johansson championship fight, but asking questions in it is like making love in Grand Central Terminal. The President is confronted by a firing squad of television cameras. Behind him are two long-distance microphones that look like antitank guns and between him and the reporters is a moat as wide as a canyon.

In the Indian Treaty Room you could see the whites of the President's eyes, and even if Mr. Eisenhower never finished a sentence, you knew when he was through. Then, too, the reporters jumped up and said "Mr. President," but he was close enough so that when he looked directly at a man, everybody knew which one he was recognizing for the next question.

This is no longer true. When Kennedy looks beyond the first couple of rows and indicates the next questioner, there are at least a dozen men in his line of vision, and the one who gets in is usually the character with the loudest voice and not necessarily the best question. Sometimes a shy and retiring fellow like William H. Lawrence of *The New York Times* will get in with a philosophic question, but not often.

There isn't much that can be done about all this. The President is the master-force of this Administration. He is the chief spokesman and newsmaker. He is releasing not only important news of the White House, but, as a device to limit the questioning, secondary news of the departments as well. Accordingly, he is attracting at every conference many more reporters than Eisenhower's norm.

It is difficult to limit them: the small dailies have as much right as the big dailies to be represented. It is hard to go back to the Hoover system of written questions without losing spontaneity. And it is too much to expect the President to call the questioners by name, though he is tending to do that more and more.

Of course, it wouldn't hurt if the reporters learned from Kennedy the arts of brevity and precision of speech. Many of them are now following the example of the old lady who said, "How do I know what I think until I hear what I say?" And some of them are hogging the cameras to wow the folks back home.

Pending a revolutionary transformation of human nature, however, there are really only two practical ways to solve the problem. The first is to ban all reporters from *The New York Times*, or if that is too radical, cut the *Times* down to ten reporters. This would solve the crush at a single stroke.

The second is to build in the cellar of the Executive Office, or in the courtyard of the old State Department across the street, a small theater-in-the-round, with steep sides like an operating theater in a teaching hospital. This might be regarded by the Appropriations Committee as an expensive substitute for good manners, but it would bring the President close to the reporters where we could whisper decorously and dissect him in comfort.

A Cool Summer Visitor
from Washington

IN THIS SUMMER POLITICAL CAPITAL EVERYTHING IS COOL AND IN-
formal, including the President of the United States.

This Cape Cod village is obviously President Kennedy's home,
a safe tribal harbor in a stormy world. The hedges around the
Kennedy compound are green, high, and private. His Republican
neighbors are discreet and tolerant, half resentful and half proud.
There is an air of opulent simplicity about the place, all expen-
sively concealed, and in this setting he relaxes much more than
in the clamorous hustle of Washington.

It is now just three months since he met Nikita Khrushchev in
Vienna. Since then the jovial evaporationist has been threaten-
ing, every hour on the hour, to obliterate the human race, but
Kennedy remains calm and even confident.

He seems perplexed about Khrushchev rather than angry.
What puzzles him is why he cannot get down to rational discussion with the Soviet leader about the factual situation in Berlin
and central Europe. Kennedy's approach to the problem is highly
pragmatic. He would like to discuss in tangible terms Khrushchev's problems and explain to him his own problems and then
see whether an honorable accommodation is possible. But
Khrushchev did not approach the impasse in this way in Vienna,
and he has said nothing since then to persuade Kennedy that
Moscow is ready for this kind of talk.

Nothing could be further from the truth than Moscow's representation of Kennedy as a reckless and combative young man
spoiling for a fight. The striking thing about him is that, after

seven months of disappointing negotiations with the Russians, the allies, and the Congress, he is taking his frustrations with such equanimity. He has not got the military build-up he wanted from the allies in Europe; he has had to divert his attention from Berlin to wheedle votes out of the House Appropriations Committee for foreign aid; he has got nothing from Khrushchev but threats and misrepresentations, but he is not personal or vindictive in any of his comments about these things.

Behind this impersonal, almost detached, approach, however, is a fairly simple yet severe analysis of the Berlin problem. This is that if the Soviets want to negotiate an honorable accommodation, he is ready to go along, even though he realizes that any new accommodation may be interpreted by his political opponents as something worse than now exists, and therefore as appeasement. But if Khrushchev and his wholly owned subsidiary in East Germany try to block the West's access to Berlin the risk of war will be taken.

The main danger is that this calm Kennedy appraisal of his responsibilities may be misjudged in Moscow. Official reports from there indicate that Khrushchev believes the United States would not resort to nuclear war unless American territory were attacked. The only trouble with this belief is that it just happens to be totally wrong.

Any action which closes U.S. access to Berlin will certainly lead to counteraction by the West, first in the UN, then in the field of economic countermeasures, then, if necessary, with an airlift or conventional military action on the ground to force the passage of supplies.

Any assumption, however, that the U.S. would acquiesce in the defeat of its command on the ground without resorting to the ultimate weapons of nuclear power would be highly reckless. For nuclear war in such circumstances is not "unthinkable." It is, in cold fact, being thought about and planned, and Mr. Khrushchev, unless he wishes to preside over a Soviet wasteland, next door to 800 million Chinese, would be well advised to take this into account.

One gets the impression that Kennedy is not wedded to any formula for Berlin save the genuine preservation of its freedom and the preservation of the honor of the United States. His mind is not cluttered up with rigid commitments to the technicalities of the past. His emotions are not engaged in the defense of lines on the map or even in rushing to the aid of the East Germans who had fifteen years to get out of their jail. He will negotiate in good faith but he will not be bullied.

He has been trying now ever since Vienna to make this clear to Khrushchev without success. He has rejected advice to tear away the barbed wire between East and West Berlin and has withheld economic sanctions or appeals to the UN. But these are questions of tactics and timing rather than of principle, as Khrushchev will discover if he tries to close the access routes to the former German capital.

The ironic thing about all this is that it is Kennedy, rather then Khrushchev, who is ready for peaceful and competitive coexistence. It is Khrushchev who is trying to direct the course of history and Kennedy who is ready to accommodate himself to history on the basis of "coexistence." The question is whether Khrushchev will allow an honorable accommodation to take place.

APRIL 29, 1962

The New Kennedy Style in Diplomacy

EVER SINCE THE DAYS OF EMERSON AND THOREAU, AMERICANS have been writing about the importance of developing a distinctive "American style" in literature and diplomacy. And after watching President Kennedy during the visit of Prime Minister

Harold Macmillan of Britain, there are a lot of people around here who think that maybe Kennedy is beginning to accomplish just this in the field of diplomacy.

The President has changed the mood and the tone of political expression in the capital and he has done it with an unusual combination of informality, dignity, and wit. In the past the visit of a British Prime Minister to Washington was usually a solemn procession, full of hands-across-the-seas clichés, formal meetings and dinners, and vapid communiqués. Harold Macmillan's visit here this time, in contrast, was like a house party and at times almost like a spree.

The White House correspondents' dinner for the President and the Prime Minister Friday night illustrates the change. It was the biggest, noisiest American blowout since the Inaugural Ball. For once nobody made an English-Speaking Union speech about common heritages or the threat of "atheistic Communism." In fact nobody even mentioned Khrushchev, which is progress. The comics mimicked both Kennedy and Macmillan; the President and the Prime Minister laughed at themselves; and, while one more dinner like this would probably paralyze the whole alliance for a month, the informality and absence of pretense were almost worth the hangover.

The decline of pretense and pomposity is the main thing. In the past these occasions have tended to be as ritualistic as English banquets in the Guildhall, with the great men spouting heroic pipe dreams or noble nonsense. But there is a little more reality now. Differences are not only acknowledged but expressed. Difficulties are recognized and discussed, and there is even a vague concession of the obvious point—always concealed or denied before—that the world's problems are probably bigger than the men who have to deal with them.

Much of this new mood here comes out of Kennedy's humor, which is not the usual American humor of exaggeration but a kind of bold and ironical self-deflation and even self-mockery. For example, the savage Kennedy criticism of Big Steel for raising its prices was paraphrased dead-pan Friday night by the President and applied to the $2.50 rise in the price of the correspondents' dinner. Similarly the President observed that he had just returned from consulting with his rich constituents in Palm Beach, Florida, and announced that "I'm now against my entire program."

If this were merely a change of style it could be welcomed as an agreeable new aspect of political manners and forgotten, but it is more than that. It is a reflection of a serious effort by Kennedy to dispel some of the illusion of political life and deal with things as they are.

Kennedy's approach to Macmillan in their informal but searching private talks was: "Tell me what you can and cannot do about joining Europe, and I'll do the same." This is precisely the politician's approach he took to Khrushchev at Vienna, without noticeable effect, but he continues to try to cut away the fat and get down to the bone.

This is probably a hopeful sign. There are still a lot of illusions befogging the relations between the United States and Europe. Washington is probably too confident that Britain will join the Common Market on almost any terms. Europe, likewise, is probably far too confident that it can have the advantage of an economic boom while leaving it to America to furnish most of the manpower for the defense of the prosperous Continent.

In the relaxed, let's-get-down-to-it style of Washington today these things can be discussed frankly, and in this sense the atmosphere of the capital is not only a thing of manners but of political substance.

President Kennedy, though out of New England, is no Henry Thoreau. No two American lives could be more different than theirs, but the President is expressing in his own way Thoreau's love of reality. "Be it life or death, we crave only reality," Thoreau concluded. "If we are really dying, let us hear the rattle in our throats and feel cold in the extremities; if we are alive, let us go about our business."

How to Overbalance
the Political Scales

THE INCREASING POWER OF NATIONWIDE MASS COMMUNICATIONS
is obviously working to the political advantage of the Kennedys.
Not only is the President dominating the political news on national television, but his only competition in the national magazines seems to be his wife, Jacqueline.

The big, colorful magazine racks in the streets of Los Angeles
today illustrate the point. *Harper's* magazine proclaims from its
front cover "The Kennedys Move In on Dixie." The cover on
McCall's carries a picture of Mrs. Kennedy and her two children,
and *The Saturday Evening Post* advertises "A Feminine Chat
With Jackie." In fact Mrs. Kennedy's only competition at the
moment seems to come from Governor Nelson Rockefeller of
New York on the cover of *Newsweek*, and from Nikolai Lenin,
of all people, on the cover of *Look*.

On top of all this, the advent of a nationally circulated daily
and weekly press is clearly adding to this trend. The *Wall Street
Journal* is already publishing five days a week on the Pacific
Coast and circulating *The National Observer* on Sunday. *The
New York Times* will start publishing six days a week in Los
Angeles in the autumn, and this is already having a visible effect
on the Pacific Coast daily press. They are increasing their coverage of national and international news. They are adding more
nationally syndicated columns, most of them originating in
Washington, and all this gives the President an even wider audience than he had before.

This is something new in American political life. Franklin

Roosevelt had national radio and the will and ability to use it effectively. But he didn't have television. Harry Truman and Dwight D. Eisenhower had both radio and television but used them sparingly and kept the Washington press corps in formal channels.

President Kennedy, however, is exploiting all the new mass communications. He had an audience of 85,000 for a speech at the University of California the other day. Over 200,000 turned out to see him in New Orleans last week. He was all over the TV screens from Atlantic City today. Tomorrow his press conference will be televised nationally, and after that it will be a big Presidential rally in Madison Square Garden, with many of the stars of Hollywood and the New York theater as his supporting cast.

This conscious policy of dominating the news is apparent enough in Washington, but it is even more striking out here— especially in the absence of a popular national figure in the political opposition. Former President Eisenhower has receded into the well-earned and agreeable shadows of retirement. Governor Rockefeller is still a remote regional figure at this distance, and even former Vice President Richard M. Nixon, showing off his new house to the press here last night, seemed less of a national figure than he did when he came to within 100,000 votes of the Presidency a little over a year ago.

This is a serious problem for the Republican party. It is being overwhelmed in the field of publicity, which is the battleground of Presidential politics. The Democrats have passed power from the men born in the nineteenth century to the new generation born in the twentieth, and the GOP has not. Also, the Republicans have to deal not only with an articulate young President in the White House but with the whole Kennedy clan.

Not since the days of Teddy Roosevelt and his "Princess Alice" has there been anything like it, and the Teddy Roosevelts didn't have instant communication with the whole continent. But now the Kennedys are getting more publicity than the Prime Minister and the Queen of England combined.

Some of this publicity is of course adverse, particularly in the national business and financial papers, and especially since the steel-price controversy. But the mass-circulation magazines are treating the Kennedys like a royal family and overwhelming the voice of the smaller critical journals.

It is true, of course, that the President has usually dominated the news of all generations. What he says and does commands the front pages, even if he does not open the White House and its staff to the press and TV reporters, but there is a new dimension now. As the daily newspaper goes national, many of the large city newspapers that used to concentrate on local news have to move into the world to meet their competition. And Kennedy, being an astute politician, is exploiting the trend as much as he can.

As this trend continues, the dangers are obvious. The opposition can continue to express its feelings on the floor of the Congress, probably in the presence of a handful of members and spectators, but the President has an audience of millions at his command any day he likes. It is not a situation that promises to maintain a political balance of power in the United States.

FEBRUARY 18, 1963

The Hard Education of
John F. Kennedy

A STRANGE KIND OF MALAISE NOW PERVADES WASHINGTON. THE exuberant optimism of the first few months of the Kennedy Administration has vanished. Even the sense of a new beginning, so evident at the start of this year, has given way to doubt and drift.

Not only at the top of the Administration, but down through

the Congress as well, there is a feeling that something is seriously wrong, that men are trapped in institutions, that the habits of the past are dominating the present and future, that power is balancing power to the point of paralysis, and that events are controlling men rather than the other way around.

Both at home and abroad, the President is in trouble. He bet almost everything on a tax cut and tax reform, and it now looks as if he will get just enough of a tax cut to be blamed for planning a budget deficit but not enough of a cut to achieve the objective of stimulating the economy.

Overseas, his grand design has been rejected by De Gaulle and there is very little he can do about it in the immediate future. For West Germany, Britain, and to some extent Italy are now deeply preoccupied with domestic politics and with passing power from one generation or one party to another.

Meanwhile, the political temperature is rising in this country, and before long, the subjective considerations of the 1964 Presidential campaign will be diverting policy into political strategy. Wherever the President turns, he seems to be blocked. He is deeply and sincerely committed to an educational program that will deal with the starting rise in population, but he cannot overcome the opposition of his own church.

He is decidedly unhappy about what he calls the "myths" of both management and labor, but he is not prepared to use all his influence against all myths but only against the myths of his political opponents. He is neither happy with the policy of subsidizing agriculture nor willing to risk the consequences of not subsidizing it. He is in despair about the organization of Congress and the tyranny of the conservative committee chairmen on Capitol Hill, but he is unwilling either to attack the Congressional "establishment" or reconcile himself to it.

None of this is surprising. The President is driven both by events and by tradition. He is a moderate confronted by radical facts. In his mind, he knows that the country is being convulsed by a population increase of more than 3,000,000 people a year, by a social revolution between the races, by a scientific revolution in industry, and by politicians who are not only necessary but cantankerous.

He knows also that he is dealing with a new industrial and political revolution in Europe by an alarming social revolution in Latin America, Africa, the Middle East and Asia, and by the turbulent passing of the old generation of world leaders: Adenauer in Germany, Nehru in India, Franco in Spain, Macmillan in Britain, and maybe even De Gaulle in France, Khrushchev in Russia, and Mao Tse-tung in China.

In his heart, however, he can not bring himself to confront radical events with radical policies. De Gaulle is willing to defy events and try to bend them to his will. Kennedy, being younger and more modest, is not. There is something both attractive and dangerous in this. He puts a limit on his aims, which is attractive, but tries to compromise with everybody—labor and management, De Gaulle and Adenauer, Khrushchev and Keating, North and South—which is both attractive and dangerous. For the result is that he may very well come up to the 1964 election without having achieved any of the objectives he dramatized so confidently before he knew how complicated the big world was.

The prospect now is that his compromises will give him trouble both with a whopping budget deficit and an alarming army of the unemployed, trouble both with the conservatives and the liberals who think he has not gone far enough, and trouble with the Communists and the Alliance. This is why the exuberant optimism of the first few months of the Administration has vanished and why the Republicans are now beginning to whoop and holler. But even the Republicans are not too confident. It is easier to defeat Kennedy's legislative program than to agree on an effective alternative; it is much easier to beat Kennedy in Congress than to defeat him at the polls, and Kennedy knows it, which is his sole consolation.

Nevertheless, he is depressed. For he thought, even at the beginning of the year, that he was gaining on history, and now, after only a few tumultuous weeks, history seems to be gaining on him.

Kennedy and the Scientists

IN SOME WAYS THE MOST INTERESTING CONFLICT IN WASHINGTON today is not the political war between the parties or even the cold war between the nations, but the Quiet War between the policy-makers and their expert advisers.

This takes many forms: President Kennedy versus the scientists over the allocation of the nation's money and brains; McNamara versus the Joint Chiefs of Staff over the TFX fighter plane; the Joint Chiefs versus the Pentagon civilian intellectuals over whose advice is to be taken on military strategy; the Commerce and other civilian home-front departments versus the Pentagon, the Space Agency, and the Atomic Energy Commission over research and development funds for military or civilian purposes.

"Let us explore the stars, conquer the deserts, eradicate disease, tap the ocean depths," said the President in his inaugural. It was a noble passage, but the problem is one of priorities: which comes first—the moon or the slums, the unexplored or the unemployed, security or solvency?

The range of choice is endless and conflict over priorities is inevitable and maybe even healthy, but it is almost impossible here to find any logical pattern to the Administration's methods of deciding how science can serve the nation best. Each department fights for the largest possible share of money and scientific and engineering brains. Each can make a good case for a larger share than it has.

For example, James E. Webb, administrator of the National Aeronautics and Space Administration, had some of his critics in for dinner this week to explain that his agency could not only justify the $5.7 billion budget this year but much more. He made a good case, too, but when the main question came up about whether the agency's man-on-the-moon project was as important as other worthy scientific projects here on earth, even his own space scientists disagreed.

Theoretically, the President's Assistant for Science and Technology, the Bureau of the Budget, the President's Science Advisory Committee, and the National Science Foundation are all competent to survey the larger question of how science is to serve the nation—to answer the basic question of priorities for defense, space, foreign aid, and the home front.

But if the President has put the question of priorities to these institutions, there is no public evidence of it. On the contrary, there is a great deal of evidence that men like Jerome B. Wiesner, the President's Assistant for Science and Technology, Dr. Alan T. Waterman, director of the National Science Foundation, and leading members of the Science Advisory Committee are dissatisfied with the present allocation of funds and talent.

Sir Charles Snow, the Cambridge University physicist, has pointed up the importance of this question by noting that most of the life-and-death decisions of modern political life "have to be made by a handful of men, in secret, and at least in legal form, by men who cannot have a firsthand knowledge of what those choices depend upon or what the results may be."

This was true of the decision to make and use the fission bomb, to make the fusion bomb, and to produce intercontinental missiles. But it is also true of an increasing number of other scientific questions, beginning with the first: how are the immense forces of sciences to be used?

Since the question of priorities has not been resolved by the President, it is not surprising that there is constant conflict between the departments and even within the departments between the policy-makers and the experts.

This is not to suggest that the scientist and engineers should take over the policy decisions of how their skills are to be applied. These decisions have to remain with the elected officials of the Government, even if, as Snow says, they lack firsthand knowledge of "what those choices depend upon or what the results may be."

But this is all the more reason for confidence that the President has at least an orderly method of deciding the question of scientific priorities, and there is no such confidence in Washington today. The Quiet War merely goes on, and it is getting noisier every year.

NOVEMBER 23, 1963

The Assassination

AMERICA WEPT TONIGHT, NOT ALONE FOR ITS DEAD YOUNG PRESIdent, but for itself. The grief was general, for somehow the worst in the nation had prevailed over the best. The indictment extended beyond the assassin, for something in the nation itself, some strain of madness and violence, had destroyed the highest symbol of law and order.

Speaker John McCormack, now 71 and, by the peculiarities of our politics, next in line for the Presidency, expressed this sense of national dismay and self-criticism: "My God! My God! What are we coming to?"

The irony of the President's death is that his short Administration was devoted almost entirely to various attempts to curb this very streak of violence in the American character.

When the historians get around to assessing his three years in office, it is very likely that they will be impressed with just this: his efforts to restrain those who wanted to be more violent in the cold war overseas and those who wanted to be more violent in the racial war at home.

He was in Texas today trying to pacify the violent politics of that state. He was in Florida last week trying to pacify the businessmen and appealing to them to believe that he was not "antibusiness." And from the beginning to the end of his Administration, he was trying to damp down the violence of the extremists on the right.

It was his fate, however, to reach the White House in a period of violent change, when all nations and institutions found themselves uprooted from the past. His central theme was the necessity of adjusting to change, and this brought him into conflict with those who opposed change.

Thus, while his personal instinct was to avoid violent conflict, to compromise and mediate and pacify, his programs for taxation, for racial equality, for medical care, for Cuba, all raised sharp divisions within the country. And even where his policies of adjustment had their greatest success—in relations with the Soviet Union—he was bitterly condemned.

The President somehow always seemed to be suspended between two worlds—between his ideal conception of what a President should be, what the office called for, and a kind of despairing realization of the practical limits upon his power. He came into office convinced of the truth of Theodore Roosevelt's view of the President's duties—"the President is bound to be as big a man as he can."

And his inaugural—"now the trumpet summons us again"—stirred an echo of Wilson in 1913 when the latter said: "We have made up our minds to square every process of our national life with the standards we so proudly set up at the beginning and have always carried at our hearts."

This is what the President set out to do. And from his reading, from his intellectual approach to the office, it seemed, if not easy, at least possible.

But the young man who came to office with an assurance vicariously imparted from reading Richard Neustadt's *Presidential Power* soon discovered the two truths which all dwellers on that lonely eminence have quickly learned. The first was that the powers of the President are not only limited but hard to bring to bear. The second was that the decisions—as he himself so often said—"are not easy."

Since he was never one to hide his feelings, he often betrayed the mood brought on by contemplating the magnitude of the job and its disappointments. He grew fond of quoting Lord Morley's dictum—"Politics is one long second-best, where the choice often lies between two blunders."

Did he have a premonition of tragedy—that he who had set out to temper the contrary violences of our national life would be their victim? Last June, when the civil-rights demonstrations were at their height and passions were flaring, he spoke to a group of representatives of national organizations. He tolled off the problems that beset him on every side and then to the astonishment of everyone there, suddenly concluded his talk by pulling from his pocket a scrap of paper and reading the famous speech of Blanche of Spain in Shakespeare's *King John:*

> The sun's o'ercast with blood: Fair day, adieu!
> Which is the side that I must go withal?
> I am with both; each army hath a hand,
> And in their rage, I having hold of both,
> They whirl asunder and dismember me.

There is, however, consolation in the fact that while he was not given time to finish anything or even to realize his own potentialities, he has not left the nation in a state of crisis or danger, either in its domestic or foreign affairs. A reasonable balance of power has been established on all continents. The state of truce in Korea, the Formosa Strait, Vietnam, and Berlin is, if anything, more tolerable than when he came to office.

Europe and Latin America were increasingly dubious of his leadership at the end, but their capacity to indulge in independent courses of action outside the alliance was largely due to the fact that he had managed to reach a somewhat better adjustment of relations with the Soviet Union.

Thus President Johnson is not confronted immediately by having to take any urgent new decisions. The passage of power from one man to another is more difficult in other countries, and Britain, Germany, Italy, India, and several other allies are so preoccupied by that task at the moment that drastic new policy initiatives overseas are scarcely possible in the foreseeable future.

At home, his tasks lie in the Congress, where he is widely regarded as the most skillful man of his generation. This city is in a state of shock tonight, and everywhere, including Capitol Hill, men are of a mind to compose their differences and do what they can to help the new President.

Accordingly, the assumption that there will be no major agreements on taxes or civil rights this year will probably have to be revised. It is, of course, too early to tell. But it is typical and perhaps significant that the new President's first act was to greet the Congressional leaders of both parties when he arrived in Washington and to meet with them at once in the White House.

Today's events were so tragic and so brutal that even this city, which lives on the brutal diet of politics, could not bear to think much about the political consequences of the assassination. Yet it is clear that the entire outlook has changed for both parties, and the unexpected death of President Kennedy has forced Washington to meditate a little more on the wild element of chance in our national life.

This was quietly in the back of many minds tonight, mainly because President Johnson has sustained a severe heart attack, and the constitutional line of succession places directly back of him, first Speaker McCormack, and then the President *Pro Tempore* of the Senate, 86-year-old Senator Carl Hayden of Arizona.

Again this note of self-criticism and conscience has touched the capital. Despite the severe illnesses of President Eisenhower just a few years ago, nothing was done by the Congress to deal with the problem of Presidential disability. For an all too brief hour today, it was not clear again what would have happened if the young President, instead of being mortally wounded, had lingered for a long time between life and death, strong enough to survive but too weak to govern.

These, however, were fleeting thoughts, important but irritating for the moment. The center of the mind was on the dead President, on his wife, who has now lost both a son and a husband within a few months, and on his family, which, despite all its triumphs, has sustained so many personal tragedies since the last war.

President Kennedy was, even to his political enemies, a wonderfully attractive human being, and it is significant that, unlike many Presidents in the past, the people who liked and respected him best were those who knew him the best.

He was a rationalist and an intellectual, who proved in the 1960 campaign and in last year's crisis over Cuba that he was at his best when the going was tough. No doubt he would have been re-elected, as most one-term Presidents are, and the subtle dualism of his character would have had a longer chance to realize his dream.

But he is gone now at 46, younger than when most Presidents have started on the great adventure. In his book *Profiles in Courage*, all his heroes faced the hard choice either of giving in to public opinion or of defying it and becoming martyrs. He had hoped to avoid the bitter dilemma, but he ended as a martyr anyway, and the nation is sad tonight, both about him and about itself.

There is one final tragedy about today: Kennedy had a sense of history, but he also had an administrative technique that made the gathering of history extremely difficult. He hated organized meetings of the Cabinet or the National Security Council, and therefore he chose to decide policy after private meetings, usually with a single person. The result of this is that the true history of his Administration really cannot be written now that he is gone.

He had a joke about this. When he was asked what he was going to do when he retired, he always replied that he had a problem. It was, he said, that he would have to race two other members of his staff, McGeorge Bundy and Arthur Schlesinger, Jr., to the press.

Unfortunately, however, he was the only man in the White House who really knew what went on there during his Administration, and now he is gone.

The Nation's Guilt

A TALE OF TWO CITIES. AND TWO MURDERS. IN DALLAS: VIOLENCE and anarchy. In Washington: sorrow and humiliation and anxiety. Running through the private and public comments here today was a single theme: that this decent country has been made to look uncivilized; that there is a kind of rebellion in the land against law and good faith, and that private anger and sorrow are not enough to redeem the events of the last few days.

The doctrine of an eye for an eye has prevailed in Dallas, and the civil authorities in neither of these two cities have promised the nation a full objective inquiry into the deaths of President Kennedy and Lee Harvey Oswald. But thoughtful men here are not satisfied. They are determined to explore the question of public as well as private guilt in these two cases.

The Chief Justice of the United States raised the question of public responsibility for the present atmosphere of lawlessness in his eulogy to the murdered President at the Capitol today. We do know, he said, that such acts of assassination and murder "are commonly stimulated by forces of hatred and violence such as today are eating their way into the bloodstream of American life."

The grandson of President Woodrow Wilson, Dean Francis Sayre of the Washington Cathedral, put the point more directly in his sermon this morning.

"We have been present at a new crucifixion," he said—this one following on the murder of Medgar Evers in Mississippi and the bomb murders of eight Negro children in Birmingham. "All of us," he added, "have had a part in the slaying of our President. It was the *good* people who crucified our Lord, and not merely those who acted as executioners.

"By our silence; by our inaction; by our willingness that heavy burdens be borne by one man alone; by our readiness to allow evil to be called good and good evil; by our continued toleration of ancient injustices . . . we have all had a part in the assassination."

The American people saw two scenes on the television today that illustrate the dualism of American life, the nobility and tenderness on the one hand, and the brutality on the other.

Jacqueline Kennedy arrived in Washington years ago merely as a beauty and is leaving it, as she demonstrated at the Capitol today, as a beautiful spirit. Out of the crowd she stepped under the vaulted ceiling of vast Rotunda, a trim and pale figure in funeral black with the golden Caroline on her hand, and kneeled ever so slowly before her husband's flag-draped coffin, and stretched out her hand and touched the flag and kissed the coffin; and then rose as gracefully as a young girl and walked away. At least that was the way the people in Washington saw it through their tears.

In Dallas, another scene: murder at point-blank range of the handcuffed human being suspected but not convicted of assassinating President Kennedy. This was being shown all over the world tonight, and people here were so sick of it that the tendency was to punish the culprit and be done with it. But these two murders raise fundamental questions in the minds of reflective men and women here and cannot be forgotten so easily.

Is the evidence on Lee Harvey Oswald to be left with the Dallas police and the FBI? Is the public not entitled to know what was said to and by Oswald in the Dallas jail? Cannot a Presidential or some other objective commission carry on a private investigation, interrogate Oswald's wife and brother, and finally present its findings to the nation?

The Dallas side of the tale cannot be left where it is without adding to the moral confusion Chief Justice Warren and Dean Sayre talked about today.

More than the policemen and the politicians, the jurist and the philosophers here are insisting that the "inalienable rights" of the individual in this country, as the Founding Fathers insisted, came not from the state but from their Creator, and that nobody has a right to take them away.

The point at issue here was defined very clearly by Walter Lippmann. "The decay of decency in the modern age . . ." he wrote many years ago, "the treatment of human beings as things, as the mere instruments of power and ambition, is without doubt the consequence of the decay of the belief in man as something more than an animal animated by highly conditioned reflexes and chemical reactions.

"For, unless man is something more than that, he has no rights that anyone is bound to respect, and there are no limitations upon his conduct which he is bound to obey. This is the forgotten foundation of democracy in the only sense in which democracy is truly valid and of liberty in the only sense in which it can hope to endure. The liberties we talk about defending today were established by men who took their conception of man from the great central religious tradition of Western civilization, and the liberties we inherit can almost certainly not survive the abandonment of that tradition."

Both Dallas and Washington have forgotten the foundation, and this is the point the preachers and the jurists were trying to make today. The President of the United States, said Chief Justice Warren, is "chosen to embody the ideals of our people, the faith we have in our institutions, and our belief in the fatherhood of God and the brotherhood of man."

This is probably the single hope in the tragedy. For it may be that only the shock of this ordeal can help the nation recover a clearer vision of how a free and civilized people must live.

Better to Light a Candle
Than Curse the Darkness

PRESIDENT KENNEDY WAS CAREFUL ABOUT PREPARING A SITE AT Harvard for his library but, unfortunately, he was not so careful about preserving the material to go into it. That task will now be undertaken, but the scholars cannot do it justice unless they get a great deal of help fairly soon from the vast company of Kennedy friends and colleagues who have special personal knowledge of what he said and did in the White House.

The main lines of his Administration are, of course, fairly clear. It was a brief but dramatic chapter in the exercise and defense of Presidential power against the challenges of the states (Mississippi and Alabama), the challenge of the Communists (Cuba, the Congo, and South Vietnam), the challenge of big business (the steel crisis), and the constant challenge of the Congress (civil rights and taxes).

All these challenges were faced and met, but not always or even usually in formal meetings of the Cabinet or the National Security Council. Kennedy was not a committee man: committees bored him. He was not primarily a writer, but a reader and a talker; and much of the real story of his Administration was worked out in private meetings between President Kennedy and a great number of other officials and friends who came to his office in ones or twos.

Most of the time no records were kept of these important but intimate meetings, and the full story of this remarkable period in American history cannot be written unless a major effort is made fairly soon to record the memories of those who saw him in the preliminary meetings before the great decisions.

Here, then, is something tangible, something perhaps even more important than renaming capes and sports fields and cultural centers, that President Kennedy's friends and associates can do. They cannot replace his shattered memory but they can put down on paper their recollections of anything he said or did in their presence that will provide the raw material for future historians.

Many of these men loved President Kennedy not only for what he was "but for some shadow of what he was to be." Not only the decisions, but the flavor of the Kennedy Administration now lies with these men. The self-depreciating, half-mocking Kennedy wit, for example, had a way of slipping out in these private but deadly-serious meetings, and every evidence of it is worth recording because it helps illustrate that peculiar quality of courage that Ernest Hemingway calls "grace under pressure."

This is, of course, a major historical effort. It will have to be organized. Kenny O'Donnell has a record of every official appointment he made, and for those who cannot or will not write, the tape recorder can be used to capture their memories. But this takes years, and right now, while everybody is conscious of his debt to the slain President, is probably the best time for those who saw him to start getting their recollections in order.

This was the Administration of the junior officers of the Second World War. Not only Kennedy himself but a great many of his closest associates were trained and hardened then. As Walt W. Rostow has pointed out, "everything from the style of humor to the way the President organized the White House as a small unit command post went back to that formative experience."

This may not be the best way to organize the White House— many observers here think it was not—but it is important to an understanding of the Kennedy Administration, and may be to the future of the Presidency, to record and analyze how the system worked, and this cannot be done unless those concerned provide the basic information.

Even the story of President Kennedy's worst hour—the first Cuban crisis—and his finest hour—the second Cuban crisis— cannot be told without a major effort to find out what went on in those private meetings before the Bay of Pigs and the confrontation with Khrushchev.

No doubt several accounts of the White House command post in the week before the blockade of Cuba have already been written privately by men who attended, but the blockade was only the most dramatic in a long series of events. Khrushchev risked the Cuban adventure—or so it seems—not because he had Kennedy on the run, but because in Berlin, Southeast Asia, Africa, and the arms race, Kennedy had boxed him in, and all these events have to be reported in detail before the Kennedy Library at Harvard can really meet its purpose.

At the moment, the history of the Kennedy Administration is merely a majestic memory and a confused heap of facts. The job of linking cause and effect, personality and action, remains, and this is the really important light that has to be lit to his memory. For "it is the cause and not the death that makes the martyr," and it is "martyrs who usually create faith, and not faith that creates martyrs."

DECEMBER 1, 1963

The Mood of the Capital: Change and Continuity

THE MOOD OF WASHINGTON NOW IS STRANGE AND PARADOXICAL. IT is full of both vitality and nostalgia; half Johnson and half Kennedy. The major theme is continuity, but everything else is contrast.

In less than three weeks the new President has become a legend, almost a Texas "tall story"—Lyndon conquering George Meany and Henry Ford, Martin Luther King and Harry Byrd, the savers and the spenders, Wall Street and Main Street.

Meanwhile, the Kennedy Legend grows and deepens. It is

clear now that he captured the imagination of a whole generation of young people in many parts of the world, particularly in the university communities. Even those who vilified him now canonize him, and many of his political opponents who condemned him are now seeking a candidate who looks and sounds like him.

People here do not like to compare the old and the new for the time being, but they cannot help it. To talk about President Johnson's genius with Congress somehow seems to imply a criticism of President Kennedy; to dwell on President Kennedy's grace and style similarly seems to suggest a criticism of President Johnson; and most people want to do neither.

Yet comparisons are unavoidable because time somehow seems to have moved backward rather than forward in the last few days despite all the momentum. . . .

Most reflective people here feel this change in time and mood, but some regret it much more than others and some do not regret it at all. For it was the very newness and youth of the Kennedy approach and the Kennedy players that pleased part of Washington and displeased the rest.

Kennedy was a critic of the poker game in the back room. He played it, but he gave the impression that it was often a waste of time, and that he might even like to change the rules. He was the handsome young stranger from the East, who sounded as if he'd like to clean up the town, and a lot of the old players were dubious and even suspicious.

"Before my term has ended," he said in his first major address to the Congress on January 30, 1960, "we shall have to test anew whether a nation organized and governed such as ours can endure. The outcome is by no means certain." Here was the young skeptic wondering out loud whether the country didn't have to be reorganized and reformed even before he had settled into the White House. It is hard to imagine President Johnson saying any such thing.

Johnson may in the end reform things more than his predecessor, but he doesn't look or act like a reformer to anything like the same degree. He seems to be a part of the old system, almost to be a symbol of it, comfortable with it, determined to make it work, and confident that he can make it work.

Perhaps this is why, in his first three weeks, he has been able to defend the Kennedy program and still get a sympathetic reaction from Congress and the business communtiy. Somehow, they feel that he is more a part of their world.

This is why the mood of Washington, the feel of the place about men and ideas is so important. President Kennedy thought of himself as being pro-business, and also as being pro-labor, and pro-Congress, but he also thought they needed to reform and change. He approached the State and Defense Departments—even the Presidency—in the same way, but this was the way of the critic and the skeptic, neither of whom has ever been very popular in history.

Yet this is precisely why Washington, in its common sorrow, is still vaguely divided. For some men believe that all we need is somebody who can make the present organization of the Government and the country work, and others wonder with Kennedy "whether a nation organized and governed such as ours can endure."

It is a fundamental question. It was being asked here before Kennedy arrived and will probably be asked after President Johnson is gone. Kennedy did not deal with it, but he gave the impression that he wanted to deal with it, and is mourned by many here still not only for what he was, but maybe even more for what he might have been.

"Love," said Santayana, "is very penetrating, but it penetrates to possibilities rather than to facts."

Farewell to Camelot

THE CAPITAL IS SAD ABOUT MRS. JOHN F. KENNEDY'S LAWSUIT TO stop publication of William Manchester's book on the assassination of her husband. No personal or political controversy about the Kennedys—and there have been many—has produced such unanimity in Washington. Everybody understands and sympathizes with Mrs. Kennedy's objection to certain parts of this ghastly story. But even the people who love her the most and are now rallying to her support—including Bobby Kennedy—are sorry she has insisted on taking this controversy to the courts. They deny this, of course, but it is true.

There are a number of reasons for this, the first of which is very practical. There are simply too many copies of Mr. Manchester's transcript of *Death of a President* in circulation to be suppressed, no matter what the courts say. Twenty-five copies of his transcript were sent to magazine and other editors to see whether they wanted to pay between $500,000 and $1,000,000 for the right to publish excerpts of the book. These have been read by thousands of editors, who are a competitive and gabby crew. How many more copies have been reproduced at night by junior editors and even officeboys in this Xerox generation is beyond calculation.

Mike Cowles and Bill Attwood at *Look* magazine, Cass Canfield at Harper & Row, and all the other principals in the controversy will play it straight, no matter how irritated they are with each other at the moment, or how much the publishers have to lose—which could run into millions—but what is going on in other publishing houses which had copies of the original manuscript, even their bosses cannot know.

The world is full of bootleg book publishing companies, which pay no attention to the copyright laws of the West. In Formosa and Eastern Europe, publishers with cheap labor and materials think nothing of printing *In Cold Blood* or any other best seller by the millions and selling it for a fraction of the cost in the United States, without permission from, or compensation to, the author.

It is not hard to imagine the temptation and profits involved in reproducing "the original manuscript unedited by the Kennedys" of the Manchester book by such companies. Millions of dollars are involved. One American company alone offered $1,000,000 for the American paperback rights.

Thus, Mrs. Kennedy could easily win her case in the American courts and lose it in the world. And if she is worried about Mr. Manchester's frank disclosures about what the Kennedys thought about Johnson during the assassination crisis, she can forget it, because Bill D. Moyers, the President's press secretary, has already read the offending passages, and no doubt the President has been told what he already knew or suspected before Mr. Manchester ever got involved in this unhappy incident.

So much for the practical reasons of not trying to stop the unstoppable. The personal aspects are even more interesting. Mrs. Kennedy naturally wants to emphasize everything that perpetuates the good and minimizes the bad in the Kennedy story. She has a contract that says she can compel this with Manchester. The legend of Kennedy is more wonderful than the political history of Kennedy, and her contract with Manchester has deceived her into thinking she can make history conform to legend. No good wife would do otherwise, but she is holding up her hand to the avalanche. Kennedy is not only a husband but a President, not only a personal figure but a historical figure, and while the courts can interpret contracts, they cannot command history.

It is not difficult to understand Jacqueline Kennedy's desires. No President's family has ever approved its biographers. She can do nothing now about the death of the President. What she is faced with is the death of Camelot, the killing of the myth. It is intolerable but also inevitable, and the lawsuit is only going to make the inevitable even more intolerable, especially for such a private person.

This is really the difference between Jacqueline Kennedy and

Bobby Kennedy—and it has been a much more savage difference than the presentations to the court suggest. Bobby would like to preserve the Kennedy legend too—he is riding it to the Presidency—but he is primarily interested in the future and she in the past, and therefore he accepts the reality which she quite naturally rejects.

Both are right in their own terms, but the Kennedys are now too important in the political life of the country to put legend ahead of history. They cannot rely on legal contracts. It is time to get down to reality. Manchester shows them at last not as a united clan, but as a human family with all the differences and yearnings and weaknesses of most families, and in the end, that may be even better than the Kennedy myth.

NOVEMBER 15, 1964

The Kennedy Legend

TIME SEEMS TO BE TRYING TO MAKE AMENDS TO JOHN FITZGERALD Kennedy. Robbed of his years, he is being rewarded and honored in death as he never was in life. Deprived of the place he sought in history, he has been given in compensation a place in legend. What was a monstrous personal and historic crime a year ago is now something even more elemental and enduring: it is a symbol of the tragedy and caprice of life, and it is likely to be remembered by the novelists and the dramatists long after the historians have gone on to other things.

Will he seem different to the historians from the way the dramatists will see him? What are they likely to say of his conduct of foreign affairs, domestic affairs, the Presidency itself? Are we already confusing myth with reality, as he was always telling us we should not do?

Probably we are, but this is only fair and maybe even natural. For there was always something vaguely legendary about him. He was a story-book President, younger and more handsome than mortal politicians, remote even from his friends, graceful, almost elegant, with poetry on his tongue and a radiant young woman at his side.

He was a sudden and surprising person. He never did things when other men were doing them. He went to Congress and the White House earlier than most. He married much later than his contemporaries. His war record, his political record, and his personal life were marked by flashes of crisis and even by a vague premonition of tragedy. He always seemed to be striding through doors into the center of some startling triumph or disaster. He never reached his meridian: we saw him only as a rising sun.

Accordingly, it is not easy to make an estimate of his 1,000 days in the White House. He didn't have a fair chance and he didn't even give himself a fair chance. He often made his decisions alone after a series of private talks with several individuals, none of whom shared the whole process of his thought. Oddly in one who had such an acute sense of history, he was disorderly about keeping records of what led up to his decisions, and though he had a great gift for conversation, he seems to have spent little time talking to his closest associates about how he had decided things in the past.

All this complicates the task of placing him in the catalogue of the Presidents. We do not have the record. We do not have the full story of the two Cuban crises, or his meeting with Khrushchev in Vienna, or the reasoning behind his gambles in Vietnam, or the communications that led up to the atomic test-ban treaty with the Soviets. We have only our clippings, memories, and impressions, and these can be uncertain guides.

Historians—and here we are in the realm of opinion—will probably rate President Kennedy's handling of foreign policy higher than his contemporaries did. It is a spotty record. He dreamed occasionally of an interdependent Atlantic world, and this has become part of the legend, but the reality is that the alliance was in poor shape during most of his Administration. He courted Latin America like a thoughtful lover, but, again, the Alliance for Progress was more dream than reality.

Even so, he had a feeling for the way the world was going. He understood the challenge of change. He was fascinated by the political revolution produced by the liberation of the colonial peoples: sometimes too fascinated with it, and too inclined to give it a higher priority than it deserved. He studied and understood the intricate problems of the atomic revolution and the scientific revolution, probably better than any of his predecessors.

Yet this keen, analytical intelligence was not always a help. It enabled him to see the problems, but it often depressed him about finding the answers. I always thought—perhaps wrongly—that his intelligence made him pessimistic. The evidence that science was transforming the world seemed so clear and overwhelming to him that he was irritated by the failure of men and institutions to adapt and keep up.

In his very first State of the Union message, ten days after he had been sworn in, he told the Congress and the nation: "Before my term has ended, we shall have to test anew whether a nation organized and governed such as ours can endure. The outcome is by no means certain. The answers are by no means clear."

His bungling of his first foreign-policy gamble, when he tried to help the Cuban refugees overthrow the Castro Government, made him all the more conscious, not only of the complexities of political decision, but of the possible consequences of failure.

The events of the Bay of Pigs contributed to his natural caution, and added to his problems with the Communists for most of the rest of his days in the White House. It is impossible to be sure about this, but I was in Vienna when he met Khrushchev shortly after the fiasco of the Bay of Pigs, and saw him ten minutes after his meeting with the Soviet leader. He came into a dim room in the American Embassy, shaken and angry. He had tried, as always, to be calm and rational with Khrushchev, to get him to define what the Soviet Union could and would not do, and Khrushchev had bullied him and threatened him with war over Berlin.

We will have to know much more about that confrontation

between Kennedy and Khrushchev, one now deprived of life and the other of power, before we can be sure, but Kennedy said just enough in that room in the embassy to convince me of the following: Khrushchev had studied the events of the Bay of Pigs; he would have understood if Kennedy had left Castro alone or destroyed him; but when Kennedy was rash enough to strike at Cuba but not bold enough to finish the job, Khrushchev decided he was dealing with an inexperienced young leader who could be intimidated and blackmailed. The Communist decision to put offensive missiles into Cuba was the final gamble of this assumption.

The missile crisis brought out what always seemed to me to be Kennedy's finest quality and produced the events on which Kennedy's place in history probably depends. There is a single fact that repeats itself in the Kennedy story like the major theme in a symphony: he was always at his best in the highest moment of crisis.

He could be ambiguous and even indecisive on secondary questions. He obviously trifled with the first Cuban crisis. He also temporized with the Vietnamese crisis, partly supporting those who wanted to intervene "to win," partly going along with those who reminded him that the French had suffered 175,000 casualties against the same Communist army, but never really defining his aims or reconciling his power with his objectives.

Yet always in his political life he acted decisively when faced with total defeat. He was supremely confident, almost presumptuous, in going for the Presidency in the first place against the opposition of the most powerful elements in his party. He was bold and effective when first Hubert Humphrey, then Harry Truman, and finally Lyndon Johnson challenged him publicly during the campaign for the nomination. He probably won the Presidency in the critical debates with Richard Nixon. And this same quality came out in the missile crisis in Cuba.

Then he was, as Robert Frost had urged him to be, "more Irish than Harvard" but with a dash of Harvard intelligence, too. If the first Cuban crisis was the worst example of the uses of American power and diplomacy in this generation, the second Cuban crisis was the best. And the significance of this fact can be understood only in relation to the longer perspective of war in this century.

Twice in this century, the leaders of the free world have been confronted by the menacing power of a totalitarian state. From 1912 until 1914, and again from 1935 until 1939, Germany made a series of moves that clearly threatened the peace and order of the world, and during those critical testing periods, Britain, France, and the United States failed either to raise enough military power or to show enough will power to avoid the holocaust. The resulting tragedies of the two great wars transformed the history of the world.

The Soviet decision to place long-range missiles in Cuba, capable of firing atomic rockets into almost any part of the United States, was a similar and in some ways even more ominous test. This lunge into the Western Hemisphere was clearly an effort to change the world balance of power in Moscow's favor, and Kennedy faced it at the risk of war and turned it back.

It is ironic that he went to his grave with many of his fellow countrymen condemning him for failing to get rid of all the Communists and all the defensive missiles in Cuba as well as all the offensive missiles. Yet this view has not been shared by most of the political leaders and historians of the world.

I saw Prime Minister Macmillan of Britain just before he resigned and before President Kennedy was murdered. "If Kennedy never did another thing," Macmillan remarked, "he assured his place in history by that single act. He did what we failed to do in the critical years before the two German wars."

Within a year of Kennedy's death, Khrushchev was removed from power partly as a result of his humiliating defeat in the Cuban missile crisis, but something important and maybe even historic remained: The Communist world was relieved of the illusion that the United States would not risk atomic wars to defend its vital interests. This new awareness greatly reduced the danger of miscalculating American intentions and led almost at once to the first really serious steps to bring atomic weapons under control.

Mr. Kennedy was more at ease in the larger world of diplomacy and the struggle between nations than he was in the world of Congressional politics and the struggle between contending national forces. He had more freedom of action in foreign than in domestic policy. He did not seem to mind the small talk of ceremonial meetings with heads of state or foreign students at the White House, and he had a rare combination of informality and dignity that made him very effective in this role. But blarneying with pompous Congressmen bored him and he simply would not take time to do it, as his successor, President Johnson, has with such marked success.

This was odd, in a way. He was a superb politician in planning and running a Presidential campaign, but he didn't really know the deck on Capitol Hill and he did not really like to play the political game there. Even though he spent most of his political life in the House and the Senate, he was always sort of a nonresident member of those peculiar clubs, always a back-bencher with a high truancy record and an excessive respect for the chairmen of the committees and the other elders of the Congress.

The very qualities of appearance, style, and cast of mind that won him the admiration of the intellectual and diplomatic worlds somehow marked him as an outsider in his dealings with the Congress. He had little patience for the tiresome loquacity and endless details of legislation, and he never cared much for the boisterous bantering and backslapping of the cloakrooms.

He had a kind of gay magic as a political speaker, most of it as carefully contrived as it seemed spontaneous. He was good at the arts of Hollywood and Madison Avenue, and this delighted his fellow politicians, but he was a little too polished, ambitious, and out of the ordinary to escape the envy and criticism of the Hill.

Congress likes typical Americans and Kennedy was not one. In his mature life, he probably crossed the Atlantic more often than he crossed the Allegheny range. He never seemed at home in the West. The America he understood best was bounded by Harvard Yard, the State Department, Park Avenue, and Palm Beach. His political style and humor were not based on the exaggerated language and gymnastics of the American hustings but on the gentler models of the House of Commons.

Maybe these things had nothing to do with his troubles in

getting a legislative program through the Congress; maybe it was just the old stubborn resistance of the Congress to change—"the government of the living by the dead"—but the fact remains that his domestic program was in deep trouble when he was killed, and some of us despaired that Capitol Hill would ever be his field of triumph.

Part of the Kennedy legend is connected with his introduction of the most radical legislation on behalf of Negro equality in this century. But again the reality is less romantic. He did not normally like to take on anything more than he had to tackle, no matter how worthy. Oddly for a man who wrote a book celebrating the heroes of lost causes (*Profiles in Courage*), he was always saying: "Why fight if you are not sure to win?" The Negro demonstrations in the summer of 1963, however, forced his hand, and he went along when some Republican leaders and his brother Robert urged that action was necessary.

Yet, on the home front, as in the foreign field, he did start one major innovation of transcending importance. At the urging of Walter Heller, the chairman of the Council of Economic Advisors, he broke with the traditional economic concepts of Capitol Hill and plunged for a large tax cut and a planned budget deficit. Liberal economists in Europe and in the American universities had been arguing for years that it was no longer necessary to redistribute the wealth of the rich in order to elevate the poor, but that the total production of wealth could be increased to the benefit of everybody if modern technology and fiscal measures were applied.

Kennedy was not by temper a fiscal reformer. He came to the White House as a rather timid liberal, but the longer he was in office the more he cried out against the restraining economic and fiscal traditions of the past and the more he appealed to the country to deal with the world as it is. He never saw his tax bill go through; he died before it was passed. But he was largely responsible for heading the country into the most prolonged period of peacetime prosperity since the last World War. There was a recession when he took over in 1961. Unemployment was up to almost 7 per cent of the work force. There was a balance-of-payments deficit of nearly $4 billion. The outflow of gold to other countries in 1960 totaled $1.7 billion. But by the time he died, this trend had been reversed, at least in part as a result of his initiatives.

Yet even if he turned the tide of the cold war toward the control of nuclear arms, and started the trend toward acceptance of the new economics of increased production and general prosperity, this is not the Kennedy story that is likely to be remembered. These things were only dramatic symbols of his critical mind. He was a critic of his age. He did not think we could deal with the menace of nuclear weapons unless we searched constantly for means of accommodation with the Communists. He did not think we could employ our people in the midst of a revolution in labor-saving machinery unless we changed our attitude toward Federal budgets and Federal deficits.

He did not think we could deal with the pressures of Communism, rising population, or galloping automation, or that we could contain the rising expectations of the nonwhite races and the new nations unless we moved faster to integrate the races at home and the nations of the free world abroad. In short, he did not believe we could deal effectively with a transformed world unless we transformed ourselves—our attitudes of mind and our institutions.

This was a youthful mind asking the big questions. He was not one for big plans and grand designs, though contemporary writers often professed to see such things in some of the speeches of Ted Sorensen. Incidentally, it was always difficult to tell where the soaring rhetoric of Sorensen's bolder and more liberal mind left off and the more cautious Kennedy mind picked up, but Kennedy was not a great planner.

I once asked him in a long private talk at Hyannis Port what he wanted to have achieved by the time he rode down Pennsylvania Avenue with his successor. He looked at me as if I were a dreaming child. I tried again: Did he not feel the need of some goal to help guide his day-to-day decisions and priorities? Again a ghastly pause. It was only when I turned the question to immediate, tangible problems that he seized the point and rolled off a torrent of statistics about the difficulty of organizing nations at different levels of economic development.

Yet there is a puzzle in all this. For while he wanted to transform the thought and institutions of the nation, and regarded the machinery of the Congress as almost an anachronism, he concentrated on working—not, on the whole, very successfully—with the Congress, and he never really exploited his considerable gifts as a public educator.

"Give me the right word and the right accent," said Joseph Conrad, "and I will move the world." This was Churchill's way, and nobody admired it more than Kennedy. But while he made a few glorious trial flights, something held him back, some fear of appealing to the people over the heads of the Congress, some fear of too much talk (he hated verbosity), some modesty, maybe—always so apparent in his embarrassment before applauding crowds.

The essence of the tragedy, however, is perfectly clear. What was killed in Dallas was not only the President but the promise. The death of youth and the hope of youth, of the beauty and grace and the touch of magic.

The heart of the Kennedy legend is what might have been. His intelligence made people think that the coming generation might make the world more rational. It even made it hard for the intellectuals of Europe to be anti-American. His good looks and eloquence put a brighter shine on politics, and made his world relevant and attractive to young people all over the world.

All this is apparent in the faces of the people who come to his grave daily on the Arlington hill. In the world of their dreams, Presidents would be young and heroic, with beautiful wives, and the ugly world would be transformed by their examples.

John Finley, the master of Eliot House at Harvard, sent me a letter which sums up this sense of loss better than anything else:

"No doubt like innumerable people, I felt suddenly old without Mr. and Mrs. Kennedy in the White House. On reflection, ours seems a society of older people; it takes a while to reach the top in science, law, business and most other things. Yet, paradoxically, only the young have the freshness to enjoy and not be wearied by the profusion and vitality of present American life.

"Not only by ability, but by sheer verve and joy, the Kennedys imparted their youth to everyone and put a sheen on our life that made it more youthful than it is. Mr. Johnson now seems Gary Cooper as President—'High Noon,' the poker game, the easy walk and masculine smile. But even Gary Cooper was growing older, and the companions and adversaries around the poker table reflect a less fresh, if no doubt practical and effective, mood. All will be well, I feel sure . . . but it is August, not June. . . ."

Always we come back to the same point. The tragedy of John Fitzgerald Kennedy was greater than the accomplishment, but in the end the tragedy enhances the accomplishment and revives the hope.

Thus the law of compensation operates. "The dice of God are always loaded," wrote Emerson. "For everything you have missed you have gained something else. . . . The world looks like a multiplication table, or a mathematical equation, which, turn it how you will, balances itself. . . . Every secret is told, every crime is punished, every virtue rewarded, every wrong redressed, in silence and certainty."

INDEX

A NOTE ABOUT THE AUTHOR

JAMES RESTON was born in Clydebank, Scotland, in 1909. His family moved to the United States in 1920, settling in Dayton, Ohio. Mr. Reston was graduated from the University of Illinois in 1932. He held a number of news and publicity jobs in the Middle West before going to New York in 1934 as a sportswriter for the Associated Press. Three years later the AP sent him to London, where in 1939 he joined *The New York Times*. In 1944 he was transferred to the Washington bureau of the *Times*, and he succeeded Arthur Krock as bureau chief in 1953. Mr. Reston won the Pulitzer Prize for his news dispatches in 1944 and 1956. He married Sally Fulton of Sycamore, Illinois, in 1935. They have three sons, two of whom are newspaper reporters.

A Note on the Type

The text of this book was set in Electra, a typeface designed by W(illiam) A(ddison) Dwiggins for the Mergenthaler Linotype Company and first made available in 1935. Electra cannot be classified as either "modern" or "old style." It is not based on any historical model, and hence does not echo any particular period or style of type design. It avoids the extreme contrast between "thick" and "thin" elements that marks most modern faces, and is without eccentricities which catch the eye and interfere with reading. In general, Electra is a simple, readable typeface which attempts to give a feeling of fluidity, power, and speed.

W. A. Dwiggins (1880–1956) was born in Martinsville, Ohio, and studied art in Chicago. In 1904 he moved to Hingham, Massachusetts, where he built a solid reputation as a designer of advertisements and as a calligrapher. He began an association with the Mergenthaler Linotype Company in 1929, and over the next twenty-seven years designed a number of book types, of which Metro, Electra, and Caledonia have been used very widely. In 1930 Dwiggins became interested in marionettes, and through the years made many important contributions to the art of puppetry and the design of marionettes.

Typography and binding design by Guy Fleming. Composed, printed and bound by The Haddon Craftsmen, Inc., Scranton, Pa.